BUSINESS
PLANS
THAT
WORK

Includes Actual Business Plans That
Successfully Attracted Financing

Joan Gillman
with Sarah White

Published by
Adams Media Corporation
260 Center Street, Holbrook, MA 02343 U.S.A.
www.adamsmedia.com

ISBN: 1-58062-457-X

Printed in the United States of America.

J I H G F E D C B

Library of Congress Cataloging-in-Publication data
available upon request from the publisher

Many of the designations used by manufacturers and sellers to distinguish their products are
claimed as trademarks. Where those designations appear in this book and Adams Media was
aware of a trademark claim, the designations have been printed in initial capital letters.

This publication is designed to provide accurate and authoritative information with regard to
the subject matter covered. It is sold with the understanding that the publisher is not engaged
in rendering legal, accounting, or other professional advice. If legal advice or other expert
assistance is required, the services of a competent professional person should be sought.
—From a *Declaration of Principles* jointly adopted by a Committee of the
American Bar Association and a Committee of Publishers and Associations

This book is available at quantity discounts for bulk purchases.
For information, call 1-800-872-5627.

Visit our exciting small business Web site: www.businesstown.com

CONTENTS

Acknowledgments

The best part of the work I do is the wonderful people I get to work with. I've had the privilege of working with an incredible group of clients over the years. I believe I've learned more from you than I've given. I'm privileged to work with a terrific group of colleagues from all over the United States and the world. They are not only terrific people to work with but good friends who have enriched both my personal and professional lives. Without all of you, this book would never have been written. Special thanks to Tim Baye, Bob Sheppard, Joan Winn, and Howard van Auken for sharing business plans; they've added so much to the book. Andy Bangs, Tim Baye, Bob Brockhaus, Hattie Bryant, Denny Dennis, Joline Godfrey, Rod Heller, Chuck Hofer, Frank Hoy, Fred Kiesner, Don Kuratko, Terri Lonier, Mike Meeks, Dale Meyer, David Zach: my thanks for sharing your time and invaluable insights. You've all given me so much over the years; I'm pleased to have you as colleagues and friends. I can't finish this list without special thanks to Jack Reiners, who came to the Small Business Development Center (SBDC) to see how he could help and we drafted him into service. Jack, you are a terrific role model; many thanks for all your help, guidance, sharing, and support.

I need to thank my family and friends for putting up with me during the writing of the book. Writing a book and a business plan have a lot in common: one must give up things while going through the process. And last but by no means least, thank you, Sarah White, my first client many years ago and now my first collaborator. You've been a godsend to this process. Thank you for taking my thoughts and ideas and turning them into a book. Every one of you needs a Sarah White looking over your shoulder.

And thank you for reading this, doing the work it takes to get started. You embody the entrepreneurial spirit that makes this world work. Best of luck to you.

partONE

Setting the Stage

Allow me to introduce you to the business planning process, and with the help of my crystal ball, explore tomorrow's business environment and how it may affect your plans.

Let's start by investigating what business planning is and how a variety of individuals and businesses face the planning challenge.

chapterONE

Introduction

WHAT YOU WILL FIND IN THIS CHAPTER

- Who needs a book on business planning
- How this book is structured to help you learn
- Who has participated and why
- What business sectors offer most growth potential today—and tomorrow

Some of us are just naturally preoccupied with business. I am a teacher, trainer, consultant, and mentor of businesspeople. Entrepreneurship has been my life since I was born.

My father became a businessman when he and his sister took over from their mother a women's and children's clothing store. From an early age, I worked in the store, too. At age six, I was making boxes for Christmas; at eight, I was selling on the floor. I don't know why they bought from a chubby eight-year-old, but they did. By age 13, I was running the cash register, and at 16, I was the buyer, making trips to New York.

The family business dominated our lives for a long time, affecting us all and on many levels. I grew up immersed in small business.

Reluctant Entrepreneurs

My grandmother started the business in Homestead, Pennsylvania, right across the river from Pittsburgh. We were smack in the middle of the steel capital of the world at that time.

She was a wife who lost her husband quite early. She had four daughters and my father, who was her only son. It was a successful business. She started it really out of need, having four daughters that she had to clothe. We catered to the women of the steel mills. Most of them were single, since married women seldom worked in the mills, and most had a large discretionary income. They spent quite a bit of money on clothing for themselves and for their nieces and nephews.

Grandmother retired early, and turned over the business to her daughter and son-in-law (my aunt and uncle), and to my father. Aunt Frances and Uncle Sam ran the women's department, and my father ended up with the children's department. But to equalize things, because equality is very important in my family, my grandmother apportioned the building separately from the business. She gave two-thirds of the building to my father, and one-third to my aunt and uncle. As a result, they paid my father rent, which countered the imbalance caused by the fact that children's clothing makes a lot less money than does women's clothing.

Dad was not enamored of business. He wanted to be either a doctor or an actor—I was never quite sure which. He was not a good businessman. He didn't understand cash flow analysis. He didn't understand inventory control. But despite that, when my aunt and uncle retired, they sold my dad the entire business.

My dad lacked another ingredient a successful entrepreneur needs: health. My dad wasn't a well man. If he'd had more stamina, he could probably have overcome his other shortcomings. Instead, he had five heart attacks. The last one killed him in 1967. When he died, he left my mother with three children and $100,000 in debt. I was the oldest at 21, a senior in college, and engaged to be married.

My mother asked me if I wanted the business, and I said no. She asked my sister and brother, and they also said no. So she turned the business around by herself, made a profit, paid off all debts, and then sold the business. She went on to become an art teacher at a junior college in Pittsburgh.

My dad was given a successful business but not the passion for entrepreneurship. My mother, out of terror perhaps, found that passion in herself. As a result, she was able to take a failing business and remake it into a successful, sellable enterprise. She was able to remake herself as an entrepreneur, on the fly, while coping with the loss of her spouse and the demands of her growing family. Not bad for an artist.

Those two people, that setting, the buying trips to New York, and the inventory-clearance sales in Homestead, Pennsylvania, created me. My interest in entrepreneurship has taken me from a small, failing family business to a passion to make sure that others didn't make the mistakes my father made. It's a real joy now to work with small and medium-size businesses. I like having a part in helping them.

Since 1986, I have been involved with the University of Wisconsin School of Business and its Small Business Development Center—first as a counselor and teacher, and later as the center's director. In 1993, I developed the university's Family Business Center, and took charge of the Agribusiness Executive Management Program. Today, I am faculty liaison for the Family Business Center. But I do have a life outside the university. I serve as the executive director of the U.S. Association of Small Business and Entrepreneurship, a group of 550 people who teach entrepreneurship. I travel frequently to Europe and the Middle East, consulting, teaching adults, and advocating for business development.

That's who I am. Who are you?

A Book for Born-to-Be Entrepreneurs

If you've picked up this book, you've identified yourself as an entrepreneur. You may not have your own business—yet—but you've heard the call. Or maybe you've been landed in business by circumstances beyond your control, just like my mother.

Some of you are at the dreaming stage. Others are planners for prospective or existing businesses. What each of you shares is the ambition to fit the

---

KEY CONCEPTS

Are you looking to finance a new business?
Do you need a strategy to guide your
  growth plans?
Are you preparing to start a business?
Then you need a business plan.

---

definition of an entrepreneur. You want to be the one who organizes, operates, and assumes the risk for a business venture.

What sort of business? It may be a start-up or an existing business. It may operate in the retail, wholesale, distribution, manufacturing, or nonprofit sector. It may be a "mom-and-pop shop" or a business with ambitious plans for growth.

Your gross sales might be anywhere from $0 (still on the drawing board) to $50 million or more. You might employ no one, one person, or 100 people. Your trade area might be your town or the globe, or anywhere in between. Size—whether you measure it by sales volume, staff, or trade area—does not change one fact about you. To survive you need to plan.

A need for planning

The urge to plan usually begins with an outside stimulus. You may be facing a business life cycle issue, such as start-up, expansion, or responding to a move by a competitor.

You may be looking for financing, or for a way to communicate the essence of your company to managers and staff. You may be preparing for growth, or simply striving for greater understanding of where to direct your energies today.

Whichever of these scenarios is true for you— and it may be more than one of these I've described—you know one thing. You need to plan. The question is how?

That's where this book comes in. On completing this book, using the tools and concepts presented, you will be ready to write a thorough business plan to guide you. In fact, I'll bet you'll already be halfway there. Your notes and worksheets completed along the way will provide the basis for completing your own written plan.

Is this a book on how to write a business plan, or how to plan a business? You can't do the former without the latter, so this book will of necessity be about both. In my classes on business planning, I tell my students: "The plan is worth nothing. The planning *process* is worth everything." Most successful entrepreneurs find themselves revisiting their plans every six months or so, adjusting forecasts, changing objectives, evaluating new threats and opportunities as events and their implications become known. In some businesses, especially those that are Internet based, that planning cycle is collapsed to every three months or even less.

My point is, in this competitive and fast-paced business climate, it's much more important that you know *how to plan* than that you know how to *write* a plan.

Unfolding the Planning Cycle

I love teaching. I wish we could be in a classroom together, benefiting from the energy of motivated minds focusing together. But few entrepreneurs have time for classroom study, and that's where this book comes in. As much as possible, I will present the subject of business planning for you as I would in my classes. I'll tell stories, as I would in class, and some of them will curl your hair. People in business take some pretty scary risks. Wise people in business learn from the experiences of others.

Some of the stories come from the business plans that are included in this book in part four where you can read them just as they were submitted to bankers, consultants, and others. Throughout the book, we'll draw on these plans as examples. Their formats vary, as all business plans will. Each business is unique. Further, each audience for whom a plan is written has its own unique needs. Written plans are of necessity tailored to speak to a specific audience. The plan you show your potential investor will emphasize financials, whereas the plan you show the fellow you want to hire as marketing director will obviously include more detail on your sales and marketing objectives.

The deep questions

There is no "ideal" business plan format, as the plans included in this book will show. From the wide variety of these example plans, you will come to see the planning cycle that ties them together.

You will see how each individual or group of individuals sat down and faced the deep questions: Why are we doing this? What do we want out of this business? Why do we believe we can succeed? What steps are we taking to increase our chances of success? Who will buy our product or service? How much will they buy? When will they buy it? How much money am I likely to make?

You will see how the basic opportunity that creates a business is explored; how strategies to exploit that opportunity are designed; how resources must be marshaled and allocated; how threats must be anticipated and weaknesses strengthened; and how feedback must be gathered to learn from the outcome of previous initiatives and to guide the development of further initiatives. It's a grand endeavor. And like doing the dishes, it is never done.

How to Use This Book

This book is divided into four parts:

[1] Setting the Stage
[2] The "Three-Legged Stool"—marketing, personnel, and finances.
[3] Get Going
[4] Real-World Business Plans

The first section of the book sets the stage. I'll introduce the planning process, and with the help of my crystal ball, place it in the context of tomorrow's business environment. This section concludes with an outline for a comprehensive business plan, with an explanation of the reasons for what is included and the order in which they are included.

The second section of the book takes you deeper into the "three-legged stool" that supports every business activity: *marketing*, *personnel*, and *finances*. As we look at excerpts from business plans, we'll explore critical success factors in each area. As you read, you'll grow in understanding of what *your* specific plan should include.

The third section of the book is geared to help you get started today. A variety of business plan reviewers and supporters of entrepreneurship share their insights. Our parting advice will give you the edge you need to write a winning business plan. And I don't mean "winning" in the sense of academic competitions or compliments from your friends and neighbors. I mean a plan that gets the results you want, whether that is the support of investors and bankers, the cooperation of partners and staff, or your own better understanding of what to do and how to do it. When you finish the third section, you will be ready to write a plan that will guide your business to its next level.

The final section of the book reproduces business plans prepared by real-world businesses under real-world pressures. Where the plans' authors made mistakes, such as typographic errors or flaws in grammar, those errors have been left intact. My comments precede each plan, to help you see these business plans through the eyes of experienced reviewers. You will learn from the planners' mistakes as well as from their successes.

A word about structure

Each chapter in this book starts with a summary of key topics, called "What You Will Find in This Chapter." Then as each topic is discussed, supporting examples are drawn from the business plans. Actual names of businesses and their owners have been changed to encourage greater frankness by contributors. Each chapter ends with a conclusion, called "Thoughts to Take Away."

Each chapter features specialized sidebars for your browsing pleasure:

- **Key Concepts:** summarizes an important concept from the text
- **Resources:** points you to books, Web sites, government institutions, and other helpful sources
- **Voices:** many of my peers have contributed their expertise to this book; enjoy their insights, in their own words

At the back of this book, you'll find an appendix section that includes a generic business plan outline, blank planning worksheets to photocopy or set up as computer spreadsheets, a list of resources, and a glossary of common terms.

Who Has Participated and Why

The plans included here were submitted by colleagues from around the country.

By allowing their plans to be included, the entrepreneurs in these various businesses have given you the opportunity to look over their shoulders. Step into their doubts and dreams, and be inspired by them. Then take a step back, and consider these plans from the vantage point of their intended reviewers. If you were the banker who could approve this loan, would the plan answer any questions that might affect your decision? If you were one of the employees forging a common intent to purchase and run this business, how would this plan help you? The more you try on these "what-if" questions, the more you become a participant in the book and the more you'll learn from it.

I have sought out my friends and contemporaries, other teachers and consultants in entrepreneurship, to offer you far more insight, and more diverse perspectives, than I could have assembled on my own.

The participants in creating this book are an eclectic group. They include would-be and current entrepreneurs, teachers, commentators, and successful businesspeople. But the most important participant in this book is you.

No look-alike plans

The business plans I've chosen to include are meant to illustrate the various business concepts we'll cover. They represent useful models for you, but not a template for you to copy. Business planning doesn't work that way.

A man called me and said that he had read five business planning books. He thinks he has finally put together the ideal business plan outline. I said, "I wish you had called me earlier. You don't need five books. You only need one. Read one book to get a basic business plan outline, and then get to work. Take that outline and work your way through it."

That's the best advice I can give. It's really important that you take an outline and make sure you do all the work it calls for. Most business plan outlines are very similar. There isn't a perfect outline, and there's not even a perfect business plan.

When I was teaching art (a previous career), I would teach about the body's proportions so that people could draw faces and human forms. I explained some of the rules of the face. I drew an oval on the board, and divided it in half lengthwise. Then I divided it in half the other way.

I explained that the horizontal division is where the eyes go. And halfway between the eyes and the chin is the nose. And halfway between the nose and the chin is the mouth, and I drew lines in the appropriate places. "Now draw a face," I said. And I got 30 faces that looked exactly like the face that I had drawn. They just followed the rules (like a business plan outline) without adding their own personalities and unique differences that would have made the faces individual.

If you follow a prepackaged business plan template, you'll get a plan like those 30 faces. That's not the purpose of a business plan. The purpose is to express your thoughts. There are some basic rules—that's the plan outline—like the face whose general proportions are the same, but what's important is that you write *your* plan. A lot of people think they can hire somebody to write it for them. I'm not a proponent of that.

If you have someone else write the plan for you, then it's not your plan. You need to be an expert on your business. I don't expect you to be a full-fledged accountant or attorney when you finish writing a plan, but you need to have some basic knowledge of these fields. You need to be able to speak "accountant-ese" and "legal-ese" and, if you're going to be hiring people, "human resource-ese." You must understand and know all you can about your business. If you hired someone to do it for you, then that person becomes the expert on the subject matter. You, the business owner, are always playing catch-up. I can't emphasize this too strongly. Do every bit of research yourself, or do as much as you possibly can. Get help where you need it, but write the plan yourself. The real value of planning is in the process.

What Business Should You Pursue?

For those with a passion that verges on obsession, the choice of what business to pursue has only one answer. This is the case for many entrepreneurs. But there are also those of you who feel that you would enjoy the challenge of business ownership, but have not yet decided on a product or service that fits.

I can't tell you how many people have asked me, "What business should I go into?" My favorite story concerns a friend of mine.

A basketful of dreams

My friend Carol called me up and asked if I would come over and have lemonade on her back porch. It was a beautiful June day as we sat and drank lemonade, and she said she wanted to bounce a business idea off me. It isn't unusual for people to invite me over and then want to talk business but I don't mind—I really love what I do.

Carol's business idea was that she wanted to give talks to help parent–teacher organizations (PTOs) around the country. I asked her my usual questions.

I usually start from the end and work backwards, so I said, "How much money do you want to make?" and she told me. And I said, "I think we have a problem because, in order to make that amount of money—and that is the amount it would take to sustain you, in the fashion you want to be accustomed to, or the amount that makes it worthwhile if you're going to do this—there are some things you have to consider." When we worked it backwards, it was pretty clear that she would need to charge a great deal of money. One thing that's common knowledge about PTOs is that they don't have a lot of money, and they want everything on the cheap.

It wasn't a feasible idea. It would be an excellent social idea if she wanted to volunteer her time, and expenses, but unless she was going to become her own charitable foundation, she wasn't going to be able to make this a success.

Voices

Entrepreneurs are really children who have never given up the ability to play, but have combined it with the ability to add value.

—David Zach

For Carol the bottom line was she wanted a profitable business. She was willing to consider other ideas besides the PTO talks, so we kept brainstorming. As we were talking, I said what I would really like to have is a gift basket that I could purchase (this was several years ago, before the big gift basket craze hit) and then send to my child in college. It was the end of my daughter's freshman year in college, and I had just experienced my first brush with "supermom" and the looming empty nest. Her freshman year, I had been supermom. I had written a letter a week and sent a gift package every month. September's was a back-to-school basket; October's had all kinds of Halloween decorations for her room; November's had Thanksgiving treats and knick-knacks; December's was Christmas lights and decorations; and on around the year.

It took me a lot of time. I would go to 15 different stores to pick up all the goodies, and pack up the box to send to her. My friend Carol thought that was a terrific idea, but after she thought about it, she realized she wasn't looking for something she would wholesale into gift stores. She took the idea and added her twist: a direct-mail business. The problem was Carol failed to plan sufficiently. She didn't really think through her idea, even with the advice she got from me and others.

Carol faced three dilemmas, and they involved the key aspect of any business: customers.

The first is really quite simple: finding the right customers. If you're going to do a direct-mail business, the most important thing that you have is your list. Compiling a list of college students' parents is difficult. Carol had a lot of friends who had kids in college, but not enough to support her business. The commercial mail lists available had only students' names and addresses, not their parents' home addresses. Compiling the list turned out to be very difficult because she didn't want to sell to the students, she wanted to sell to the parents.

The second dilemma concerned price. These baskets were expensive by the time she put them together, a little higher than the price point I and people like me were looking for. That meant that in order to be successful she needed to find not just parents of college students, but a subset of that group—the *rich* parents.

The third dilemma concerned her market's ability to produce repeat customers. Doing a business plan will teach you that **the most valuable customer you have is the repeat customer**. Well, people like me are terrific freshman moms, but by sophomore year we are a little less into being supermom. Even though I wrote my daughter letters and called once a week, by that second year I found a florist in her college town and arranged to have flowers delivered once a month, and let it go at that. Much easier and easier on my budget. Junior year she spent abroad, and senior year she got flowers and telephone calls but not so many letters. The need to be supermom fades quickly. I was supermom longer than most.

Carol's business didn't succeed. It was too difficult to get the mail lists. The brochure and the marketing materials were just too expensive. Carol had a fabulous garage sale when she went out of business. If she had done a little more research, she might have designed the business differently. A written business plan with a detailed marketing section would have brought to light the flaws in her business concept. If she had addressed those flaws in her prestart-up plans, this story might have had a different ending.

If you plan to start it, plan to run it

I have seen a lot of clients who had deep pockets, and it causes most of them trouble. It makes it easy to get into business. They don't need to think it through; they don't need to plan. A lot of them plan to be absentee owners; that is, they plan to keep their "real" jobs and hire other people to run their businesses. Wrong. Especially in the start-up stage, a business needs the owner's hand. A business needs the owner's guidance. It's very difficult to be a successful absentee owner.

You don't get the feel for the day-to-day traffic, the day-to-day issues and problems. I once worked with a man who came from a rural town and opened a framing business. He kept his normal job during the day and hired someone to work from 9:00 A.M. until 5:00 P.M. He'd get there at 5:00 P.M. and take over the business until 9:00 P.M. That was his regular routine.

One day he got there at 5:00 P.M. As the day-shift salesperson left, she said, "it's been a really slow day," but she didn't say how slow. He looked in the cash register. Not a sale had been made. The register had never been opened all day.

As he was leaving that evening, after spending four hours alone in his shop, he felt that his life was over and this business was not going to be successful at all. But as he stood outside locking the door, the neighbor next door was locking his also, and spoke up. "Really slow day. There was absolutely no one on the street." Our man realized it wasn't just his business, after all. But by not being there all day, he didn't have a feel for the street and what was going on.

You need to be there and to spend a good deal of time in your business if it's going to be successful. It's hard to delegate a start-up business. That fellow had made plans based on what he thought he knew, before he opened for business. It proved absolutely critical that he be there in those first start-up months in order to learn quickly where his forecasts needed to be revised.

I can't tell you what business to go into, but I can suggest where opportunities might present themselves. Certain business sectors are growing; certain trends, from demographics to immigration to recreation and leisure patterns, are fueling growth for many entrepreneurs. Several of my friends weighed in with their opinions about emerging opportunities for business. Find a way to adapt these ideas to your business concept, and prosper with my best wishes.

Growth Potential

You may have a great product idea, but in today's fast-paced world, you need more than a great product—you need one with staying power.

"There have been whole industries that have come and gone in 10 to 15 years," said Fred Kiesner.* "Take, for example, the fax. The fax has only been widely used for 10 years or so, and in the next five years it will be dead. Who needs a fax when you can do attachments to e-mails and share documents over the Internet?"

---

*To simplify this discussion, the background and credentials of each interview contributor are described in appendix A.

In chapter 5, we'll talk more about the product life cycle. Meanwhile, let's examine several business concepts with potential for growth.

Help people get things done

As we continue our evolution from the Industrial Age to the Knowledge Age, most new products will be services, not tangible objects at all. Futurist David Zach sees the emergence of the concierge: "a new industry of people who help you get things done."

Already corporations are providing a concierge service that helps their top-level managers with everything from taking care of laundry to having a car's oil changed.

In Peter Drucker's work he mentioned that at the turn of the last century, one of the largest occupational categories was "servant." Then that category went away. The need for those services didn't go away, but rather was fulfilled by the homemaker. Then as homemakers have increasingly gone away, again, the need for those services hasn't gone away. It's got to be filled by somebody. So either we stop being so obsessed with work, so we can spend more time on our home and life care activities, or we become people who'll pay for that. The concept of servant will re-emerge, but this time with a higher professional status. Someone who knows how to navigate in that great wide world out there.

Apply new technology to solve old problems

In addition to the demand for concierge services, Zach foresees the evolution of new industries made possible by advances in technology.

Two industries are emerging that are wonderful: distance learning, as well as logistics management.

With distance learning, it's all about exploring how you can educate people when they're not really there physically, sharing space. More and more, we're bringing things to people as opposed to bringing people to things. That may be a total transformation of the economy in that we've figured out how to move things and ideas amazingly well. A lot of people no longer have to go someplace. Distance learning brings the educational environment to the person.

Logistics management is an emerging new science. For example, people are figuring out how to eliminate warehouses. With better and better information about production, transportation, and consumption, you can basically eliminate a warehouse.

Domino's Pizza may be the ultimate model of manufacturing in the future. They have taken the concept of factory, broken it up into little pieces and put them in people's neighborhoods, then guaranteed customized delivery of any product within 30 minutes to your doorstep. If we can do it with pizzas, why can't we do it with cars, or computers, or furniture?

A good example is a machine from Xerox and IBM that could change the way we produce and distribute books. They have a machine that can print books from start to finish. You download the book into the machine and it comes out with a four-color cardstock cover that looks as good as any paperback you'd buy in a bookstore. Could Barnes & Noble become a kiosk? And not have to have inventory because they can print up the book right there? It doesn't mean we eliminate books. We eliminate warehouses all over the world, where inventory goes and sits, and then an amazing amount of books end up getting destroyed because they didn't sell. If we don't produce it until it's consumed, that's a huge cost savings.

Provide "third places" for socialization

Before you go into mourning over the loss of your bookstore, read on. Zach went on to point out a fundamental of human nature.

We will still have bookstores, because bookstores have become what are called "third places." It's not home, it's not work—it is a transformation of the traditional marketplace, in that it is a place for people to go and physically share space with others. Check out a Barnes & Noble on a Friday night: it is a kind of singles night. People will adapt. That's the wonderful thing. You throw a monkey wrench in the path and they find a new path. Coffee shops are another third place. The sociological term for it.

Great opportunities lie ahead for businesses that provide that "third place" for people to socialize and share ideas. Just consider the wave of baby boomers now approaching retirement age, and think about that many people (115 million by the year 2020, according to AgeWave Communications) with time to finally go out for coffee and keep up with friends. Add to that population the number of students and "SOHO" (small office/home office)

businesspeople who use coffee shops as a place to work, and you have quite a growth trend.

Serve demands for education, health, finances, home, and leisure

The most obvious social shift we will see in coming years is the aging of the baby boomers. The experts predict increased demand for services related to life-long learning, health, finances, home, and leisure.

Education. Not so long ago, graduation from high school or college signaled the end of learning and the beginning of a life of work. Today, that model is being replaced by a new one. Work and learning are increasingly blended together throughout our lives. Corporate training is a vast and growing field. Providers of education after retirement, for example, Elderhostel, are experiencing tremendous success. How can you get in on that action? Think about what you know, then turn it into training. If you have technical expertise, package it as a training offering, and teach others a skill. If your talent lies in the area of organization, become a packager of training programs that other people present. You could market a series of "brown-bag" luncheons on life skills, like money management or juggling work and family for corporations as a benefit to their employees.

Health. The health and wellness trend may have been around for a while, but there's still lots of life left in this product/service category. The baby boom generation built its identity around youthfulness, and it isn't going to age without a fight. Any product or service that fights aging—from diet supplements to cosmetic surgery—is going to sell very well.

Finances. Financial independence is also important to boomers. Many delayed serious work during their 20s, and later found their income absorbed by growing families. Today, many boomers are focused on catching up via investments. Aggressive income growth is important to them, as is protecting what they have. For some the question is capital generation—for others, it's what to do with what they've got. Baby boomers are in line to inherit more than $10 trillion, according to some sources, as their parents pass on. Generation X members are accumulating savings, too, proud of their 401Ks and their stock market investments. Serving the financial needs of people like these will make portfolio management, insurance, cash flow analysis, and estate planning a boom town for years to come.

Home. Remodeling is big business as boomers find themselves with empty nests. Amenities like whirlpools and home theaters are selling like hotcakes. Kitchens and baths need adaptations to help older people stay in their homes longer. More diverse housing options, including "mother-in-law apartments" and clustered retirement living, are emerging as the boomer population ages. Famous for their independence throughout their lives, boomers will want to maintain that independence as they age. Adaptation of the home environment to changing needs will continue to power the home products and remodeling industries.

Leisure. It's hard to imagine a leisure business that won't make money in coming years. Again, it's those baby boomers—with increased time, money, and an ingrained habit of spending on recreation, every conceivable leisure business stands to prosper from them. Cultural attractions, performing arts, travel purveyors, restaurants . . . all up, up, up. Sports and hobbies, too—anything that helps us relax and feel refreshed, whether it's rock climbing or bird watching, will experience growth. Offer a product or service that enhances leisure, and you can't go wrong.

I can't tell you what business you should go into. You must follow your passion. If you have passion, and a little luck on your side, your will find a successful match with needs and desires of a population large enough to support your ambitions.

Passion and a plan. That's what this book is all about.

Thoughts to Take Away

- The impetus for planning usually begins with an outside stimulus, such as a need for funding, or a response to a competitive threat. But once you have begun to plan, you must make it an ongoing habit. Successful entrepreneurs review and revise their plans every six months, or even more often than that.

- There is no one ideal format or outline for a business plan. Each business is unique, and each audience for the plan is unique. This book offers guidance and examples to help you choose the planning model that works best for *you*.

- Throughout this book, you'll hear the voices of my contemporaries, commentators, and researchers in the field of entrepreneurship. We've collaborated to bring you the cutting edge concerning business success. But the most important participant is *you*. As you read, make notes, try the exercises, fill in the worksheets.

- No one can tell you what business to go into—you must follow your passion. Certain sectors are primed for success, and if you can adapt your business concept to take advantage of these trends, your passion will prosper.

chapterTWO

Deep Questions

WHAT YOU WILL FIND IN THIS CHAPTER

- Why entrepreneurs engage in business planning
- Who should be involved in the business planning process
- When planning is most appropriate in the life cycle of a business
- How the planning process is conducted and the written plan generated

When we love something, thinking about it is fun. When we go on vacation, we do a lot of preparation. First of all, we decide where it is we want to go. We choose a destination we're excited about and want to experience.

Then we talk to everybody we know about that place. Whether it is New York City, or Las Vegas, or Europe, we talk to everybody to find out who's been there. Then we ask what they liked and didn't like. What restaurants they went to. Where they stayed. We pump them for everything we can learn about the destination.

Then we go and get books from the library and the bookstore, and we read about the place. We go on the Internet and check out sites that tell us more—where to stay, good prices for travel. We rent a car. We make our hotel reservation. We check our credit card limit to make sure we have enough money to cover the trip.

We do a lot of talking and planning and preparation—all for a one-week vacation!

I find that people go into business having done a lot less preparation than they do for their vacations. I suggest you put in at least that much effort. Business planning takes time. The success rate improves dramatically when you plan. And—this may surprise you—many parts of the process are fun.

Why Plan?

Too many people believe the only reason to write a business plan is that the financial community wants to see one when you ask them for money. It's true most plans are written in anticipation of a search for loans or investors. But there's a reason lenders and investors want to see a plan: They're smart. Why should anyone trust that you know what you're doing if you can't articulate your plan in writing? How will you know that what you are planning is feasible, and the costs associated affordable, if you don't buckle down and research those questions?

The people most likely to shortchange their planning efforts are, sadly, those with the deepest pockets. People who have a lot of money cannot plan. They are less likely to take the time to think about what they're doing.

One client came to me. He was extremely wealthy, with a large trust fund. He was interested in going into business with a woman who already had a very successful small business. They would become partners. Their area was going to be fancy high-end desserts, fancy cookies and specialty cakes. His idea was to sell them to country clubs and hotels, and also to have a catalog business.

He commissioned a market research company to do a study. He was very proud of the study they brought back. But it was boilerplate. The research company had given him a fill-in-the-blank marketing study, and it even compared his product to the wrong types of products. It wasn't very useful, and yet he had paid a great deal of money for it—$25,000.

He also produced a beautiful full-color brochure that was obviously very expensive—another $25,000 gone. But he hadn't thought about where his business would be based. He wanted to have a retail outlet, but hadn't rented a space. He had a beautiful brochure, but there was no address on it. He hadn't thought through his business plan, and he was spending money quickly.

He came to my office and asked me questions, and I gave him the best advice I could, and then he would go and do his own thing. I remember he always came in wearing a plaid flannel shirt and jeans. And yet the product he was representing was extremely high-end, better suited to a three-piece suit.

He would go home to his family, who lived in another state, and that was problematic also. He would spend two weeks on the business, and then he would disappear to have some time with his family at home. There was no continuity to his involvement in the business. He was good at hiring people—he kept hiring and hiring—but there was nothing for them to do because he hadn't developed his business.

I hadn't seen him in about three months, and he came to my office and he dropped a bomb. "I'm $100,000 in debt, I've gone through my trust fund, and my family won't back me. What do you think I should do?"

My advice to him was to get a job. It was quite clear to me that he was not cut out to be in this business. The unfortunate part is that it not only affected him, but it affected his business partner. She lost the business as a result of his mismanagement.

For want of a plan, a thriving business vanished. Why should you plan? Because failure to plan can kill you. Going through the process is critical to success.

What are you doing this for?

There are probably as many motivations for entrepreneurship as their are entrepreneurs. A business planning process gives you the opportunity to examine your own motivations, to do a "reality check." Do your motivations match up to the realities of the entrepreneurial lifestyle?

Many people gravitate toward business ownership for the opportunity to live a life more in tune with their values. You may feel that by getting away from a big corporation, you will be able to do what is important to you. Running your own business allows you to experience self-reliance and independence in way that being a part of the corporate "rank and file" never will.

There's a conflict there, and Michael Meeks, an inveterate entrepreneur who is now a doctoral student at the University of Colorado–Boulder, describes how he sees it:

I believe one of the things that drives entrepreneurship and makes the economy boom is the sheer elbow grease factor. The sweat equity put into entrepreneurial firms. It's not uncommon for business owners to work 70 to 80 hours per week. When you get out and talk to entrepreneurs, many are working 100-plus hour weeks.

If your vision of the entrepreneurial lifestyle is that you will have greater freedom, think again. "Sure, you have freedom. You have the freedom to work any 80 hours a week you want to," a friend of mine says.

Starting a business will affect your every waking moment (and most likely your sleeping moments, too). There is always something more you could be doing, or thinking about, or worrying over. Your entrepreneurship will affect your family and friends, for better or worse. Sadly, many personal relationships have been disrupted by the demands business ownership places on an individual.

This is not to say that you must resign from your marriage and friendships when you start your business. Family and friends can help you tremendously, if you open up to them. Don't shield them from the concerns that you experience. Rather, allow them to become your sounding board and pep squad.

Many businesspeople find themselves unable to spend as much time with family and friends as they would like. This is reasonable during a business's start-up or high-growth phases. If it continues year

Voices

Optimism is what causes us to run our own businesses, and optimism is what brings our pain. We don't want to deal with reality. We don't want to look hard at the numbers. We want to pretend everything's wonderful.
—Hattie Bryant

in and year out, however, something is wrong. The owner has not learned to delegate or is using the business as an excuse to avoid meaningful relationships. It's possible that the business is not truly viable—it is merely being kept alive by heroic transfusions of the owner's lifeblood.

Are you willing to give up your life to gain your business? Most of us are ready to make that sacrifice for a time. Will the business be worth it? No one can answer that question for you. In the business planning process, you will explore what rewards the business has potential to generate, both the tangible financial rewards and the more intangible rewards of business ownership—satisfactions such as independence, accomplishment, and community service.

Terri Lonier has been self-employed for close to 20 years, most recently as CEO of Working Solo, Inc.

When small businesses start, usually the individuals start because they have a passion to do something, whether it's to be a carpenter, or a caterer, or they love gardening, or whatever it is. They have this passion to do this. That is the sphere they think they're going to be operating in. All of a sudden they get into business and they realize there's this whole other sphere, which I call "the business of making a business." That's the marketing. The taxes. The government forms. All of the paperwork. All the stuff you have to do to run a business has to take place. They find out they're being dragged out of their passion sphere into this business sphere. They really resent it.

Lonier has made it her mission, through Working Solo, Inc., to help these individuals spend more time in their passion sphere.

Isn't doing more important than planning?

Why should you stop to plan when you could be—should be—running your business? As I said before, there is always something more you could be doing. If there are orders to be packed and shipped, or a big proposal that's due in a couple of days, wouldn't it be wiser for you to work on those rather than stop and work on your business plan? Those tasks are indeed urgent, but by no means are they more important than the long-range health of your business. Part of your job as

---

**KEY CONCEPT:
MOTIVATIONS AND TRADEOFFS**

What do you want out of the business? What will you be giving up to gain it? Many people think business ownership will allow them to live a life more in tune with their values. But once they are caught up in their new business, working long hours and worrying all the time, they experience doubts. Are you ready to invest the "elbow grease" necessary for your business concept to succeed?

---

a business *manager* is to understand what Stephen Covey (author of *The Seven Habits of Highly Effective People* and *First Things First*) has called "the tyranny of urgency." Time management and delegation are key skills that will help you understand when you should pack orders and when you should do the work you're responsible for as the enterprise's top visionary.

Covey has used the analogy of "sharpening the saw" to highlight this problem. It goes like this. Lumberjacks are working away on a huge pile of logs. A two-man team draws the saw back and forth, over and over. The first day they produce a huge pile of timber ready to ship. The second day the pile is somewhat smaller, although they have worked as hard—if not harder. The third day the pile is smaller still. "What's going on?" the foreman asked. "The saw's getting duller," they replied, "but with so many logs to do, we don't have time to sharpen it."

Writing a plan is taking time out to "sharpen the saw." By taking time out to plan, you will produce more, not less.

Assumptions in planning

There are two parts to the planning process we are discussing: the mental work of planning and the documenting of the plan in a written form. When we produce a written document, we produce it tailored to the needs of a specific audience. When Dr. Seuss wrote *One Fish Two Fish Red Fish Blue Fish*, he chose a different language and pacing for his story than Herman Melville chose for *Moby Dick*.

In the planning process itself, the "audience" is irrelevant. But once you begin writing, you must make some assumptions about who will be reading the plan and what their interest in it will be. Are you preparing the plan to be reviewed by lenders? Key managers? Is this plan tied to a financing proposal, or does it serve other purposes? Perhaps there will be several versions—one for each audience. You may even prepare a plan summary simply to encourage supporters—your family and friends—to believe in you.

How honest should you be? If your creditors are lined up around the block, and you are preparing the plan in a last-ditch attempt to secure a bank loan to satisfy them, you will naturally be tempted to depict your business in a rosier light than your situation would indicate. A no-holds-barred review of the situation would very likely reveal that your business concept has failed. In this situation, unjustified optimism will do more harm than good.

Don't get me wrong. Optimism is a good thing—in fact, it's a personality trait shared by almost all entrepreneurs. But there are situations where our optimism stands in our way. It clouds our vision just when we need to be more sharp-sighted than ever.

When you are in the planning stage, it's time to be fearlessly honest. If your research leads you to observations that frighten you, your fear is a message worth listening to. You may choose to go ahead in the face of frightening odds—business owners do it all the time. The successful ones do so having done their level best to find out what the risks are, thereby allowing them to strategize their best responses to those risks.

When you are in the documentation stage, finally assembling a written draft of your plan, it's time to allow your natural optimism to shine through. Don't allow your writing to be dominated by empty hyperbole, but do allow your passion to show.

Financial projections are a critical component of the business plan. Our natural optimism is most likely to run away with us when it's time to prepare pro formas (projected financial statements). And that's just the moment when we need pessimism most. Typically, pro formas are cast in three scenarios—best case, worst case, and most likely. I wish I could tell you how many people find that hitting their worst-case projections would be a relief compared to how poorly their real-world performance is going. When you are preparing your projections,

take off your rose-colored glasses. Examine your assumptions, and proceed with care. Chapter 7 covers the process of preparing pro formas in detail.

Many business owners make the mistake of thinking that a change of strategy will turn the business immediately in a new and better direction. But businesses turn like boats, not bicycles. A change in strategy today may not show up in financial statements for six months or a year.

Cash flow planning is too often our downfall. We may hire a new person to deliver a product or service, or we may take on inventory in a new product line and think that it will sell immediately. Financial projections we prepare while in this optimistic state of mind are likely to overstate the results of those strategic decisions, both in how much new sales will result and in how soon they will be realized.

A business plan is written with a specific audience in mind. If your plan will be reviewed by different people with different concerns, plan on creating different versions for each audience. Tailor the content, and the degree of optimism, to each reader. But always be brutally honest in the version you write for yourself.

Who Plans?

You do. Although there are plenty of people who will offer their help, in my opinion, you should say "thanks but no thanks" to most of them. Business consultants can bring expertise in the preparing of business plans, and contacts in the financial community, but no amount of conversation with you will give them everything a plan requires one to know about a business, its key personnel, and their dreams.

You may have a friend in business who says, "I've done a plan; let me help you with yours." Again, a friend may be able to help you, but don't count on him or her to know your business as you do. Ask that person to help you as a friend can. A friend or consultant can be most useful when acting as your sounding board. Getting someone to play "devil's advocate" is a useful counterbalance to your own optimism. Regular meetings with a consultant or friend could be the critical ingredient that gets you going and helps you successfully finish an effective business plan. By all means solicit help—but remember, nobody can birth this baby but you.

Software is available that will "write the plan for you." That's all right if you use it to help you draft the written plan. Just don't rely on it to give you strategic insights. You want this to be *your* plan, not boilerplate.

Business structures

The key personnel of the business are responsible for planning. If you are the sole owner of your business, then it's obvious who will conceive the strategies that become the business plan: You will. If you share responsibility for the business's direction with other key personnel, then you will most likely create a strategic planning group and charge it with the task of writing the business plan.

How is your organization structured? Businesses are typically structured as sole proprietorships, partnerships, corporations, or limited liability companies. Whichever you choose will be a major factor in how you keep your books, how you share risk and rewards, how you plan, and how your business is taxed. A lawyer should advise you on the appropriate structure for your business, depending on your situation. Factors involved in choosing a business structure include your exposure to risk, your access to capital, your purpose for forming the business, and the laws in your state.

Partnerships

Many people who want to start a business consider starting with a partner. Maybe it's the "buddy system" we learned at summer camp—we think having a business partner will help us avoid the risks of "going it alone." Although I wish this weren't true, going into business with a buddy is seldom a good idea. Your business buddy is likely to be a liability more often than an asset.

Hattie Bryant, creator of the *Small Business 2000* series on public television, has seen too many partnerships run aground:

One of the most common mistakes we see is someone taking the wrong partner. On Small Business 2000 we've done stories where business divorces have had to take place. It's so painful. It goes back to too much optimism, not enough evaluation of values and common qualities between the two partners, that causes the divorce. Everyone who's been running a sustainable business over time, that I know, would say—better no partner than a partner.

KEY CONCEPT: OPTIMISM VERSUS REALISM

Each business plan is published for a specific audience. A plan for review by potential lenders will focus on different highlights than a plan prepared for review by potential staff members. Tailor the content, and the degree of optimism, to each audience. But always be brutally honest in the version you write for yourself.

Don Kuratko offered these cautions about partnership:

It can be very exciting during the courtship, when you feel that you've found someone who shares your enthusiasm. To find out later on you really did marry the wrong person is horrible. The only thing worse is marrying the wrong person and knowing you could have done your homework better, realized some things. A partnership situation can be even more important than a marriage. You're talking about your whole life's work. I would be very, very cautious getting into a partnership.

Good partnerships do exist. To build one, make sure there is clear value added by each partner, and clear delineation of functional responsibilities. In such a situation, the result is greater than the sum of the parts. Partners should bring different skills to the table. These skills need to benefit the business's strategic direction. When looking for a partner, look for people who have skills different from your own. You're not looking for your mirror image. When the situation changes, and the partnership no longer adds value, a well-planned partnership agreement provides the structure for an amicable business divorce.

Partners, LLC, corporation, sole proprietorship—whatever your initial choice of business structure, it doesn't have to stay that way. As your business develops, your structure most likely will change. It's a good idea to have a lawyer work with you at the start, and through any major transitions, to be sure you choose wisely. It's important that the documents of your chosen business structure are properly completed and filed with appropriate agencies—another job for your attorney.

Form a strategic planning group

If you're in an existing business, you can recruit a strategic planning group from the officers of your corporation, or the partners in your partnership, or the key personnel who manage the functional areas of your business. This team will formulate the strategies and participate in the writing of your business plan. It's not uncommon for different individuals to submit portions of the plan relating to their functional areas. Your head of sales can research the marketing section, while your human resources director works up the personnel section, and your chief financial officer prepares the pro formas for the financial section. No one should do his or her work in a vacuum, and the business planning process is no exception. If you are a sole proprietor writing a plan on your own, consider asking your accountant, marketing consultant, or other advisors to be part of your strategic review group.

When Do People Plan?

With an existing business, too often planning is a function of pain. Planning starts when something is going wrong. The people responsible are looking to understand what and why and how so that they can get it back on track. And too often, the result is a good strategy applied too late.

With a start-up business, planning is a function of pleasure. It's fun and exciting to think about a revolutionary business concept, to dream about taking control of your life's work.

Whether pleasurable or painful, people expend effort in planning when their business is making a transition. Businesses move through stages, from start-up to expansion to plateaus and breakthroughs. When they make these transitions successfully, it's a sure sign that there was good planning in advance. While the planning process is functionally the same at any stage, each has its own emphasis.

Startups

With a start-up business, the planning emphasis is on feasibility. Will there be customers who want to buy what you're offering? Will there be enough of them to allow you to be profitable offering it?

What is the industry like—are there trends afoot that will affect the feasibility of your idea? What about competitors? Why will people buy from you instead of them? In chapter 5, we explore feasibility analysis in more depth.

Several of the business plans we've included were prepared by start-up businesses. If you are the force behind a start-up business, look at the plans for The Artful Fly, the Whole Fish & Seafood franchise, and Blue Sky Travel.

Expansion

It takes money to start a business, and more money to expand it. Very often the start-up expenditures are funded by the resources of the entrepreneur. When you've exhausted the investment capacity of your family and friends—and you've proved the feasibility of your concept—your expansion plans will almost certainly involve seeking either bank loans or capital investors. I rarely see a successful business expansion that is funded solely from the cash flow of the business.

A business that plans to grow recognizes there are opportunities that could lead to increased efficiencies and profits. Businesses typically grow in one of two ways—either by expansion of the primary location or by expansion into new market areas with multiple additional facilities. In other words, either you do what you've always done, but on a bigger scale, or you do the same thing you've always done, but in more places. Either way, your goals are likely to include greater return on investment for you and your backers.

Voices

A business plan isn't written so much as it is compiled. Each part of the plan has its own process. Write down the thoughts as they come to you. You will find where they belong in the organization of the written plan later. Plans have different orientations. Do whatever is going to work for you.

—Jack Reiners, business counselor,
UW–Madison SBDC

If you are considering an expansion strategy, look at the plans for O'Toole's Machining and Red's Automotive.

Plateaus and breakthroughs

The solution to a plateau may be to shrink rather than grow. A medium-size importer might choose to concentrate on a few successful products, for example, while discontinuing the marginal product lines. A breakthrough could mean a new way of handling operations that improves profitability without expansion.

Fred Kiesner has observed that the Internet poses a challenge to traditional small businesses, which must respond with a breakthrough in strategy or face a decline:

I'm on the board of a little business right now. He's had a wonderful business, he's 63 years old, and he wanted to sell, get out. All of a sudden, before he could sell, his business declined and he got in big trouble. Why? Because he wasn't on the Internet, and everybody else in his field was. So he's quickly trying to catch up and get a Web presence. He was saying "I've had this great business for 30 years. I'll sell it now and have a good retirement." And before he could get his good retirement, the damage was done. He didn't catch on.

Another example. I have a wonderful student that I taught 10 years ago. He went out and bought a declining business and revitalized it. He was doing extremely well. But all of a sudden he just—not long ago—said "This business is going to die in the near future if I don't get on the Internet." It hasn't even begun to go down yet, he's doing wonderfully well, and he's still realized the Internet is his future and he's absolutely concentrating on converting his business to the Internet. They'll still do the old stuff alongside, until it dies out, but he's a catalog guy. He mails out hundreds of thousands of catalogs. He's all of a sudden saying, "Uh-oh, if I don't get on the Internet, I'm out of business."

The search for breakthroughs motivated the business plan for BizCopy. The firm is doing fine day to day, but sees alternative courses of action that could fuel growth, and must decide which strategy to pursue.

**KEY CONCEPT:
HAVE A PARTNERSHIP AGREEMENT**

If you do take on a partner, plan the divorce when you plan the marriage. A partnership agreement may be included in the business plan and should describe a process for valuing the business and for arbitration should the partners be unable to negotiate satisfactorily.

Changes in ownership

Changes in ownership occur for many reasons, including succession from one generation to another, acquisition by an outside business, or merger with another existing business to form a new company. I mentioned earlier that the business structure is likely to change when such a change takes place. Along with the new business structure, the company is likely to need a business plan. The plan may be written to seek support for, or to structure the process of, transition, or it may be written by the potential new owners, in which case it closely resembles a "start-up" business plan.

When planning, keep in mind . . .

You'll need money when you start a business, grow a business, and at times throughout its life, as you guide the business through competitive storms and other breakthroughs. At some point, you will look for funds outside your family and friends—whether by applying for a bank loan or preparing a prospectus to raise venture capital. You will need money, and that means you'll need a business plan with a sound financial focus.

Looking for money is not, of course, the only reason to write a business plan. The planning process is always an opportunity to rethink your business from the ground up. A business in a comfortable

---

Voices

One of the most important factors in success, and I wish we could bottle it, is persistence and willingness to work hard.
—Charles Hofer

plateau may engage in a planning process simply to shake things up. Look at this business as if you were outside, considering buying in. Think "outside the box." What would have to change for you to want this business? Try on this mental change of perspective, and see what ideas present themselves. Perhaps by outsourcing certain functions, or bringing others in-house, new areas of opportunity for profit or efficiency will emerge.

Difficulty can catch up with you from any direction. Competitors can open across the street. The city can close the street for repairs, or reroute your high-profile traffic corridor and leave you with a long lease on a dead end. Innovations happen every day. Most business failures occur because a manager did not see something coming that he or she should have seen—if the situation had been properly analyzed. When everything is going well is a good time to start working on your business plan.

How Do People Plan?

Start planning your business in much the same way you start planning your vacation. Choose a business concept you're excited about and want to experience. Choose something you're really good at. Build on your strengths.

Talk to everybody you know—don't let worries about someone stealing your idea force you to work in isolation. It's pretty unlikely someone else will feel so passionate about your idea that he or she will quit his or her day job and beat you to the punch. It's important that you get some real-world reactions to your ideas, from potential customers, suppliers, lenders, and investors. It's important that you learn what others know about your "vacation destination."

Check out the resources available at the library, bookstore, and on the Internet. But don't spend too much time looking up information about the planning process—remember, this isn't brain surgery, and what you know today is probably adequate to get you started. Instead, concentrate your research efforts on understanding your industry, your competitive environment, and your customers. Assess the threats and opportunities found there. Assess your own strengths and weaknesses where your business concept is concerned.

Many people take classes in business planning, such as those my colleagues and I teach. In your community, you will probably be able to find offices of the Small Business Administration (SBA), and Service Corps of Retired Volunteer Executives (SCORE). Check your nearest campus or chamber of commerce. Small Business Development Center (SBDC) locations may be found on the Web within the Small Business Administration site, *www.sbaonline.sba.gov*. Any of these organizations is likely to offer classes. The classroom environment allows you to go through the planning process with a support group, to learn from others, and to access a teacher who can give you one-on-one coaching.

But most of all, continue reading this book! It's designed to break the planning process into bite-size pieces. The example plans I've included should give you plenty of opportunity to compare your planning process to those of other business owners. The examples will show you that no two plans are alike, and no single format is considered correct.

Good plans start with an executive summary. Think of the summary as the book jacket to the book you are about to buy. If you like what's on the jacket, you buy the book and read on. The executive summary is your commercial—a chance to sell the reader on your concept. Usually, the executive summary is written last, hitting on a few high points that have arisen in the writing of the plan. The executive summary identifies the business concept, and places it in context of the industry, competitive situation, and potential markets. It will summarize the current situation and the purpose for preparing the plan. The summary allows a reader to learn quickly what the plan involves.

Voices

Being an entrepreneur is tough. You get kicked in the teeth every day, nothing goes right, there's always a problem. You're in over your head most of the time. You've just got to believe you're going to make it work. Have passion for what you can do. Believe that you can do it.

—Fred Kiesner

The next sections are the "meat" of the plan, analyzing the business with regard to its market, its personnel, and its financial situation and prospects. Depending on the purpose of the plan, some sections will be emphasized over others. As a planner, you focus on the area that really matters to the success of your business. If an area is relatively stable, unaffected by threats or opportunities, the plan will describe that and move on to more dynamic areas of the business. When the plan is prepared for several audiences—a version for investors and a version for recruiting managers, for example—the relative emphasis in the plan will shift. You may find yourself preparing both a detailed and a summary version for each section of the plan.

The written plan concludes with a summary, followed by any necessary supporting documents, attachments, and appendixes.

How do people plan? By thinking, researching, talking, thinking, writing, researching some more, talking some more, thinking some more. If you enjoy intellectual challenges, self-reflection, and conversation, you are going to enjoy this process. Few things are as fun as designing the course of your life, if you open up to the experience.

Conclusions

Is there a way to jump-start a business? In my opinion, no. But there are factors that, if present, will tell you that you're on the right track.

When you go into business for yourself, make sure you know something nobody else knows. Do something better than anybody else. Develop a unique idea or a unique marketing position.

You may know a skill better, or have leased a location that is superior to competitors, or have designed a certain strategy you are going to adopt that is superior to anything your competition is doing. If you have that edge, have confidence. Your efforts in planning will not be wasted.

Behave ethically

Ethics and honesty have been concerns for business for as long as there has been commerce. Is it wrong to lie in business? Is it wrong to take advantage of information you may have gained through unscrupulous means, or to proceed where you may have a conflict of interest? If "all's fair in love and war" and "business is war," as people say, is it fair to do whatever it takes to win?

No. Before you attempt to justify acting unethically, ask yourself: Is this how I want to be treated by others? A good reputation and a clear conscience are worth more than any temporary advantage you might gain.

Frank Hoy advises any company writing a business plan to be absolutely and unquestioningly honest and ethical:

There are countless opportunities to compromise. You'll have any number of opportunities to shade a deal, where you can get an inside track, operate on inside information, maybe you perceive that bribes are necessary . . . . You never know where those things are going to come back to haunt you. You never know if one of these days you'll decide you want to run for public office. Look at any local

---

**TYPICAL COMPONENTS
OF A BUSINESS PLAN**

Note: A complete generic business plan outline is included in appendix C.

- Section 1: Front matter
  Executive summary
  Business description
  Vision, mission, core values statement(s)
- Section 2: The market
  Market analysis
  Products/services offering description
  Marketing plan
- Section 3: Personnel
  Key management personnel
  Staff needs and organizational plan
- Section 4: Financials
  Profit and loss
  Cash flow
  Balance sheet
  Other
  Assumptions and comments
- Section 5: Closing
  Applications and effects of loans
  Supporting documents

community. Look at the people who sit on city councils and other government bodies. There are all kinds of business owners there. Maybe that will be you one of these days. Or there will be another opportunity for you to be in a prominent position. Are you prepared to expose your background and have it checked out?

Do you want to do business with people who are unethical? Keep in mind, people want to deal with people who are ethical. If you're not, sooner or later they will catch you, and they will spread the word.

Business relationships of all kinds—those between you and your customers, you and your suppliers, you and your employees, you and your advisors—depend on trust. Trust depends on ethical behavior. Your success absolutely demands that you adhere to moral principles and standards to guide your behavior. You must "do right" no matter what the pressure to do otherwise.

Thoughts to Take Away

- Why? You plan to analyze what you want from the business and what you are willing to give up, and also to help you speak to various audiences to gain their support for your plan.

- Who? Those involved in planning will be those who have input on the future of business. These may include business partners, key managers, future or existing customers, and outside advisors. Even the solo entrepreneur should seek input when writing the plan.

- When? Plans are typically created or revised as businesses pass through life stages. These include start-up, expansion, plateaus and breakthroughs, and changes in ownership.

- How? People plan by pursuing research, talking with others, reading books, taking classes, and otherwise devoting their time to creating possible strategies, evaluating those possibilities, and writing their conclusions down in the format of a business plan.

chapterTHREE

Small Business Tomorrow

WHAT YOU WILL FIND IN THIS CHAPTER

- Where is the Internet leading us?
- What can women and minorities expect to find in tomorrow's business environment?
- Will independent retailers survive the competition from national chain discounters?
- What do franchises offer the entrepreneur?

- Is it smart to "SOHO"—to operate a small or home-based business?
- Can families survive a family business?
- How should you address these themes in your business plan?

To have a successful business, you need to have an edge—to know a skill better than most, or have a location that gives you an advantage, or develop a strategy that is superior to anything your competition is doing. Writing a business plan requires that you research the industry and marketplace in which you compete. One goal of this research is to find unbiased support for your belief that you have that strategic advantage.

A section of your written plan will be devoted to a discussion of the industry and market, giving context to your plan, and communicating the strategic advantages of your business concept. The research you do in preparation for writing that section of the plan may help bring to mind business opportunities, such as new markets, or product extensions, or better ways to do what you do, which you will then want to explore. This is what we call "strategic thinking."

To get you started thinking strategically, I've asked my colleagues in entrepreneurship to peer into their crystal balls and share their visions of challenges and opportunities that lie ahead. The themes that surfaced in these discussions concern the impact of the Internet, prospects for economically disadvantaged groups, strategies for independent retailers facing competition from national giants, the future of franchising, changing patterns of work made possible by technology, and the special challenges of family businesses.

One or more of these themes may be having an impact on your business already. One or more may spark a breakthrough in strategic thinking that gives you the competitive edge you've been looking for. I can promise you these trends will be affecting the world in which you live—and so, affecting you.

Here's what we see coming. We're telling you now so that, as you go through the process of writing your plan, you develop strategies with these trends and influences in mind.

Scene: Early Morning, the Office, One Day in 2010

Your office may be a room in your home, the front seat of your car, a converted warehouse, or a corner office suite. Your sales may take place in your showroom, or over a Web site, or in your customer's boardroom. Your business may employ no one, one person, or 50 people. Regardless of your individual circumstances, if you are the owner of a small business, you are a powerful player.

Most people don't realize how significant a role small business plays in the American economy. Studies by the National Federation of Independent Business (NFIB) show that small business is a powerhouse of job creation. Two-thirds of the net new jobs, over the last 25 years, have been created by small business. Overall, small business employs more than half of the private work force. These well-established trends show indications of continuing for years to come.

Who are these small businesses, what are we doing, and how are we going about our work?

The Internet

In every corner of the business world, Internet use is an important aspect of operations. My colleagues and I are finding that virtually everyone is going online to research decisions, make connections, and participate in commercial exchanges. We worry about the unrestrained "Wild West" atmosphere and the legal issues surrounding copyrights and copycat competitors. We dream about the seemingly limitless potential for small businesses to think big. And for most of our clients and students, we have one recommendation above all: Get in the game soon.

As a professional futurist, David Zach is used to speculating about future developments. He cautions:

It's very important to go beyond the first set of implications. The first set of implications for a change almost always look backwards, studying impacts on trends already in progress. But what are the implications of the implications? I try to identify not what is the exact specific future that's going to emerge, but what are the choices and possibilities. I believe the future is not something that just happens. It's something we build, step by step, day by day. The question "where do we go from here" is not so much trying to identify a forecast, as it is identifying principles and values of "what do we want?"

The age of information is not about getting more information. It's about understanding. How can I get information that is exactly what makes me comfortable, instead of confused? This should not be an impossible task, given our growing understanding of information sciences.

But getting just the information we want has so far proved to be difficult.

Once search capabilities have been refined, the Internet will take its place as a new means of sharing information, joining the printing press, the telephone, and the fax machine. We can't tell you if

someone is going to come up with a way to organize that information tomorrow. But when that happens, the Internet will come of age.

In the meantime, while we wait for the perfect search engine, Web sites that rate other sites are helping to fill that information need—and becoming successful Internet businesses in the process. Evaluation sites such as *www.gomez.com* save you from having to discover relevant sites on your own, and provide you with an evaluated list, guiding you quickly to sites that suit your needs.

Changing business relationships

To make the Internet a valuable tool for small and medium-size businesses, we will have to understand a new way of doing business. We may find ourselves removing the middle man from our business relationships. New roles and responsibilities previously assumed by that intermediary may now be yours to manage. You may face a need to form strategic alliances with companies all over the world, to fulfill the promise of business activity unhampered by geographic location.

An unrestrained Wild West

The Internet has opened a frontier where the people who protected our safety as consumers in the past cannot go. There are so few restrictions, so little oversight, that it makes many of my colleagues nervous. Said Don Kuratko:

The Internet has presented us with a challenge, and we're excited, but it's also time to pull back a bit and consider the legal ramifications. What is protectable and what is not? On the Internet you can be copied so quickly, which has raised a lot of legal questions. But the law will move at its regular speed—warp speed behind us.

Voices

I've had a home-based business for 21 years. I am now just at the point where my business is big enough for me to consider outside space. The idea of having a split between work and life is very appealing to me.

—Terri Lonier

It will be interesting to see how our government reacts to all this. Already the debate over lost sales tax revenue is forcing states to take a close look at sales transactions over the Internet. Intellectual property laws, consumer protection in cases of product safety, determinations concerning monopolies and other forms of unfair competition—all are in need of regulation. Frank Hoy posed the question, "Whatever would pass through a legislature, it's going to be obsolete in terms of what's going on in the technology and the environment, by the time it's put in place. Will those laws hinder or help the Internet and the creation of business?"

Add to that the question of boundaries, or the lack of them. Almost any activity that relies on the Internet can be carried out anywhere in the world. That opens up tremendous possibilities—but with them come challenges. Since Internet companies can be located anywhere in the world, who can—and who should—regulate their activities? If we make it more difficult to do business within the United States, will companies move their operations overseas, beyond federal control?

One of the biggest players in the cellular phone industry is Nokia, of Finland. Here is a huge player, coming from a very small country. Your competition could be coming from anywhere—and their "where" might be an environment without laws regulating labor, consumer safety, truth in labeling—you name it. Remaining competitive while maintaining the high standards for business conduct we experience in the United States is a challenge facing each of us.

Internet-specific businesses have unique concerns

One out of every six businesses that starts today is a "dot-com" business—one with no ties to traditional ways of doing business. (Amazon.com is an example of a dot-com business, and Barnes&Noble.com is an example of a traditional retailer building a Web presence as an extension of other operations.)

One out of every six new businesses could be planning to compete with you. Meeting that competitive challenge requires that you integrate Internet technology into your own plans. The cost of designing, maintaining, and publicizing a Web site will increase as sites become more plentiful and more sophisticated. The sooner you enter the fray, the better.

KEY CONCEPT:
HOW BIG IS SMALL BUSINESS?

Relatively little statistical material about small businesses exists, and what does is confusing. We don't even know how many small businesses there are. A "ball park" estimate is the best we have. The term *small business* means different things to different people.

If everyone who files a U.S. tax return with business income is included in the definition of "business," then more than twenty-one million businesses exist. If just those whose principal occupation is owning or operating a business are included, the number falls to just about twelve million. Approximately seven million of those twelve million work for themselves, but don't employ anyone else. That leaves about five million employers. How many are small? Most. Fewer than 80,000 businesses employ 100 or more people.

Source: William Dennis, *A Small Business Primer.* Washington, D.C.; NFIB Foundation, 1993. Reprinted with permission.

But once you're there, competitors will almost immediately begin to copy your moves. For Internet-specific businesses, there are few barriers to entry, which presents an opportunity matched by a threat. It has become easier to start a business. They may be located anywhere, or nowhere. But as a customer of these businesses, you have no assurance that you are dealing with a reputable and reliable firm.

These are just some of the concerns facing Internet-specific businesses and those who compete or do business with them.

Competing with the dot-coms. Hattie Bryant hopes traditional retailers who now face competition from the dot-coms will study their competitors:

If you sell baby clothes, you now have to compete with "BABY.COM." You've got to face that competition squarely. Study your competitors on the Web just as you study your competitors in real life. Figure out how they're doing what they're doing, and what is their potential to affect your market share. I would start surveying my customers who walk in the door, and saying, "Have you been to Baby.com?" And if they have, ask did they purchase any-

thing, what they liked about it; ask "What could we do, to keep your business?" You can't go to sleep at the wheel.

Anyone who starts an Internet business must count on facing competition. "If you have a good idea, you'll have competitors. Acknowledge that," said Don Kuratko. "The question now becomes, what significant competitive advantage do you see for yourself?"

Because of the ease with which people can copy and compete with you, the Internet alone is not enough to give you a strategic edge. You must now demonstrate how you use the Internet to express your other competitive advantages. What else do you have? Your technical knowledge, your service, the backup you provide, or the follow-up? Even if somebody did copy the idea, what else are you going to be doing to outmaneuver competitors and serve customers better?

Cheap to get in, expensive to grow. The Internet has provided an opportunity for people with limited capital to get into business. People with computer skills and creative ideas have been able to get started cheaply, often building a business from home.

But the cost to develop a truly good Web site is going to accelerate in the next few years, Bob Brockhaus advised:

As sites get more sophisticated, as customers demand more and more variety of products, and easier access, and easier transactions, there are going to be some pretty nice bells and whistles coming along. As we get more high-speed transmission, people are going to be looking for more information, because it won't take so long to download it. The cost of maintaining a site that is competitive is going to grow. You'd better find some deep pockets. You won't need it from day one, but you will as your business grows.

Dot-com companies face the same challenge traditional businesses do in terms of marketing. Once you're there, how do your customers find you? Advertising and marketing expenses are turning out to be one of the largest categories of cost for Internet-specific businesses.

Whom are we really dealing with? To customers, the credibility of Web companies is a concern. Europe and other developing regions are producing many new Internet companies. When I talked with

Frank Hoy, he had just returned from teaching several intensive courses at two different universities in Finland. "In both places I came across students who are starting Internet-based businesses while they're still in school. About half the students I taught were Finnish, and half were exchange students from literally all over the world."

With dot-coms being started by everyone from students to Fortune 500 companies, in every corner of the globe, how do we as consumers know we can trust the companies we find on the Web? For centuries, we have relied on reputation and personal experience as we placed our trust in local merchants. With the growth of the mass consumer culture, we formed relationships with national brands, extending our trust beyond the borders of our local communities. The reputations of these national brands were built largely through advertising expenditures. We will not easily extend our trust to every unfamiliar dot-com name that turns up in our search engines. New Internet businesses will need to find new ways to gain customer trust if they are to succeed. Those firms that can spend enough on advertising to build brand awareness will have the edge—but real consumer confidence can't be bought. It must be earned, and that takes time. How long will it take in the hyperdrive time frame of e-commerce? Will those with the biggest advertising budgets succeed, driving out small but viable competitors?

RESOURCE: *WWW.GOMEZ.COM*

Web sites that rate other Web sites can make your Web research missions more efficient. Check out *www.gomez.com*. This site evaluates various e-commerce sites. For example, if you're looking for cars, hit "autos" and the site shows a list of auto sites ranked by many factors, including ease of use, customer confidence, on-site resources, relationship services, and more. It even tells you which sites are best for the serious shopper, the "tire-kicker," the first-time buyer, and the auto enthusiast.

Sites like these are a great way to check out what your competition is doing on the Internet. Check now and check often—Web sites change daily.

FOUR REASONS TO TACKLE THE INTERNET

Hattie Bryant shared these thoughts from her presentation, "Four Good Reasons to Use the Internet to Build Your Business."

• "The first reason the small business owner needs to embrace this is just to be there." Buyers of both consumer and business products and services are going online to research purchases. The Internet presents a wonderful medium for finding information and comparing offerings. Your customers will most likely find your competitors on the Internet. And that's the first reason you should be there.

• "The second reason is to generate leads," Bryant continued. Many small business owners use their Web sites to stimulate interest in their products, then offer some incentive for people to e-mail them, thus beginning the sales cycle. Business owners move toward more personal communication as the sales cycle progresses, and in many cases, turn those e-mails into customers.

• "The third reason is to actually get the cash register to ring," Bryant stated. The ability to make purchases over the Internet has been a reality for some time now, but consumer confidence in the safety of e-commerce transactions was slow to follow. Finally, growing trust in the privacy and reliability of transactions is allowing the Internet to become a point of purchase. It's very inexpensive to collect money via the Internet. You can outsource your transactions to companies that specialize in e-commerce. Many telephone companies and Internet service providers will handle the transactions for you, in exchange for a little piece of the action.

• "The fourth and last reason—the best reason for a small business—is to actually use the Internet to do their back-office business practices," Bryant believes. A business Web site can be accessible to the whole world, but it doesn't have to be. Some areas of the site can be protected, accessible only to those with a password. Businesses are using private areas of their Web sites to streamline internal operations. They are using Web applications to do their accounting, their ordering, their billing, and to pay their bills and vendors. Some companies make their personnel manual available online, and allow individuals to check the status of benefits and retirement accounts through password-protected files. Private areas of the site allow workers in different physical locations to have access to the same files and information, making telecommuting and virtual work groups a practical reality. "All the business of running a business is going to be made much easier and more efficient by the Internet," Bryant concluded.

Consider, for example, the business plan for Resume.com. This Internet employment service plans to compete head to head with "established" employment firms like Monster.com and Hotjobs.com and, according to their plan, "to create a specific niche for itself in order to obtain the greatest percentage of market share possible." ("Established" takes on new meaning in Internet time: These "established" competitors were start-ups just one year before the Resume.com plan was written.) If Resume.com fails to earn consumer confidence, either through a failure to deliver real added value or simply through a failure to connect with potential users, it will never get a chance to "create a specific niche." Its dreams of obtaining market share will go unrealized.

The winner in this instance is likely to be the firm with the largest advertising budget that delivers the promised value. If all goes according to plan, Resume.com will be that provider. But Resume.com's founders may find their business subject to a buyout offer by a competitor in a round of consolidation moves before they've reached that goal. Or if they are less fortunate, Resume.com may simply become a casualty of an industrywide shakeout. No one can guarantee that the marketplace will give a business the chance to earn the credibility it needs to survive.

Not interested in the Internet?

The Internet's most visible impact for many of us will be its role as a communication vehicle, following on the heels of the telephone, television, and e-mail. Its unique appeal lies in bringing the sight and sound capabilities of television together with the interactive capabilities of telephones and e-mail. Through a Web site, a company can interact with its customers—and track those interactions. And therein lies a Trojan Horse as significant as the convenient communication we enjoy thanks to the Internet.

Tracking of online interactions presents a tremendous opportunity. If you learn to collect and use this information appropriately, it can bring new levels of sophistication to your business practices. Fewer and fewer businesses will be able to maintain a competitive edge without the depth of insight into customers, products, and purchase transactions that Web site data can produce. You will be able to predict accurately what the market is for any product or service, where the peaks and valleys in demand will fall, why one plant places more orders than another plant. Such "data mining" will be the source of many of the new insights and innovations that come along. If you are interested in maintaining a successful business, you need to take an interest in the Internet.

No one prescription concerning the Internet will be right for all, however. Some people are going to be better off designing their businesses around an Internet-specific commerce model; some are going to be better off pairing a Web presence with a physical presence; and some will be best served by waiting until a shakeout takes place. "Then they can look at what the best practices are, and say 'now I can see what's cost-effective. That's the route I'm going to take,'" observed Frank Hoy.

The Internet and your business plan

When you're writing a business plan, how do you incorporate the Internet? No matter where you stand with regard to this new forum of commerce, you need to address that variable in your plan. Don Kuratko offered this advice:

If it is not an Internet-specific business, do some research within your industry. Find similar firms that are using the Internet to their advantage—selling, or advertising, or providing information for consumers, or whatever. Use that information in your business plan.

If it is an Internet-specific business, and you're claiming there's nothing like it out there, I'd still recommend you do the research as you would for a traditional business. Ask yourself, within the Internet industry, what are some similar businesses? How do you plan to maintain your strategic edge?

The Internet offers tremendous opportunities, and unforeseen threats, in every corner of the commercial world. Read about it, discuss it with your peers and advisors. Keep asking the entrepreneur's favorite question: "what if . . . ?"

Opportunities for Women and Minorities

Opportunities in entrepreneurship are at their brightest for those who have in the past been kept on the sidelines of the economy, including large numbers of women, and racial and ethnic minorities. Those who have entered corporate American life have found that access to the top level of power and influence is still difficult to attain. Those who become frustrated in their corporate jobs are taking the skills and experiences learned there and applying them to starting businesses.

Women's work

Women in the corporate workplace have been gaining knowledge and skills, and have established a track record demonstrating their competence in business. In corporate settings, hierarchical management styles have given way to more team-based approaches. Women's strengths in communication, working with people, networking, and coordinating multiple tasks have come to be valued. Our track record and strengths have prepared us for the challenge of entrepreneurship.

At just the right moment, the Internet has arrived to provide women with a vehicle to grow businesses. "Take the skills and talents that women have, and give them that kind of a tool—we are going to see some incredible advances by women entrepreneurs in the next 10 years," Don Kuratko predicts.

Statistics show women are starting businesses at a rate faster than men these days, but this trend has its dark side. Terri Lonier observed:

Having a business is not something that can be a sideline. To create a thriving business takes a lot of focus and

Voices

The Internet is in some ways the classic low-cost-of-entry wedge. People who have some computer skills and some creative ideas have been able to get in cheaply, with home-based kinds of businesses. They've had the freedom to experiment, because the risk tends to be small, with less capital investment.

—Frank Hoy

a lot of time. Many times it has to take priority over home life. Sometimes friends and family don't understand it. Many women find they get a huge thrill out of running a business, and they're very empowered, and yet—the people within their circle who depend on them don't really understand what it takes to run a business. It will be an incredible challenge.

Opportunity in diversity

History teaches us that racial and ethnic minorities have always been entrepreneurial. Due in part to discrimination by the dominant culture, these groups have had to create their own jobs. In doing so, they have contributed greatly to the economic health of the United States. The Asian immigrant community has been the most successful in the business world, when compared to other minority segments, but others are coming on strong. The Hispanic population is the largest ethnic group in the United States, and faces special challenges in entrepreneurship. Frank Hoy, in his position as dean of the College of Business Administration at the University of Texas at El Paso, works closely with Hispanics in business and has this to say:

The Hispanic population has not come in with the same entrepreneurial attitudes, in terms of creating their own enterprises. But that is changing. More and more, there has been greater encouragement and more role models for Hispanic business creation. Various Hispanic and Mexican-American chambers of commerce, and other leadership roles that Hispanics are beginning to take on, are driving that.

We look at Hispanic entrepreneurship as the key to economic development throughout the Southwest. There's going to be a limit to the number of high-paying jobs that come out of this region, so if we're going to have economic health and increased levels of education and prosperity among Hispanic immigrants, they're going to have to create their own companies.

Some of my contemporaries have concerns that minority cultures have not emphasized education to the extent our society demands. "Education is now becoming extremely critical to success in the future. You've got to have an education, to be in charge of knowledge. If you're not in charge of knowledge in the future, you're not going to make it," Fred Kiesner declared.

> ### KEY CONCEPT: INTERNET COMPETITION
>
> Whether you are doing business on the Web or not, you almost certainly face competition from businesses that are doing business there. Studying your competitors on the Web is just as important as studying your competitors next door. If you have a good idea, believe me, you'll have competition.

Given the right educational background and entrepreneurial encouragement, minority individuals have the opportunity to develop businesses within their culture, and to attract those outside the culture as well. Of course, their opportunities go well beyond businesses focused on specific subgroups.

Said Michael Meeks, "Being a minority myself, a Native American, and being involved in minority groups, I see a problem in that we focus too much on being minority groups. That causes a myopic view. The playing field is being leveled, and I see minorities playing a larger and larger part. There's a huge opportunity now for us to start businesses."

With opportunities for minorities plentiful, the question will soon become—who is a minority any more? As a culture, we may find ourselves categorizing groups by their relative access to social and economic advantage, rather than patterns of ethnicity, race, or gender.

"A lot of our notions of things like race may be bound up in a chronological cohort," David Zach said. "Views of what is race, or what is a particular group, change over time. A tremendous number of people in the U.S. are marrying people of a different race. The melting pot is not a myth. The next generation will be of mixed race, and cool with that."

Entrepreneurship will continue to be an important means of blending new arrivals into the contemporary American business stew.

Never a better time

Access to capital has been the greatest barrier to entry into entrepreneurship facing women and minorities, and this concern is not going away. There remains a degree of bias in the old establishment against investing with minority businesspeople. As a result, new business growth is more likely to be found in small "mom-and-pop" businesses that require less start-up capital.

Disadvantaged groups find it harder to come up with a social network that will help them finance major ventures. In the next decade, we will see government moving away from financial assistance programs targeted toward women and minorities, so relief will not come from that quarter.

But I predict these barriers are crumbling. The baby boom generation, because of their success in investment markets, represents a source of new capital coming into the game. There's a great opportunity here for our culturally diverse entrepreneurs to jump in and channel some of the rewards of our healthy economic environment toward themselves.

Internet businesses are the recipients of much of that new capital. It lends itself to marketing to special niches. Building customer relationships is going to be very important. Minorities that can bond with commonalties of their customers could be very successful. Investors will recognize this potential, and capital will be available for those with strong business concepts in which to invest.

Are you white, are you male, are you sorry you can't serve yourself up a share of this bubbling pot of opportunity? Don't despair. Although membership in a special group gives certain individuals a competitive edge, it also provides an identifiable market niche others can target with products and services. Look for a need you can fill. Busy businesswomen need concierge services, elder care, logistical support . . . you name it. Minority businesspeople need help connecting with mentors, role models, and investors. Specific groups have unique needs, from makeup that flatters Asian complexions to legal expertise in workplace discrimination. Where there's a need, there's an entrepreneurial opportunity. Where there's a group with common characteristics, there's likely to be a niche that can be served.

Independent Retailers in the Land of the Giants

If only the news were so rosy for independent retailers. We have watched with dismay as across

America, Main Street shopkeepers close their doors in the face of competition from big discount stores on the edge of town. We cluck sympathetically as we drive to those big stores for their unbeatable prices and huge selections.

Some industries have been hit harder than others. Family-run restaurants are rare compared to national franchises; independent coffee shops are yielding to Starbucks with hardly a whimper. Today, your local druggist is more likely to work for a regional chain of pharmacies than for himself or herself. Among the hardest hit have been retailers in the book business. First, the bookstore giants Barnes & Noble and Borders moved in with their megastores; then the e-commerce pioneer Amazon.com stole a piece of their very large pie. The visions of large selections at discounts that only massive buying power can achieve have seduced customers away from independent booksellers all over America. Who will be next to go?

Don't let it be you. There are ways for a David to compete with a Goliath, and the good news is the battle isn't always won with dollars, but with savvy. Retailers who read their customers like books will thrive, as will those who outsmart the competition and master the latest weapon in the arsenal—you guessed it, the Internet.

Know your enemy: Big-box discounters and category killers

Big-box discounters live by a simple motto: "Stack it deep and sell it cheap." A no-frills approach to retailing keeps overhead low, and national buying power keeps huge inventories arriving just in time to match demand. The result? Low, low prices. Discount stores have made big-box consumer goods like washers and dryers, big-screen televisions, computers, and air conditioners affordable to almost every family. In their own way, they've done a lot to improve our overall quality of life.

Category-killers blend the big-box discount store concept with a focus on specific retail segments, such as electronics, toys, pet supplies, books, office supplies, or hardware. Category-killers have brought hard times to niche businesses, raising consumer expectations of wide product selections and cheap prices.

Big-box retailers and category-killers are succeeding because they do a lot of things right. They make goods available in a cost-efficient manner. They use technology to their advantage, controlling inventory management and product line distribution. It's not surprising that small retailers are feeling threatened.

"Retailers with one to four employees, and to some extent the five-to-nine employee retailers as well, are taking a huge beating," acknowledged William Dennis, a researcher with the National Federation of Independent Businesses. "The proportion of retailers in our membership has gone down from about 35 percent back in the mid-1970s to about 23 percent today. If you're a retailer selling goods that are mass market, you'd better have something that's really special or different about you."

It's a fact of life that commodity products, where price is the sole factor driving the purchase decision, will probably never again be viable for independent retailers. The national giants have taken that ground, and wise independents will leave it to them. Never compete on price against the big boys because you'll always lose.

But as Frank Hoy reminds us:

Retailing is an evolutionary thing. As soon as one type of business seems to dominate everything, some new initiative enters in. Because there's always a weakness. There's always a gap. Whether it's office supplies or bookstores, there will always be an opportunity for niche businesses that emphasize service over product, because people will pay a premium for that.

**KEY CONCEPT:
THE INDEPENDENT ADVANTAGE**

Commodity products, where price is the sole factor driving the purchase decision, will probably not be viable for independent retailers in the future. Successful independent retailers find ways to compete other than on price.

How David fights Goliath

The essential strategic insight for independent retailers fighting giant chains is simply this: Find ways to compete other than on price. In a competition for best quality, or personal service, or staff knowledge, you are quite possibly able to offer something the big discounters can't match.

Smaller outfits can compete with big-box megastores, but they have to find creative ways to do it. For small businesses, a key advantage is their creation of a personal atmosphere. Consumers truly enjoy dealing with the owner of the company. That's part of human nature. Successful small retailers understand that, focus on that, and become very customer focused.

"The discounters may try to give the family business feel, but they don't have the heart, soul, and emotion that an independent store does. They will always come across as phony. The real advantage to independents is to cherish and use those special aspects you do possess," said Don Kuratko.

Hattie Bryant agreed. "We cannot compete on price, and we will refuse to. Instead, we will have a merchandise mix that is so original, people will come back just to see what's new. Big-box retailers are predictable. Independents will succeed by being unpredictable, and surprising our customers."

Voices

The barriers to entry for minorities have been dropped, or significantly lessened. I believe that we now have opportunities that we have never had in history, and it will only continue to improve.

—Michael Meeks

Bryant sees a move toward what she termed the holistic shopping experience. "There is a return to the city, a revitalization of urban areas. We want to come back to a sense of community, a feeling that this is where I belong, where I fit in, where they know my name. Revitalized areas are proliferating, and providing a place for specialty retail to thrive."

Location has always been of critical importance to retailers. Location may prove to be the attribute that allows independents to survive the inroads of retail giants. Independents will sidestep their competitors through locating in vibrant specialized shopping districts, or through a Web site that literally brings the world to their door. Who's to say you have to compete only in your community? You can now go global and find customers all over. You're not pinned down by your local big-box competitor any more.

I can hear you saying, "but they're all over the Internet, too, and they can afford a bigger presence than I could ever dream of." I'm not suggesting that small business can compete directly with big business on the Internet. You don't go toe to toe. You do the end run.

Bob Brockhaus suggested that very narrow niches offer large opportunity for the business that commits to specialization:

If I were only going to sell supplies for left-handed plumbers—there aren't that many left-handed plumbers within five miles of my stores. But with the Internet, I can now have a market worldwide of left-handed plumbers. It's a very small niche, but it spans the world. If I can get the product to them in a timely fashion and there's no one else trying to serve that niche, I may do very, very well.

Entrepreneurs are finding worldwide narrow niches in areas from biotechnology lab supplies to sheet music for folk guitar players.

Small businesses using the Internet to deepen relationships with current customers are on the right track. If you think about the Internet as a service portal, not a sales portal, as a small business owner, you will win.

Find your niche, consider the world your location, and then serve, serve, serve. And count your blessings. Societal trends, including a return to holistic values and a growing comfort with the Internet, have arrived just in time to save many independent businesses from extinction.

Franchises

Entrepreneurship carries a double-edged sword: risk and independence. As an entrepreneur, you have the freedom to pursue any strategy you want, but you run the risk that what you want to do is a mistake. Franchises offer the opportunity to minimize your risk of mistakes in exchange for a degree of independence. Franchising allows individually owned businesses to operate as part of a large chain. The products and services offered, and many other aspects of the operation, are held to a standard imposed by the franchiser.

A franchise operation can generate a reliable income for its owner, making it a popular option for the individual whose goal is to replace working for somebody else with self-employment. A single franchise operation will not likely take that individual to millionaire status, however. The big bucks come to the individual who owns multiple franchises, or who creates a business concept with the intention of becoming a franchiser, like that of the Whole Fish & Seafood business plan example. Every business should examine, in the planning process, whether growth through franchising is a possibility.

The popularity of franchise establishments relies on the fact that franchises make everything alike, and people like that. We want to be assured of consistency in many aspects of our lives. Although we may complain about the homogenized aspect franchises are giving America, we appreciate that whether we are in Atlanta or Duluth, our buying experience at a McDonald's or a Jiffy Lube will be reassuringly predictable.

On becoming a franchisee

What you're buying, when you purchase a franchise, may be an operating procedure, or a license to a particular process, or the brand name and market

Voices

Populations mix. Cultures do not ever really stay the same over time. They adapt, and they blend, if they wish to survive.

—David Zach

acceptance that the franchise organization has developed. You are getting, in essence, a business by kit.

People buy franchises because they remove much of the possibility of failure. The "school of hard knocks" lessons that entrepreneurs experience in their start-up years are handed to the franchisee, neatly packaged. Can this really be considered entrepreneurship? "All you have to worry about is hiring people and making sure they show up. And that's one of the least attractive parts of the whole business," said William Dennis.

Franchises are great for people who want systems. With the franchise you get guidance and parameters within which to work. You can get into business, get some training, and by virtue of the franchise's national reputation, get your operation properly positioned right from the start.

Franchises work well for people who want to be part of a larger team effort. Some of us just do better as part of something big.

Franchising is, objectively, the most efficient way for an idea to proliferate. Each franchisee who buys in contributes dollars that are used to grow the entire business. The franchise organization's investment in marketing and advertising goes a long way in building brand identity, positive associations in consumers' minds that benefit each franchisee. These are big advantages for the small retailer who doesn't mind trading some independence for a greater chance at success.

If you're buying a franchise. No business venture is without its risks, of course. Making sure you buy the *right* franchise is a critical factor to consider. First of all, you've got to love the "stuff" of the franchise. If it's not something you can feel a personal passion for, don't even think of it.

Make sure the franchise organization you consider is making money based on franchisees' profits, not making money by selling lots of franchises. If all they're doing is selling franchises, you're not going to get the support you need. You want somebody who will be profitable because *you're* profitable.

When you've created a "short list" of franchises you could love, research the companies carefully. Call the home office. Call other franchisees. Call the Federal Trade Commission. Each franchiser is

---

KEY CONCEPT: FRANCHISER AND FRANCHISEE

A company that creates and sells franchises is called a *franchiser*. An individual who has purchased a franchise is called a *franchisee*. A franchisee acquires the rights to a "business in a box." The "box" typically includes the franchiser's product or service, and use of the franchiser's trade reputation and operational systems. The franchise agreement usually gives the franchisee exclusive rights to a specific geographic area in return for a fee and usually a percentage of gross sales.

---

required by federal law to provide documents that demonstrate their history and track record. Dig down and find the good, the bad, and the ugly. Weigh it all out. You won't find a perfect company, but you should find one or more that fit your goals. A word of advice: As you research franchise organizations, ask would you be buying a single franchise in a network that has nothing else but multiunit franchisees? You may be setting yourself up to get pushed around by others with more clout in the organization.

Choosing a franchise doesn't excuse you from doing your homework. Even if the franchiser provides a business plan, you need to prepare your own. Ask, and answer, your own deep questions. Study the marketing, personnel, and financial aspects of the franchise in relation to your unique situation. It may be a great franchise offer—but not right for you.

On becoming a franchiser

Some businesses create themselves from the start with the intention of becoming franchisers. Others discover franchising as a means to grow. Take the example of Computer Tots. Two women educators believed that young children have the ability to learn simple computer skills. As a low-cost alternative to day care, they created Computer Tots. Their intent was simply to start a business that would replace their "day job" incomes. But the lawyer they found to handle their incorporation happened to specialize in helping businesses franchise their concepts. Consequently,

---

**KEY CONCEPT:
FRANCHISES OFFER LESS RISK**

The rule of thumb is that, on average, 80 percent of new businesses fail within five years. The typical failure rate for a new location of an existing franchise falls under 30 percent. With many franchisers, the failure rate is below 20 percent. Your likelihood of success is statistically much better in a franchise than in your own business.

---

after two years, the women were able to use his expertise and expand into a franchiser role, selling around the United States. Their start-up became a highly successful national franchise operation.

There is danger in a growth strategy based on selling franchises, however. Ambitious entrepreneurs run the risk of taking on too much, too soon. Consider the example of Boston Market. The franchisers announced they would open 500 stores in one year. It's very hard to control that kind of growth. They floundered in a big way, and have now sold a major portion of their operation to McDonald's. As they discovered, maintaining standards while growing at that kind of pace is very difficult.

Every existing business ought to examine itself for a franchise opportunity. Franchising may be a viable strategy for growing an organization, if the risks inherent in rapid growth are managed well.

Frank Hoy contributed this insight: "If people look at franchises thinking they want to build wealth, they want to expand and grow, then they should look at the multiunit route. Almost any franchise organization in the United States will have a multiunit franchisee whose net worth is larger than that of the franchiser."

The future of franchising

Hoy observed that franchising as in terrific export industry for the United States:

You can go anywhere in the world and see U.S. franchises. There are concerns about cultural imperialism, everybody in the world is becoming Americanized. But I see franchising as an incredibly beneficial tool to third-world countries where there has not been sufficient education or economic background for people to develop

managerial skills. With a franchise, if somebody is placed in a management position and given an operating manual and follows that to the letter, they tend to be successful. They've followed a successful model. This can be very valuable in training managers for an economy, who will subsequently start their own businesses as they develop their skills and build equity.

The franchise operation you start today, and expand overseas tomorrow, may play a key role in fostering economic health in other countries in years to come.

Many of us hold personal values that make us dubious about franchise operations. We have concerns that franchises, like big-box retailers, are homogenizing society in a way we would rather reject. But David Zach offered a different vision of the future. "I've wondered, can somebody take the concept of a franchise, and put it behind the scenes, so that it allows for what's up front to be more unique and more indigenous? So the system is organized efficiently, but the presentation of the product or service has more unique value, that people can relate to, at that spot?"

Zach looked to the hotel industry for an example:

You go to a Marriott anywhere in the world, and you know you're in a Marriott. It looks the same. It smells the same. On the other hand, consider Preferred Hotels. They are an affiliation as opposed to a chain, an affiliation of unique hotels throughout the world. They are quite often the showcase hotel in the area. In Milwaukee, the Pfister is a Preferred Hotel. When you're at the Pfister, you know you're in Milwaukee, you know you're in an elegant, beautiful, hotel. It's a unique experience.

Preferred Hotels might be a really good model for the future, in terms of how we allow for uniqueness to

---

**RESOURCE:
FRANCHISE DISCLOSURES**

To learn more about information franchisers must reveal to potential franchisees, write to the Division of Marketing Practices, Federal Trade Commission, Washington, DC 20580, or call 202-326-2502. Visit their Web site at *www.ftc.gov/bcp/conline/pubs/invest/buyfran.htm.*

---

come through. We can have the display of a franchise be more personalized to the individual owners and the individual community.

My colleagues and I believe that in the future, franchises will allow more latitude to customize the offering to local demands. We will see the efficiencies of chain operations supporting unique individual franchisees that are customized to reflect local interests and tastes.

The SOHO Phenomenon

Small offices and home offices—the world of SOHO—make up the fastest growing segment of the business environment. In basements and garages, in spare bedrooms and in cars and in coffee shops, the workers of SOHO can be found. International Data Corporation (IDC) projects an expected fifty-one million SOHO businesses by 2002. IDC reports 1,200 new SOHOs are forming every hour of every business day. What has produced this activity? The intersection of two trends. Our transition to a knowledge-based economy has created business opportunities where physical inventory is not required, greatly reducing a business's need for space. Technological advances have brought us business equipment that is affordable and simple to use, even portable enough to allow us to do business wherever we happen to be. Wireless communications complete the picture. Working from anywhere we please has become a practical reality for many people.

Terry Lonier is the founder of Working Solo, Inc., a business that in her words "works within a triangle bounded by technology, marketing, and small business." She is my main source for news from the land of SOHO. She identified three general categories of SOHO businesses: the perennials, the transitionals, and the telecommuters:

Perennial SOHOs are those companies that never want to get larger than 20 people. Transitional SOHOs are the start-ups that are blasting right through that limit. It's a matter of choice. Then there's the whole realm of telecommuters. There are more than ten million of them now. They are SOHOs as well, working out of home offices, but they're really corporate workers. They're an intriguing mix.

KEY CONCEPT: PROS AND CONS OF SOHO

The low fixed costs associated with running a business in the home increases the likelihood of success for a SOHO business. Starting a SOHO requires relatively little capital. However, the isolation of SOHO work isn't for everybody. It may even be illegal in your community. Research your plan carefully if you are considering a SOHO enterprise.

We tend to think of SOHOs as technology based, but that's not necessarily true. Home-based companies have long operated in areas like construction, lawn care, janitorial services, accounting, and insurance. The arrival of Internet communications has simply made the SOHO choice practical for an even wider range of pursuits.

Lonier predicts that technology will open up even wider horizons, as application service providers become established:

You will be able to connect to the Internet and have all of your data and applications sitting up on some "Cloud 9." Any time you want to be at work, wherever you are, that's your office. That opens up enormous possibilities—you can be in Phoenix on Monday, and Seattle on Wednesday, and Cancun on Friday. You can be just as productive, because your files are always with you, wherever you are. It's going to be really powerful.

SOHO business owners are a very individualistic breed. If you ask them what they are, they don't say, "I'm a business owner." They say, "I'm a Web designer, I'm a dog groomer, I do wallpapering." They identify with their talent, their skill, their craft.

They are very independent thinkers. They start businesses not just for the financial rewards, but for the flexibility and they freedom the hope the SOHO choice will bring.

Pleasures and perils of the SOHO lifestyle

SOHO work could be considered a return to a very traditional idea. The shopkeeper who lived above his shop, the farmer on his land, were essentially SOHO businesspeople. People have only worked away from home for the last hundred years or so. Increasing numbers of people will choose to return to SOHO because they are craving a life that integrates home, family, and work into a more balanced whole.

SOHO work is an option for many people outside the typical entrepreneurial mold. Younger people, older people, immigrants to this country—all are finding that the start-up of a SOHO business requires little capital and can often be done without a bank loan.

The low fixed costs associated with running a business in the home increases the probability of success for the SOHO venture. "One of the reasons SOHO businesses have a higher rate of success is because of their very low overhead. What they aren't spending on rent and utilities they can put back into marketing. Or into their pockets," Lonier added.

The dark side of SOHO. The SOHO opportunity has its dark side, however. It may even be illegal in your community. William Dennis explained the issues:

There's a major concern here, regarding zoning, the environment, land use. There's going to be increasing pressure to restrict the impact of one person's residence on other people's residences. You run into trouble with the neighbors. Maybe the UPS truck stops once too often. Or say you're a piano teacher, you've got people walking in and out every hour. Neighbors don't like it. There are huge environmental issues. It will have to do with what you sell, the transportation it takes for your customers to get to you, land use—we're seeing these issues now, but they'll be in spades in the next 20 or 30 years.

Frank Hoy pointed out that the isolation of SOHO work isn't for everybody. "Studies have documented that we are social animals, and we like the physical interaction we have with people. Even at companies that allow people to work at home, those people still come to the office, just for that social exchange." Companies that encourage their work force to spend part of the week at home and part of their week in the office in face-to-face interaction report that their employee satisfaction is very high. Such companies have had to overcome workspace productivity issues to keep expensive real estate from being underutilized, however. Shared-use offices, a practice sometimes called "hoteling," is one answer to the part-time presence of the work force.

Independent SOHO workers, lacking even the part-time social life of a workplace, must find their own ways to cope with isolation. David Zach reported that "working solo provides the entrepreneur with choices, almost on a daily basis, of who to work with. A critical part of successful 'sohoing' is maintaining connections." Successful SOHO operators combat the isolation with an intuitive love of connecting, making time to network with potential clients and strategic partners, and to commiserate with fellow SOHOists. Some simply take their work where people gather, perching at coffee shops with a laptop, a cell phone, and a cappuccino.

Terri Lonier's firm Working Solo, Inc., recently asked SOHO entrepreneurs to comment on their greatest fears. Their top three responses were:

- Not having enough money to keep the business going
- Long-term illness of self or key employee
- Losing customers to a larger company

All three responses relate to maintaining a sufficient flow of work and cash in the business, a primary burden for SOHO firms.

How do SOHOs grow?

Every business plan must address the subject of growth. Your strategic approach to growth may be to run from it like the plague—it's not unusual for a small craft business, like that of our example The Artful Fly, to make a conscious effort to restrict the business to a size the founding craftspeople can manage. It is also not unusual, since the arrival of e-commerce, for a business to start in the garage,

Voices

Women are very busy; we make our own incomes, we're not going to stress ourselves to save a dollar per pound on oranges when we could go to a smaller, more accessible place, and have a more holistic, pleasant shopping experience.

—Hattie Bryant

take over the whole house, and be in an office complex employing 200 people within the span of a year.

Neither will happen without appropriate planning. Chuck Hofer described the dilemma that growing SOHOs face, and proposed a solution:

If you've got a business you started in your home office, and you've found out that there's a bigger market and you need additional employees, it gets difficult to expand such a business under traditional methods. You have to have your employees come to your home, which leads to zoning problems, and so after a period of time, if you want to grow, you need to set up a "real" office. The point is, you lose the circumstances that allowed you to work from home.

But with the World Wide Web, you could potentially add employees, who also operate out of their homes, with the transfer of business records and so forth going over the Internet.

If your plan does call for growth, make sure you build the cost of "real" office space into your pricing structure. Just because you don't have occupancy costs in your home doesn't mean you shouldn't charge as if you did. Build those cost centers into your pricing structure from the start, or you'll face a rocky transition when you make the move into commercial space.

SOHOs benefit society

My colleagues are excited about the potential of SOHOs. Fred Kiesner said:

We've got to get the managers, the executive types in the world, to understand that you don't have to be at your desk in an office to be working. People in the big businesses don't understand that. The employee is going to be able to go out and be independent, not have to work for one company any more, instead do contract work for six, eight companies. I see a lot more people having their own little businesses and making a nice living out of it.

George Solomon pointed out the advantages of this system to the employer. "With outsourcing I don't have to employ you anymore. I'll make you a contractor and make you responsible for all those overhead costs that I used to be responsible for, like vacations, and health insurance and medical insurance and everything else." Both employer and

---

TOP MYTHS ABOUT WORKING SOLO

1. I won't have a boss.
2. I can set my own work hours.
3. I won't have to work as hard.
4. I'll be able to charge a lot more money.
5. I'll be able to take long vacations.
6. No one will be able to tell me what to do.
7. I'll be on my own.
8. I'll only need a few customers.
9. I can figure things out as I go along.
10. I'm good at what I do; how hard can it be?

From *Working Solo* by Terri Lonier, published by John Wiley & Sons

---

employee—or call it client and service provider—are happy with the new paradigm.

But Michael Meeks is thinking even bigger than that:

I believe SOHOs are the next avenue to solve a lot of global problems. Example: transportation. We're seeing gridlock situations in big cities. The mayors of Denver and Atlanta are investing in technology to create situations that enhance SOHOs. If you've got someone working at home, or in decentralized small offices, you can decrease the number of people on the road.

But SOHOs have a larger benefit. There's also a low entry barrier for a lot of people to develop entrepreneurial skills, even if they're working for someone else out of their home office. We've gotten to the point where over 70 percent of families are two-income, and in most cases, that's two people working away from home. We'll see more people going back to the home, trying to establish the family values we had decades ago. SOHOs and technology are going to allow that.

Family Business

If you're thinking about a family business, you need to be aware that, like it or not, you're going to play three roles. If you drew three overlapping circles, like a three-leaf clover, and labeled one circle Family, one circle Business, and one circle Ownership, you'd have the three roles you play as a family business owner. It's much more complicated to participate in a family business because you must play these three roles simultaneously.

For one thing, you're always a family member, regardless of the business. That's the role in which you worry about the health and prosperity of your family. Continuity is very important to the family. Your participation in family life and in the community is important. All these can be whittled away by the other roles you play in a family business.

You're always a business manager, regardless of the family. You worry about operations, finances, employees, suppliers, customer relationships, and all the other concerns. The business's plans for growth can have tremendous impact on the family. The business may simply be an income-substitution type of enterprise, which will end when the primary family members involved retire or pass away. But quite possibly the business is intended to grow. Is the goal to sell the business when it reaches a certain level, or to have it remain in the family?

If one of the goals that you set for your business is continuity from one generation to the next, then you need to plan for that right up front. And that's where ownership comes in.

Who owns the business? Do you and your spouse own the business? Do you, your spouse, and your children own the business? With ownership comes additional problems, such as liquidity, capital allocation, and assuring succession. Who is going to take over this family business if something were to happen to its leader? Even those of us who know business planning rarely think about those eventualities. Certainly in my own family's business, this was true. My father thought he was immortal, right up until his fifth heart attack killed him. Somehow the first four didn't motivate him to make plans for training anyone to take over the family business.

How do you keep these roles separate? How do you manage your competing priorities so that you still have a family *and* a business? Communication makes a family business work. How we talk about the business among our family members determines whether we are going to be successful at balancing our three roles.

Bob Brockhaus weighed in on the importance of communication in family-owned businesses:

It's a concept that a lot of entrepreneurs don't have in mind initially, when they are just starting a business. But also, in the back of everybody's mind, if they have children, is the idea that someday this might be one that's run by their kids.

As time passes, it becomes more likely and more unlikely at the same time. The father may assume that his oldest son is going to take over the business some day, but doesn't really discuss it with that son. The son really down deep wants to be a concert pianist, but doesn't even share that with his father. They are going down two separate roads, but thinking they are both on the same road. The father then becomes disappointed when the son doesn't take it over, or the son does because he owes it to his parents, but it isn't really his choice.

The solution is really early communication. What is the business really like? What are the problems, the opportunities, so that the second generation gets a more realistic view? Often times they see it simply as a cash cow that gives them a good life, or, as something that takes their father, even their mother, and their money, away. Because all the profits are going back in the business, Mom and Dad are working umpteen hours a week, never having time for relaxation or activities with the family. Dad comes home, sits around the dinner table at night, complaining about all the things that happened at the business. Not talking as much about the good things that happen. The kids are hearing this, and saying "this ain't gonna be me when I grow up. I'm going to do something else." Inadvertently, the father is leading the son away. Early com-

munication, honest and complete communication, is the best thing that can be done to prepare for succession.

When it is determined there will be succession to a second generation, then the strategy needs to incorporate the desires of that junior generation. The son may want to go international, but the father goes on developing the local company by opening more stores but all in the locality, doing nothing to prepare for doing the international business. When the son gets the business and wants to go international, they've lost five or 10 years of preparation.

Brockhaus acknowledged that today, such a scenario is as likely to happen from mother to daughter—and the issues will be just as sticky.

Conclusion

In this chapter, my colleagues and I have taken today's business and social trends and we've imagined possible futures based on them. As you project your business concept into the future, consider the impact these trends may have on you. We've explored the future of the Internet; changing prospects for women and minorities; strategies for independent retailers, franchisees, SOHO workers, and family businesses. Each of these themes reveals specific opportunities for cer-

tain businesses, and other opportunities for those businesses that figure out how to market products and services to them.

Study these themes for needs and characteristics that identify a target market you can serve. In the next two chapters, we'll explore how you go about matching your business offering to a market segment that needs that product or service. It's likely one or more of these trends are creating opportunities for you.

Study these themes for personnel strategies, such as contracting with independent SOHOs instead of hiring employees, or recruiting managers among minority groups. Consider these trends with regard to your access to and need for capital. Later chapters will pick up this thread.

Your written business plan will communicate how your business concept leverages these trends.

The future is not something that happens to us: It is something we as a society build. It is our responsibility as individuals to hold values and express them in ways that contribute to the shape of that future. You have more control than you think. Where you live, where you shop, how you work, what you sell—all help sculpt the future you will live in. Entrepreneurs have a very direct role in creating the future. And that is one of the greatest satisfactions of entrepreneurship.

Thoughts to Take Away

- The Internet is as essential to your business as your telephone. Your business plan must incorporate a strategy for maximizing your opportunities and reducing your threats from this rapidly changing frontier.
- Women and minorities can expect increased opportunity as cultural barriers fall away. Diverse entrepreneurs with big visions will have more access to capital to grow big businesses, whereas those who wish to start small will find the Internet and SOHO phenomena making their dreams practical and realistic.
- Independent retailers who focus on unique merchandise mix, customer knowledge, and personal service will find they have competitive advantages over big-box discount stores.
- Franchises present tremendous business opportunities both here and abroad. Considered from any angle—single-unit income replacement, multiunit wealth building, franchiser business concept—franchising holds promise. Those who explore customizing franchises to local environments will find themselves at the cutting edge.
- Small offices and home offices (SOHOs) give entrepreneurs who value their independence a low-cost-of-entry business opportunity. Thinking small is big business today.
- Family businesses succeed when there is strong communication among affected family members. Good communication is essential when there is a planned succession from one generation to the next.

chapterFOUR

How to Make a Business Plan

WHAT YOU WILL FIND IN THIS CHAPTER

- Thought-provokers and idea-starters to get you in the right frame of mind for planning
- What a vision is and how it affects a mission
- An outline for a business plan and why no plan follows it exactly

If you were a trucker, you wouldn't leave the driveway without a road map. If you were a builder, you wouldn't start construction without a blueprint. If you were a pilot, you wouldn't take off without a flight plan. Get the picture? Planning is essential wherever leadership is involved. Whether it's you leading yourself in your own one-man band, or you and your management team leading your 200-person work force, the plan is the critical element in getting where you want to go.

Planning is the act that makes all subsequent actions go well. Planning is how we forecast the future, anticipate problems, identify opportunities, and get things done. Planning keeps day-to-day activities on the front line aligned with overall company goals.

Effective planning is proactive rather than reactive. It is focused on predicting what will happen, maximizing opportunities, and preventing problems. An effective plan describes values that will guide the organization in coping with the unexpected.

Problems that arise because of poor planning have their costs in time, money, and morale. It is almost always easier and cheaper to do things right the first time. Good planning improves performance across the board. It prevents problems, reduces costs, and increases the satisfaction of everyone involved—customers, staff, and vendors.

Have I got you convinced that you need a plan? Then let's talk about how you go about making one.

The Planning Process

Planning involves assessing the current situation, setting objectives for the future, then determining steps to reach those objectives. A plan can be short range or long range. "Long" usually means 10 to 15 years, whereas "short" typically covers a period of one to five years. It's important that a short-term plan look beyond the next few months. The future is coming: Aim for a spot on that horizon, even while you cope with the situation in which you find yourself today.

The business plan is not just a tool for start-up businesses. Every successful business engages in planning on a regular basis. The result is a written business plan that is a living document. A business plan is an important tool not just for guiding your activities, but for communicating your company's story to employees, strategic partners, and the financial community. It helps you make key decisions.

Once you have created a written business plan, refer to it and revise it periodically, throughout the life of your business. "It's not necessarily that the plan changes, but that it gets better. I just finished updating our plan last night. I put in some of our new partnerships, some of our new hires. You want to keep that baby ready for the next round," said Rodney Heller, of Foodusa.com. His plan just earned him $3 million in venture capital—and he plans to go back for more in the next 120 days. (Read more about this online business and its search for capital in chapter 7.)

When you encounter changes in your industry, your competitive environment, the economy, or any other factor that can affect your business results—reexamine your plan.

Each section of the business plan has its own process. The marketing plan, the personnel plan, the financial plan—each represents time spent in planning. Different people may be involved in assembling each section. Key managers in each area may be involved, or different business advisors. It's quite likely that you will be working on each section simultaneously, creating first rough notes, then written portions, before the actual "Business Plan Draft No. 1" comes together as a complete document.

Celebrate that fact! You do not, after all, have to type "My Business Plan" at the top of a blank piece of paper and start writing. Just as an artist creates sketches before beginning to paint, just as a composer improvises before committing musical notes to paper, a writer does a lot of preparation before beginning to write. You need not be stymied by the blank page, the empty canvas, the silence in the air.

If you look at business planning as a two-part process—first the strategic work of planning, then the methodical work of documenting the plan in writing—you will find it easier to begin.

Know your audience

First and foremost, you are creating a business plan to provide yourself with a road map by which to navigate in the months and years ahead. Once you start implementing the strategies outlined in the plan, you will find yourself absorbed in other activities. You'll be doing, not planning. Especially if you are in the first stages of a business start-up, you are about to enter a hurricane. Soon you will be working long hours and wearing every hat imaginable. The written business plan helps keep you on track in that storm of activity. You are writing this plan for *you.*

When you engage in the business planning process, you move from what Terri Lonier calls "your passion sphere" into your business sphere. If possible you pull back from day-to-day operations so that you can find the vantage point of higher ground, the perspective of the longer view. You allow the wise, far-seeing side of yourself to come out, and you listen to what that self has to say. You allow the stu-

**KEY CONCEPT:
THE PLAN LIVES ON**

Business plans are not just tools for start-up businesses. Once you have written a business plan, refer to it and revise it periodically, throughout the life of your business.

dent in yourself to emerge, and seek out teachers, research, answers to the questions that arise. You write the business plan almost as a letter to your "other" self, the one who, when caught up in daily operations, could use a wise counselor to lean on.

In most cases, the business plan will have audiences other than yourself. Are you preparing the plan as part of a financing proposal? A business plan is one of the first pieces of information investors and bankers will want to see. The financial community demands an objective, in-depth analysis of your business. They want to know about the opportunities and risks. They need substantiation of the feasibility of the business concept; the want to see projected return on investment. This audience will give the financial section of your plan close scrutiny.

Are you preparing the plan to be reviewed by potential managers? Recruiting key personnel means communicating your vision in a way that makes them want to be a part of your team. Use your plan to explore what rewards the business has potential to generate. Those rewards should include tangible financial rewards, plus intangible rewards like affiliation with an innovative company, and the fellowship of good coworkers. The marketing and personnel sections of your plan will be of interest to this audience.

A business plan may be requested by a potential landlord, by key vendors, or by advisors such as your accountant, lawyer, or spouse. In other words, everyone you are asking to believe in you will have an interest in seeing your plan. Make some version of your plan available to everyone—even include it with your employee handbook.

There will most likely be several versions of your plan. You may create a summary document for certain audiences, and more detailed background that can be incorporated when the particular reviewer has a deeper interest in one or more areas.

How much is enough? In most cases, a business plan will run 25 to 50 pages in length. The thicker plans I see are fat with supporting data, not long-winded writing. Don't let your writing become bogged down in examples and details best attached as appendixes. Keep the main narrative clear and concise. Your aim is to enlighten and inform, not to make experts of your readers. Keep the plan itself succinct. You want it to be read, not skimmed.

Long or short, keep the tone of your writing factual. Avoid hyperbole. No one is going to buy your claims if you can't back them up with facts. Do your homework, then let the facts speak for themselves.

What business are you really in?

In chapter 2, we began to explore the business planning process. I posed questions that I hope clarified for you the who, what, why, when, and how of planning. In chapter 3, we explored external trends and influences that may affect your business plans. I hope these chapters have gotten you started figuring out what business you are in, and why, and where you'd like it to take you.

Whom do you buy from, and whom do you sell to? There are two general "spaces" in which commerce is transacted—the business-to-business (B to B) space and the business-to-consumer (B to C) space. All around you, businesses are selling products and services to other businesses. They might buy (or sell) raw materials, or finished goods, or machines for making raw materials into finished goods, or accounting services or delivery services to move those materials and goods—you get the picture. Meanwhile, retail businesses are taking those products and services, creating merchandise assortments from their pick of the crop, and selling them to end users. What little (or large) corner of this commercial space do you occupy?

In one sense, every entrepreneur is in the same business—the business of figuring out what our customers need and want, and what we can do to provide some portion of that better than any competitor can. This has always been true, but today, there's a new twist. Not only are you in the customer-satisfaction business, you're in the technology business. More and more, businesses are depending on a technological component in the solutions they offer their customers. Even your neighborhood florist is using computers and the Internet, for internal systems as well as communication with customers.

It's a new world, and it's changing rapidly. People who have been successful for a long time must master new roles, or risk failure. Today's entrepreneurs are asking, "How will I use technology to serve my business and my customers better?"

Hattie Bryant sees the challenges entrepreneurs face:

Technology implementation into all the fibers and layers of your work is going to be critical, even if it's just a matter of using technology to manage your business efficiently. . . . We'll see baby boomers just sell their companies and walk away, because they know they don't want to do this much, to work this hard, anymore. You've got to do it all, and it's harder than ever. To sustain a business takes a full court press on all fronts. The flip side of the coin is, people who have always embraced technology are acting like 18-year-olds; they're so excited about this. The prospect of change thrills some people and scares others.

Today's business environment requires that you either learn a lot about technology yourself or hire someone who will maintain that knowledge, or outsource the task via freelancers. Through one or more of these routes, your business must have a plan for staying current on technological developments—and maximizing them in your operation.

What are your plans for growth?

If a business plan is a road map, this is the point at which you have to ask, "where to?" No business stays in the same place forever. It grows, or fails to grow; it masters new challenges, or it falls prey to its own weaknesses. Your business plan should include plans for the evolution of your business.

"But I don't know what will happen. How can I plan for the unknown?" I can hear you saying. How can a business plan help you prepare for a future that no one can accurately predict? By helping you focus on your distinctive strengths, that edge that gives you confidence in your business concept. With your uniqueness firmly in mind, you are well positioned to leverage events as they unfold. External analysis—studying the opportunities and threats your environment presents—may reveal strategic opportunities. Internal analysis—reflecting on your own strengths and weaknesses—will help you determine if these opportunities are right for you.

How far into the future should you plan? Like the captain of a ship, you need to keep your eye on a point far enough out that, if you see a threat, you have time to react to it. The planning horizon is the time required to put in place a strategic change. Realistically, there's not a lot of point laying detailed plans beyond that horizon since external changes will simply make you do that work again. On the other hand, if you set your planning horizon too close, you may miss out on opportunities. It is typical for businesses to form detailed plans for the upcoming 12 months, sketchier plans for the subsequent year or two, and simply define visions and values that will guide their choices beyond that horizon.

You need to think where you'd like to be 10, 20, 50 years out. Those decisions guide how you run your business. Consider these questions: How big do I want to be? Do I want to grow this business to sell? Is this business to be passed on to future generations? If so, when? There is not, of course, one right answer to these questions. There's nothing wrong with starting a small business with plans to keep it that way.

New roles for the entrepreneur. We don't assume that a one-man band can direct a full orchestra. Yet we tend to assume that as entrepreneurs we have the skills to take our businesses from bright ideas to Fortune 500 companies. Why? It's that entrepreneurial optimism thing. Thank goodness we have it—otherwise the dynamo of small business might grind to a halt. But it does represent a challenge. Starting a business is the only job I can think of where there's no possibility of on-the-job training. Says George Solomon:

It's one of the most common mistakes I see. The owners can't grow the business anymore because they are incapable of managing it. Physically and psychologically, they haven't created a structure capable of maintaining high growth. They have always been in charge of everything, micro-managing everything.

When the business grows to where they have to delegate, they are incapable either because they're unwilling to let go or because they can't figure out how to let go.

KEY CONCEPT

Business planning may not be effective at predicting the future, but it's a good way of assessing the present. A plan:

- Reveals tradeoffs that may be necessary
- Sets boundaries of the possibilities to be considered
- Simulates plausible scenarios
- Generates ideas
- Forces you to think about consequences

Solomon sees this crisis occur at predictable stages:

In terms of years, it's somewhere around three or four years old. In terms of dollars, it's around $1 or $2 million in sales. In terms of product line, it's when you want to get past a single product line or single location, to two locations, or two product lines, and beyond. The enterprise has grown past the level any normal person can effectively handle alone, and the original manager hasn't delegated any of this. A lot of entrepreneurs can't get away from being the person who did everything, to become the person who envisions everything and delegates everything.

Businesses that grow quickly often create for themselves cash flow problems, or customer service problems, or supply problems. All are major mistakes that require strategic planning to avoid.

I asked Don Kuratko what an entrepreneur should include in the business plan to help with the growth factor: "Make sure the quantitative parts are there. How the financial projections match up from cash flow to needs. The plan should quantify what kind of resources can be realistically anticipated. Some people think they're going to grow with the same base of resources they have today and that's impossible."

Growth takes money. Very few businesses pay for their growth out of cash on hand. There is a strategic threat inherent in this, which Bob Brockhaus pointed out:

As you need more money, you suddenly run out of your own equity to put in. Banks at some point say *"your debt level is as high as we want to take it." Now you have to look for new equity funds, outside of yourself and your friends and families. As you look for that equity, it's not always easy to find venture capital funds. Even an informal venture capital fund today is probably not interested in putting in anything less than a million dollars. If you only need $600,000, or $700,000, or half a million, that can be hard to raise in equity.*

If your business plan calls for rapid growth, make sure you are positioning yourself from the start for the venture capital hunt that will come with your success.

And what about you, the owner? How, in the plan, have you visualized yourself at five and seven years of growth? Will you fall into the one-man-band syndrome? So many entrepreneurs start out that way, and take satisfaction from how well they manage their multiple responsibilities. But down the road, growth means adding personnel at senior levels of management. How are you going to delegate? How are you going to educate and train your personnel? Staff development is a key component of any plan for growth.

There's a saying, "You never step in the same river twice." Each time you wet your toes, new water is flowing past them. In a business, like a river, the environment is fluid. Even if your goal is to remain the same, you must work to stay where you are, or you will find yourself swept along with the current.

Components of the Plan

A business plan should include the following main components:

- Front matter
- Marketing
- Personnel
- Financial
- Closing

In this chapter, we'll talk about the first and last components. The marketing, personnel, and financial sections will be the focus of the next three chapters.

If you've taken a speech class, perhaps you've heard this "rule of three" about presenting information: "Tell them what you're going to tell them, then tell them, then tell them what you told them." The executive summary is the first phase, "telling them

what you're going to tell them." The middle sections are the second phase, "telling them." And the closing is, of course, the final phase, "telling them what you told them." As a structure, it's proven effective. The rule of three communicates information in a way that allows people to learn. Although there is no perfect outline for a business plan, this three-times format has been adopted by most plan writers because it maximizes reader comprehension.

The middle section, describing plans regarding marketing, personnel, and finances, make up what I call the three-legged stool of business planning. A three-legged stool doesn't wobble. A business plan that gives adequate attention to each of these areas should prove to be a steady base for your operations.

Each of the "legs" of marketing, personnel, and finances will require its own strategic planning process. You will research possible strategies, evaluate those possibilities, then summarize your conclusions in the written plan. Since each leg must reflect the shape of the other two, these planning processes are necessarily intertwined and overlapping.

It's enough to drive you crazy! Where do you start when every possibility depends on other choices? I have two thoughts on that.

First, begin with a pencil, not a chisel. In other words, don't start with the assumption that you are carving your decisions in stone. Try out different strategies and see where they take you. Ask "what-if" questions, and pursue plausible answers. You can then weigh the pros and cons of different courses of action before you choose the final strategies for your plan.

Second, focus where the action is. Where are the dynamics of your business undergoing change? Are you experiencing a shift on the competitive front? Are customers' needs evolving, presenting new ways

Voices

Quite honestly, if you're in business and you're looking at doing a business plan, that means you're successful. Because if you're not, you're so busy putting out fires you're probably not going to do a business plan.

—Bob Brockhaus

for you to serve them? Is technology opening up new ways your operation could function more efficiently? Are you preparing to hire key personnel, or to look for new investors? Let your "what-if" process begin where the action is.

Section 1: Begin at the Beginning: Front Matter

Flip to the business plans in the back of this book, if you like, and take a look at how business plans begin. Each is unique, but we find essentially the same elements grouped at the beginning. If the plan is being sent to a reviewer, the very first thing inside the envelope will be a cover letter followed by a nondisclosure statement. These are essential to get the plan directed to the right reader, to get that reader oriented to the subject, and to inform that reader of your expectation that he or she will keep the plan's contents confidential.

Then the plan itself begins. First will come the title page. Here I recommend you list the name of the business, the names of those who prepared the plan, and the date of the plan. Some people put the number of years the plan covers on the title page, or a contact phone number and address. Resist the temptation to add other information or design elements.

A table of contents page should follow the title page. I like it when the table of contents includes page numbers. But do this only if you promise you will check and revise it each time you revise your plan. A "typo" here will raise doubts about your thoroughness and carefulness in preparing the plan.

Anyone experienced with preparing business plans will tell you that the front matter is the last section of the plan to be written. If you write following an outline, your table of contents should closely resemble that outline.

Typically, the front matter of a business plan will include the following:

- Cover letter
- Nondisclosure statement
- Title page
- Table of contents
- Executive summary
- Business description
- Vision and mission statements

KEY CONCEPT: PLAN FOR THE UNKNOWN

A business plan helps you prepare for a future you can't predict, by mapping out your approach to the unknown. Planning prepares you to respond to events as they unfold.

The executive summary. The executive summary is just that—a summary that allows a busy executive to learn quickly what the plan involves. This portion of the plan summarizes the business concept, the current situation, and the success factors that give this business a competitive edge. The executive summary alerts the reader to the purpose for which the plan was prepared. If the plan is written to support a search for loans or investors, the financial needs of the business are spelled out here. If the plan is written to consider strategic alternatives, the executive summary states that.

The executive summary functions as an advertisement for the business concept described in the plan. Like a book jacket, it "sells" the reader on spending some time with the plan. If the reader doesn't like the executive summary, he or she is unlikely to read on.

The executive summary is usually written last. Why? It's a summary of the plan. It's hard to summarize something you haven't written yet. Plan on including an executive summary—but don't plan on writing it until you are nearing completion on the other portions of your plan. Each point mentioned in the executive summary must be elaborated on later.

The executive summary typically conveys the business concept, its current situation, its key success factors, and the purpose for which it has been prepared, although not necessarily in that order.

Compare these examples from two of our plans.

The executive summary for Red's Automotive briefly recaps the history of the firm, leading to a statement of the current opportunity in the fourth paragraph.

Recent analysis of market conditions, potential and Red's market share (Appendix A) indicates that, while Red's sales will continue to grow, replication of sales growth rates of the previous three years is unlikely . . .

This market environment prompts consideration of product-line expansion, establishment of operations in a different trade area, or both, to foster continued business growth and development. Given this scenario, Red's is planning on establishing a new operation in the Teal City trade area, targeting the retail, commercial and heavy duty truck repair market.

For a different example, consider the first paragraph of BizCopy's executive summary:

The purpose of preparing this plan was to provide BizCopy, Inc. with a plan and vision to grow sales past the 1 million dollar level to 2 million in sales while remaining profitable. In preparing this plan we examined the financial makeup of BizCopy, the marketplace, products, pricing, and promotion. We discovered what activities and products are contributing to growth and have created a plan to leverage these to accelerate growth.

A **business concept statement** may do any or all of the following: identify the business or industry you are in; identify who your target customers are; describe basic facts or characteristics about the business; and tell what sets it apart from competitors. This must be as brief and clear as you can make it. Do not confuse this with the mission statement still to come, where your goals, vision, and philosophy will be discussed.

A **current situation statement** presents facts about the business and puts it in the context of the larger business scene. If it's a start-up business, this statement describes projected activities. If it's an existing company, it describes the situation in terms of the most relevant characteristics. Depending on the purpose of the plan, this statement might describe your business in terms of its sales and profits, its competitive position relative to other firms, or major challenges you foresee.

A **key success factors statement** tells the reader your basis for optimism. What has been responsible for your success so far? What gives you your edge, now and in the future?

A **purpose of the plan statement** specifies the "why" of it all. If there are financial needs, describe them in this statement. Give your reader a quick financial snapshot of the company. Whatever the purpose for the plan, the statement here is its intro-

duction. More detail will follow in the relevant middle sections of the plan.

However you combine these statements to create your executive summary, keep it brief. It's quite unusual for an executive summary to run longer than one to two pages. About four or five paragraphs should be adequate in most situations.

As a study of the example plans in this book will show, the components of the executive summary may appear in any order, and may be touched on in more or less depth depending on their relative importance.

Let's take our discussion deeper with a look at the plan of The Artful Fly. Here is an executive summary in its entirety. This short text covers each of the essential ingredients of a complete executive summary:

The Artful Fly is a new business producing visually dramatic presentations of artificial fishing flies. (Note how concisely the writer has summarized an unusual business concept.) *The business is a corporation coequally owned and managed by Jim Fisher and Jane Angler. The Artful Fly obtains its fishing flies from four sources. These are:* **antique flies** *from fishermen who have gained historical prominence in the history of fly fishing,* **famous flies** *from fishermen who have recently received acclaim through their books about fly fishing and fly tying,* **professional flies** *from fishermen whose flies have demonstrated outstanding fly tying skills and standards, and finally* **customer flies** *from customers who forward their flies for framing. The Artful Fly mounts and frames these flies for sale to fly fishermen and their families.* (This entire paragraph represents a clear, thorough, business concept statement.)

The Artful Fly estimates sales of more than 1000 units during the first year of its operation. Gross sales are expected to be $187,421. On these sales The Artful Fly projects gross profits of 7 percent for its first year of operation. Net profits for the year are expected to be 18.6 percent. First year's return on equity is projected at 40.33 percent. (Here the writer presents the current situation, focusing on the financial projections for the first year of operation of this start-up business.)

The Artful Fly projects a healthy profit in its first year of operation because it is the first national company whose business is mounting and framing fishing flies. Two companies compete with The Artful Fly customer flies only. They do not, however, mount and frame customer flies, nor do they sell flies from other sources. The Artful Fly plans one special offering for Christmas. It is a combined offering of an autographed book by widely read fishing author Tom Troutman and four of his hand tied wet flies attractively framed. Arrangements have already been made with Mr. Troutman. (This paragraph combines current situation with key success factors.)

The Artful Fly seeks debt funding of $44,000 at 11 percent annual interest for a term of five years. The funds are needed to purchase equipment, inventory, and advertising. Because of the high profitability of its products, The Artful Fly anticipates repayment within two years at the ordinary interest rates. (This closing paragraph states the purpose of the plan, which in this case is a financial need.)

The business description. Many business plan writers insert a business description section after the executive summary. A business description gives you an opportunity to paint in broad strokes, filling in background for your reader. A business description can be longer than an executive summary. Discuss the industry and where your company fits in it. Describe your location, operations, your business and legal structure. Provide a clear description of your product or service, and your customers and suppliers. Identify your niche. State the specific advantages that set you apart from your competition.

In our sample plans, you will find fairly typical business description sections included in the plans for Whole Fish & Seafood, O'Toole's Machining, and The Artful Fly. The plan for BizCopy contains several sections devoted to the business description, under headings "Background Information" and "Organizational Matters." Given that the purpose of this plan is to weigh alternatives, it makes sense that there is considerable emphasis on the current operations of the business in this plan.

The business description might include a history of the business, descriptions of key supplier or customer relationships, an explanation of the ownership of the business, a discussion of seasonal factors, or any other critical information that will help the reader understand your plan. This is the place for a brief description of the facilities. If you intend to operate a home-based business, this would be a good place to explain why, and to show that you understand the issues facing you as you work at home. (See chapter 3's discussion of SOHO businesses if you're not sure you understand!)

See Worksheet 4.1 in appendix D for idea-starting questions to assist you in writing your business description.

Vision and mission statements. If you're reading more than one book on business planning, you're likely coming across words like "vision" and "mission" used to describe a core value statement to be included in the business plan. Are we all talking about the same thing? How is a vision different from a mission? The dictionary definitions clarify the issue. *Vision* is "intelligent foresight," whereas *mission* is "a self-imposed duty." Sounds like you want to have both, doesn't it?

The way I see it, your vision helps you identify your mission. A vision statement describes a positive picture of a possible future. This statement describes a vision of your preferred long-range outcome. A vision can be complex or simple, elaborate or concise, but it must be compelling and sincere. It must be ambitious enough to require a stretch. A vision gives you something to reach for.

Your vision statement describes where you want to be; your mission statement describes how you will get there. It helps you stay on track when unexpected opportunities or threats demand response.

The mission of a business is the fundamental, unique purpose that sets it apart from other firms of its type and identifies the scope of its operations. It is a means for aligning what the organization says it does, what it actually does, and what the rest of the world believes it does.

The mission includes only the one or two most critical purposes, leaving out many less important purposes. It needs to be brief in order to be memorable. The primary thrust of a mission statement is external, focusing on markets and customers, but it is an important internal source of motivation as well. A mission statement describes the ground rules, so to speak, by which the game will be played by this company.

Having these statements helps your business in two ways.

First, the statements help you communicate both inside and outside the firm. It's very important for your employees to know what you believe, and what values you expect them to share. It's important for employees to know what your plans are, and how they fit into those plans. These statements help staff to understand their roles. Even more important, they force you to articulate what you expect their roles to be.

Second, these statements commit the company to a stated philosophy. Like a New Year's resolution, these statements represent a promise to yourself and to your future. By creating vision and mission statements, you provide a banner around which your team can rally.

To determine your vision and mission, the best course of action is, of course, to book a week in a delightful place where you and your key stakeholders can retreat to do this work. Failing that, many businesses book two half days or a day (or better yet, two or three days) in a conference room away from their place of business. A facilitator can be very helpful with the process of envisioning (exercising your "intelligent foresight"). Workshops and seminars are available, and so are consultants who can guide you through this process.

I consider it vitally important that you leave the office to do this work. If all you can do is to retreat to your home and spend a day in bed with a notepad, then do it. You cannot do your best work surrounded by the day-to-day distractions of business.

If a business plan is a road map, then these statements are your compass. They guide actions and decisions. They connect what a company is capable of achieving with the needs of its potential customers.

See Worksheet 4.2 in appendix D for questions that will stimulate discussion about your company's vision and mission.

From all the questions on that worksheet, you'd think these statements would be as lengthy as the business plan itself. That's not the case. Once you've pondered those questions, you must boil your thinking down to a few well-chosen and highly evocative words.

The Steelcase office furniture company had a mission statement that said "Our mission is to provide the world's best office environment products, services, systems, and intelligence designed to help people." Their new mission statement says "We help people work more effectively."

At the University of Wisconsin–Madison Small Business Development Center, my home base, we have developed this mission statement:

Our mission is to enhance the success of small business owners and managers in our service area, Dane, Sauk, and Columbia County, and to encourage growth in our economy. Our mission is to be a valuable and innovative resource for business, recognized by the business and economic community as a major contributor to the economic health of our service area. We will achieve our mission through practical, customer-focused management education, training, counseling, and networking.

When we come up with new ideas for programs or other things we want to do, we consider them against this mission. Often we say "good idea, but it doesn't fit." It has kept us out of some markets, prevented us from exploring certain products, but it has served us well.

In our sample plans, you will find a mission statement included in the plan for BizCopy. Here it is:

At BizCopy, our mission is to provide superior, knowledgeable service and innovative solutions to businesses and professionals in the Corporate Valley at competitive rates. To accomplish this, we will work harder to improve all facets of our trade. We will be vigilant in finding new ways to exceed the rising expectations of our clients and prospects. By doing these things, we expect our business to grow and prosper, while we achieve a higher level of job satisfaction.

Statements like these help newcomers to a company grasp the personality, culture, and ambitions of a firm.

There is no one right format for every plan. Look at several of the other example plans, and see if you can identify the components of a mission statement.

I like seeing mission statements displayed all over. Some firms print theirs on their business cards. Some have it engraved on a plaque in an area where customers are. It's also good for employees to see. A good mission statement reminds all of us why we're here—and that's what it's for.

The front matter of your business plan distills your whole grand vision down to a concise executive summary, a business description, and perhaps a vision and/or mission statement. It is obviously difficult to distill what doesn't yet exist—so rough in this section with notes, perhaps do the worksheets, and then move on to the next sections of your plan.

Rodney Heller of Foodusa.com described how he went about writing his plan:

I bought a book; it gave me an outline. I went through and I wrote the plan, but I didn't have it in any sequential order, nothing. I just wrote what I thought. On marketing. On staffing. Market opportunity. Potential yields. On this and that, right on down the line. Then, once I was done with writing all that, I started piecing it together and putting it in order.

I wish we could show you the Foodusa.com plan—but unfortunately, it's top secret. As I've mentioned with regard to Internet businesses, the danger of copycat competitors is all too real. Heller's efforts paid off in over $3 million in venture capital investment, and more is flowing in. "If you've got a good plan, it exudes enthusiasm," Heller concluded.

Section 2: The Market

In this section of the plan, a business is analyzed through the lens of the marketing function. This section may include any or all of the following:

- Market analysis
  - Industry analysis
  - Competitive analysis
  - Customer analysis

> ### KEY CONCEPT:
> ### THE IMPORTANCE OF VISION
> ### AND MISSION
>
> Potential investors, lenders, employees, customers, and vendors all want to know what your vision of your business is. But most of all, you want to know. If you find you have difficulty with this section of the plan, work through it—don't give up. This may be the most important work you do in your business.

- Products/services offering description
- Marketing plan

In chapter 5, we'll pick up the work of creating a marketing strategy. But before we move on to the next topic, I want to share with you a story from my own family's business.

When I was 16 years old, my father took me to New York and he told me I could be the buyer for the store. That was really exciting for a young woman. I went into the market, and I bought everything that I liked—and I bought all in my size. That didn't turn out to be a very successful season for the store. The problem was, the things that I liked were not necessarily the things that our customers liked. The size I needed was not the size they needed. That was a very important lesson for me.

Our customers were 35 to 55 years old, single, and wanted professional clothing. I was 16 and wanted to dress like a 16-year-old. It's a good thing that my sister and my mother wore the same size I did because we all had a fabulous wardrobe from the things that didn't sell. But I learned how important it was to keep the customer in mind, not my personal taste. A lot of businesspeople make the same mistake. They buy what *they* like, and put together the environment that *they* like. Now that's important because this business is where you're going to spend your life, but you have to make sure you're offering what the customer really wants and is comfortable with.

The marketing section of the plan will be the road map that keeps you on the highway toward customer satisfaction. If you stray into the scenic territory to either side of that road, you may have a fascinating trip—but you won't arrive where you need to go.

Section 3: Personnel

A business plan is only as strong as the people who execute it. The purpose of the personnel section is to build faith in the business's management team. The personnel section demonstrates that you and your team have the skills to run your marketing, operations, and financial functions. Typically, the personnel section of a business plan will include the following:

- Management team
- Staff team
- Plans for growth

Depending on the emphasis of the plan, more or less detail will be provided on these topics.

The most important is the background of key personnel. In this section, you provide the information that will give your team credibility. Some plan writers choose to include resumes of each member of the management team. Other plan writers choose to write short biographies, including anecdotes to demonstrate each team member's most important skills or characteristics. Relevant degrees, certifications, and prior experience should be noted, whether in resume or biography form.

Each person's role in the company should be described. If you have job descriptions, include them in the appendix. An organizational chart can be included to make clear how the company's functions are covered. Anyone with a financial stake in the company should be identified as such.

The personnel section should discuss the organizational strengths of the business. Describe your own personal strengths and weaknesses, and explain how you're going to compensate for your weaknesses. It's better to take the lead and show honest self-knowledge than to let others point out your weaknesses to you. If you're like me, not much of a financial person, you might want to say that you've hired XYZ Accounting to work with you, and that your first hire is going to be somebody who has a strong financial background. In your plan, deal with the strengths and weaknesses of key managers as well.

> ### KEY CONCEPT: STRONG PEOPLE MAKE A STRONG PLAN
>
> A business plan is only as strong as the people who execute it. In your personnel section, discuss the organizational strengths of the business. Provide the information that will give your team credibility.

If a plan stresses marketing as key to their success, but lists no one "in charge" of marketing, this gives the reader a clear message that the plan's writer hasn't thought through a critical aspect of the business.

If the company has aggressive plans for growth, that growth will almost certainly bring the need for recruitment and training of staff. A human resources plan for staffing requirements is extremely important, especially in areas where low unemployment makes hiring a "buyer's market."

If the company considers good customer service part of its mission—and if it doesn't, it won't be around long—then a plan for maintaining a high level of service is a good idea. This is extremely important to businesses in the service sector, where individual performance can have a critical impact on the overall success of the company.

Facilities issues can have a big impact on worker productivity and other aspects of the business. Situations such as outgrowing an old facility, or deciding to purchase rather than lease space, can provide the occasion for a new business plan. You may want to address facilities issues here, as you describe the workflows of your operations, as well as in your business description.

In our sample plans, you will find a strong personnel section included in the plan for The Artful Fly ("Organizational Structure, Ownership, and Management"), and the plan for BizCopy ("Management Team," a subsection under "Business Structure, Management, and Personnel").

The plan for Blue Sky Travel describes a start-up business in the service sector. In this situation, the background of the managers is absolutely essential to the credibility of the plan. The owners address it early on in their plan, under the heading "Management and Ownership."

Personnel is not a difficult section to write. You may want to approach this section quite early in your process. Because if you don't know yourself and your partners, and the key things you are going to do, you are really in trouble. Might as well find it out sooner than later.

Section 4: Financials

Financial data is how the game of business is scored. The financial section reports on how the company has performed in the past, and projects how it will perform in the future. If your company is up and running, your plan should include income statements and balance sheets for the last three years. All plans, whether for a start-up or an existing business, should include projected financial statements (called pro formas) for the next three to five years. These projections should realistically indicate the highs and lows you expect as a result of your current strategies. It's typical for projections to follow two or three scenarios, often labeled best case, worst case, and most likely.

The financial section of a business plan should include some or all of the following:

- Profit and loss statement
- Cash flow forecast
- Balance sheet
- Break-even analysis
- Assumptions and comments

In chapter 7, we'll examine each of these pro formas. Financials are more than important—they're the life or death of your business. Whether you're a "numbers person" or not, I want you to know each of these statements so well you can take one apart and put it back together in the dark, so to speak.

I'm reminded of two clients I've dealt with over the years, a husband and wife. They came to me saying they'd lost a little money, a couple of thousand dollars. I asked for copies of their financial statements. They said they were still with the accountant, and they'd get them to me. Unfortunately, I made the mistake of not asking for last year's statements instead—I agreed to wait for this year's. We talked about marketing, the issue they wanted to discuss, for about two months. Then I asked again for the financial statements, and they gave them to me.

KEY CONCEPT: FINANCIAL PROJECTIONS MUST BE REALISTIC

You must be realistic when putting together your financial information. Don't let your optimism run away with you. Your projections, like your mission statement, are promises you make to yourself. Don't make promises you feel you may not be able to keep.

It was quite clear that they couldn't read a financial statement. They had beautiful file drawers full of beautiful colored folders for each month, and they dutifully took the statements from their accountant and put them in the appropriate colored file. But they never looked at them or read them.

They didn't lose a little bit of money. They lost $150,000 over the course of several years. They had been losing a little bit of money every month for a very long time. If they had been able to manage their business through their financial statements, their situation would have been very different. Financial statements aren't about taxes. They're about managing your business.

Most of the business plan examples in this book include financial sections. In chapter 7, we'll examine how they are prepared and help you accomplish this important aspect of your planning process.

In the meantime, this advice from Rodney Heller should increase your confidence:

"Essentially, putting financials together is nothing more than ratios. If you sit down with somebody who knows the ratios that are standard, three-quarters of your financials are already done. Just get those ratios. Sit down with somebody who knows what is standard in your industry."

Section 5: Closing

Beginning, middle, end. Just as your plan starts with an executive summary, to tell the reader what you're about to tell them, your plan will close with a round-up of the key facts and a final statement of purpose for the plan. If you flip to the back of most business plans (and that's what most bankers do), you will find yourself in a thicket of attachments, appendixes, and pro formas—rather a messy finish. A summary can be included there to act as a guidepost in that thicket. This can be quite short—even a bullet list of key points will do. The business plan for BizCopy concludes with "overheads" from a presentation of the business plan—a nice touch.

Following a summary "guidepost," if you choose to include it, will be any appendixes you choose to include. These vary quite a bit from plan to plan, but often include a statement summarizing the applications and effects of loans, if the plan has stated financial needs, a personal financial statement, resumes, positive newspaper articles about the business, and other credibility-builders.

A typical final section of a business plan might include the following:

- Closing summary statement
- Applications and effects of loans
- Supporting documents

Always double-check your work to make sure that any appendixes or attachments you have mentioned in your earlier sections really do appear where you said they would.

Conclusion

Writing a business plan requires a substantial investment of your time and thought. The process can take as long as six months, or even more. After all, you can't do a thorough analysis of every facet of your business in a weekend or two. To make the process more enjoyable, and to make your plan stronger, involve others in the effort. Get feedback and advice

> ### *Voices*
>
> *You've got to husband your resources. Many companies, after the first wave of success, suddenly begin behaving like they've arrived at the end of the rainbow. There's a natural tendency to think, "I've sacrificed so much. Now I can begin to get it back," and the point is right now is when you probably need to sacrifice a bit more.*
>
> —Chuck Hofer

> ### KEY CONCEPT:
> ### USE GRAPHICS
>
> Want your business plan to be understood? Use graphics to tell your story. You might reproduce your ads in the marketing section, show organization and processes with charts in the personnel section, or use graphs to show trends in your financial section. All will help your plan to come alive for the reader.

on your plan. Show it to the advisors you work with, such as your banker, your accountant, and your local Small Business Development Center or Service Corps of Retired Executives consultants well before you finish the document. You may find their perspectives help you invest your effort more efficiently.

Michael Meeks has this advice for you:

Most business owners are like firefighters all day long. It turns out that 80 percent of those fires don't give any returns. If they would focus on the 20 percent that matters, they'd be much better off. You need to focus. And, you need to know what's going on. Look at all the information about your own internal processes that you can—accounting, inventory, project management. Software is available, and affordable. It's really valuable if you learn to manage your business by it.

Planning is doable if you break it into manageable tasks, and in the next chapters we'll help you do just that.

The best reason for planning is that it forces you to set goals. Remember in Lewis Carroll's *Alice in Wonderland* when the Cheshire Cat and Alice meet, and the Cat is sitting up in a tree with an enigmatic smile on his face? Alice is lost, and she's come to a fork in the road, and she's not sure quite which way to go. She notices the Cheshire Cat and she asks for directions. The Cat asks her, "Where are you going?" and she says, "I don't know." The Cat says, "If you don't know where you're going, it doesn't matter which way you go."

If you don't have a goal in mind, you're not going to reach that goal. Defining goals and means of achieving them is what business planning is all about.

Thoughts to Take Away

- The written business plan demands that you choose an audience, then write with their needs and interests in mind. Still, you are one of the most important audiences this plan will have. Always write the first version of the plan for *you yourself*.

- Your business plan must reflect a clear vision of your goals for growth and for incorporation of technology in your business.

- Though there is no perfect outline that works for every business plan, most follow a basic order, starting with an executive summary, moving through discussions of marketing, personnel, and finances, and closing with supporting material that provides background and supports the credibility of the plan.

part**TWO**

The Three-Legged Stool

Let's build a "three-legged stool" to support your business activity. A three-legged stool doesn't wobble. A business plan that gives attention to each of these areas—marketing, personnel, and finances—should provide a steady base for your business operations.

In this section we will explore critical success factors in each area, illustrated with examples from the real-world business plans that appear in Part 4. As you read, you'll grow in understanding of what your specific plan should include.

chapterFIVE

Marketing

In the souks of Africa, in the piazzas of Europe, in the smallest of small towns, in the strip malls of America, you'll find it—the marketplace. Wherever crossroads facilitate the coming together of buyers and sellers, marketing is taking place. Today, those crossroads need not even be physical locations. The Internet is the hottest souk in cyberspace.

If you balanced a bundle of fabrics on your head in the morning and set out for your stall in the square, you would be doing business as your ancestors have for thousands of years—and you would be wrestling with marketing issues that are as timely today as ever. It's critical that you stock your small space with the fabrics most likely to sell if you don't want your scarce cash or display space tied up in slow-turning inventory. It's imperative that you make the right call when a customer offers to trade feathers for fabrics, regardless of your need for feathers. You are making marketing decisions, striving both to serve your customer and to protect your own best interests. You may not want feathers at all—but you don't want your customer going to your competitor across the square either. If you expect to be successful with your fabric stall, you will need a sophisticated understanding of the industry, the customers and competitors who inhabit it, and the unique attributes of the goods you put on offer. Together, these components make up the marketplace.

When you write the marketing section of a business plan, you size up the marketplace in which you, your customers, and your competitors come together. The marketing section of a plan may include any or all of the following. The order will not necessarily be that shown here:

- Market description
  - Industry description
  - Customer description
  - Competitive description
- Products/services offering description
  - Product
  - Price
  - Place
  - Promotion
- Marketing plan

The purpose of this section is to describe the marketing strategies you plan to implement, and to show why you believe these strategies are your best response to the situation in which you find yourself.

Who are your customers? Why will they be attracted to your product or service? What is your pricing structure, and why? The reader of your plan should be able to find the answers to these questions in the marketing section of your plan.

A marketing section should touch on the demographics of your target market, industry trends, competition, and future outlook. Your plan should spell out what you believe to be the best ways to reach your potential customers. This might include direct marketing, advertising, special promotions, or personal selling—or more likely, a mixture of these elements.

My colleagues and I who review business plans find the marketing section is often a weak point in the plan. This is unfortunate because businesses succeed or fail as much on their ability to market themselves as on any other factor in the equation.

What Marketing Is All About

What is marketing, anyway? In marketing textbooks, you'll find a definition along these lines: "Marketing is the process of creating a product, then planning and carrying out the pricing, promotion, and distribution of that product by stimulating buying exchanges in which both buyer and seller profit in some way." That's a lot to swallow whole, so let's break the definition into its component parts.

The process of creating an offering . . . Central to most businesses is the creating of a product or service for sale. That offering may be an entirely new product or service idea, or a new twist on an old idea, or an infusion of new managers who shake up "business as usual." For a retailer, it's not one product, but many. Successful retailers have the ability to create a merchandise mix so imaginative it seems fresh even to repeat customers. For a manufacturer, the offering might be a new way of distributing an old product—like when type foundries began selling fonts to graphic designers as electronic files, immediately available for downloading over the Internet. Whether the idea is new or old, the product one or many, marketing begins with finding a way to fill a potential customer's need with something you can sell. You're providing something different, or making something different, or adding your touches to something that may already exist, to create an offering that is unique and appealing.

. . . then planning and carrying out the pricing, promotion, and distribution of that offering . . . The marketing plan is the result of insights into the pricing, promotion, and distribution of a product or service offering. The strategic thinking creates the plan, goals, tactics, and individual activities in pursuit of strategic objectives carry out the plan; Marketing implies a process of planning and implementation that guides the potential customer and the product or service offering toward an encounter.

. . . by stimulating buying exchanges . . . Once potential customer and offering have found each other, the customer must experience desire for the benefits that ownership of the product will confer. Only then can the buying exchange take place. Everyone in your company who is involved in buying exchanges is a marketer. The sales clerk on the floor stimulates buying exchanges when he suggests a tie to go with a shirt; the art director stimulates buying exchanges when she dresses up a photo of a grilled steak to make the meat appear more appetizing. Marketing should be integrated into every level of your business.

. . . in which both buyer and seller profit in some way. If both aren't profiting, one or the other will be reluctant to repeat the experience. The buyer should profit by receiving the anticipated benefits the purchase was intended to deliver. The seller should profit by selling the product or service at a price that includes a margin for earnings, beyond covering the costs of making and delivering the product. The seller also profits from intangibles like increased brand awareness, and goodwill resulting from excellent customer service. The entire buying exchange must be transacted profitably for both parties.

The marketing function is successful when it increases the sustainability of a business, while making life better for its customers. And every day, marketing is becoming more and more critical to sustain businesses. The old days of "build a better mousetrap and they'll beat a path to your door" are gone. We shouldn't forget that some people have skills that they do extremely well, and want to offer to the world. The adage goes "there's a lot out there, but if you're the cream, you rise to the top." But convincing people you're "the cream" requires marketing.

Today's new product and service offerings are different from the "better mousetraps" of the past. For most categories of goods and services people already have "mousetraps" that do the job quite well, thank you. Today more than ever, marketers must create messages that persuade potential customers to solve problems they didn't even know they had. When this is done without conscience, it leads to a throw-away culture that gives marketing a bad name. When it is done with a strong ethical component, it leads us toward a future where our lives are better than we ever thought possible. Who knew that heated car seats, gourmet microwave meals, and Velcro closures would make life so good? Who knows what innovations the next few decades will bring, allowing us to customize our experiences to our own definitions of "the good life"?

Marketing is the essential ingredient that connects end-users to the offerings that make life great. Marketing, like the other areas of a business operation, benefits from planning. You need to assess your current situation, set objectives for the future, then determine steps to reach those objectives.

Market Analysis

You don't conduct business in a vacuum—you do it in a world already inhabited by buyers and sellers, where buying exchanges have been taking place all along. What's going on at the party before you get there? That's the question this section of the plan is designed to address.

In this section, you describe the customers, competitors, and trends affecting the marketplace in which you operate. You might begin with a market description, giving the size of the market in terms of dollars; or distinguishing what product groups are rising or falling; the relative stability of the marketplace; and other factors you deem important. You might concentrate on major trends that affect your business, such as emerging markets, shifts in competition, consolidations among suppliers, or demographic shifts among customers. This discussion of the marketplace gives context to your plan. It may help bring to mind business opportunities, or new markets, or new product/service areas. Carefully analyzing changes in the marketplace around you can open your mind to possible opportunities and threats—while you still have time to choose strategies that maximize the former and minimize the latter.

Industry description

Prepare a brief summary of facts about the overall industry in which you compete. It's important that the readers of your business plan understand the nature of the industry, so describe it clearly. Are you operating in the business-to-business space or the business-to-consumer space?

If the industry is extremely competitive, for example, this will affect you. Is it easy for new businesses to enter the field? Is the industry dominated by a few key players? Do you intend to challenge the established leaders? Explain the basic nature of the industry.

Situations resulting from recent and ongoing changes are important. Describe where you think the important trends in your industry may lead. Call your trade association, your library, or your banker, if you need help spotting the trends. I've included a discussion of general business trends in chapter 3 of this book to get you started thinking strategically about your industry and your market potential.

See Worksheet 5.1 in appendix D for idea-starting questions to help you write this section. Be warned: These questions will call for some thorough research. Statistics and other information from respected sources will support your statements and lend credibility to your plan. (Be sure to identify your sources.)

Frank Hoy sees weak industry analysis as a common mistake among small and new businesses, and tells the tale of a successful entrepreneur who avoided this mistake:

We see people who think that the world is going to stay the same forever. You don't have to be terribly sophisticated to see new trends, to see what's happening in your industry, in your own community. Sit down and think it through for yourself. "How is this going to impact my business? Maybe I'd better change."

Here in El Paso we're identified as the city that has lost more jobs as a result of the North American Free Trade Agreement (NAFTA) than any other city in the United States. Our dominant industry here used to be the garment industry. It's all moved across the border. We have an independent business owner here who had been extremely suc-

cessful in a jeans-washing business, getting contracts with Levi's and other manufacturers. Now Levi's has downsized, they've shut down nearly all their plants here. In order to be competitive, the local businessman has found he's had to open a jeans-washing facility in Mexico, and downsized his operation here. This guy is a lifelong El Pasoan, committed to this area, a good business citizen of this community. He intends to stay here. As he's changed his operations, he's also looked for alternative investments. If you can see that you're in an industry that's in decline, and moving, and you want to stay, ask "what business is reasonably recession-proof?" Well, he bought a beer distributorship. That will keep him and his family here, while they're still able to run their other facilities in Mexico.

He's constantly keeping an eye on what's going on. Making sure he won't go down the tube as a result of events beyond his control. He adjusts and finds other business opportunities.

Start a file immediately. Clip any articles that are remotely connected to your industry and your business idea.

Customer description

Your description of your marketplace and industry would be incomplete without an in-depth look at the people who make up the "buying" half of the buying exchange.

It's vital to the success of your business that you understand who your customers are. What benefits bring them to buy from you? What level of quality are they looking for? The answers will not be the same for every customer, of course. For that reason, it's important to distinguish between the different customer groups you serve.

These customer groups can be identified by traits they share—traits like geographic location, product usage, demographic profile, and lifestyle. When we attempt to identify what traits buyers have in common, we are engaging in *market segmentation,* or another way of saying it, *target marketing.* When we pursue a target marketing strategy, we look for the traits that predict the ways a customer group will behave. We know the targeted segment will probably respond in a similar way to a specific offering, or marketing message. The key is to understand who is responding to what, and why, so we can use that knowledge to design our marketing strategies.

KEY CONCEPT: SEGMENT YOUR MARKET

Lumping all of your customers into one mass market leads you down the wrong path—trying to be everything to everybody. Segmenting your market helps you serve specific niches better.

This is true for consumer products and services, and also true for business-to-business buying exchanges. Businesses can be grouped by identifiable traits just as individuals can.

Typical factors for distinguishing market segments include consumer demographics, psychographics, and for businesses, industrial demographics. Consumer demographics include age, sex, family size, family life stage, income, occupation, education, religion, race, nationality, social class, and geographic location. Psychographics include needs, attitudes, activities, interests, opinions, and lifestyle choices. Industrial demographics include Standard Industrial Classification (SIC code), location, sales volume, number of employees, net worth, and number of plants. You may find other traits beyond those listed here that are valuable predictors for *your* customers.

Where do you find this information? You may want to start at the public library. Find your SIC code and that of your industrial customers. Study the census data for each group that concerns you. Ask reference librarians to help—that's what they are there for.

Once you've identified your customer groups, determine how large each group is and what each group is buying. Study the characteristics of their purchases. What are the benefits they value most?

For each customer group you've identified, describe the product/service attributes those customers require. Try to define the level of quality they expect, and the price range they consider reasonable. If they expect customization of the offering to their needs, describe what that entails.

Finally, look at the profitability of each group you've identified. Some may be more profitable than others—and what you learn as you analyze this question may surprise you. The largest group is not necessarily the one most profitable to you. Select the groups that are most worthy of your focus, then make them your priority in terms of your marketing strategies and the resources you allocate to each target market.

Worksheet 5.2 in appendix D will help you write this section.

Chuck Hofer recommends increasing the attention you give to understanding your best customers' buying motivations:

Businesses need to make sure, once they've identified that target customer, they know the exact and precise and primary reasons why that customer is buying their product. Make sure you understand all different factors a customer will be buying for, but particularly that you understand the priority order. Knowing that, make sure you're selling is based on positive appeals, rather than negative appeals. Positive appeals are what keep the customers coming back. The negatives may help you get them in the door, but they aren't the thing that will help you close the sale. You need to make sure you understand the positive appeals.

Example. A company was going to sell to gill-net fishermen a device that would keep whales and other sea mammals, like porpoises, away from their nets. There were some federal regulations about to go into effect that might require the use of devices such as this. One of the mistakes that company made was to emphasize "we'll help you avoid the regulations" aspect.

The fishermen, who were very anti-government anyway, got very turned off by that. It was very difficult for the company to actually sell. The primary appeal, it turned out, was that if a whale crashed into your net it did a whole lot of damage. Actually, and this company didn't realize this, fish have sensing devices. While they couldn't tell the "pings" that this device made, the whales also give off sounds, and one of the things that turned out to be true is that if you take whales away from your nets, you actually catch more fish. Since fish can sense the whales, they will try to swim away from the whales. Bottom line—keep whales away from your nets and you'll have a better chance that fish will swim into them.

Ultimately that business succeeded, but it didn't happen until they began emphasizing the two positive appeals: significantly increased catches, and significantly reduced damage to your nets. Not the fact that you would comply with government regulations.

If that company had spent more time learning *why* fishermen bought their product, they could have experienced more success, and sooner.

Competitor description

Who are your primary competitors? A list probably comes to mind even as you read those words. Businesses that are always matching your prices, or offering to honor your coupons, or buying ads just a little bigger than yours.

If your business is local, check out the Yellow Page listings in your category(ies). Many people use a map and push pins to identify competitors' locations. Try this—you'll likely gain new insights.

Rank them, or categorize them into distinctive groups that compete with you in specific areas. Direct your analytical efforts to those firms you compete with most directly. Look for indications of the strengths and weaknesses of each firm, indications of their future plans, and how they might react to your next moves. If one firm seems to lead the pack, see if you can identify why they have been successful. Do they have a particular advertising approach? Are they targeting a particular market segment? By studying where they are focusing their energy, you might find a way to do an end run around them, or to beat them at their own game.

Your direct competitors aren't the only ones giving you a run for your money. Competition might be affecting you from areas you don't even realize. Are there products or services that substitute for the ones you and your direct competitors offer? For an example, think about the grocery store where you usually shop. Who is their competition? Many would name other grocery stores—their direct competitors. But others would name convenience stores. Others might say the family-run supermarket down the street, or the mega-store that's been built in the area. Those are all direct competitors. But that leaves out the indirect competitors. There are also the fast-food restaurants. You could spend your food dollar in the supermarket buying food, or you could spend it in a restaurant. The supermarkets know that—that's why we now have roasted chicken and salad bars and other home meal replacements in the grocery. Supermarkets are going head to head with small and not-so-small restaurant chains, providing a growing array of ready-to-serve products.

Another example? An auto repair business experiences competition not just from other auto repair shops, but also from "shade tree mechanics" who would like to do the job themselves.

We recommend you keep files on each of your key competitors. "But how do I find out about them?" you're asking. It's easier than you think. Here are a few suggestions.

- Seek out published information. I mention this first, because this research will have you better prepared when you move on to the next suggestions. Your library reference desk will guide you to useful resources, such as business directories, directories of professional associations, and online services. This book's appendix B lists many useful resources, both online and traditionally published.
- Consult your trade association. Associations compile and disseminate data about the industry. If your competitors belong to the trade association, you may find profile data available to you.
- Read the newspaper. Business articles reveal strategic initiatives of your competitors.
- Keep tabs on the promotional efforts of competitors. Look at their phone directory ads. Seek out their ads in local media. Track what they are offering. What does the ad copy focus on? What is emphasized in the sales pitch? What do their salespeople focus on when they compare their products to yours?

KEY CONCEPT: KNOW YOUR COMPETITION

What is it you most want to know about your competitors? Why they are able to get customers, and how they are able to keep those customers happy.

- Send a "mystery shopper" to visit competitors.
- Speak to suppliers, such as temporary staffing agencies, who do business with both you and your competition. You won't, of course, ask for trade secrets—but casual questions will gain you useful information.
- Other members of the business community, such as real estate developers, are likely to be in the know. General trends, and even quite specific information, are easy to obtain if you stay in touch with your peers in the community.
- Your employees may have more information than you—or they—know. They may have friends in similar jobs with your competitors. Anyone who has contact with customers is likely to hear what the other guy is offering.
- And last but not least—ask your customers! Individually or in a group, ask customers to tell you about their attitudes, experiences, and impressions of the firms you compete with for their dollars.
- You may see an opening to win share of market from your competition, by recruiting their customers to become yours.
- Knowing their marketing strategies, including marketing mix and segmentation strategies, improves your ability to make your own marketing strategies unique, not "me-too."
- By observing your competition over time, you have the opportunity to learn from their mistakes.

Bob Brockhaus offered this advice for start-up companies on researching their competition:

Work for them. Get some on-the-job experience with the people you're going to be up against, if you can possibly do that. Network in the industry, with potential suppliers and customers as well as competitors. That is the best preparation for understanding the market you're getting into and the financing sources and the trends in the industry, so you can have a better chance to make a success of it.

My friend Judy did exactly that. She worked for a travel agency, she learned the business, she spent a year with them finding what she liked and didn't like. You have to be careful with noncompete clauses, and you have to think about whether you are able to do this or not, but it is an extremely effective way to build your expertise. Judy learned the business, and even found a partner. The two of them went off and founded their own business. It happens every day, in every industry. My friend Judy is very successful. She grew her agency; her partner decided to do something else, and now she's the sole owner, and has been in business for over 10 years. It's great to learn on someone else's nickel.

However you do your competitive research, be sure you understand thoroughly the playing field on which you will compete.

Worksheet 5.3 in appendix D will help you write your description of your competitive situation.

Examples from our business plans

The result of analyzing the market by looking at industry trends, customers, and competitors should be the discovery of a business opportunity, or confirmation of one you believed to exist. The analysis should also reveal the relative strengths of your business concept vis-à-vis these elements in your environment. You may decide to revise certain aspects of your offering, based on what you have learned in this analysis phase. Better to do so now while you're still in the planning stage.

Among the example plans included in this book are several with strong market analysis sections.

Two plans that deserve your attention were prepared with the counsel of Tim Baye, who in his work as an associate professor in business outreach with the Southwest Wisconsin Management Education Program of the University of Wisconsin–Extension, counsels entrepreneurs just as I do. As you look at the two plans, one for O'Toole's Machining and the other for The Artful Fly, notice both the similarities and differences in the market analysis sections.

O'Toole's Machining. This plan's market analysis section contains subtopics labeled "Existing/Historic Customers," "Prospective Customers/Markets," "Competition," and "Industry Trends." The market analysis section begins

O'Toole's Machining's current and near-term future overall market is best defined as transportation/agricultural/industrial machinery original equipment manufacturers (OEM) located in the Upper-Midwestern United States. O'Toole's Machining perceives that it can best compete in these industrial segments within a five state region, including: Illinois, Indiana, Iowa, Minnesota, and Wisconsin.

A secondary market for O'Toole's Machining is to continue to serve as a subcontracted machining service provider for other upper-midwestern machining firms whose capacity and/or capabilities are not adequate to meet the needs of their own customers. However, O'Toole's Machining believes that future prosperity resides in targeting the OEM market, rather than the machining subcontracting market.

This introduction neatly condenses a complicated and technical industrial niche into a summary that orients the reader to the market analysis that follows in the plan. Later in this plan, a section on "Market Opportunities" spells out specific strategies for leveraging the insights introduced here.

The Artful Fly. This plan's market analysis section contains subtopics labeled "The Industry," "Fly-Fishing Consumer," and "Profile of Competition."

Consider this introduction to the fly-fishing consumer, under the heading "Demographics and Lifestyle":

The market which the Artful Fly has targeted is the fly-fisherman. The economic demographics for fly fishing are

second only to polo and are ahead of skiing and golf. The average fly fisherman is a white male who is married, a college graduate, and 40 years of age. His average income is $84,600. His average household income is $113,000. Most fly fishermen hold an administrative or management position. The majority has at least two major credit cards. (National Sports and Recreation Industry, 1990 study)

The description of the fly-fishing consumer continues with information regarding his media usage, his attitudes toward tradition and innovation, his geographic distribution, and other relevant information. Notice how this plan's author has cited the source of his information.

BizCopy. This plan is organized a little differently. Industry background and future trends are discussed in one section, labeled "Background Information," while other market analysis information is discussed in a later section titled "The Marketing Plan." Here a section labeled "Market Analysis" contains the customer and competitive analysis, plus a description of market potential.

This brief customer analysis hits the important points, and refers the reader to a customer survey in an appendix, from which the conclusions in this short paragraph were drawn.

BizCopy's customers are both male and female professional representatives of local businesses. BizCopy's customers shop for their documentation needs during normal business hours—generally Monday through Friday: 8:00 A.M. to 6:00 P.M. The main reason for purchase is business necessity. Quick-print customers weigh quality, price, convenience, and other factors when choosing a quick-printer.

Including the customer survey in the plan was an excellent idea. I only wish the tabulated results of the survey had been included as well. Instead, the author has omitted these, including only his conclusions drawn from the survey results.

Resume.com. This plan focuses heavily on industry analysis, in part because, as an Internet-based business, it is planning on entering a very new industry. Readers are likely to need orientation to the subject. The section titled "Industry Analysis" includes paragraphs labeled "Threat of New Entrants," "Power of Buyers," "Power of Suppliers," and "Industry Conclusions." Consider the following excerpt. Where do you suppose the author went to do the research found here?

Rivalry in the industry is a strong force. There are several companies that provide the majority of the same services. The competition is currently very strong in this industry with approximately eighty-seven on-line employment service providers listed under the Yahoo! employment page alone. Appendix 1 provides a list of the industry's major players and a brief description of the competition. Some of the larger companies are headhunters.net, careerpath.com, and monster.com; these are Resume.com's main competition.

The Resume.com plan failed to convince me that this company had the necessary competitive edge. Take a look at it and see what you think.

These plans will come up again as our discussion of marketing continues.

Products/Services Offering Description

Until now, we've been discussing the environment you find yourself in. Now it's time to turn our attention to the other half of the equation—the environment you create for yourself. If the market analysis studies "what's going on at the party when you get there," then this section of the plan studies "what you bring to the party."

For many years, marketers have described "what we bring to the party" as the marketing mix, which consists of four elements usually referred to as the "four Ps" of product, place, price, and promotion. A full marketing strategy consists of decisions regarding each of these elements. The marketing mix shifts your focus from the environment to the components that *you* control.

P = Product (and/or service offering)

A product can be a bandage or a band, a concert or a concept. Your product may be a tangible thing, a combination of tangibles and intangibles mixing products with services, or solely existing in the dimension of service. That's why I like the term *offering*. It's clumsy, but at least it's inclusive. A dress off the rack is a product. A dress altered to fit you is a product combined with a service. A specialist who creates a wedding dress to your order is delivering more service than product. A person who teaches sewing so you can make your own dress is providing a service—no products attached. See if you can think of other examples on the product/service continuum.

Products and services typically have a life cycle. Products are invented, introduced, and grow. At some point, they reach maturity, and eventually pass into decline. The fax machine was introduced, gained wide acceptance, and is already in decline—not even 20 years later. A new innovation came along—the Internet—and drove a stake through the fax machine's heart.

Not just products, but whole product categories go through this cycle. Think about hair. In the late 1960s, men began wearing their hair much longer, and barbers experienced a corresponding lack of demand for their services. Traditional barbers either went out of business or adapted to the times by learning what beauty parlor operators knew about the longer styles. What had been an industry strictly segregated by gender became largely unisex. And it happened pretty quickly. Few barbers had business plans—and more than a few went under.

Your plans considering your product/service offering need to acknowledge the life cycle of your offering and its industry. Whatever you are offering, expect it to evolve in tune with customer needs.

When your product is a service. In today's knowledge economy, your offering is more likely to be a service than a product. The majority of offerings combine elements of both. Restaurants provide a tangible product, but the service they provide, from food preparation in the kitchen to waiters at your table, add the elements that distinguish one restaurant from the next. The whole experience of dining in a specific establishment becomes the "product," as chains like Chuck E. Cheese have proved.

Service-only offerings exist everywhere you look. Out my window, a Federal Express agent is exchanging greetings with the mail carrier—both providing services. One is bringing me solicitations from people who want to clean my furnace vents and shampoo my rugs. The other is bringing documents I must deal with immediately.

I present workshops for professionals who will defend me if I have legal trouble; organize me if I have messy drawers; counsel me if I succumb to stress. All are providing services with no substantial connection to a product.

While all offerings, both products and services, exist to fill customer needs, services have characteristics that make them very different from products. Consider the following characteristics of services:

- **Intangibility.** Purchasers can't touch, taste, see, or feel a service before they agree to buy it. It's difficult for them to measure its quality. What they get in the buying exchange is initially a promise of satisfaction. Once they can determine whether the promise has been fulfilled, the water is pretty much under the bridge. It's hard to return a bad haircut. There is a heavy requirement that the buyer trust the seller when services are involved. You can counter this by stressing competence, professionalism, and experience in your selling messages.

- **Inseparability.** Services are typically delivered by people. Have you ever followed your hair stylist when she's moved from one salon to another? It's the person you trust—not the institution she works for. Employers in service businesses must respond to inseparability with an emphasis on collaboration and teamwork. The Internet is changing this dynamic for some of us since it enables us to provide services without face-to-face contact. Keeping the personal touch—without encouraging inseparability—will force some service providers to master this high-wire balancing act.

- **High perishability.** Products sit on shelves waiting for buyers; services don't. If you're a psychic and you expect a client at 4:00 P.M., and that client fails to show, you can't resell that 4:00 P.M. slot to someone else (unless you're an extraordinarily good psychic, in which case you already knew this would happen). You may respond to perishability via several strategies, including offering early-reservation discounts and charging for no-shows. In selling services, timing is everything.

• **Difficulty of quality control.** It's impossible to standardize a service offering, especially once you hire employees to help you deliver your product. Your management of personnel becomes critical at this stage. You must set performance standards, perform appraisals to make sure standards are being met, and find other ways of ensuring quality control wherever possible.

• **Involvement of customer.** When you're having your hair cut, do you chat with the person cutting your hair? Over time, we become friendly with the people who provide services to us. If service slips, we're likely to feel uncomfortable complaining because of this involvement. It's psychologically easier for us to find another supplier than to approach the problem head-on. Unfortunately, this is costly for the business we leave behind. Replacing a customer costs much more than retaining one.

Each of these characteristics is a factor to consider when you are selling a service offering. You must deliver not only a high quality of service, but also manage the service encounter so that the process is as satisfying as its eventual result. The good news for you in the service business is that you are typically in closer touch with your customers than are those who offer products. This gives you a constant source of feedback, new ideas, and inspirations that will help your service offering evolve.

Feasibility. For new businesses, and for existing businesses considering new offerings, a key element is determining the feasibility of the offering. Are there customers who want to buy this offering? Are there enough of them to make you financially viable? If this offering is already available elsewhere, why will people buy from you instead of your competitors? You must look at the trends around you, as discussed in the market analysis section, for objective proof that your offering has a compelling reason to exist. This means finding your competitive edge—that thing you do particularly well.

My colleagues are quick to emphasize this point.

KEY CONCEPT: FEATURES AND BENEFITS

Customers value products and services not for what they are, but for what they do. Concentrate on the benefits of your product or service. What makes it useful? What problem does it solve? And most important, what makes your offering deliver the benefit better than any competing offering can?

George Solomon contributed, "There are two powerful motivations for businesses to get started and succeed—the consumer must believe that business will either save them time, or provide them knowledge. If you save the consumer time, or provide them knowledge, you'll have a successful business."

Dale Meyer said, "Make sure you're really offering something that has value added. You must really be providing value that was not there before."

The Artful Fly's business plan describes a product that, though unusual, appears to be highly feasible given the market analysis factors presented in the plan. A description of The Artful Fly's product appears on page 133.

Features into benefits. We value products and services not for what they are, but for what they do for us. We don't like big black boxes sitting in our living rooms—we like the news and entertainment the box dispenses. We don't really want an elaborate two-part liquid container on our kitchen counter—we want coffee. There's a saying along these lines: "a man doesn't buy a drill bit, he buys a hole."

I ask you to stop thinking about the features of your product and concentrate on its benefits. What makes it useful? What benefit does it deliver? And most important, what makes your offering deliver the benefit better than any competing offering can? Figure 5.1 shows an example of features translated into benefits for a common product: the ubiquitous credit card.

FIGURE 5.1 Features into Benefits Example: Credit Card

Feature	Benefit
Accepted at many locations	Freedom, flexibility
Large credit line	Purchasing power
Works like cash	Convenience and safety
Compact size	Easy to take anywhere
Frequent flyer tie-in	Saves money, increases opportunities
Picture ID	Security
One monthly bill	Saves time

Now you try it. Worksheet 5.4 in appendix D is an exercise for you to practice translating features into benefits for your own product or service offerings. Consult the list in Figure 5.2 to stimulate your thinking about benefits people might value. (Remember that saving time and gaining knowledge are likely to be highly valued by your customers.)

FIGURE 5.2 Common Benefits and Motivators

To be liked	Security	Health
To be appreciated	To be attractive	To gratify
curiosity		
To feel important	To be comfortable	Convenience
To make money	To be distinct	To be sexy
Save money	To be happy	Fear
Save time	To have fun	To gain knowledge
Guilt	Greed	To make work easier

Worksheet 5.5 in appendix D will help you write a description of your product or service offering. Later, when it's time for you to create advertising and promotional programs, this list of benefits in Worksheet 5.5 will be helpful to you.

P = Place (location and distribution issues)

What does *place* mean anymore, in this era of the global village and Internet commerce? This P is really ready to retire—or at least evolve into a more relevant letter. This P stands for all the aspects of getting product/service offerings to their end users. The right goods must get to the right place, in the right quantity, at the right time, for the lowest possible cost, without sacrificing quality or customer service. This requires planning—and that's what this P is doing in your business plan.

Place factors vary a great deal by business type. Retailers are highly concerned with locations convenient to customers, unless they've chosen to locate on the Internet. Manufacturers and distributors are also concerned with location, but their concerns are different. Convenience to customers, availability of raw materials, access to suitable employees and support services, impact of existence of government regulations—all will be important to relative degrees, depending on the business category in which you operate.

How much you emphasize the place aspect in your plan will depend on the unique challenges facing your business. Place is likely to be either highly critical or unimportant to you—there does not seem to be much middle ground.

Several of our example plans fall in the category for which place is highly critical. In the plan for BizCopy, location as it relates to growth is a driving force for the business planning effort. This excerpt from the plan's statement of purpose explains:

The purpose of BizCopy's business plan is to outline a strategy for growth in the commercial printing industry

If BizCopy is capable of growing . . . how will this growth take place? Should BizCopy open a new location? What geographic area should BizCopy open a third store in? . . . should BizCopy consolidate the two existing stores into one? Could the territories be covered with outside salespeople?

Voices

If less than 20 percent of your customers are complaining about price, then you're not charging enough.

—Jack Reiners

The plan delivers on its promise to analyze these questions, then draws conclusions to create a strategic plan for reaching company objectives.

Another example of place as a critical issue can be seen in the plan for Red's Automotive Service. Red's is opening a new operation in an adjacent trade area, and also adding a new distribution channel through the purchase of a tire truck, allowing Red's to better serve the agricultural/commercial tire market.

Sometimes, the place story is really about connecting places—connecting buyer and seller.

Foodusa.com (profiled in chapter 7) serves the distribution needs of the meat industry, replacing a traditional chain of supply with an Internet-based market exchange. "I replace numerous people—salespeople, buyers, credit departments, transportation departments, brokers and traders. I remove cost from the system," said Rod Heller. By reducing the costs incurred in the old system, this start-up company has secured for itself a promising business niche.

If place is an important issue for you, take a look at these plans for inspiration. Then use Worksheet 5.6 in appendix D to help you plan your place (distribution) strategy.

P = Pricing strategy

Your customer's goal is to obtain the most benefits for the price paid for a product or service. Your goal is to obtain the most price for the benefits. Somewhere in the middle, you meet for that mutually profitable buying exchange.

RESOURCE:
BUSINESS INCUBATOR LOCATIONS

Business incubators provide a place for new businesses to "hatch." They are a great way for community development to blossom, and an intriguing way for a business to get the esprit de corps of other small businesses in the incubator. You get the "water cooler effect." Incubators typically offer resources such as trained managers and shared support services. You can't stay there long (usually about three years) but it's a great place to start, or an interim step for a home business preparing to grow.

KEY CONCEPT:
PRICING FOR PROFIT

Pricing an offering requires you know both your fiscal break-even point and the nature of market demand for that offering. Set your prices at or below the break-even and you will have no profits. Set your price too high above that point, and you may be out of reach of too many buyers.

Many entrepreneurs think that price is a function of math—you take what it costs you to produce the product, you tack on a percentage for profit, and that's your price. But that doesn't work if the price doesn't meet the value expectations of the customer who's going to buy. Another way of pricing is to look at what that customer expects to pay, then work out what you can afford to deliver at that price, while protecting your percentage for profit. Either method requires that you know your break-even point on each product/service line—a subject we'll take up in chapter 7.

Pricing puts you in the land of supply and demand. If there is high demand for what you sell, and relatively few alternatives or substitutes available, then you will be able to charge a high price. Marketers term this *inelastic demand*. If, on the other hand, there is less demand for what you sell, and/or plenty of alternatives and substitutes available, then you are facing *elastic demand*. If your price is too high, your customers will simply choose an alternative or do without. The nature of elastic demand limits your ability to charge a price higher than that of your competitors.

As purchasers of goods and services, price has become our most quantifiable way of measuring the value of an offering. We really believe, in most cases, "you get what you pay for." When it's hard to kick the tires, as when purchasing a service, we're suspicious of low-price offerings.

How do we define value? We weigh the benefits of a purchase against its cost to us. The benefits may be tangible, or intangible—the status that the purchase conveys, for example. The cost is only partly monetary. We also must factor in the time and energy it took to decide on that purchase.

Many of us will pay more to avoid unpleasant tasks because we value our time more than money.

All the elements of an offering contribute to the value customers perceive it to have. Its form (stylish or utilitarian), its functionality, its availability, added niceties like free assembly, or customization—all lend value to the offering. If you want to raise your price (and your profits), look for an aspect of the offering that can be tweaked to increase its value in the potential buyer's mind.

In today's "save me time or give me knowledge" environment, service is often the component that adds the value that allows you to charge a higher price. Consider the purchase of a bicycle. You could purchase a bike from a discount store—and find yourself spending hours trying to assemble it at home. You could pay more to purchase one from a bicycle shop—and find yourself enjoying a personalized, custom fitting, before you take home a bike that's instantly ready to ride. You will also feel you have a place to go when you have questions about bicycling—unlikely with a discount store purchase. Service, and the perception of value it conveys, makes the difference.

Don't compete on price if you can help it. Unless you're starting your own big-box discount store or category killer, concentrate on competing on other factors than price.

Chuck Hofer commented on pricing strategies for new and small businesses:

Most new ventures are successful because you're providing something the customer wants, better than your competition. There are a large number of benefits that small businesses provide. A great mistake is undercharging for those. In almost no circumstance is the primary benefit of a small business that you provide the service less expensively than established competitors, and that's why you need to understand your primary benefit. When you understand it, you understand why you can charge a higher price.

What are the alternatives to competing on price? You can personalize. You can customize. You can specialize. You can offer better financing or better guarantees. You can offer more convenience. You can raise the perception of value by promoting an upscale image. You can even raise your price, and communi-

cate that you charge more because you're worth it. If the demand for what you sell is reasonably inelastic, you'll do fine. In situations of elastic demand, competition will unfortunately always focus on low price. Faced with this situation, make sure you address it adequately in your strategic plans.

Price is much more than the dollar figure you print on a tag. Price is a strategy that includes discounts, surcharges, payment terms, negotiability, variable cost estimates, and more. Your pricing strategy can help you obtain organizational objectives like increasing your market share, maximizing profits, building up a new product line, or remaining competitive.

The example plan from Resume.com gives an excellent look at the relationship between pricing and other factors in an operation. In this business, the majority of revenue is generated by subscribers' fees paid by companies who pay for access to a database of job-seekers' resumes. Resume.com has structured their subscriber fee differently from competitors, thus achieving an advantage that they are counting on to attract larger corporations. This will increase the desirability of supplying resumes—thus pulling the suppliers (job seekers) to provide the "product" for customers.

Your pricing policies will affect your sales volume goals, and thus affect the projections in the financial section of your business plan. An in-depth analysis of the pricing function is beyond the scope of this book, but well worth your attention.

Worksheet 5.7 in appendix D is designed to help you frame your pricing strategy.

P = Promotion

This P covers promotional activity from planning your advertising to training your sales staff. Promotion is the element that communicates the availability and desirability of whatever it is you offer. Depending on the situation in which you find yourself, this section of your product/service description might mention your plans to use paid advertising media, or to offer sales promotions like contests and coupons, or to rely on personal selling or public relations activity to "get the word out." You'll get a chance to expand on the promotional strategy you plan to adopt when you write the marketing plan section, coming up.

In my opinion, the key to this P lies in yet another P—the concept of *positioning*. Positioning is the component that keeps your promotional activity coordinated—dancing to the same music, pulling in the same direction. Positioning takes your product or service and promotes its uniqueness in the marketplace.

What is positioning? Jack Reiners described positioning as "the act of designing the company's offering and image so that they occupy a meaningful and distinct position in the customer's mind." Positioning is how potential customers differentiate you from your competitors. Positioning is by its nature competitive—it is always chosen relative to positions held by competitors.

Voices

When you pay too little, you lose everything, because what you bought was incapable of doing the thing it was purchased for . . . if you deal with the lowest bidder, add something for the risk you run.

—John Ruskin, *Common Sense*

Positioning works as a promotional strategy for a simple reason: Your customers are human beings. Basic psychological insight teaches us that we humans can't hold two conflicting beliefs. We refuse to believe that two different shoe stores have the broadest inventory imaginable, even if both state that in their advertisements. A corollary of this is the fact that it's better to be first than best. Once we human beings have made up our minds about something, we hate to change our opinion. As a consequence, whichever shoe store first convinced us it has the broadest inventory will be the shoe store whose claims we continue to believe, until absolutely forced to change our minds.

Developing a promotional strategy for your business should start with choosing the position you want to hold in potential customers' minds. Consider the positions held by your competitors: On what dimension are they considered "best"? They might be known for product features, or selection, or convenience—you get the idea. Positioning is about finding or creating a dimension in which you can become known as "best."

Positioning reflects the personality you've created for your business. This personality comes from the tone of your advertising, your customers' experiences with you, what they tell others about you, what your employees say about you, the appearance of your store, your Web site, and your personnel—in other words, practically everything you do has the potential to strengthen the position you hold in public perception.

A new business has the opportunity to create a position from scratch. An existing business already has a position, whether it has proactively chosen that niche, or simply been assigned it by the community's experience of that business.

The success of your promotional activity absolutely depends on controlling your position and using it to your advantage. Every communication and experience customers have with your company should be consistent with the position you've chosen to project.

Worksheet 5.8 in appendix D is designed to help you explore the concept of positioning further, with regard to your own competitive environment.

Brand identity is an extension of the idea of positioning. A brand consists of the associations and expectations that come to mind when exposed to a name, or a logo, or a package. Through repeated exposure, brand identity comes to represent the positioning you want your customers to think of when they see your brand. Branding is absolutely essential if you want to stand out in an ever-more-crowded marketplace.

In the age of Internet commerce, brands are becoming more and more important because they establish a recognizable identity and build trust between buyers and sellers.

William Dennis identified the advantage that accrues to a brand identity: "When I'm buying something over the Internet, I'm buying a pig in a poke, unless I recognize a brand name. So as long as I get something from IBM, I know who they are. I know that they're real. I know they won't rip me off. When I see Joe Schmoe's place, I don't know if that place even exists. How do I return something?" A recognizable brand name conveys credibility.

Building a brand and a position is relatively simple if you're doing business in a centralized geographic area, easily reached by mass media advertising. Building a brand is much more difficult if your market is geographically dispersed, or you dream of conquering the national scene. You can take the hard road, and build your own brand name and credibility, or you can take a shortcut and buy an existing franchise. Part of what a franchise gets you is a leg up on that long process of gaining a position in public awareness.

A main purpose of advertising is to build brand identity. Dot-com companies advertise in the traditional media to publicize their brands; traditional companies advertise on the Internet to reach consumers where they work and play. To participate in this high-stakes competition for consumer awareness, everything you do must reinforce your brand and the positioning behind it.

Worksheet 5.9 in appendix D will help you draft a simple positioning statement, which you can use to guide your other promotional efforts.

Message distribution. If the promotions P is about communicating the availability and desirability of your offering, how do you do that? You may rely on yourself and your staff in personal selling situations. You may also find yourself turning to mass media, including broadcast, print, and Internet vehicles, to distribute your message beyond the ground you and your staff can cover in person. When planning your message distribution strategy, think about what goes on as an individual is converted from an ordinary "Joe" to a buyer of your product. Figure 5.3 illustrates the process of conversion that takes place.

FIGURE 5.3 The Sales Conversion Process

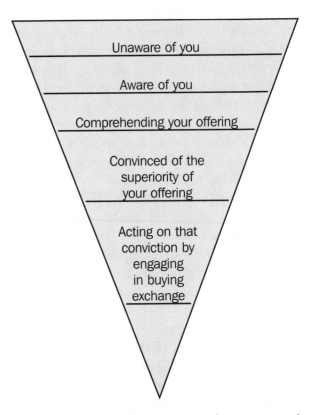

Some promotional activities are better at moving a person from unaware of you to aware of you; other activities are more successful at convincing that person to want your offering, then act on that desire. Broadcast advertising, trade shows, and conventions are good at creating awareness. Print advertising and direct mail are good at building comprehension. Personal contact is excellent in the final stages of convincing and closing the sale. When you plan the distribution of your marketing message, keep this "funnel" in mind. Don't assume one sales postcard will take that "Joe" from top to bottom in one move.

More than a few of the plans included in this book give promotions "a lick and a promise." As a plan reviewer, when I see a phrase like "promotion will be accomplished by word of mouth" I question the depth of marketing knowledge on the part of the plan's writers—and I worry about their ability to hit their sales projections.

Of the plans included in this book, only a few give much detail about promotional plans. The Artful Fly plans to market its framed flies through selective magazine advertising, and the plan explains what magazines, why, and when.

Resume.com faces the challenge of marketing itself not just to employers but also to job seekers. This plan does an adequate job of laying out promotional goals and showing how goals will be met, as does the plan for Blue Sky Travel.

The marketing plan section of the BizCopy plan includes this enlightening statement: "Although BizCopy is currently advertising on television, . . . BizCopy has established that the use of television and radio are not efficient means of advertising. Rather, the most effective method of advertising is through continued direct sales efforts—both personal sales attention, and direct mailing to current and potential customers." I find this description more confidence inspiring than a generic "will rely on word of mouth" statement.

Your Marketing Plan

People who start businesses tend to be really gifted either in marketing or in finance. Few have equal talents in both areas. (Surprisingly, strength in the other "leg of the stool," personnel, is even rarer among entrepreneurs. I have come to think this is because people who are naturally good at managing people find themselves happily fulfilled working in larger corporations.) Where are the talented marketers when it's time to write the business plan?

Given the complexity of the marketing function, and its importance to the success of a business, I'm surprised how few business plans contain a thorough marketing plan. Short-change this section, and you run the risk of raising questions in the minds of your plan's reviewers. What's the use of

---

KEY CONCEPT: THE OUTLINE FOR YOUR MARKETING PLAN

Your plan should include each of these three major headings. Depending on the emphasis of the plan, you may or may not touch on the subheadings.

- Market description
  - Industry description
  - Customer description
  - Competitive description
- Products/services offering description
  - Product
  - Price
  - Place
  - Promotion
- Marketing plan
  - Goal statement
  - Strategy statement

---

making detailed financial projections if you have no idea how you will induce the buying exchanges on which you'll build that future?

Mind you, I'm not saying a business plan must include a marketing plan complete with objectives, goals, tactics, and implementation activities. I am suggesting that you do the work necessary to create such a functional marketing plan, then summarize that plan in the business plan document.

I know that sounds like a lot of work. But look at it this way: The more competitive your environment, the more important marketing is to your survival. Work on that marketing plan as if your life depended on it.

If you don't know, find out. All the components of marketing—analysis of the external environment, design of your internal response to that environment—depend on your knowing what's going on around you. That knowledge is the result of research.

Ask among the businesspeople you're acquainted with. Who has used market research, and how? Research can guide many decisions, helping you hit the ground running, or get where you want to go faster. It can help you answer questions like:

- Should my ads feature price, quality, reputation, or what?
- Where are my competitors' weaknesses?
- Who are my most likely customers, and why do they buy?
- Which geographic areas are growing in importance, and which are dwindling?

Research helps us understand buyer behavior, competitive moves, and industry trends.

Research can be conducted by consulting primary or secondary sources. We suggest you begin with secondary research—information that has already been collected by someone else. Secondary information may be lurking in your own business records—in production, financial, or sales figures, for example. External sources of secondary research can be found in computer databases, periodicals, government documents such as census reports, and in specialized sources like trade publications and associations.

If secondary research does not yield the information you need, then move on to primary research—information you gather yourself. Primary research can be qualitative (open-ended research such as a focus group) or quantitative (questions asked in numerically measurable terms).

Knowing what question you are trying to answer is, of course, the critical starting place for any research project. With that in mind, you can choose your research technique, develop your research project, collect and analyze the data it generates, and likely derive real knowledge from the result.

BizCopy did primary research by conducting surveys in the course of its planning process. "The quick-print industry is highly saturated with cutthroat competitors," this plan states, and for that reason accurate and timely information is essential. One survey involved asking competitors to quote prices for hypothetical jobs, allowing BizCopy to double-check its pricing decisions. Another survey involved phone calls to print buyers in the community, determining whether or not they were currently using BizCopy, then asking detailed information about their buying behavior. This phone survey produced information that helped BizCopy to better understand their niche in their community. Through these research vehicles, BizCopy was able to tailor their pricing, products, and service enhancements. The text of the customer phone survey should be included in the business plan document. This statement from their plan demonstrates the type of management insight direct research can produce: "The key to increasing the quick-print trade area is to offer a quality sales staff who can convince outlying customers that location is not as important as quality and price when choosing a quick-printer."

Market research is a broad subject, but further discussion is beyond the scope of this book. I'd highly recommend you set yourself a personal goal to study research techniques in greater depth. Here's why.

In a small town in a time long ago, a hardware store owner conducted a simple research project. He gave everyone who came in his store a handful of peanuts. Then, at the end of the day, he studied where the piles of peanut shells fell. This "data" told him how customers moved through his aisles, where they paused, and for how long. He was able to make sophisticated retailing decisions based on that simple technique.

Today, your Web site is that store. Each user leaves a trail of data, just like those peanut shells. This information opens a window on your customer relationships, internal processes, vendor accounts—whatever functions your site is used for. Learn how to look through that window. Developing and using information from research data—often called "data mining"—is gaining in importance every day. It presents one of the best sources for innovative thinking in your enterprise. Use it to your profit.

Anticipate growth

Some businesses create themselves with the intention of reaching a certain level and then cruising steadily at that altitude. But those are the exceptions. Most businesses are created with the intention of following a continual path of growth. If your business is designed to grow, make sure the marketing section of your plan conveys a sense of how this growth will be supported.

Franchising is a means for growth. If you've been able to build good brand awareness for your company, and a replicable way of operating, you may decide to position your company for an eventual franchise offer. The concept for Whole Fish & Seafood is built entirely around the idea of growth through selling franchises.

Strategic alliances. These "partnerships without the marriage" are increasingly important for new and small businesses. An alliance allows businesses to leverage their assets by aligning with partners who bring strength in areas where they lack depth. If a strategic alliance is part of your thinking, you may mention it in the marketing section of your plan. Focus your discussion on how the alliance adds value to your customers or provides an edge over your competitors.

When you're considering strategic alliances, what do you need to look out for? For one thing, make sure that there's truly an advantage to be gained. "What is the value added?" should be the first question of the proposed alliance. If you can't describe the advantage clearly, I'd advise you not to proceed

Don Kuratko cautioned: "Don't give away the store. Make sure when you get into the contractual arrangements of the alliance, that you understand what is being said. We would strongly recommend some legal advice. You've got to be careful you're not getting trapped into something you would regret later on."

Dale Meyer added this warning: "Be very clear about your own goals. If you're technology based, and all you're looking for is a cash infusion, ask for a shorter-term alliance. Structure it the right way legally. Both sides have to be very careful, talking about what the benefits are to each. That's the beginning of building trust. Distrust, from one side or both, will make an alliance into a terrible relationship."

By proceeding with caution, some businesses find breakthroughs via strategic alliances. Consider the pairing of Barnes & Noble with Starbucks coffee shops—a natural fit of products, and a combination that adds value to both offerings.

Strategic alliances figure in several of our example business plans. The Artful Fly plans to leverage relationships with recognized flytieing authorities to give

> **KEY CONCEPT:**
> **STRATEGIC PARTNERS**
> **MUST ADD VALUE**
>
> Before you consider a strategic alliance, ask what value is added by each partner. Be very clear about your own goals, and seek to understand those of potential partners. Make sure that there is truly an advantage to be gained by the alliance.

their products added value. Whole Fish & Seafood must have alliances with seafood purveyors to maintain their product quality.

O'Toole's Machining is in the exciting but challenging position of relying on a key customer as a strategic ally in growth. O'Toole's Machining has been approached by a major agricultural equipment manufacturer to be a primary machined component vendor. This offer creates a platform for O'Toole's Machining to expand significantly—definitely value added for both partners—but opens O'Toole's Machining to the risk of relying too heavily on one source of sales. This plan addresses this risk and others in a straightforward manner.

Marketing Recommendations

Several of my colleagues expressed strong feelings about the importance of the marketing function.

Dale Meyer felt:

Most new businesses are started by people who have had some significant experience and immersion in the area they're marketing and selling to. These people come with an understanding of the subtleties of an area. It may be software, or health care, or telecommunications. They know where the market is not being served. Where value can be added. Their success comes from having the ability to act and react relatively quickly due to a good knowledge basis.

Rodney Heller of Foodusa.com offers a great example:

We're in the business-to-business space, on the Internet, in the food industry. In this space, you do not need to have a technology background; in fact, it works against you. What you do need to have is what we call "domaine expertise."

I have to know the food industry. I was able to take my background as a food broker, and combine it with technology, to come up with a more efficient solution for the sales and distribution of meat products.

Not surprisingly, futurist David Zach voiced his concern about the future. He worries about marketing's power to create or destroy trust:

Lots of times people put an emphasis on marketing before they put an emphasis on quality of production. If you look at young people today, "trust no one" is one of their foundational understandings of the world. Because everything has become marketing, and there's a lot of lack of content behind much of it, it's just the ability to spin a wonderful story. There seems to be no requirement that there be substance behind the spin.

Marketing has to be honest. If it is based on the desire for personal gain as opposed to production of value, you are asking for trouble—asking for, at some level, failure.

The marketing section of your business plan has three purposes. First, it gives your reader an orientation to your marketplace, by examining the industry, the customers, and the competitors found there. Second, it gives you an opportunity to explain to the reader how you intend to shape your product or service offering to fill a need in that mar-

ketplace. This is where your competitive edge shines. And finally, the plan records your commitments to strategic marketing objectives and tactics for achieving them.

Few plans, in my opinion, are as strong in marketing as they should be to support the ambitious plans of the entrepreneurs. Increasingly, as we move toward a knowledge economy where the majority of "products" are services, marketing is becoming one of the most important aspects of your business.

KEY CONCEPT: KEYS TO MARKETING SUCCESS

Examine your marketing plan for these keys to marketing success:

- Good product or service
- Meet a perceived need
- Enough potential buyers
- Advantageous timing
- Brand awareness
- Differentiation
- Salable at a profit
- Persuasive communications

Thoughts to Take Away

- The market analysis section of your plan describes "what's going on at the party when you get there." These are the factors in your environment that are beyond your control. This section should include a discussion of your industry, your customers, and your competitors.

- The product/service offering description section of your plan describes "what you bring to the party." These are the internal factors of your business that you control, typically called the marketing mix or the "four Ps." This section should include descriptions of your product, place, price, and promotion issues.

- The marketing plan section of your business plan (which may include the previous two sections, or may be a separate section following the market analysis and product/service offering description) gains its strength from two key factors: the research you have done to ground the plan in reality, and a persuasive discussion of how you plan to achieve your projected growth. Consider forming strategic alliances that add value so as to augment your ability to grow.

chapterSIX

Personnel

WHAT YOU WILL FIND IN THIS CHAPTER

- The necessary functions of management
- The issues that arise when you become an employer
- The three roles of family-involved business relationships
- How a strong personnel plan contributes to the success of your business

The personnel section of a business plan shows how the work of the business will be accomplished in each functional area. Though the personnel section of a business plan is relatively easy to write, sadly, too often this section gets neglected. It's very important to prove not just that you have a viable business idea, but that you're the right person to be in this business.

An electrical contracting firm wanted to transfer ownership to a group of its employees. These were very bright technical people with almost no business background. The plan this group produced contained a succinct management plan that described how daily functional decisions would be handled, and describes bi-weekly members' meetings to discuss larger issues and major business decisions. This section states that the incumbents in the firm's managerial positions will continue in their jobs. The intact work force was in my opinion as a reviewer, essential to the viability of this plan.

I would suggest that, given the importance of building confidence in these tradespeople-entrepreneurs, including more background on them would be a good idea to show where they have strengths, and where weaknesses should be addressed. Experience in management and leadership can be gained outside the job. If these individuals have chaired local fundraising efforts, or held officer's roles in service clubs, or been active in other organizations, I as a reviewer would find that information welcome. I want to believe they can run the company, but on what basis will I be convinced to extend my trust?

What's Your Job? Management

The owner, the general manager, the president, the creative director . . . whatever you call your position, you as the leader of your business are responsible for leading the dance. The classic business school definition of management lists "planning, organizing, directing, and controlling" as the functions of management. These are the steps of the dance.

These management functions take place regardless of the size of a business. These functions do not magically create themselves when a business reaches a staff of five, or a million dollars in sales, or any other milestone. Each of these functions exists even in a one-person consulting business.

Some functions of management include:

- New product and service development
- Operational oversight, specifying job processes and workflows
- Sales—prospecting, presenting, closing
- Marketing—identifying likely buyers, analyzing them for potential target niches, directing promotional efforts to reach them
- Finances—bookkeeping, administering vendor contracts, monitoring cash flow and budgets

- Human resources—hiring, training, disciplining, and motivating
- Management—planning, organizing, directing, and maintaining control

For the business planning process, and the written plan that results from it, consider who comprises the management team. In a start-up business, or an intentionally "micro" business, that "team" may consist of only one or two people. Regardless of the size of a business, what are the managers' qualifications for the traditional functions of management?

The description of your management team should identify who has an ownership role in the business, and explain how owners are compensated. Do you have a board of directors? Who is on the board? What expertise do they bring?

Who are your advisors and consultants? To whom will you turn for advice? By describing these relationships, you address any shortcomings in qualifications of key personnel.

Worksheet 6.1 in appendix D is an internal assessment of capabilities. The object of this worksheet is to cause you to think specifically about certain skill sets, and whether your company has adequate resources where those skills are concerned. Honestly rate the abilities of your management team.

Bear in mind that not everything is "very important" in every business. As you fill in this worksheet, indicate the importance of this function to *your* organization's overall health.

A manager of a restaurant filling this out might respond, "We have had a lot of turnover, so employee morale is really low." In that business, there would be significant "bang for the buck" if morale improved. This manager would rate these areas poor in performance, and high in importance.

On the other hand, a company marketing children's sleeping bags might respond "for us technical competence is poor, but unimportant. We buy the manufacturing from outside stitchers. If it's off by half an inch, it doesn't matter." The product manager's knowledge of the actual sewing operation is relatively unimportant. Equipment isn't important to her either. On the other hand, supplier relationships and distribution systems are quite important.

For any area in which poor performance is paired with high importance, you had better be doing something. Your business plan should reflect how you're going to address that weakness.

The management portion of the personnel section of a business plan answers the questions: What are all the things that are going to go on in your company, and how are they going to be managed? If the management team lacks depth in some of these areas, how will that weakness be addressed? Who are the players with stakes in the game? Who will be coaching from the sidelines?

What kind of manager are you?

It's one of the cruelest ironies of entrepreneurship: The skills and traits that make us good at *starting* companies tend to get in the way when it is time to *run* them. When our business grows to where we need to delegate, it can be extraordinarily difficult for the entrepreneur to let go.

Managing a successful, growing enterprise means operating with and through people. Old "I'm the boss, do it my way" attitudes have proved ineffective in today's economy. More and more, managers focus on cooperation, team building, and delegation of responsibility and authority to the lowest possible level in the organization. These managers find themselves spending more time on other activities, such as trend spotting, planning, and implementing improvements.

Women tend to find this new leadership style more comfortable than men do. Joline Godfrey, CEO of Independent Means, states:

I'm always a little uneasy about making generalizations, . . . but women's comfort with lack of hierarchy means we are not re-training ourselves how to operate in this new economy. Women, particularly women who are in their 30s and older, actually come to the workplace with an outlook and perspective and set of values that may be particularly well suited to our times.

Figure 6.1 summarizes some characteristics of old and new management styles.

FIGURE 6.1 Managerial Style: Old vs. New

Old-Style Managers	New Managers
• Think of themselves as boss	• Think of themselves as sponsors, team leaders, internal consultants
• Follow a chain of command	
• Work within a set managerial structure	• Deal with anyone necessary to get the job done
• Make most decisions alone	• Change in response to market changes
• Hoard information	• Invite others to join in decision-making
• Demand long hours	• Share information
	• Demand results

Source: "The New Non-Manager Managers," *Fortune*, 12 February 1993, 80–84.

If you show signs of being an old-style manager—and as an entrepreneur, it's likely you have at least some affinity for these old-style management traits—how will you make the transition to a new style of management as your business grows? Self-development is just one more of the many responsibilities you have signed on for, along with a business loan, a lease, and the many other tangible and intangible "contracts" entrepreneurship implies.

Observations on the manager's role

"It's so difficult balancing all the things I have to be knowledgeable about. How can I do it all?" It's a complaint I hear from many, many, business owners. You need to understand money, and technology, and your industry. You have to bring incredible stamina to the task, matched with a willingness to make sacrifices. It's tough not to become too identified with the "baby" that takes so much of your time, and so much of your heart, in its birth and early development.

I asked some of my colleagues how entrepreneurs can prepare themselves to be great managers.

Technological know-how. More than a few of my colleagues observed that today, we're all in the technology business, in addition to whatever business niche we fill. Almost every business, small or large, relies on computer-based operational and adminis-

> **KEY CONCEPT:**
> **THE OUTLINE FOR YOUR**
> **PERSONNEL PLAN**
>
> Your plan should include each of these three major headings. Depending on the emphasis of the plan, you may or may not touch on these subheadings:
>
> - Management team
>   - Background of key personnel
>   - Outside consultants and advisors
>   - Duties and responsibilities
> - Staff team
>   - Staff needs
>   - Job descriptions
>   - Organizational chart
>   - Compensation
> - Plans for growth
>   - Operational expansion
>   - Recruiting plans
>   - Succession plan

trative systems, hardware, networks, and more. William Dennis felt that technological expertise is one of the first areas in which delegation pays off:

We are finding out that people who have a separate technology expert in their business do better than when the owner is the person who is most knowledgeable on computer technology. That's not a problem when you have 20 employees, because by that time you can afford to put someone on technology. But when you have six employees, that's different. You can't afford a specialist. What happens when something goes down? You call tech support. If you've got six people and you're the most knowledgeable of them, where's tech support?

Outsourced support relationships can be an important transitional step for small-but-growing businesses.

Know your industry coming in—then stay on top of it. If technology is the first thing to delegate, industry expertise should be the last. Frank Hoy summed up the sentiments of many:

One of the most common mistakes I see is people who have the wrong experience for the business they want to start. I can't tell you how many people have come to me with the desire to start a restaurant, who have no restaurant experience. They come in with no understanding of the cost controls involved in restaurant management, no understanding of the fact that the restaurant industry has the highest failure rate of any industry in the United States, no recognition of what competition they will face, or how to draw people into the business, or how to maintain quality.

Hoy went on to emphasize the need to monitor industry trends and prepare for changes:

There are people who think that the world is going to stay the same forever. They don't adjust to the category killers, and the impact of the Internet, and so on. . . . If you simply read the daily paper, and maybe the Wall Street Journal *or* Business Week, *or watch* CNN *and* Wall Street Week *and other programs, you don't have to be terribly sophisticated to see new trends, particularly if they're happening in your industry, your own community. Sit down and think through for yourself, "Okay. How is this going to impact my business? Maybe I'd better change."*

Bob Brockhaus echoed Hoy's opinion: "Are you really watching where your industry is headed? Trying to get right up near the front of that wave, and not so far behind? Oftentimes if you're not there early, you're not going to be successful. You're just another me-too."

Stamina and sacrifices. Managers are the monks of a new priesthood—a cult of business that is starting to demand "24/7" attention. "A lot of people just aren't willing to work hard enough," Hoy stated. Bob Brockhaus agreed, and added that family sacrifices are part of that picture. Successful managers, he says, have:

... the willingness to make personal sacrifices, and a family that's willing to allow you to make the sacrifices, in terms of time and focus on the business, as opposed to the other things in life. Your kids might not have the nicest clothes or participate in the activities that are more expensive, or that require more parental time for them to be part of. Those are all real sacrifices. A lot of times, those sacrifices have to be made in the early years of a business.

At the end of this chapter we'll pick up the discussion of families and business—an important component of the personnel picture.

I agree with my colleagues' assessment of the difficult roles entrepreneurs must juggle. But there's an additional point that must be made. People are separate from their businesses.

Separation anxiety. We are in a sense the small businesses we run—but only up to a point. It's really important, given the failure rate of small businesses, that we maintain a sense of our own identity separate from our businesses. It can be very unhealthy for you *and* your business if you become so identified with it that its success or failure is your personal success or failure. You must be able to recognize, when grim times come, that "I didn't fail, I had a business that failed."

Insufficient separation can be just as hard on the business that succeeds. Running a business without sufficient separation between principals and the business entity makes it impossible to transfer the business to new managers or owners later on.

My friend Greg Peters presents an example. He started Greg Peters Coffee, and when he first started his business, he was always in the store. Everybody who came in was on a first-name basis with Greg. When he grew to a half dozen outlets, his charismatic leadership was one of the fundamental reasons for that success. But as his business grew, he spent more time in his corporate office and wasn't so visible in the stores anymore. People stopped identifying with Greg personally.

When he first chose to call his business Greg Peters Coffee, he chose to lend his personality to that business. Customers, in a way, demanded that he remain as the personality of the business even though his role as its manager had changed significantly.

How you structure your business, and the role that you as the owner play in the business, become very important. You have a choice to be a visible figurehead of your business, or not, and there are pluses and minuses to that choice. A plus, for Greg Peters Coffee, was that his name made people feel a personal relationship with his place, in contrast to a big national chain. They saw, "here's Greg's store, and here's Greg in it." But the minus for Greg was that it grew beyond what he alone could handle. Greg now must decide whether to delegate other managerial duties, so he can remain a "roving ambassador," or to attempt to reposition his business in a way that depends less on his personality.

In almost any town, you can find local examples of businesses so closely identified with their founders that the value of the business would be lost without them. The car dealership, or the appliance store, usually bear names familiar in that community. Did those business owners set out to become so identified with their businesses?

Duties and responsibilities: Who does what, why, and for how much?

For the business plan document, you will need to prepare a description of managerial duties and responsibilities. I suggest you describe your own role in the business first, then proceed to describe your other key managers, their duties and responsibilities, and who reports to whom. This discussion should make clear who has authority to make what decisions. Issues critical to market success, such as quality control and assurance of customer satisfaction, should be listed as responsibilities assigned to yourself or another key manager.

This section of the business plan should give your reviewers a clear sense of who does what, who is responsible for what, who supervises whom, and how each key manager is compensated.

Compensation may be in the form of a salary, or in the form of stock options, a win–win situation for some ambitious employees and employers. Rodney Heller of Foodusa.com shared his experience. "My early hires all took pay cuts to work for me. One guy was making $120,000 a year, and I said 'I'll give you $80,000. But here's your options.' He said 'I'll take it' because he loved my story. Another officer was making $300,000 a year. He's making a dollar a month with me. He's got good options. He'll be a very, very wealthy individual." The strength of Heller's business plan convinced talented managers to join his firm. The strength their backgrounds contributed to his business plan is fueling further interest among venture capitalists.

> ### KEY CONCEPT
>
> Of the sample plans included in this book, no individual plan has everything we recommend in its personnel section. For several of the businesses described in these plans, personnel issues are critical, and yet their personnel sections fall short of the forceful presentation that would convince a reviewer that critical needs have been understood and addressed.

Setting of salaries is part of the management function. Of course, if you're a sole proprietor or a partner in a business you don't get a salary—you are entitled to shares in the profits. If you issue yourself a "paycheck," you are really receiving a "draw against earnings." If there are no earnings—guess what? No "paycheck."

As you work out the details of owners' draws and salaries and benefits for key employees, you will make assumptions that affect your financial projections. Your decisions here will show up as line items in your pro forma profit and loss statement. Meeting your forecasted payroll will be a key concern in monthly cash flow budgets. Salaries represent the "intersection" where personnel planning meets financial planning. If you are writing the personnel section early on in your process, as I suggest, you will probably need to revisit the salary statement in this section after you work on your financial projections.

Resources available to your business. Who are the people who could help your business become more profitable? An advisory team can be very helpful if you are an inexperienced manager. I recommend advisory boards—in fact, I recommend having more than one advisory team, for reasons I will discuss in chapter 8. Advisors are good under one condition: that you are willing to accept their advice. If you don't accept their advice, your board will say, "Why are we here?" and they will leave. They can't be window dressing. They need to have a function.

Worksheet 6.2 is a management planning tool to guide you in drafting the duties and responsibilities section of your business plan.

The goal: credibility

In your business plan, you need to showcase your strengths, and address your weaknesses. Worksheet 6.3 in appendix D covers what a reviewer of your plan is likely to want to know about you. What have you done with your life that has a bearing on your managerial abilities? A reviewer has deep interest in who you are and what you bring to the table. You must convince that reader of your ability to handle the managerial and technical aspects of this business. The same goes for each key partner or employee.

Are you physically up to the job? This is particularly important to me. My father had a heart condition and was in and out of hospitals for 11 years before the fifth heart attack killed him. He couldn't take care of his customers from that hospital bed. Show your plan's readers that you have the physical stamina for the work required.

Question 7 in Worksheet 6.3 is important to the plan for two reasons. You're going to be running your business by this plan, so you'd better understand what your personal financial status is. Further, if you're going to be seeking equity or debt investors or key employees, each will want to know how much of "you" stands behind the business. This section of the plan should indicate your financial strengths as an individual. Remember, it's important to differentiate between you the person and you the business.

The management portion of the personnel section shows that you understand the functions of management, that you've planned for them in your business, and that you have the wherewithal to manage this business.

The business plan for Blue Sky Travel presents a simple statement of management and ownership. In three paragraphs, owners Cecilia Cielo and Nadine Nuvole describe their ownership participation, and confront head-on the principals' lack of direct experience in the travel agency industry. "The need for an experienced travel agency business manager is quite apparent," the plan states. The plan sets an objective of hiring a full-time business manager by the third year of operation. As a reviewer, I find myself asking "by the *third* year? How do you expect to get to the third year without that expertise?" but I do appreciate their forthright approach to the question.

What's Their Job? The Staff Team

A business plan should contain information regarding your staffing needs, now and in the future. This may take the form of an organizational chart, a human resources plan, or simply a narrative within the personnel section of the plan. It is appropriate to discuss what positions need to be created and filled, and what your policies will be regarding hiring, salaries, and benefits. Typically, the plan details the individuals and job functions in key areas, without sinking to descriptions of every cook and bottle-washer on board. The point is to show that you have assessed and planned for the personnel necessary to a successful operation.

Worksheet 6.4 in appendix D covers what you in your planning process should consider, and what a reviewer will want to find documented in your plan regarding employee hiring needs.

Hire the right people at the right time. The availability of appropriate labor is very important to any labor-intensive business. What are your recruiting plans? How are you going to get these people, making the assumption there are people available? How many are you going to need? How are you going to train them? What will their job duties be?

It's not uncommon for small businesses to use a mix of staff and outside suppliers to accommodate the peaks and valleys of the workload. Freelancers or independent contractors, if available, help you manage periods of high demand without permanently swelling your staff. Some new entrepreneurs fail to anticipate how difficult it is to let go of individual employees when the need for them is reduced. We make a serious commitment to one another when

Voices

A lot of people get into franchising because they think they can buy their way to success, and they won't have to invest a lot of time. Successful franchisees, if they've started a successful business before on their own, will tell you running a franchise takes at least as many hours. It takes years before they get to a position where they're making good money off the business.

—Frank Hoy

we enter into employer–employee relationships. We trust and expect that person will be loyal and productive, working with our best interests at heart—and he or she expects the same. Saying to a good employee, "I'm afraid we no longer need you" is one of the hardest tasks you'll face. To avoid it, too many managers delay action, sometimes at a considerable cost to the organization.

It's critical that you understand whether you can *afford* help, before you begin recruiting help. How much will salaries, benefits, and other costs of employment raise your break-even point? Will more help mean more productivity, matched by profitability? Not necessarily. Your financial projections have considerable impact on allocation of resources to salaries and other costs related to adding jobs.

Job descriptions

When you do hire people to work for you, you want to get value for every penny you pay them. To make their endeavors productive, they need direction. The clearer their understanding of what they were hired to do, what they are responsible for, and how they are expected to perform, the more benefit you will derive from their presence. Therefore, even in very small businesses, I recommend that you create written job descriptions.

A job description is a list of all the tasks, duties, and responsibilities involved in a specific job. It may specify "nuts and bolts" like hours of work, supervisory relationships, and when salary and performance will be reviewed. It may include specifications of the knowledge, skills, and abilities that a candidate for this job should possess.

A job description can also describe training goals for a position. I find many businesses spend a great deal of time on the hiring processes, and then spend little or no time on training once someone is hired. That's sad because employees want to do well, but often don't know what that means. The job description is the first step. It tells the individual what is expected. Too often, as employers, we wait till we "really" need someone before we hire. Then we are "too busy" to take the time to train him or her. A job description describes the significant contribution each employee makes in the operation. It can

KEY CONCEPT

When you're doing that strategic thinking of "where do I want the business to be," you have to include your ongoing role in the business in your thinking. Will you be a visible leader, or will you do your work behind the scenes?

help both employer and employee see where training would increase productivity, or enable individuals to take on more responsibilities.

A good business plan will include job descriptions of key employees, both in operational and managerial positions. This is just another way you show the plan's reviewers that you have planned for staff needs and have a thorough understanding of how the "work" of your business will be accomplished.

There is a considerable amount of governmental and legal regulation that affects you when you become an employer. Your plan should show you are aware of these issues.

The business plan for BizCopy contains a reasonably well-prepared personnel section. In the section on "Organizational Matters," the business structure, management, and personnel of BizCopy are briefly described. Consultants to BizCopy, including advisors for accounting, legal, banking insurance, and marketing functions. In addition, participants on the advisory board and map group are listed.

Growing the Team

Your business plan lays out how you will manage growth in your human resources. Don't underestimate the challenge that growth represents.

So many of the businesspeople I talk to complain about how difficult it is to work with people. Handling people isn't easy. We're all different. It's wonderful to say that you have a vision for your business, and all of your employees are going to share that vision. But employees come with different thoughts and different desires.

You as a business owner get so caught up in your business. You have a passion. You will work 14 hours a day, seven days a week, if that's what it takes. Don Kuratko hit the nail on the head:

We get kind of a funny look when our employees are punching out at 5:00. We act like they shouldn't be doing that. We tend to forget that they came for a paycheck. While we look at them going out the door and say "slackers!" they get in their cars and say "nut case." They can't believe that we're staying the late hours.

There's always going to be a difference in thinking between entrepreneurs and employees.

Good interpersonal skills. To succeed in business, you need a talent for human resources. All other factors being equal—adequate market demand, adequate capitalization—it is the people who work for you who make the difference in your business success.

David Zach shared his insights into the interpersonal skill most critical to entrepreneurs—the ability to trust:

The ability to trust others and to encourage trust in others is present in successful entrepreneurs. Maybe there's a chicken and egg element there. You learn to trust by trusting. Still, a lot of people go into business mistrusting people. One of the great gifts of America to the world is that we, to a great extent, build the ability to trust. It is our foundational freedom, more than anything else. Our ability to trust has allowed us to connect with others. You cannot connect unless you are able to trust. But it means that we must increasingly demand honesty, not just of ourselves, but of the people around us. When we find dishonesty, we must call it.

Dale Meyer added:

Take care in who you bring in with you. Often the people who start the business are technical people, without a whole lot of business expertise. You want a team that, even though you're not all alike, you can at least appreciate and work with each other, in the heat of battle. If the people aren't somewhat compatible in very basic ways, can't become a true team, that can unravel the whole thing.

Growing beyond physical limits. When you add employees, you have to add places for them to work. At some point, the growth of your staff will tax your current facilities. In some cases, you can compensate by redesigning work environments and processes for greater productivity. Administrative functions can be automated to reduce support staff and the space they work in, for example. For some companies, allowing people to work from their homes solves the space problem. Roughly ten million corporate employees work by telecommuting, according to Terri Lonier. Many of these workers are pioneering the "hoteling" concept, which allows a blend of work from home and work in-office, without dedicating valuable workspace to people who are not often present. Instead, individuals needing to spend some time in the office "check in" to a workspace stocked with the necessary supplies, but devoid of personal attachment—just like a hotel room. Making such accommodations allows staff to expand without expanding your overhead in real estate.

Another way to avoid adding overhead is simply not to employ the people who work for you. Many businesses, instead, participate in subcontracting arrangements. Although you may pay a higher hourly fee to a subcontractor, you avoid the hidden costs of employment: real estate, a computer workstation, bonuses and benefits, administrative overhead, and payroll taxes among them. Expect this trend toward subcontractors in place of employees to grow.

David Zach reported on this phenomenon from the subcontractor's perspective:

As we become more sophisticated about what the Internet can do for us, we will not be defined by singular jobs but by a portfolio of abilities. That concept of ad-hoc organizations, where you come together, you do certain things, and then you move on—that's not for everybody, but that whole concept of free agent nation is appealing. I personally love being able to work with a lot of different organizations.

Voices

Many fledgling entrepreneurs say, "I don't need to pay attention to the personnel function because I'm not going to be big enough to need managing, and I'm not going to have employees to manage." These functions don't go away. They just descend on one person.

—Jack Reiners

Subcontracting arrangements allow you access to high-quality, self-motivated individuals, while maintaining your flexibility and keeping your fixed costs low.

One word of caution, however. It's extremely important for you to be aware of the legal issues surrounding the difference between an employee and an independent contractor. Serious mistakes can be made by not properly withholding income and social security tax for an individual you think is an independent contractor, but is actually an employee. It's not just that you and the employee/contractor agree as to the status. There are specific factors that, when weighted together, determine that status. Consult an attorney, a Small Business Development Center, or your state's Department of Revenue, to make sure you understand and are in compliance with the law.

Finding and keeping good people

Does your community have the people you need to fill the jobs you create? If not, how will you respond to this challenge?

One answer is simply to accomplish more with less—to automate tasks so that each individual can be responsible for greater output. Many clerical positions have been eliminated through automation of office activities like telephone call routing and formatting of correspondence. Today, mid-level managers simply e-mail each other, whereas in the past, they might have had secretaries typing letters and mailing them back and forth.

Another answer: Think outside the box on who's employable. Hire someone from a neglected or stigmatized group. Might you find suitable workers among these groups?

- Students
- Immigrants
- Minority communities
- Retirees
- Criminals
- Former welfare recipients
- The physically or mentally disabled

Skilled immigrants, labor analysts say, are necessary for American business to keep up with demand.

KEY CONCEPT: MANAGING THE PEAKS AND VALLEYS

Many businesses use a mix of staff and outside suppliers to accommodate the peaks and valleys of the workload. Independent contractors can help you accommodate periods of high demand without your having to commit to additional permanent staff.

Congress is considering increasing the number of U.S. work visas, allowing more immigrants to work in the United States. But David Zach points out the complexity behind such a simple suggestion:

. . . suppose we throw the doors wide open on the country. We fill that labor need with immigrants. I don't think that works ultimately in the long run. Particularly for those countries the brains are being drained out of. Then their economies don't develop. What it's doing is shifting the solution to one area and shifting the problem to another.

Each population brings with it special needs, ranging from language training to flexible hours, but also contains individuals who are highly motivated to work. By hiring them, you can be a good citizen and fill your labor needs, too.

Keeping people by keeping people happy. As a rule, most small business owners aren't in a position to pay employees what they would like to pay. It's not a question of what that employee is worth, but what the business can afford. Moreover, in smaller businesses you don't have a lot of opportunities to promote people. With little opportunity for advancement, and marginal pay, why would someone want to work for you? You have to figure out nonmonetary ways to keep people. That's really hard.

What motivates us as entrepreneurs is likely to be entirely different from what motivates our staff. We must find ways to motivate them through their personal goals. Many employees report that they want opportunities to grow on the job. The more employees see potential for growth, the more they feel they're not just working but also learning. And if they're learning, they're growing. And if they're growing, the job becomes exciting. So they stay.

You need people to stay. The cost of replacing an employee is very high. Called "opportunity costs," they include the ads in the paper and everything else related to finding applicants, the organizational time devoted to planning for and conducting interviews, evaluating and negotiating a hire, and then training the replacement. In these days of low unemployment rates, even finding perfectly qualified applicants is not a sure thing.

What can you do to get good people to stick around, without offering wages and benefits you can't afford? Offer more personal control over time, opportunities for education and training, and the possibility of future promotions. Lifelong learning for key personnel benefits everyone.

BizCopy sets a good example. In the business plan for BizCopy, the "Goals and Objectives" section includes "Employee Based Goals," in which the following statements are made:

- Provide a good work environment. Fast-paced and fun with a variety of job duties.
- Promote teamwork.
- Business growth allowing employees job rotation and promotions.
- Cross-train staff to be able to assist in overloaded areas.

It's not hard to see how such goals promote retention of good workers. BizCopy exists in a highly competitive industry niche, in which advances in technology demand fast response just to stay current. Their business plan shows that they are aware of the challenge this presents. "If BizCopy does not keep up with digital technology, or technology in general, its competitors who do will gain a competitive advantage," the plan states. The BizCopy plan reflects the imprint of owners who are committed to lifelong learning in order to keep their technology-driven business at the cutting edge.

The Team and the Family

Every business is a family business. Even if your family members are not employees or officers in the business, they are involved—because you are. If nothing else, someone in your family is going to be affected by your involvement in the business. If it's the Smith Company and their last name is Smith, they have concerns about what's going on.

If you're thinking about a family business, you need to know that you're going to play three roles, as shown in Figure 6.2. It's much more complicated to be involved in a family business because of the interplay of these three roles. Which role are you playing, when you are talking about a particular matter with a relative or coworker? Are you the family member? Are you the business owner? Are you the business manager?

FIGURE 6.2 Three Roles of Family Business

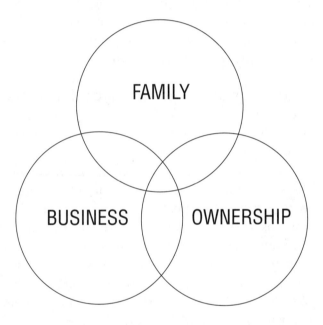

You are at all times a family member. You must keep in mind the health of your family, its prosperity, and its continuity no matter what other roles you play.

Voices

Many people have told me—never hire one person. When you hire one person, you get the problems of four or five. You might as well wait until you need several, then hire. Because the book work and government regulations are such that it's just not practical to hire one individual.

—William Dennis

When you are responsible for a business, you are never far from that role either. Where you're worrying about operations, finance, employees, suppliers, or customer relationships, you are always "on the job" looking for ways to improve your business. Somehow you must keep this role separate so that you have a family, and a business—and an individual identity of your own.

And finally, you have the issues of ownership. Who owns the business? You and your spouse? Your children, too? How about aunts, uncles, cousins? With ownership comes specific concerns—of liquidity, capital allocation, and assuring succession. Who would take over this family business if something were to happen to you? Ownership carries with it responsibility for strategic direction, financial performance, and long-term security of investments. These are very different concerns from those of the family member or the business manager.

Family business counselors talk shop. When I counsel family businesses, most of the discussions center on issues of succession, communication, and developing leadership—not about finances or marketing. The emphasis falls on interpersonal skills. If there are multiple family members in the business, it really gets involved. In larger family businesses, from day three on, the questions are, "Who will succeed me?" and "Who has authority, and when?"

Tim Baye has worked with a number of family businesses as well. He shares insights and techniques gleaned from his counseling practice:

There's an exercise I've found to be very helpful, I have the individuals write job descriptions for each other. Then, slide that job description across the table and read what each person wrote. This helps to do two things: First, it clears the air of unspoken expectations of all the people involved. Then, it starts identifying gaps that nobody wants to take responsibility for. Like accounting, or dealing with the bank.

Another exercise Baye prescribes involves writing statements of lifestyle, personal, and financial goals. Worksheet 6.5 in appendix D summarizes the questions Baye is likely to ask his counseling clients regarding their goals and expectations. "If their goals aren't in sync, that's a pretty good eye-opener for the family members. My tech-

> **KEY CONCEPT:**
> **KEEP GOOD PEOPLE HAPPY**
>
> To keep good staff members, offer benefits they want and you can afford. Offer more personal control over time, opportunities for education and training, and the possibility of future promotions.

nique is to look for the common denominators. We try to find one area of understanding first, then build on that."

Even if spouses aren't planning to go into business together, it's important to clarify each spouse's view. Often as not, there is a hidden agenda, or set of expectations, regarding the family relationship and the degree of support the family will give the business. In states where marital property law applies, there is joint ownership of all assets. Even if one spouse is not interested in being involved, he or she must at least acknowledge sharing the liabilities and assets of the business. He or she should have some understanding of what goes on in that business.

Communicate. The more information you share, and the more positive the information, the better for all concerned. If you are always going home and complaining to your family about what's going on, you are less likely to get the support you need. A positive attitude both at work and at home becomes important.

If a major development is likely to occur in the business, share it with your spouse, even if he or she is not involved in the day-to-day operations. Show that you respect your spouse as a sounding board. If for no other reason, share information because it is going to affect the family. Some business matters may cause changes in schedules or time commitments. Others may cause dips in compensation or disposable income—matters that will affect the family's expectations. More information is typically better. Don't be afraid to share it with your family.

Planning for succession

The passing of a business from one generation to the next can be helped or hindered by the founders.

Succession works best when the founders are able to professionalize the organization, moving it away from the chaotic entrepreneurial model, early on. In situations where the founder has developed an overall business strategy and plan, has identified specific titles and job descriptions, I've seen that the conflicts between family and business are more readily resolved.

Today's family businesses are breaking the stereotype of a senior son taking over his father's business. Now we're seeing the elder daughter, or younger brother or sister, or cousins, or all of them going into the business together. That second generation is becoming more of a team concept. Team building and communication skills are vital in the new family business.

Each individual participates in answering: How do we balance family and business? What information do we share? Should we go public, that is, have outsiders in the business, or just keep the business in the family?

Tim Baye related an example of a classic family business, dealing with succession issues.

It's a fairly large manufacturing firm, in which the primary bottleneck is the owner, because all decisions flow through him. He is attempting to restructure his organization so that his two sons can assume more responsibility. If they decide that they don't want to be part of the business, he has redesigned the business's organization in a manner that would allow him to recruit from the outside, and move rather quickly in filling these positions that he would have expected his sons to take. As a result of the business planning process, he's taking a step back. He's starting to evaluate new business opportunities, the competitive environment he is in, and starting to develop a much more effective marketing function in the company.

This example underscores the reality that many times it's not the business plan itself but the process of asking the questions that are contained in the plan that is more important.

Planning for the unexpected. One does have to plan, especially if you're in a family-owned business, for unexpected eventualities. I remember one of my colleagues, who taught business with me, decided that what she really wanted in life was to build a bed-and-breakfast in northern Wisconsin.

She and her husband spent two years drawing up blueprints; they drove the six hours up there and walked the land and sited the house; and they did all the wonderful planning needed for her dream to take shape. She left working with us in April and moved up there and opened the B & B in May. And in July, she was diagnosed with cancer. Three months later, she was gone.

Nowhere in their planning had they talked about or thought about what would happen if one of them wasn't there. She taught business planning, but even so, she avoided thinking about the "what-ifs." Today, her husband is left running the bed-and-breakfast without her.

Even those of us who know business planning rarely think about those eventualities. Certainly, in my own family business, I think my father, even though his fifth heart attack killed him, believed he was immortal. He didn't make plans for training my mother, or 21-year-old me.

One of our example plans proved crucial in a similar crisis. Tim Baye's client Mike O'Toole engaged in a planning effort in part to raise funding for expansion, but also to reinvent his company, and himself as a cutting-edge manager. His planning process, and the document generated as a result, were comprehensive and detailed. The expansion funding was secured. Then tragedy struck. Mike O'Toole died in an accident. As Baye related:

That plan allowed O'Toole's widow to assume a position of management in the company, and to have some degree of understanding what she was getting involved with. She had a very strong emotional need to continue the legacy of her husband, and keep the company together, as well as to provide future employment and a source of income opportunity for her son. The plan that

---

RESOURCE

People interested in family businesses should contact one of the Family Business Centers located around the United States. A great site for finding out where family businesses are, and hooking up with other family business issue links, may be found at the Family Firm Institute Web site, *www.ffi.org.*

I developed with the founder provided her a basis to come up to speed very quickly. It also helped her understand all the key issues in running the company. She's now in the process of contacting all her customers, looking for new business opportunities, as well as conducting a comprehensive industry and trend analysis, to be able to identify both service lines and new industries that her company can pursue.

None of us know what tomorrow holds. As these examples show, a good business plan can be crucial in keeping a steady hand at the helm when a business encounters rough seas.

Your Personnel Plan

The personnel section of your business plan serves two functions: one internal, one external. The external function is the simpler of the two. For outside reviewers, the purpose of the personnel section is to build faith in the business's management team. Each element that you include in the written document should serve this purpose.

The internal function is rather more demanding—and more critical to the success of your business. For internal purposes, the personnel section defines who has authority and responsibility for managerial and operational functions. It addresses when and how additional staff will be hired, what they will be hired to do, and where this might lead. This part of the process forces the planner to consider how weaknesses will be addressed. It raises the hard questions concerning growth, succession, and unforeseeable events. Writing this section of the plan requires the business principals to see themselves as individuals separate from their business, hard as that may be to accomplish.

Once the hard thinking is done, this section should be relatively easy to write. The exception may be if you are involved in a family business. In these cases, the work becomes more difficult—but even more necessary. Many times, it is not the business plan itself, but the process of asking the questions that are contained in the plan, that is more important. It's not the document, it's the process of developing the document, that's important.

Conclusions

The personnel plan shows how the "work" of a business will be accomplished. It defines what management will do, what staff is needed, and how issues of growth and succession will be handled. In family businesses (and there's a family behind almost every business), clear role definition is particularly important. Good communication is the key—and good communication is fostered by the business planning process.

The management section of the personnel plan should contain a description of managerial duties and responsibilities. The owner's role in the business, whether as visible figurehead or behind-the-scenes manager, should be clearly explained. This section builds management's credibility by demonstrating what skills and background they bring to the job and how they will go about addressing weaknesses. A reader should get a clear message that "these people have what it takes to manage this business."

In the staff team section of the personnel plan, the plan should show a thorough understanding of the operation's processes and human resource needs. The plan should reflect awareness of an employer's responsibilities with regard to governmental and legal regulations.

As a plan reviewer, I want the personnel section to show me that no important function is left uncovered. I want to see assurances that quality control and customer service have been planned for. I want to see a clear delineation of authority and responsibility where each of the "three legs" of business are concerned: marketing, personnel, and finances. But most of all, I want to feel that I have met the management team—and that they have inspired my confidence.

Thoughts to Take Away

- You must successfully make the transition from entrepreneur to manager as your business grows. Self-development is one more of the many responsibilities you have signed on for as a business owner, as well as responsibility for planning, organizing, directing, and controlling—the necessary functions of management.

- Issues arising when you become an employer include finding and keeping good people, creating job descriptions for them, developing your own supervisory skills, and choosing when to use independent contractors or hire more staff as you grow.

- Families engaged in business find that they play three roles: family member, business manager, business owner. Each role carries with it responsibilities, and demands clear communication about the complex issues involved.

- The personnel section of your business plan serves two functions: one internal, one external. The external purpose is to build faith in the business's management team. The internal purpose is to define who has authority and responsibility for managerial and operational functions, to define how and why additional staff will be hired, and to answer hard questions concerning growth, succession, and unforeseeable events.

chapterSEVEN

Financials

WHAT YOU WILL FIND IN THIS CHAPTER

- The key financial statements, and how to create them
- How to project cash flow to better manage your operation

- How budgets help you monitor performance and manage exceptions
- What the financial section of your plan is really saying to your reviewers

My colleague Tim Baye likes to say, "The key to understanding financial statements is understanding marketing." That may surprise you a bit. But as he explains, financial statements and projections are like report cards. They report on how well you've chosen a market in which you can compete, how well you put together the right set of resources to pursue that opportunity, and how well you're doing at implementing your plan.

Preparing the financial projections for your business plan is a two-part process. First comes the strategic work of researching the financial needs and activities of the business. We analyze the past history of our business, and others like it, to give us a solid basis on which to make assumptions about the future. "Past performance is the best indication of future performance," I've heard many a banker say. With our assumptions as well researched as we can make them, we proceed to the number-crunching work of making projections. With spreadsheet software, it is not difficult to generate the columns and rows of numbers that represent the future financial activity of your business.

How can I make you comfortable with the business of numbers when your passion lies in the more creative aspects of business? Perhaps by emphasizing how the "numbers business" is interwoven with the other aspects you love. And by reminding you that, when it's your future at stake, financial analysis becomes "the greatest story problem ever told."

Marketing plan affects financial projections. Your marketing plan is the essential tool in making projections of sales. Following research, the marketing plan reports on the sales potential in your marketplace, and explains how sales will be accomplished. Only when a marketing plan has been developed can sales resulting from marketing be projected, and budgets drafted.

Tim Baye described how he guides his clients in gathering information about the marketplace so that they can make informed projections of future market potential. The first step he recommends is to talk directly with potential customers:

It's a relatively simple process of making a phone call, sending a letter, saying "I'm J. Smith, I want to establish the XYZ Company. I've identified you as a prospective client. I'm in my feasibility phase and I'm trying to identify what is the best way to serve people like you. If I could have the opportunity, I'd like to call you next week and see if you'd be willing to discuss your purchases in my general area of interest." Ask them about their historic sales. Ask them about the vendors they currently

KEY CONCEPT

Financial *projections* represent goals and expectations. Financial *statements* record how well you did at meeting those goals and expectations.

use. Ask about the strength of those vendors; ask what they wish those vendors did differently or better. Then conclude by saying: "If you were to consider me, and my business, what criteria would I have to meet?"

Baye instructs his clients to interview as many as four times the number of customers they think they could reasonably serve within a year's time frame:

By repeating that process, you gain some strong information. You identify what are the buying trends, by size and type of organization. By compiling this information, and then comparing it with some secondary data for those firms you weren't able to contact directly, you can come up with a pretty good estimate of market potential. You can also develop a fairly good estimate of existing market share, by your competitors.

These insights help you identify trends or expectations within the market. "Then you can go back to your associations, your publications, within the industry, and say—am I unique here? Is what I'm hearing right? Is this a trend that I should be paying attention to?"

The next step Baye suggests is to assign projected sales figures for each specific market opportunity. If you are planning for several lines of products or services, you will want to project sales figures for each category on your "laundry list."

Seasonality. An estimate of next year's sales is a useful reference point, but when and how will those sales be realized? Projections by quarters or months are more useful, if you are to manage the cash flow of your business. What seasonal factors affect your sales? In construction, the bulk of sales will naturally take place during good weather. In retailing, the bulk of sales will be heavily loaded into the fourth quarter. Your understanding of the nuances of your industry will tell you what you can expect in terms of seasonal effects on revenue.

With a seasonally adjusted forecast of sales, you are ready to begin making financial projections and setting the budgets by which you will manage your business.

Your projected sales may not be equal to the capital needs of your business—in fact, with a start-up business, I'd have sincere doubts about your plan if

---

KEY CONCEPTS

Seasonal factors may create some months in which you are cash-poor, even though your business is performing well overall. Projections by month or by quarter are more useful than yearly projections, when it comes to understanding your cash flow.

■ ■ ■

You need solid financial projections because you do not know what the future will bring. Projections provide the budgets that help you manage the unexpected.

■ ■ ■

Accounting is the art of recording, classifying, and summarizing in a significant manner and in terms of money, transactions, and events which are, in part at least, of a financial character, and interpreting the results thereof.
—*Accounting Research and Terminology Bulletin* no. 1 (1961)

---

you did show such healthy sales in a first year of operation.

The process of preparing financial projections enables you as a businessperson to have a much better understanding of what your opportunities are, what strategies you need to pursue, and what the financial implications are.

On top of that, you are better able to communicate your financing needs to the outside world in terms that relate to your business operations. Financial projections assist you in gaining financing from outside resources. Take that information and go to financial institutions, be it for equity or more likely in search of a commercial loan, and say, "This is the amount of long-term financing we need, this is the amount of equity we need, and according to our projections, in about three months, we're going to need to exercise a line of credit in this magnitude. We will keep you apprised."

Financial Statements

Financial statements describe your business from several angles—its assets and liabilities, its trends toward profitability or indebtedness, the nature of its cash flow. The statements derived from past data are like photographs, capturing what was "really there" as seen through accounting's lens. Financial projections are more like architects' renderings, depicting "what will be there" in the future. Financial statements record past events of the business; projections express the anticipated results of your plans. Financial projections can be used as budgets for managing your business, and as pro formas to show business plan reviewers your anticipated future. Projections are prepared in the format of financial statements for ease in comparing projected versus actual performance.

I can hear you now: "But I don't know what's going to happen. What good are projections?" You need solid projections exactly because you don't know what will happen. Budgets help you manage the unexpected.

Even when we feel that our projections are based on guesstimates and gut hunches, we express them in formal quantitative terms to help us spot problems and to set specific targets for short-range and long-range activity. We do all the research we can to make sure our projections are grounded in reality. In a start-up business, that means researching the industry and marketplace. In an existing business, we do that research, but also rely heavily on studying our own past financial statements.

Your statements

Financial statements are the product of the accounting function. They are by their nature summaries, providing not a complete picture of the business, but one in which unimportant details have been assimilated into an overall view. There are two statements you as a business owner should be intimately familiar with—and one more statement you would do well to add to your vocabulary.

The income statement. Also known as the profit and loss statement, or the statement of operations, this statement summarizes the operations of a company over a specified time period. In this way, it is like those pairs of "before" and "after" photographs. The income statement shows the results of a series of events over time—a month, or a quarter, or a year of operations. The purpose of the income statement is to compute the net income

(profit or loss) of the operation between the opening and closing dates of the chosen time period. It lists revenues, minus costs of goods sold, minus expenses (overhead), to arrive at the much-talked-about bottom line—the numerical figure that, positive or negative, is the "grade" on your "report card" for that period.

An income statement will consist of four main sections:

- Revenues—inflows from the routine operations of the company, commonly referred to as sales.
- Costs of goods sold—the costs directly tied to production of the company's products or services. In a manufacturing concern, this will take the form of beginning inventory minus ending inventory; in a service business, it is more likely to include subcontractors or other job-related purchases that are rebilled to the client. These are **variable costs**.
- Expenses—any costs incurred in business operations, resulting in the production of the revenues listed in the first section. These are **fixed costs**, and typically include selling, administrative, and occupancy costs.
- Net income—the output of the income statement. This result becomes an input to the balance sheet.

An income statement is necessary, but, like "before" and "after" photographs, has limited usefulness as an aid to decision making, unless you compare one time period to another. Depending on the business you are in, you may find it useful to compare previous quarter to current quarter; previous year this month to current year this month; previous year to date to current year to date—you get the picture. Because this is a summary of operations over a time period, it is more useful to track similarity to or variance from other time periods than to get excited about a particularly large or small net result.

Figure 7.1 shows an example of an income statement. Worksheet 7.1 in Appendix D gives a blank template for your own spreadsheet. I recommend that you set this up on your computer.

The balance sheet. The balance sheet, also known as a statement of financial position, shows your financial position, weighing the balance of assets to liabilities. Unlike the income statement, which covers a time period, as a video does, the balance sheet captures a moment frozen in time, as a photograph does.

A balance sheet will consist of three main sections:

- Assets—resources controlled by the company, for use in its operations.
- Liabilities—claims on the resources of the company by outsiders.
- Owner's equity—what's left when liabilities are subtracted from assets. The owner "owns" (has equity in) any remaining resources of the business.

Assets and liabilities are separated into two categories: current (within one year) and long term (outside the current year). Owner's equity also comes in two flavors: invested (provided from the owner's pocket) or earned (generated from the profitable operation of the business).

The balance sheet yields a simple yardstick of financial health called the "current ratio," which is arrived at by dividing current assets by current liabilities. Current assets are those that will convert to

KEY CONCEPT

When preparing a cash flow budget, record all cash inflows and outflows on the date when cash is expected to change hands.

cash in a year or less. Current liabilities are those that will be payable in a year or less.

Watching the rise and fall of the "owner's equity" line can be as engrossing as watching the Super Bowl if you're the one whose pockets are being filled or emptied.

Figure 7.2 shows an example of a balance sheet. Worksheet 7.2 in appendix D gives a blank template for your own spreadsheet.

Cash flow budget. The cash flow budget summarizes the cash inflows and outflows for a period of time. Typically, the preparer uses the same time period covered by the income statement. A cash flow budget will consist of four sections:

- Beginning cash balance—the amount of cash available to the business, typically the sum of balances in bank accounts.
- Cash inflows—cash sales, collection of accounts receivable, proceeds from loans, and any other cash received.
- Cash outflows—payments made to vendors, employees, taxes, loan repayments, capital expenditures, and any other cash dispersed.
- Ending cash balance—the result of adding inflows to and subtracting outflows from the beginning balance.

Investments or draws taken by owner(s) are shown as cash inflows or outflows. All inflows and outflows are dated as of when cash is expected to change hands. (In other words, you would record an anticipated cash outflow for the day you plan to pay an invoice, not the date when you receive that invoice.) The cash flow budget can be more useful for managerial decision making than the other statements. The cash flow budget will be of interest to lenders and investors, who will look to your cash flow for assurance that interest

FIGURE 7.1 Income Statement

PRO FORMA INCOME STATEMENT for O'Toole's Machining, Inc.
This document produced on:14-Jul-97

	Sep-97	Oct-97	Nov-97	Dec-97	Jan-98	Feb-98	Mar-98	Apr-98	May-98	Jun-98	Jul-98	Aug-98	YEAR	% of Sales
Expected Monthly Sales	470,654	494,889	512,622	411,782	371,631	380,320	425,513	421,300	408,662	412,875	512,622	429,725	5,252,596	100.0%
Cost of Goods Sold	228,096	241,999	246,815	198,392	172,103	184,750	207,218	204,869	197,822	200,171	246,815	209,567	2,538,618	48.3%
Gross Profit	242,558	252,890	265,807	213,390	199,528	195,570	218,295	216,431	210,840	212,704	265,807	220,158	2,713,978	51.7%
Overhead Expenses	83,919	83,919	83,919	87,869	87,869	87,869	87,869	92,016	92,016	92,016	92,016	92,016	1,063,313	20.2%
Utilities & Telephone	6,000	6,015	6,030	6,045	6,060	6,075	6,091	6,106	6,121	6,136	6,152	6,167	72,998	1.4%
Insurance	2,000	2,005	2,010	2,015	2,020	2,025	2,030	2,035	2,040	2,045	2,051	2,056	24,333	0.5%
Advertising & Promotion	1,000	1,003	1,005	1,008	1,010	1,013	1,015	1,018	1,020	1,023	1,025	1,028	12,166	0.2%
Travel & Entertainment	3,000	3,008	3,015	3,023	3,030	3,038	3,045	3,053	3,061	3,068	3,076	3,084	36,499	0.7%
Repairs & Maintenance	5,500	5,514	5,528	5,541	5,555	5,569	5,583	5,597	5,611	5,625	5,639	5,653	66,915	1.6%
Shipping & Postage	300	301	302	302	303	304	305	305	306	307	308	308	3,650	0.1%
Office Supplies	8,375	8,396	8,417	8,438	8,459	8,480	8,501	8,523	8,544	8,565	8,587	8,608	101,893	1.9%
Other (inc. rents & leases)	29,505	27,755	27,847	27,785	27,801	27,882	28,012	28,130	28,130	28,206	28,409	28,369	337,776	6.4%
Property & Other Taxes	3,401	3,401	3,401	3,401	3,401	3,401	3,401	3,401	3,401	3,401	3,401	3,401	40,812	0.8%
Total Overhead Expenses	143,000	141,315	141,473	145,426	145,509	145,656	145,851	150,129	150,250	150,392	150,663	150,690	1,760,354	33.5%
Depreciation														
Machinery & Equipment	10,669	10,669	10,669	10,669	10,669	10,699	10,699	10,699	10,699	10,699	10,699	10,699	128,023	2.4%
Buildings & Intangibles	717	717	717	717	717	717	717	717	717	717	717	717	8,599	0.2%
Operating Income (EBIT)	88,173	100,190	112,948	56,580	42,634	38,529	61,058	54,917	49,205	50,926	103,759	58,084	817,003	15.6%
Interest Expense	5,682	5,662	9,600	9,554	9,506	9,460	9,412	9,364	9,316	9,267	9,218	9,168	105,209	2.0%
Taxable Income (EBT)	82,491	94,527	103,348	47,026	33,128	29,069	51,647	45,522	39,890	41,660	94,541	48,916	711,795	13.6%
Est. Income Tax Obligation**	34,564	39,607	43,303	19,704	13,881	12,180	21,640	19,086	16,714	17,455	39,613	20,496	298,242	5.7%
Tax Credits	NA	NA	NA	NA	NA	NA	NA	NA	NA	NA	NA	NA	0	0.0%
Estimated Income Taxes**	34,564	39,607	43,303	19,704	13,881	12,180	21,640	19,086	16,714	17,455	39,613	20,496	298,242	3.6%
Net Profit	47,927	54,920	60,045	27,322	19,247	16,889	30,007	26,466	23,176	24,204	54,928	28,420	413,553	7.9%

(continued)

FIGURE 7.1 Income Statement (*continued*)

SUMMARY OF SELECTED YEAR END DATA:

Total Variable Costs (CGS)	=	2,538,618
Total Fixed Costs (Overhead + Interest)	=	1,865,561
Total Net Profit	=	413,553
Total Net Operations Cash Flow	=	290,450

SELECTED FINANCIAL RATIOS:

Variable Costs/Sales	=	48.33%
Fixed Costs/Sales	=	35.52%
Gross Margin/Sales	=	51.67%
Operating Profit/Sales	=	15.55%
After Tax Profit/Sales	=	7.87%
Cash Flow From Operations/ Sales (internally generated cash flow)	=	5.53%
Sales Break Even Point ($'s)	=	3,610,581
Return on Beginning Current Assets	=	31.94%*
Return on Depreciable Assets	=	25.07%*
Return on Total Fixed Assets	=	16.87%*
Return on Beginning Equity	=	103.38%*

(1) Assumes 9.3% cost of capital and 90% debt financing, with a 5-year loan for working capital and inventory.

(2) Assumes 9.3% cost of capital and 14% debt financing, with a 5-year loan for equipment and furnishings.

(3) Assumes 9.0% cost of capital and 97% debt financing, with a 20-year loan for land and structures.

(4) 3.0% inflation rate is applied to overhead expenses.

(5) Depreciation method chosen for equipment is: straight-line. Depreciation method chosen for buildings is: straight-line. Depreciable life determined by Federal tax definitions.

(6) The enterprise simulated is assumed to be a regular corporation. Taxes are estimated based on this legal structure and the previous year's tax rates (federal, state, local, and FICA). Sole proprietor taxes include Self-Employment taxes. All other forms include only Federal and State income taxes.

(7) For monthly cashflow modeling all taxes are assumed to be withheld by the firm as monthly income is earned. This may cause monthly cashflows to be underestimated in any one year forecast which has any one or more months of net income loss. The yearly total does not reflect the actual expected amount of taxes owed for the forecasted year.

(8) Total sales are assumed to grow at a 20.0% average annual rate.

(9) Cash flow projections assume that the total amount of debt financing needed is received as a lump sum in the first month the firm requires financing, by category.

(10) Operations are assumed to begin 60 days from the current date; Jul-97

(11) Sales breakeven point are sales necessary to cover CGS, overhead, and interest expenses.

* (12) All return ratios based upon cash flows from operations, not profit.

Copyright: ReCon Associates, 1994

FIGURE 7.2 Balance Sheet

PROJECTED BALANCE SHEET: O'Toole's Machining, Inc.

Period:	Sep-97 Beginning	Aug-98 Ending
ASSETS		
Cash	4,714	308,869
Receivables	408,718	412,384
Inventory	495,849	546,622
Total Current Assets:	909,281	1,267,875
Equipment	778,649	780,625
Facilities/Bldgs	0	241,667
Deprec. Intangibles	1,328	1,063
Land & non-deprec.	8,715	60,715
TOTAL ASSETS:	1,697,973	2,351,944
LIABILITIES		
Previous Debt	1,227,021	1,089,184
New Debt:		
Short-term	190,000	568,256
Medium-term	190,000	158,662
Long-term	0	112,271
	0	297,323
TOTAL LIABILITIES:	1,417,021	1,657,440
EQUITY	280,952	694,505
TOTAL LIAB. & EQUITY:	1,697,973	2,351,944
LEVERAGE RATIOS		
Debt/Asset:	0.83	0.70
Debt/Equity:	5.04	2.39
Fixed Charge Coverage:	NA	1.84
LIQUIDITY RATIOS		
Current Ratio:	NA	7.99
Quick Ratio:	NA	4.55

New Investment in Budget Period		Financing Required	
New Investment in Budget Period	642,000		
Depreciable Equipment	130,000	Short-Term Debt	190,000
Depreciable Building	250,000	Medium-Term Debt	130,000
Depreciable Intangibles	0	Long-Term Debt	302,000
Land & Non-Depreciable Assets	52,000	Total	622,000
Working Capital/Inventory	210,000		

OTHER FINANCIAL INFORMATION

Total Sales:	5,252,596
Gross Profit:	2,713,978
Taxable Profit:	711,795
Net Profit:	413,553
Cash flow from Operations:	290,450
Sales Breakeven Point:	3,610,581
PROFITABILITY RATIOS	
Gross Margin:	51.67%
Taxable Profit Margin:	13.55%
Net Profit Margin:	7.87%
Cash flow from Operations/Sales:	5.53%
YEAR-END RETURN RATIOS	(based upon cash flow)
Return on Total Assets:	12.35%
Return on Dep. Assets:	25.07%
Return on Begin. Equity:	103.38%

Notes: Accounts payable estimates are not developed by the model. New (acquired within the planning period) short-term debt is assumed to be the only current liability.

or dividend payments will be forthcoming. Many businesses I work with don't ask their accountants for a cash flow statement. In more than a few cases this lack of information has led to trouble with a capital T.

Figure 7.3 shows the format for a cash flow budget. Worksheet 7.3 in appendix D gives a blank template for your own spreadsheet.

Sources and uses of funds. One more financial statement will be needed if you are writing your business plan in preparation for a search for money. Whether you are talking to investors or lenders, either will want to know where you expect money to come from and what the money is going to be used for. This statement is called the sources and uses of funds, or application and expected effect of funding. Its format is similar to the cash flow budget, in that it states inflows (sources of funds) and proposed outflows (uses of funds). An example is given in Figure 7.4. Worksheet 7.4 in appendix D gives a blank template for your own spreadsheet.

If you are submitting your business plan in a search for funds, you may prepare a schedule describing any expenditures for which greater detail would add credibility or clarity. A start-up or expansion plan might include a capital equipment list, explaining what will be purchased with a proposed loan.

Assumptions and comments. Any financial statement, whether historical or projected, needs explanation of how you arrived at your numbers. An assumptions and comments narrative is typically prepared when financial statements are presented for review by an outsider. In fact, I believe, even when you are preparing statements for your own purposes, it's wise to keep a list of explanatory comments.

You could include your assumptions as a set of comments at the bottom of each statement or include a separate page devoted to them. In the business plan for O'Toole's Machining, you will find a page labeled "Economic and Financial Assumptions Worksheet." Additional notes accompany the individual pro formas, shedding light on the thinking that went into these pro formas. If you study the O'Toole's Machining business plan, you will see how assumptions made in the narrative portion of the plan drive the numbers in the pro formas.

You're a busy person. Next time you pick up your plan, will you remember how you arrived at your numbers? What assumptions were they based on? In the loan review meeting, will they come to mind as needed, to answer questions? I would never leave that to chance. Assumptions are the support on which financial projections are built. Even an experienced business planner tends to get confused about where some of the numbers have come from. When it's time to do best-case, most probable, and worst-case projections, your record of assumptions shows where your hopes and fears are focused.

Using the financial statements. The income statement and balance sheet are critical to the accounting cycle, not to mention city, state, and federal tax obligations. Even if you don't care to know how your business is doing, it's likely that your accountant or tax preparer will make sure these statements are prepared on a timely basis. The cash flow budget, on the other hand, is of great importance to you, the manager, who must decide what courses of action you can afford to take, and when. For that reason, we'll discuss cash flow as a management tool in greater detail a little later in this chapter.

Do not wait for your accountant or tax preparer to ask about your statements! Ignorance of financial matters is asking for failure. Many businesses in their start-up years prepare cash flow budgets on a weekly basis, and other statements promptly at the

FIGURE 7.3 Cash Flow Budget

PRO FORMA CASH FLOW FROM OPERATIONS STATEMENT for O'Toole's Machining, Inc.

	Aug-97	Sep-97	Oct-97	Nov-97	Dec-97	Jan-98	Feb-98	Mar-98	Apr-98	May-98	Jun-98	Jul-98	Aug-98	13 Month
Cash Sales	0	0	0	0	0	0	0	0	0	0	0	0	0	0
Collected Receivables	0	47,065	449,545	495,451	501,651	412,809	374,508	384,404	422,832	420,247	409,716	422,639	499,345	4,840,212
Other Income	0	386,011	22,707	0	0	0	0	0	0	0	0	0	0	408,718
Total Operation Cash Inflow	0	433,077	472,251	495,451	501,651	412,809	374,508	384,404	422,832	420,247	409,716	422,639	499,345	5,248,930
Operation/Overhead Costs	0	143,000	141,315	141,473	145,426	145,509	145,656	145,851	150,129	150,250	150,392	150,663	150,690	1,760,354
Direct/Raw Material Costs	205,286	232,658	246,839	251,752	202,360	175,545	188,445	211,362	208,966	201,779	204,175	251,752	213,758	2,794,677
Interest Expense	0	5,682	5,662	9,600	9,554	9,506	9,460	9,412	9,364	9,316	9,267	9,218	9,168	105,207
Income Taxes Paid **	0	34,564	39,607	43,303	19,704	13,881	12,180	21,640	19,086	16,714	17,455	39,613	20,496	298,242
Total Operation Cash Outflow	205,286	415,903	433,424	446,128	337,043	344,441	355,740	388,265	387,547	378,058	381,289	451,244	394,112	49,584,980
Total Cash Flow From Operations	(205,286)	17,174	38,827	49,323	124,608	68,368	18,768	(3,861)	35,285	42,189	28,427	(28,605)	105,233	290,450

FIGURE 7.4 Sources and Uses of Funds

PRO FORMA CONSOLIDATED STATEMENT OF CHANGES IN FINANCIAL POSITION: SOURCES AND USES OF FUNDS for O'Toole's Machining, Inc.

	Aug-97	Sep-97	Oct-97	Nov-97	Dec-97	Jan-98	Feb-98	Mar-98	Apr-98	May-98	Jun-98	Jul-98	Aug-98	13 Month
Sources of Funds														
Cash Flow from Operations	0	17,174	38,827	49,323	124,608	68,368	18,768	0	35,285	42,189	28,427	0	105,233	528,203
Increase in Short-Term Debt	190,000	0	0	0	0	0	0	0	0	0	0	0	0	190,000
Increase in Medium-Term Debt	0	0	130,000	0	0	0	0	0	0	0	0	0	0	130,000
Increase in Long-Term Debt	0	0	302,000	0	0	0	0	0	0	0	0	0	0	302,000
Increase in Payables/Accruals	0	0	0	0	0	0	0	0	0	0	0	0	0	0
Sale of Assets/Investments	0	0	0	0	0	0	0	0	0	0	0	0	0	0
Cash (Equity) Contribution	20,000	0	0	0	0	0	0	0	0	0	0	0	0	20,000
Total Sources:	210,000	17,174	470,827	49,323	124,608	68,368	18,768	0	35,285	42,189	28,427	0	105,233	1,170,203
Uses of Funds														
Short-Term Debt Retirement	0	2,503	2,522	2,541	2,561	2,581	2,601	2,621	2,641	2,661	2,682	2,702	2,723	31,338
Medium-Term Debt Retirement	0	0	0	1,712	1,726	1,739	1,753	1,766	1,779	1,793	1,807	1,821	1,835	17,729
Long-Term Debt Retirement	0	0	0	452	456	459	462	466	469	473	476	480	484	4,677
To Purchase Equipment	0	0	130,000	0	0	0	0	0	0	0	0	0	0	130,000
To Purchase Bldg/Land/Intang.	0	0	302,000	0	0	0	0	0	0	0	0	0	0	302,000
Other (includes Oper.Exps.)	205,286	8,845	8,845	11,967	11,987	11,988	11,999	15,870	12,020	12,030	12,041	40,657	12,063	375,590
Total Uses:	205,286	11,348	443,367	16,673	16,720	16,766	16,814	20,722	16,910	16,957	17,006	45,661	17,105	861,334
Changes in Financial Position:	4,714	5,826	27,461	32,650	107,888	51,602	1,953	(20,722)	18,376	25,232	11,421	(45,661)	88,129	308,869
Estimated Ending Cash Balance:	4,714	10,540	38,000	70,651	178,539	230,141	232,094	211,372	229,748	254,980	266,401	220,740	308,869	308,869
Changes in Inventory (2):	205,286	4,562	4,840	4,936	3,968	3,442	3,695	1,144	4,097	3,956	4,033	4,936	4,191	256,059
Changes in Receivables (3):	0	423,588	45,345	17,171	(89,869)	(41,178)	5,812	10,108	(1,532)	(11,585)	3,159	89,983	(69,619)	412,384

NOTES:
(1) Direct/raw material purchases for each month represents the expected cost of goods to be sold in the following month, esculated by the CGS average inflation rate (Sales & CGS worksheet) 2.00%

(2) Direct/raw material purchases for the last month are assumed to be either a standard increase over the previous month or a repeat of the CGS number from 12 months prior to the last month (adjusted by inflation).

NOTES:
(1) Operation expense use of funds includes any negative operating cash flow. This assumption is intended to reflect realistic behavior to cash needs.
(2) Inventory changes affecting sources and uses of funds are reflected in cash flow from operations (direct material purchases).
This line summarizes the monthly magnitude of change (Direct Material Purchases - Cost of Goods Sold).
(3) Changes in receivables affecting sources and uses of funds are reflected in cash flow from operations (credit sale collections). This line summarizes the monthly magnitude of changes in receivables.

Copyright: ReCon Associates, 1994

close of each month, in order to spot and respond quickly to emerging trends.

The process of making financial projections

First you make assumptions, then you make spreadsheets. The formats are not difficult to master, but learning to make the right assumptions can be. That's why my colleagues and I feel strongly that *you* must do this work. You're the one with the vision for this business. If you can't see the possible futures it can bring about, who can?

It doesn't surprise me that many entrepreneurs "can't take the time" to do financial projections. After all, the work is boring to many of us. Make a few assumptions, then plug in numbers, numbers, numbers . . . and watch those totals calculate. Then adjust your assumptions, plug in more numbers, and think it through again. Sound like fun? Not my idea of it.

Still, this is some of the most important work you can do. Any potential lender or investor will want to see that you understand the numbers, inside and out. If you can't answer questions about how you arrived at your numbers, you can't expect people to trust you with their money. At a bare minimum, you have to provide the assumptions. From them, an accountant or bookkeeper can do the remaining work.

Financial projections or pro formas are essentially budgets. They project goals you hope to attain, and limits you intend to stay within. The budgeting process can be summarized in nine steps:

1. Sales forecast
2. Gross profit (cost of sales) forecast
3. Operating expense forecast
4. Capital budget
5. Financing plan
6. Cash flow plan
7. Forecasted balance sheet and financial ratios
8. Monitor performance—use reports to compare budget versus actual
9. Manage exceptions

Jack Reiners offers this advice regarding sales and gross profit forecasts: "Think in terms of units, not

KEY CONCEPT

Assumptions are the heart of a business plan. Assumptions flow from the strategies laid out in the marketing, personnel, and financial sections. These assumptions then drive the financial projections, by quantifying the projected activity in terms of income and expenses. Any business plan in which financial projections have been prepared before the strategy sections is inherently flawed.

dollars. Think of what types of units you sell. Then ask, what resources are needed to produce these units? Raw material, equipment, personnel . . . what goes into each type of unit? Thinking in terms of units helps you identify the resources going into them." Steps 1 through 7 require assumptions in each area.

Managing by the budgeting process. Steps 8 and 9 are management's response as activities during the time period covered by the projections generate actual results. As a manager, it is your job to compare forecasted performance to actual performance, and give your attention to areas where exceptions have emerged. By repeating this cycle, you evolve a deep understanding of the financial currents flowing through your business.

Developing financial assumptions

One of the more common mistakes we see made by people writing business plans is that the ideas they describe in the other portions of the plan do not correlate with the numbers they show in their financial statements. Some people even try to develop the financial statements first, then write the marketing and personnel sections afterward. *This is a terrible mistake.* The qualitative information in your marketing and personnel plans will drive your financial plan. When you quantify those activities in terms of projected costs incurred and income realized, you project the "report card" for the business plan. It is only an accurate "grade" if the financial section is driven by the other sections.

When you are developing the other sections of your business plan, each idea needs to be examined for how it will generate revenues or incur expenses.

For instance, if you have based sales figures on a marketing plan that calls for hiring a new salesperson, that assumption will affect your income statement both in gross sales and in salaries. Your balance sheet will be affected by the income statement built on that assumption. And your cash flow budget will show the salesperson's salary going out long before the new sales he or she generates are realized as collected accounts receivable.

Your owner's draw is an expense that must be budgeted for as well. We all have to eat and pay bills. Don't forget to include the amount you need to draw when you set the price you charge for your product/service offering. If you don't put it into the price it will be hard to take home.

By following a careful process of recognizing and documenting assumptions, you develop a consistent plan. First write the text, thinking in terms of revenues and expenses; list those assumptions. Then, transfer those numbers into your financial documents. Append a list of those assumptions so that any reader of the plan can clarify the "why" behind each number. If a reviewer doesn't agree with your assumptions, the whole plan is off. And if the reviewer can't see why you made a certain assumption, how can he or she know whether to agree or disagree?

Worksheet 7.5 in appendix D describes common financial assumption line items your financial projections will require.

Break-even analysis. One of the key assumptions you will be required to make is the assumption of *break-even point* for your operation. The break-even point is the point at which a company's costs exactly match its sales volume. At break-even, the company has neither incurred a loss nor made a profit. You have just covered the costs of opening your doors and making your sales. You want to know where that line is, so you can plan to stay above it.

To find out your break-even point, you will need to project your fixed costs, your variable costs, and your sales volume for a specific time period. The fixed costs usually remain constant regardless of sales volume. Rent, insurance, and salaries would be

examples of fixed costs. Variable costs vary with sales volume. Variable costs are those associated with producing and selling a product or service. For example, the labor and materials required to physically make the item, and the cost of a sales commission paid to the fellow who sold it, would be variable costs. Variable costs drop when your sales drop. Fixed costs stay fixed regardless of the ups and downs of sales.

You need an understanding of your break-even point in order to know how to price your products and services profitably. A firm's break-even point can be computed by this mathematical formula:

Monthly total fixed expenses: $ _____

Gross profit margin, in
   percentage terms: _____%

Divide fixed expenses ($_____) by gross
   profit margin (_____ %) to arrive at sales
   to break-even: $ _____

"But how do I know my gross profit margin?" you're asking. Later in this chapter, we'll explain how. Meanwhile, Figure 7.5 shows a break-even analysis in graph form.

FIGURE 7.5 Break-Even Analysis

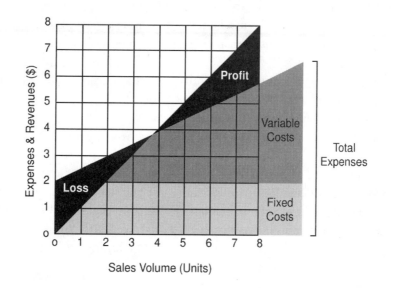

Break-Even Analysis Graph

Knowing your price per unit for various product lines allows you to extend your estimate of units sold to an estimate of total sales, based on how many you're selling of what, and at what price. You will then use projection of sales to project an income statement, and the other statements that depend on that pro forma.

The break-even analysis is an important tool for you, but it is not necessary to include it in a business plan. Of course, there's nothing wrong with including your analysis if you've prepared one.

The Concept of Cash Flow

You can be rich on paper and bankrupt because you can't pay your bills. The reason? Cash flow.

What kind of monies are you generating to flow into your business, and what kind of outflows will occur? Managing those two factors requires an understanding of the cash flow concept.

Cash outflows tend to come from four areas:

- Cost of goods sold—materials you purchase any time you make an order.
- Overhead—expenses that are fixed, or only slightly variable, from month to month.

- Debt payments—the costs incurred by paying down debt or paying interest on that debt.
- Taxes—sales, real estate, and other taxes paid by the business.

If you are running a manufacturing business, your cost of goods sold is likely to be higher than if you are running a consulting business. The nature of these outflows is very different from one business to the next.

Cash inflows tend to come from these areas: cash sales, collection of accounts receivable, and proceeds from loans.

KEY CONCEPT: COLLECTIONS INFLUENCE CASH FLOW

How fast you collect the money owed you by your customers influences your cash flow. Speed of payment can be an important issue when goods or services are delivered and an invoice is issued; only then (sometimes months later) is that debt collected.

There are two major influences on the cash inflows to a business: seasonality of sales and collection of accounts receivable. Do you tend to sell more in July than in January? Your cash flow statement should acknowledge that reality. Your business must bring in enough cash during busy seasons to carry you through your slow times.

Let's take the example of a mail-order plant nursery. The bulk of sales will take place in spring and early summer. And yet, that nursery will pay about the same costs in overhead in winter as in summer—maybe more, if the greenhouses must be heated. Furthermore, in winter, the next year's catalog needs to be produced and mailed—one of the nursery's largest annual expenses. Such a business will need careful cash flow planning to pay its bills throughout the year.

Collections also influence cash inflow. How fast do you collect the money owed you by your customers? In a strictly cash business, collection is not an issue. But in those businesses where goods or services are delivered, an invoice is issued, and then that debt collected, speed of payment can be an important issue. In some industries, slow payment is the norm. Invoices stand open for 60, 90, or even 120 days—and if the seller complains, the buyer threatens to switch to sellers more willing to accommodate slow payments.

Some accounts receivable turn out to be uncollectible. Chuck Hofer shared a sad tale:

An individual I know started his own small advertising agency. He placed ads for various customers. He ended up almost going bankrupt, and it took him almost two years to get out of it, because one his clients had him place some ads on network television, but he hadn't collected the payment ahead of time. His customer filed bankruptcy, but guess what? The television network didn't care about that. They just wanted to be paid. Since the person placing the ad was the small agency, they came back and expected payment from him. A quarter of a million dollars, and he almost lost his company because of that. You've got to remember, it's not a sale until it's paid for.

These two influences—how fast (and whether) you collect, and the seasonality of your business—have a major impact on your cash inflows.

KEY CONCEPT

Start-up businesses incur specific costs associated with getting started, like buying equipment and renovating office space. And yet, start-up businesses can expect virtually no sales to offset these costs in the first months of operation. This situation calls for thorough cash flow planning.

Some people think that if there's money in the checkbook, then their cash flow is fine. That's naive. Cash flow is a concept requiring a more insightful analysis of operations.

Several of the business plans included show statements of cash flow, including O'Toole's Machining and Artful Fly.

Start-up concerns. What should a start-up business expect in terms of outflows and inflows? There are likely to be specific outflows associated with opening the doors—costs to establish the physical facilities, equipment to buy, initial raw materials for production, as well as administrative and marketing supplies, such as stationery, shipping materials, and brochures. Fees will need to be paid for any relevant licenses or permits; for legal, marketing, advertising, and design services; cash will be needed for salaries, operating expenses, and unanticipated costs during the initial start-up period.

When will those flows out the door rub shoulders with any flows coming in? George Solomon said:

The rule of thumb for start-ups is: You can expect for the first six months to have virtually no sales. For six to nine months expect to have 25 percent of what you projected [for a typical year], for nine months to a year that will move to 50 percent, and in a year to 15 months, you finally reach about 75 percent. Finally at 15 to 18 months, you'll probably be hitting 100 percent of your projected sales.

Colleagues kibitz. Frank Hoy emphasizes the importance of cash flow in his teaching:

I make my students do three years' worth of monthly cash flow projections. I ask them: What is it you can anticipate that you're going to be required to pay? What are the various contingencies? The worst-case scenarios—

when you don't have the cash—where are you going to get it? A lot of people doing business plans just take a look at projected net income, and projected expenses, and assume that they're going to have money to cover everything. But the inflows and outflows never match.

William Dennis shared his observation: "One of the things we've found is that owners are in many ways oblivious to what's going on seasonally as well as cyclically. Believe it or not, about half [of the owners we've surveyed] can't project whether their sales are going to go up or down in the next three months."

Since I grew up in a retail business, I've seen first-hand how important it is to know whether sales will be up or down from last year. It really affects buying if you're in retail.

That's why when my dad died he was in debt. He didn't understand inventory control. If the steel mills went on strike he'd cut back, and if they didn't go on strike he'd get stuck short. And if they went on wildcat strike, he was really in trouble because all of our customers were the women who worked in the mills.

How Do I Use Financial Projections to Manage My Business?

Financial projections are budgets. As such, they are management tools. They guide each area of your operation, helping key personnel understand what you expect, and when. If your business is large enough for a level of management to exist outside yourself, the business owner, involve those people in creating their budgets. They may know nuances of their areas that will make assumptions more accurate. The more input people have in creating their budgets, the more responsibility they will feel toward them.

The last two steps of the budgeting process involve monitoring performance and managing exceptions.

Budget numbers won't run your company, of course: It's *how you react to the numbers* that runs your company. Nothing goes exactly according to plan. For that reason, spotting any variances in actual results from the projected results is key. Managers whose areas are failing to reach projected results should focus on improving performance. Managers whose areas are exceeding projections

KEY CONCEPTS

No matter what other bills you face, always pay your taxes. Part of the game is the rules. Rules mean you pay these taxes, and the government will get you if you don't. The founder of Jackalope, out of Santa Fe, keeps a little wooden sculpture on his desk. It's a skinny man inside of a jail cell. He says, "this is to remind me, this is what happens if you don't pay your taxes."

■ ■ ■

Budgets don't run your business: It's what you do with the budgets. The more input people have on creating budgets, the more responsibility they will feel to operate by their budgets.

should understand why so that successful internal strategies can be repeated, and tactical advantage can be taken of fortunate external events.

To spot variances, you must have two or more periods to compare. What trends do you observe? What assumptions were in effect; what conclusions can you draw? Give your attention to important areas where results vary from projections. In business schools, this practice is typically called Management by Exceptions. Look for changes in volume, in pricing, in timing, and take corrective action. "Trends are more important than data," Jack Reiners teaches. "Groups of trends give context to specific trends." And Tim Baye adds this advice: "There's a rule of thumb you want to follow—avoid paralysis by analysis. Don't get too bogged down." With practice, you will learn what are the important factors in your business—and how to use them to guide management decisions.

Controlling Costs

The successful business owners are the ones who control their costs. One of the most important steps you can take toward controlling your costs is to learn to use *common-size income statements* to understand where your money goes.

A common-size income statement is a recasting of the basic income statement with each line item expressed as a percentage of revenue. Simply divide each line's dollar figure by the total revenue dollar figure. Each result will represent "*x* percent of revenue." For an example, take a look at the "Comparative Income Statements" included with the business plan for BizCopy.

"This lets you take a look, from month to month, at what percentage of total revenue your wages cost you that month. What percent your postage cost. What percent of total revenue went to heating and utilities that month," said Tim Baye. Monitoring these percentages, spotting variances, and digging into why they occurred give you insight into where your money is going—and where your ship may be leaking. "That practice alone has, in my opinion, raised the general IQ of all of my clients over time. Once they grasp onto that concept, their interest in exploring additional financial management issues increases exponentially," Baye concluded.

Another important tool Baye recommends **is to calculate gross profit margin by product line**. "This is probably the most powerful financial management tool you could have in your back pocket. To calculate what you pay for a product and compare it to what you sell the product for is a simple equation. The gross profit margin is the unit's price minus the cost of the unit divided by the price." The resulting percentage allows you to spot exceptions.

Baye continued:

Start evaluating gross profit by product line. Understanding gross profit margins gives you two significant advantages: First, you can compare apples and oranges, in making decisions about what your product and service mix is. And secondly, you have an increased ability to set prices and negotiate terms. Work closely with your vendors. Impress upon them that your relationship should be mutually beneficial. I'm constantly amazed at how flexible a lot of vendors will be, but if you don't ask, there's no reason for them to offer.

Understanding gross profit margins is absolutely critical to controlling costs.

Know when to hold. Understanding when to buy the best and when to shop off-price matters to new businesses. William Dennis observed that with startups, "There are all these expenses that you didn't

---

KEY CONCEPT

Good people help your business succeed. Pay your key personnel what they're worth, even if it means paying yourself much less than you're worth.

---

expect, or that 'maybe I won't buy a used widget, I'll get a new widget instead'—by the time you add up these expenses, cost is where you get killed. Not sales. Costs."

Chuck Hofer agreed: "Many companies, after the first wave of success, suddenly begin behaving like they've arrived at the end of the rainbow. Rather than just starting the journey. You've been a little bit successful, and all of a sudden you go out and buy fancier computers or office equipment that is beyond your needs and not yet supported by the cash flow of your company."

New businesses need to know this. If you've gotten a loan, and you feel as if you have some money, that's dangerous. You may feel too free with it. You have to look at it as though you may not have that money tomorrow. Terri Lonier advised, "if your customer sees it, spend money on it. If your customer doesn't see it, don't spend money on it. Buy used desks, used filing cabinets. Put your money in stuff that will present a professional image and a high-level identity."

Salaries: a sore point

Research by the National Federation of Independent Businesses indicates that there is a direct relationship between what you earn in the business and what you pay. Not just in wages, but health benefits, pension benefits, and other expenses related to staffing. The corollary might be that "going cheap" when it comes to salaries means you are undercutting your business's earning ability. Good people help your business prosper; bad people cost you money.

Salaries for key personnel are the last area where you should pinch your pennies—even if it means paying yourself next to nothing.

According to Chuck Hofer:

People who become successful business owners are willing to work hard for low wages. Technically, there is only one job you can have in the United States where it is legally possible to work for less than the minimum wage—and that is to be an entrepreneur. If you're an employee, you must by law be paid the minimum wage. But if you're a business owner, you're the last person on the list to get paid. First you pay your taxes, your suppliers, your creditors, your payroll. What's left is yours. If it's divided by the number of hours you've worked, your average salary can legitimately be less than minimum wage.

It may be hard to face writing out those paychecks when you are taking home nothing. But the willingness to invest, take risks, and work hard to make your vision a reality is what makes you an entrepreneur.

The Search for Capital

An entrepreneur in Madison, Wisconsin, home to Oscar Mayer Foods, has answered the question "where's the beef" . . . and the poultry, and pork, and other meat products as well. The successful search for venture capital by Foodusa.com offers an example of an entrepreneur who developed a business plan and pitch that brought investors running.

Just weeks after presenting its plan at the Wisconsin Venture Fair, this Internet meat market business had garnered $3 million in investment. The business manages a meat exchange between producers, food processors, and food service distributors around the country, via an Internet Web site.

The former vegetable broker began working on a model for an Internet site brokering canned and frozen vegetables in 1996. But after more than a year's work, he discovered that idea wouldn't work because of issues of branding and labeling specific to produce. Then came his breakthrough, "Finally, a friend of mine, a poultry distributor, said 'Rod, look at meat. I think it will work,' and the more I dug into it, the better the story got. I had a couple of early victories with a very raw plan that convinced people to back me. The rest has been fast-forward. When you've got it right, it doesn't take long."

Heller's experience with venture capital taught him that it takes a combination of preparedness and personality to win:

It took me a while to get the model right. Until then, there was always a little hesitation in the back of my head going, "we've got problems with this, but we'll overcome them." When I finally got this model down, I didn't have any hesitation. I knew I had it, and it showed to everybody I spoke to. That made the difference. There's no sense in trying to hide a fault in the plan. If you can't solve that fault, the plan is no good.

Heller's success in attracting venture capital didn't happen overnight:

I spent two years trying to get money, trying to get the plan right. I was working 40 or 50 hours a week, and my gross income combined for two years was less than $4,000 because I spent so much time on my plan and so little time on brokering food. I'm married, with children. You struggle with—am I right? It all goes through your head. "I've got to contribute to the welfare of my family . . . we can't afford this, we can't afford that." But you've got to know you've got it right, before you approach any investor.

What really made it for me—I'm a great networker. You can't be an introvert. You've got to talk to as many people as possible.

Networking at conferences brought Heller in contact with another entrepreneur who had started a similar exchange for natural gas and electricity. He now sits on Heller's board of directors. His expertise has helped Heller assess his own exchange's financial potential—and built credibility in Heller's organization.

Heller's unshakable faith in the business model he's perfected gives him the kind of charisma the venture capital community responds to.

At the Venture Capital Fair, they held a practice. They said, "Okay Rod, it's your turn," and I went up there and plugged in my PowerPoint presentation and started talking about my plan. It took me 12 minutes, exactly my time allotted, and everybody said, "Wow, you were great! You've got this down pat." That was because I lived it for two years before I ever got up there. And then when I did the real presentation, it was so much fun— people coming out of there said, "You were by far the best presenter." And it showed! I got the money! I closed in 20 days on $2 million!

There's so much venture capital out there, if your story is good, it doesn't matter if you're shooting $15 million a year in expenses. Show what you think it will be, and justify it.

This example illustrates three key points on preparing a business plan to search for capital. Work on your plan until it's absolutely solid; network to find people who will build your credibility; and when the time comes to make the pitch, give it all you've got.

If You're Talking to Bankers

Is your plan being prepared to aid the search for a business loan? It's not hard to put yourself in a banker's wingtips and imagine the mindset with which your plan will be reviewed. Naturally, a banker's going to begin with money. "Who is asking for the money? How much is needed? What for? Why does this loan make sense? How will the interest be paid? How will the principle be repaid?"

As lenders seek answers to these questions, they will become interested in other sections of the plan. The marketplace, customers, products, and other marketing issues must be explained in a way that supports the financial request. The background of the business owner(s) and key managers, their fitness for the duties and responsibilities assigned to them, will be critically examined, as will staff needs and other operational issues. Throughout the plan, they

must find continuity and clarity of thought. They must finish their review with a feeling of assurance that you have considered the "what-ifs" and have adequately addressed the possible risks ahead.

What influences a lender's perception of risk? To a large extent, you do. Who you are, what you're willing to invest yourself. A lender needs to know not just that somebody can make this business concept work, but that *you* can do it.

In the past, being a female was enough to raise doubts. Getting capital is still an issue for women. According to Joline Godfrey:

Only 7 percent of all venture capital money available is going to women. But women who are driven, and have tenacity, just aren't going away. We have business structures, and networks, and resources today that we didn't have five or six years ago. The key point is—people invest in people. Women have got to present ourselves in a way that doesn't raise anxieties of the people with money. As our ideas get better and our business plans get more sophisticated, we're getting more money.

A classic mistake when asking others to invest in your business is to expect others to do what you aren't willing to do yourself. Frank Hoy explained:

What kind of equity are you putting in? People come in to my office with an idea that will require $750,000 for the launch, and when I ask how much they're putting into it, maybe it's $17,000. They don't have the equity, or they're not willing to put the equity into the venture. They fail to recognize that people have investment alternatives. Nobody is likely to want to carry the whole risk for them.

Banks are heavily regulated. They must meet very clear criteria regarding percentage of debt to equity. They can't put money into a business where the founder hasn't invested any capital of his or her own. No one is going to lend you money just because your idea is so smart. *Inc.* magazine in a survey found that 80 percent of start-up businesses get money from the owners, their families, and their friends. Only 7 percent get bank loans, and even fewer get venture capital.

If you're talking to bankers, make sure you know their lending guidelines, and make sure you're doing your part to make this a doable deal for them.

Issues of Growth

Is your business growing? Then its need for capital is probably growing too. Most people don't realize that as you grow you're likely to need more and more money to keep up with that growth. Very few businesses fund their growth solely out of the cash flow of the business. The business may already be carrying a bank loan, raising its debt-to-equity level as high as traditional banks are willing to go. Its owners' friends and families may have invested all they are able to. A desperate search for cash to support growth hardly feels like success. Unless you need a million dollars or more, venture capitalists are likely to see you as small fry when they're looking for bigger fish. "You get to an in-between place where banks don't want to fund you and you don't have more local funds to help you, you could be in trouble," said Bob Brockhaus. The solution requires ingenuity, and a big dose of charismatic energy wouldn't hurt either.

Three ways to grow

Despite the financial difficulties of funding expansion, most businesses are born to grow. Through growth you achieve increased efficiencies and greater profits. You might plan to grow through expanding operations at your primary place of business, through geographic expansion, or more rarely, through franchise operations.

Grow where you are. Some businesses plan to grow simply by growing larger. This is the most common means of growth, and will happen naturally if there is sufficient market demand for the products or services you offer. Several of the business plans included in this book exemplify this

---

approach. Red's Automotive and BizCopy are two such examples.

Several retail businesses I've counseled have grown this way. One, a toy store, and another, a hair salon, both grew by purchasing additional space in their mall locations, as storefronts became available. By doing so, they were able to increase their fixed costs in controlled increments, growing at a pace they could afford.

Grow through geographic expansion. Other businesses grow by expanding operations into new geographic areas. This approach brings the operation's products and services within reach of new customers. The business operates in the same way as before, but in more places. This approach requires more resources than growing at the original location, but can bring rewards that justify those expenditures. Several of our example business plans demonstrate this approach, including O'Toole's Machining and Red's Automotive.

Another of my counseling clients was a different toy store, very similar to the first in the quality and selection of merchandise, but this toy store chose to grow through opening stores in other communities. The new stores were all quite successful, and in a short time the owner found herself with thriving businesses in four communities, all several hours apart. After a time, she sold the distant stores, finding her hands-on management style incompatible with doing business in multiple locations.

Franchising to grow. Another, less common, means of growth is franchising your operation. A small business might create itself with the intention of becoming a franchiser, or may "stumble on" the idea at some point in its growth. One of our example business plans focuses entirely on growth through the creation and sales of franchise operations—the plan for Whole Fish & Seafood.

A franchiser can raise large amounts of capital by selling franchises. When I spoke with Don Kuratko, he had recently attended a program where the speaker was one of the founders of Papa John's Pizza: "It was started in 1984, and the major growth spurt came when they started franchising. That allowed them to raise enough capital to eventually take it to a public stock offering. The audience hearing that was obviously interested. There's a lot of businesspeople starting to think, 'maybe I should franchise my business.'"

Franchising overseas is a more realistic possibility than ever before. U.S. franchises are becoming more and more visible in other countries, and technology has vastly simplified the work of managing distant franchise locations. Although some may express concern about "Americanizing" the world with U.S. franchises, there are some benefits to the host countries. Managing a franchise operation provides education and training that local entrepreneurs may not have other means to acquire. In the United States, we tend to have a marvelously independent, entrepreneurial outlook—it's a much observed part of the American character.

Franchising may give your business the opportunity to grow beyond the level you could otherwise achieve—and could provide important entrepreneurial opportunities to others, as well.

Franchising also offers growth via the purchase of multiple franchises. Considerable personal fortunes have been made through the operation of multiple units in a franchise operation.

How do you decide which growth strategy is right for you? Few long-range decisions are based on numbers alone. Just as important are the resources available to the business, and the characteristics and skills of key managers, as these examples show. How comfortable are you with managing at a distance? Can you delegate? How do you feel about increasing your exposure to risk? All are factors that will influence the degree and the direction of your growth.

Your Financial Plan

As the example plans in this book will show you, the financial section of the plan has something "zen" about it. There are typically the fewest words here—and yet the heart of the business is beating in these numbers. The rest of the plan could be creative smoke and mirrors. This is the section that shows you know how to make money doing it. To you, those numbers may seem like a foreign language, but to a financial audience, reading those numbers is second nature. Too often, those numbers tattle on the plan's preparers, showing faulty assumptions, inconsistent logic, and other flaws the writers thought dazzling narrative could hide.

The financial portion of the plan should, in my opinion, begin with a short narrative describing what will be presented. (Remember in chapter 4, my advice to "tell them what you're going to tell them, then tell them, then tell them what you told them.") Here, that means outlining what is included with regard to the past performance of the firm, what future projections are included, and where to find documentation of the assumptions on which those projections are based. The section should end with a description of funding requirements if lenders or investors are being sought.

Quite often, this narrative is only a paragraph or two in length, referencing appendixes where the financial statements can be found. But there's no law that says you can't place those statements here, in their logical sequence, appropriately labeled. Do what seems clearest to you—and then get a second opinion.

If you find that you are stumped when it comes to making assumptions, don't give up. Your professional or trade association will have statistics that will give you benchmarks by region, size of business, and other helpful information. William Dennis offered this example:

A man who owned a liquor store died unexpectedly. His wife was left not knowing how to run the store. It came about Christmas time, and she had this terrible problem of the inventory distribution, between fifths and pints and half-gallons and that sort of thing. She had no idea how to order. She had a heck of a time trying to find out. Finally, she joined a liquor dealers' association, where she could meet and talk with people who are in the business, and that's how she managed to survive the first year. By learning about inventory from what were, effectively, competitors.

Would information specific to your industry, available in great detail, based on the experience of your competitors, be useful to you? You bet. Go and get it.

Conclusion

The financial plan details the financial requirements and potential of the business opportunity. It presents your expected start-up costs, operating expenses, and profitability potential. If you are looking for lenders or investors, it outlines "the deal." These are the most basic reasons your business plan would be incomplete without a financial section.

There are other reasons a financial plan is crucial for you as a manager.

It helps you identify and quantify the financial requirements so that you may better allocate limited financial resources. There is never enough money to do everything without evaluating how each dollar is spent—and if there is, I'm highly suspicious of the entrepreneur who would run his or her business that way.

As a plan reviewer, I hope the financial section will show me that this business is on solid financial ground. But more important, I want it to show me that its owner(s) understand how to use financial information in both day-to-day management and long-range planning.

Thoughts to Take Away

- You will prepare projections, or pro formas, for your business's income statement, balance sheet, cash flow budget, and if you are looking for financial resources, a statement of sources and uses of funds.

- You can operate without profits, but you can't operate without cash flow. Accurately projecting when inflows and outflows will take place is critical to your success.

- Budgets are important tools in managing your business, in that they provide a means to monitor performance and to manage exceptions.

- The financial section of a business plan shows reviewers the fiscal solidity of that business. But more important, the financial section shows that the owner understands how to use financial information in both day-to-day management and long-range planning.

part**THREE**

Get Going

The next two chapters are designed to remove roadblocks. I'm here to help you get over speed bumps like procrastination or being unsure of what to do first.

My colleagues join me in sharing insights and pet peeves. We'll give you the edge you need to write a plan that gets the results you want, whether that is the support of investors and bankers, the cooperation of partners and staff, or your own better understanding of what to do and how to do it.

chapterEIGHT

The Ideal Plan

I would be joking if I told you there is one ideal format for a business plan. Each plan is as unique as the business that creates it, and each audience for a plan has unique needs of its own, as well.

Certain mechanical aspects of the "ideal" plan can be described: It will be on 8½ × 11-inch paper, cleanly typed or desktop published; it will, of course, be free of typographical errors. But beyond that, what should the ideal plan include?

Tim Baye answered, "Coffee and pizza stains. I'm not kidding. Toast crumbs. Torn cover. More sticky-notes than you can count. Dog-eared pages. That's a successful business plan—one that gets used."

I like that. Baye's answer equates the ideal with success—and that's the goal of business, as well as business planning. Your ideal plan is one that you will *use* to help your business succeed.

What Makes a Successful Business Plan

A successful business plan will have the key elements we've been talking about in the last seven chapters. It will have a well-thought-out business strategy. It will honestly evaluate a company's strengths and weaknesses. It will candidly consider external threats.

Logical consistency throughout. The ideal business plan will clearly relate its overall strategy to its plans in each area—marketing, personnel, and financial. Each area will demonstrate consistency with the overall plan.

A solid marketing plan is very important. Changes within a product's life cycle must be addressed. An assessment of the market opportunity and how it will be maximized should be included. The marketing plan must complement the business strategy, and the strengths of the business.

The personnel plan should describe an organizational management structure designed to implement the business plan. I don't care if it's the best developed business concept in the world. If the founder isn't planning to delegate authority, but is expecting to see a large amount of growth, that could be the "Achilles' heel" of the overall plan.

The financial plan should be consistent with the resources needed to implement the marketing tactics and personnel needs described in the business strategy. Its projections must be reasonable, and clearly based on the assumptions proposed throughout the plan. All areas of the plan are interrelated—and the numbers should reflect this.

You may be too close to your business concept, too emotionally invested in the hopes and fears it represents, to spot inconsistencies that may have crept into your plan as you wrote the various sections. Ask others to review it with a critical eye before you consider it "final."

The executive summary is the last section to be written because everything mentioned in it must be expanded upon elsewhere in the plan. It should capture the essence of the business concept and clearly articulate what sorts of resources are needed. If the plan is being used as a solicitation for funding, state that right at the conclusion of the executive summary.

As a writer, you would ordinarily avoid redundancy. But in a business plan, redundancy is crucially important. You're not writing a novel here. Nor are you writing an academic paper. You're writing a plan. Those who use it will have different interests at different times, yourself included. Restating a key point in more than one place simply makes the plan easier for all to use. What you have to say about your company's mission, and its business strategies, should be consistent to the point of redundancy—that makes for a well-developed plan.

Finishing touches. When your writing is complete, turn your attention to the presentation of your ideas. You are temporarily taking on the role of a publisher. A publisher employs specialists to handle the technical details of preparing a manuscript for publication. A copy editor corrects awkward language, tightens run-on sentences, reunites split verbs, and generally brings the thoughts of the author in line with standard written English. Proofreaders catch typographical errors. Layout people design the appearance of pages, with an eye to niceties like consistency in heads and subheads, labeling of charts and diagrams, and so on. A technician produces the document, placing text on pages, inserting charts and diagrams, or references to material in appendixes, where appropriate. Then a table of contents is generated, page numbers inserted (and double-checked), a title page produced, and voilà! A final document is ready for copying and distribution.

Unlike a publisher, you will probably not hire others to perform each of these steps. You or a willing friend will take the draft of the plan and create the final pages, ready for that last trip to the photocopier. Make sure the manuscript is absolutely complete as it goes into the layout process. Have you included every appendix referenced in the narrative? Are all charts and diagrams (such as floor plans or graphic representations of data) ready to go?

> **KEY CONCEPT**
>
> A winning business plan will have continuity throughout the plan. All text and financial documents will reflect the same information.

Pay attention to these finishing steps. After you've gone to all the trouble of generating the important thinking the pages contain, why risk shooting yourself in the foot with a careless mistake? If you are unsure about your ability to write standard business English, ask a friend for help. Many writers suggest reading your draft out loud. Long sentences and awkward phrasing stand out when spoken.

Ask others to proofread your pages for errors. Don't rely on spell-checkers—they cannot do the job human readers do. Don't rely on yourself—you're too familiar with the project. A fresh pair of eyes are needed for this final step.

Coffee stains and toast crumbs notwithstanding, your plan is an extension of yourself. Make it present yourself as you would like to be seen.

Tips from business plan reviewers

Knowing what plan reviewers "keep an eye out for" will help you draft the ideal plan they are looking for.

An assessment of market share, based on solid research, is a good sign. Market share is one of the more commonly used benchmarks for future planning. As business counselors, my colleagues and I see firms we've worked with for 10 or 15 years evolve from start-up concerns to ongoing businesses that regularly reassess their market opportunities. Successful entrepreneurs continually reevaluate market potential and the market they serve, making comparisons of market share between themselves and their competitors, to revise sales projections.

Projections that are too hopeful are a bad sign. They show a lack of research, which would lead to more realistic projections. Optimistic entrepreneurs underestimate the strength of the competition, or they overestimate their sales potential. The temptation is always present to underestimate cost of establishing a new business, or the time required for a start-up or a major expansion to see return on investment.

Business plan reviewers are trained to spot flaws like inadequate market research or unfounded optimism.

Show, don't tell. Many of the plans I see, especially drafts in the early stages, tend to be very argumentative. Writers should be basing their rationale for the business concept on an evaluation of the marketplace. Instead, the writers rely on "why we're going to succeed" hyperbole. Why should I accept these claims? These plans would be stronger if the narrative *showed* why the beliefs of the writer are justified rather than *told* me to believe.

Try putting yourself in the chair of the reader. Imagine you're an investment banker, and you have been taught to tear apart a business plan.

The first thing you will do is read the executive summary. Then, you'll flip to the marketing section and look for an industry analysis. You're going to see how much this plan's writers have been able to teach you about their industry.

Then, you're going to look for the competitor analysis. You're going to see whether or not these planners did a good job in evaluating the competition. Do you see evidence of solid understanding based on research? If what's in those sections shows more hot air than evidence of unmet market needs, the writers have eroded the effectiveness of the education they've laid out for you. As an investment banker, you are seeing red flags all over this plan.

As Rodney Heller of Foodusa.com told me, "It has to make sense. If you find holes in it, don't run with it. It stinks! People can smell it a mile away! Fix the holes! I had to throw my first plans completely away and start over, three or four times."

Let your people shine. As a reviewer, I want to feel as if I know the people associated with this business concept. A part of your plan should show me why you're the right person to be in this business. It doesn't have to be a 20-page curriculum vitae, but somewhere the skills you bring to the table should be described. Too many of the plans I've seen don't spend enough time on the personal

strengths of the key personnel, or how they plan to recruit the appropriate people to fill out the team.

The people behind the plan are important to several different audiences. Of course, lenders and investors want to know whom they're dealing with. But you're also likely to share portions of this business plan with future employees. In a tight labor market, the business plan is a tool to convince people that "you should work with me." Make the plan available to interview candidates ahead of time so that they can recognize your abilities, without your needing to take time in the interview to brag about your accomplishments. If your background can be succinctly put into the business plan, I think that's helpful.

The personnel section is not hard to write. It's not like doing a market analysis, or crunching out the financial projections. And yet, too often, planners forget to include adequate personal information so that reviewers form a favorable impression of them.

Include personal credibility-builders, even if you have a prior relationship with the bank or source of equity to whom you submit the plan. After all, the plan will probably be read by other people who don't know you, even if some people there know you well. Almost always, a number of people have input on the decisions that involve you.

Write a plan that positions you as a real leader, with the background, skills, and vision to make your business concept a working reality.

The plan as roadmap

Don Kuratko tells his students, "You are about to embark on a journey that is going to take you not just for a financing proposal, although it could be used for that. But you're really on a journey to a strategic plan for your business in years to come.

> ### Voices
>
> *One thing I see omitted fairly frequently is an assessment of market opportunity, and its determination of market share. While that appears to be a more daunting task than a lot of entrepreneurs are prepared to do, it is often a really valuable experience.*
>
> —Tim Baye

The plan is there to be your guidepost and roadmap, and that's the most powerful thing you can have."

The plan has to be as honest and as straightforward as you can possibly make it because if you do it with smoke and mirrors, the only person you're hurting is yourself.

Kuratko went on to say, "If you were drawing a map for a good friend to come see you at your house, would you draw that map with frivolous streets and houses that didn't exist? No. You would show them the most direct route, as accurately as you could, because you want them to arrive." Remember, when you're writing your business plan, you are drawing the roadmap and you want it to be as accurate as possible. You don't need fluff in there—you need a set of instructions to navigate by.

Take a moment to imagine you're a business plan reviewer, and browse the business plans I've included. Do you see the strengths you hope to find? Look for:

- Strategies that appear rational and achievable
- Sound profitability and growth projections, formatted as bankers are used to seeing them
- Sound competitive analysis
- A sound marketing plan, based on thorough research

Form Your Advisory Board Now

Flip through any book on business planning, and you'll almost certainly find a recommendation to form a group of advisors (usually consisting of three to five people). Most small businesses don't have a formal board of directors (the liability insurance is too expensive), but most could benefit from the kind of oversight and advice a board of directors is designed to give. Even if you're incorporated and have a board of directors, an advisory board is different.

A good advisory board can be drawn from many sources. You could ask people in similar businesses to join your board, or solicit members from entirely different industries. Potential members can be academics or bankers or business consultants. Who should they *not* be? Your accountant, your attorney, your lawyer, or your banker. These are people you are paying. You'll get their advice no matter what.

**KEY CONCEPT:
THE PLAN RECRUITS THE PEOPLE**

The business plan can be an important tool in recruiting future employees. In a tight labor market, your business plan can be used to convince people to join your team. Make the plan available to candidates ahead of time, so they fully understand the professional opportunity your business offers when they come to the job interview.

You want an outside group that will take a fresh look at your business. You're building a group of individuals you like and respect who can give you advice on management. George Solomon suggested the following:

This group should be made up of people who are neither friends nor family. They should be diverse, and have skills or knowledge that will help that business start or grow. You might find the senior business loan officer at a bank has a broad-based set of knowledge. You might find the university professor who's not just a finance professor, but has consulted, or has worked in the field with emerging and growing businesses. You might find someone in your industry who you respect, and who doesn't feel threatened by your starting a business. That person can tell you about all the potholes and traps you'll be coming against. You might find someone who is a successful entrepreneur in a different industry, who's cognizant of the process of growing businesses successfully.

Your advisory group becomes an important part of your business network. They are a productive source of contacts, suppliers, and customers.

It can be frightening to open the inner workings of your business to the critical gaze of outsiders. Most likely you've carefully protected your trade secrets, financial performance, and internal problems from public knowledge. It feels like giving up a degree of control when you invite others into the mix—after all, you might have to do what they say!

Frank Hoy shared his perspective:

Research has shown, and my own personal observation dealing with successful people has emphasized to me, that the successes are people who seek advice from experts, and follow that advice. One of my professors did a study, way back, and looked at the relative success of business owners. It was a bunch of case studies, lots of lengthy interviews, but in reading through those, it just leaps out at you that the successful ones were going for advice to attorneys, accountants, bankers, belonging to professional associations, subscribing to and reading business magazines, belonging to the chamber of commerce. Those that were less successful or were failures, might solicit advice from their brother-in-law the dentist, from someone they're standing next to at the bus stop—the kind of people who don't know enough about their business to be able to challenge what the business owner already wanted to do. So when the business owner said "I've got this in mind, what do you think?" their first reaction was likely to be "sounds good to me." The reinforcement was there. If they disagree, if they said, "I don't think that's a good idea," the business owner could say, "Well what do you know? You don't know anything about my business." The key success factor is being open to information from experts, and then applying what you're hearing and learning.

An advisory board can be your eyes and ears out in the world; the board can be valuable in looking at your house and seeing where the dust is, so to speak. They see what you don't see because you live there. But when they point out a problem, you'd better be prepared to do something about it.

Advisory board agenda. I recommend you assemble your advisory board for a working meeting approximately four times a year. To keep the board running smoothly, adopt simple rules and follow them. Have an agenda for each meeting, and distribute it a few days before the meeting, so participants have an opportunity to do some deep thinking before you gather. Feel free to contact these people for advice between group meetings. A lively exchange of e-mails or phone calls between meetings can help you navigate challenges as they arise.

Each time you meet, begin by pulling out calendars and scheduling future meetings. Start and end each meeting on time; confirm at the start the schedule for the meeting, and ask anyone who must leave early to announce that, so later disruptions are minimal and expectations are clear.

At your first meeting, allow time for thorough introductions of each board member. Give people a chance to get to know each other. Then at subsequent meetings, encourage members to sit in different locations each time you meet. All members should feel a comfortable rapport with everyone in the room.

I suggest three to five people be on your board with you, and that you form it early on. Terms can be a year or two years. Bring new members in on a regular basis, so you're constantly getting fresh ideas.

In forming your team, don't hesitate to ask anyone you think could help you. In most cases, people are flattered to be asked, and you'd be surprised how readily high-powered businesspeople give of their time. There's a natural "esprit de corps" among entrepreneurs that makes the company of like-minded individuals welcome. Once you get the first advisory board member, ask that member, "Who else do you think would work well on this board?" Look for people who have been through similar experiences, or who can bring clients in, or who can bring sources for suppliers. The critical element is you must be able to accept their advice. If you are not temperamentally equipped to take advice, don't waste their time.

Don't feel you need to offer a lot of money to compensate board members. Sometimes you take them out to breakfast for your meetings. Then, as you get a little more prosperous, you take them to lunch. If you grow, then money is appropriate. No one on an advisory board for a start-up expects to be paid or to get stock options. Everybody learns by looking at your business. Many business owners are looking for ways to improve their own businesses, too. A true conversation and dialogue makes a difference.

A well-functioning advisory board can make all the difference in the success of a business.

Voices

You're not just building a business plan to seek funding or get started. You're building a strategic roadmap for your business in years to come. It's a living, dynamic document that you can go back to year after year. It will be adjusted and changed, based on the realities of the marketplace, but it's a great document to work from.

—Don Kuratko

Don Kuratko observed, "For family firms, a quasi-board to help look at things is so important. The outside voices, ears, and eyes, who have been in business and been in support roles, give family members a different perspective and pulls you out of the tunnel vision we all get into. That's extremely important."

More is better: BizCopy advisory groups. In the BizCopy business plan, two advisor groups are described: an Advisory Board and a Map Group. How are they different? The Advisory Board consists of the business's paid advisors—accountant, attorney, and banker—as well as three owners from similar copy and print firms in other cities. This board meets biannually.

On the other hand, the Map Group meets monthly. Each participant hosts the meeting twice a year to discuss whatever participants have asked to be on the agenda. This group consists entirely of business owners chosen from long-standing customers of BizCopy.

BizCopy's business plan was developed to help the owners make a critical decision shaping the growth of their firm, in the midst of intense competitive forces. There is no room for missteps in the quick-printing business—too many competitors exist, ready to take advantage of any mistakes, and technology has increased customers' ability to serve their own needs internally, further eroding potential market share.

Reading this plan, I see the hand of good advisors at work. This plan's writers have clearly articulated alternative courses of action. Statements of goals and objectives are detailed in three areas: customer-based goals, employee-based goals, and financial-based goals. Accompanying the goals are necessary steps and quantitative benchmarks. As a reviewer, I rarely see evidence of such thorough planning. You can imagine the amount of coffee and doughnuts consumed as these issues were tossed around in advisor group meetings.

A survey of quick-print customers was conducted in the course of preparing this plan. The survey helped the business's owners to assess customers' concepts of value, as well as to determine BizCopy's share of the Corporate Valley market for quick-print services. Again, I think I see the wise counsel of advisory groups in deciding what questions should be asked.

KEY CONCEPT

Take a look at your personal strengths and weaknesses. Include on your advisory board people who can mentor you in the areas where you are weakest.

I like the term *Map Group* as BizCopy has used it. If your business plan is a roadmap, why not rely on a map group to help you draw your map?

I've served on several advisory boards. I never fail to learn from the experience. I've seen advisory boards make the difference between a business's success and failure. They are an incredible extension of your network. Don't be afraid to ask for their help.

Business Associations

A source of solid advice is available to you, via professional and trade associations. These organizations bring together people who have interests and purposes in common. They are becoming more important than ever, as a means for learning to take place and relationships to develop. As the Internet allows us to connect with one another so much more readily, we are starting to form communities of interest, and professional organizations help foster this. Your membership in a professional or trade association is your passport to an extended network of people who share similar concerns and interests, and a storehouse of information, both statistical and anecdotal, about your industry and business in general.

There are three general categories of associations, and I'd suggest you explore each. The first is the industry association—national or international member organizations specific to industrial classifications, such as the National Screenprinters' Association or the National Association of Realtors. These organizations draw on their members' shared interests in that business niche. They provide in-depth research, the results of which are available to members, and also organize trade shows and conferences.

The second category is local business associations, such as your chamber of commerce. These organizations draw on shared interests as inhabitants of the same geographic region. They operate on several levels, providing opportunities for members to form business relationships and to address local political issues with a powerful unified voice.

The third category is national associations based on shared business interests, such as the National Federation of Independent Businesses (NFIB) or the National Association of Women Business Owners (NAWBO). These organizations help members master skills, access information about trends, and influence governmental policy.

All three types of associations do a lot for their members, and membership in one of each may be justified for you. Many associations publish newsletters or magazines, and maintain Web sites, where valuable information can be found. New business owners should not only join, but take advantage of the research and opportunities to network that these organizations provide.

Bob Brockhaus emphasized the importance of trade association membership:

If you're getting ready to write a plan—especially for a new business—there's a wealth of information trade associations can provide that will help you understand your competition, help you understand government regulations that affect you, especially those that are perhaps pending (in a positive or negative sense) on your industry.

With all you need to know, or spot on the horizon, your trade association or professional organization is a valuable "silent partner" in your business.

What Makes a Successful Entrepreneur

As I interviewed my colleagues for this book, I asked each to describe the success factors he or she had found among entrepreneurs whose businesses flourished. Their comments fell into several categories that coincided with business success. These traits include an ability to control costs; to focus on what is important amid competing demands; to know which trends to consider important and which to ignore; an awareness of the importance of lifelong learning; and an awareness of the importance of technology.

To these observations I add my own postscript about family business. Family business owners face an even more challenging internal business environment, and successful entrepreneurial families show additional success traits, including the ability to communicate well and to juggle the multiple roles in which they function.

Success factor: controlling costs

From the book *The Millionaire Next Door,* William Dennis drew some insights:

Most of it was based on empirical interviews. One of the things that stuck with me had to do with cost. The people who got wealthy—and most of those who got really wealthy owned their own businesses—did it, they said, not by sales but by controlling cost. The book went on to make the point that one of the reasons lawyers look so wealthy, and frequently are so poor, is that they are forced to make expenditures that other business owners wouldn't, just to maintain the trappings of a lawyer. You have to have a nice suit. You have to have a nice office. And so on. That's the price of admission. That's your investment in the business. If you don't do that, no one's going to take you seriously. And yet, those costs are exactly the kind of thing that, if you don't control them, keep you from being successful.

It is important to know what to cut. One business owner I counseled parked her rusted-out van with the name of the business painted across it in front of her business. It said to me "this business isn't making it." I'm not suggesting you do what my plumber did when he came to give an estimate in a new Corvette—that says I'm paying too much—but find a happy medium. Spend what you must to get the job done, and project the appropriate image—but not a penny more.

Voices

A common mistake is lack of focus. I do a lot of work in technology-based companies. I see an engineer or a scientist get a technology developed and rather than go into niche markets to apply it, they fall in love with their technology, so much they believe they can do everything for everybody. They don't focus enough.

—Dale Meyer

Controlling costs is like dieting. The hard work comes in knowing when to say no and what to say it to. Successful entrepreneurs regularly examine the cost centers in their financial statements, looking for "fat" to trim. Knowing where your costs are running high compared to industry averages can be tremendously helpful. The BizCopy business plan contains an excellent comparison of financial ratios, BizCopy versus industry averages, allowing the owners to see that although their gross profit margin is higher than industry averages, their net profit margin is several points lower than average. This gives them a clear indication where to begin controlling costs.

Success factor: focus

So many entrepreneurs feel as if they spend their days responding to outside demands, never accomplishing the things they meant to get to. Those who find the ability to focus amid the chaos report greater satisfaction, and show by their performance that they're onto something good.

Michael Meeks said:

I believe very strongly in the "80/20 rule." I believe that the successful business owners are the ones who know exactly what 20 percent to focus on. Because of that they are most effective and most efficient. They focus on the 20 percent of their business that generates 80 percent of the profits. They keep their eyes on what's important in their business. If the Internet is one of those things, then they need to pursue that. If not, if a Web page and technology are part of that 80 percent, then they're losing sight of what they really need to focus on. They won't be as successful.

Terri Lonier agreed. "An ingredient that helps business owners succeed is a sense of focus—they really have an understanding of who they are, what they can bring to the marketplace, and what service or product they can uniquely fulfill."

Bob Brockhaus added his vote for focus:

Look for ways to be innovative and creative in the way you run your operation. The ways to make it more efficient, so you can save a few dollars here, which will be a few dollars to your bottom line when it's all said and done. Look for ways to motivate workforce, to reduce material waste, to deliver the product more efficiently. Looking at those can be

---

> ### KEY CONCEPT
> The "ideal" business plan is written by the "ideal" business leader—one who seeks input from a panel of experts.

beneficial. All too often, they end up focusing on the day-to-day fires that need to be put out, and not looking at opportunities that save them money or increase sales or prepare their product or service for its next generation.

Focus is very important, but don't go so far that you put all of your eggs in one basket when it comes to clients or customers. Even those of us who teach this aren't necessarily listened to. My sister is a graphic designer with her own business. She has one client—a big one. Even with my repeated encouragement to broaden her base, she still has only one client. If that client goes elsewhere, she will have to start her business all over again—or close her doors.

Success factor: trend wisdom

To succeed, learn to sense which trends affect you, and which don't. Says David Zach:

This is an interesting answer to come from a futurist, but I see people paying too much attention to trends. We have become seduced by the importance of trends. It is incredibly important, for anybody who wants their success to last, to find and embrace the things that don't have to change. Think about your own business, think about the industry in which it exists, think about your community, think about your family. Think about your people, your race, your culture. Try to identify what are the things about that group or institution that doesn't have to change over time. Pay attention to trying to figure out what will last, what is wisdom . . . . If you ask the average person in business if they paid attention to the news today, 90 percent will say yes. If you ask them how many tried to find the old—did they pay attention to anything that is helping them understand a sense of what is eternal—very few of them will have done that.

Which change is progress? Most trends are unimportant to you—before you've noticed them, they're gone. You're not going to make a lot of money paying attention to those trends. We've become intimidated, whether we're being driven by the media, or our peers, to feel that we have to know all about every trend. Some trends are vitally important to you; others are not. Successful entrepreneurs learn to find and follow the critical trends.

Bob Brockhaus cautioned, "a success factor is really staying on top of the industry trends. Are you watching where your industry is headed? Are you trying to get right up near the front of that wave, and not so far behind?"

Success factor: plans for staff and self-development

In chapter 6, I emphasized the importance of lifelong learning in keeping good people working for you. In my informal survey of success factors among entrepreneurs, I was often reminded of this. Continued education and skill building are important, for both you and your staff.

Not so long ago, we associated learning with schools, and regarded work as the end of learning. That way of thinking is history. Work and learning should be blended throughout our lives.

In this increasingly knowledge-based economy, continuous learning is important in keeping our organizations at the cutting edge. We rely heavily on our employees' knowledge to provide our products or services to customers. We rely on staff to confidently make appropriate decisions, at the lowest possible level, so that the organization's time is spent efficiently. That takes training.

Terri Lonier observed, "I think entrepreneurs are lifelong learners. They are curious, and they know that every single day they can learn something else." You will experience more financial success, and more personal satisfaction, if you continue to augment the skills and knowledge that your job calls for. The people who work for you will also find skills and knowledge to be assets worth working for. Whether your organization consists of five people or 50, you need to include learning in your plans.

Success factor: plans for technology

Every business today finds itself coming to grips with technology. Whether that grip resembles an embrace or a wrestling match depends on the entrepreneur.

In chapter 4's discussion of vision and mission statements, and particularly in Worksheet 4.2, I asked you to think about your commitment to technology. Technology fits each business in a particular way. You may need to master specific technologies for your production processes, or for customer service, or simply to manage your business more efficiently.

Terry Lonier observed that even for a SOHO business, technology is vital:

These days there's a need for an understanding of technology. It doesn't have to be at the level of understanding how all the wiring happens. It's an understanding of what technology can do, and leveraging that technology. Because, for very small businesses, SOHOs, time is their most valuable asset. The way to leverage time best is through the appropriate use of technology.

Hattie Bryant related her own experience integrating technology into the operation of her public television program:

If Bruce were not a part of this company, we would not be in business anymore. Bruce has an extraordinary technology background, and put us on the Internet in 1994. If you add that up in Web time, where three months equals a year, we've been on the Web for 23 years. We're streaming video right now. You can go to our Web site and watch four episodes of Small Business 2000.

Success factors for family business

"In family business, it's a team. Team building and communication become important in a family business concept," said Bob Brockhaus. I agree. Interpersonal skills are taxed to their limit when business and family mix. Certain life skills, like expressing emotions constructively, and time management, help a family weather the conflicts their business produces. Communication is essential. So is delegation. The business will require family members to wear different hats, and juggling those multiple roles is demanding.

This demanding act becomes a little easier if your family has a sense of mission, a shared base of underlying principles that guide you in your business decisions. You could, as a family, make a conscious effort to create a mission statement, following the suggestions given in chapter 4. Or you could place your emphasis on improving family members' skill in listening, and sharing information. Over time, a sense of family mission will result.

Listening well is a skill. Too often, when we seem to be listening, we're actually busy forming our responses. We fail to take in what others are saying. Each family member needs to learn to put internal voices on hold when another family member speaks up. Old family scripts, like *Father Knows Best,* can come back to haunt the family that goes into business together. Make sure your family listens to Mother, and Brother and Sister, and Cousin, too.

Sharing information well is also a skill. The ability to share ideas in a clear, concise understandable way doesn't come without practice. When all the "baggage" of family is carried into the business sphere, sharing vital information can be difficult. During difficult times, I've seen too many business owners clam up because they "don't want to let the family down." By doing so, they cut themselves off from an important source of moral support, and hoard information that others have a legitimate need to know.

During boom times, you may find yourself hesitant to share the good news because you fear some family members "may not be able to handle it." You have visions of a family shopping spree that siphons away hard-earned profits that should be reinvested in the business. If you feel that way, ask yourself, do I trust my business partners? Because that's what your family members are, even if they're not partners in the legal sense. If you cannot answer "yes, I trust them," the next question is clear: Why are you in business with people you do not trust? Successful family businesses learn how, as a family, to work through communication issues like these.

As a family and as a business, you're going to need a clear vision and mission. You must all be able to answer "where are we going?" and "how do we plan to get there?" The business's leaders should have a definite plan to delegate, thereby increasing others' spheres of responsibilities. Clarity around roles and responsibilities must happen early on for there to be a smooth transition to successors.

A family business can be rewarding on many levels—if the family is up to the challenge. Business plan reviewers will need to understand how your family interacts, where its strengths and weakness-

> **KEY CONCEPT:**
> **BUSINESS ASSOCIATIONS**
> **ARE A VALUABLE ASSET**
>
> There are three general categories of associations: industry associations, local business associations, and national associations based on shared interests. With all you need to know, your memberships in business associations are a valuable asset.

es lie, and how, as a family, you plan to work together for your success.

Conclusion

The ideal plan will, ideally, be accompanied by an ideal presentation in person by the business owner. In chapter 7, I related Rodney Heller's experience presenting his Foodusa.com business plan to venture capitalists, who were impressed enough with his combination of solid planning and energetic personal style to lend him several million dollars.

I really want to stress positive mental attitude (PMA). You need to recognize the negative possibilities that could take place, but as the example of Foodusa.com shows, a really strong positive attitude makes a difference. You need to be aware of your own personality, and how to leverage your best characteristics to make everything come together.

It's important to believe in what you can do. If you believe you *can't,* you're making sure you *won't.* Your dominant belief has to be that you *can* do it. The plan and the planner must both project confidence. You have to feel it, and you have to get it across in the writing of the plan, and in the presenting of it to others.

In all of your dealings with people who must believe in you, from lenders to employees, wear your confidence like a designer jacket. Even if you're not feeling particularly successful, think of yourself as an actor with a role to play. This role calls for confidence and enthusiasm. You will be dynamic when speaking, focused when listening. Come in dressed for the part—conservative or creative, as the role demands.

Terri Lonier shared her belief:

Entrepreneurship is one of the most creative things that you can do with your life these days. People ask me, "How did you go from being an artist to being an entrepreneur?" I explain that I think of it much in the same light. An artist starts with this blank canvas, and all these ideas, and paints the canvas and hangs it on the wall and gets feedback. Entrepreneurs start with a blank canvas called the World, and take their ideas and refine them and instead of some art critic, the public comes and votes with their wallets and credit cards. That is the feedback.

As an artist facing the canvas of the World, paint in bold strokes.

My colleagues and I sometimes use the acronym BAGs, or Big Audacious Goals. Some BAGs were included in the brochure summary of the business plan for Farm Credit Services (FCS). "They're so bold, they make you gulp," their brochure states.

> **KEY CONCEPT:**
> **A SENSE OF MISSION IS**
> **CRITICAL IN FAMILY BUSINESS**
>
> A family is better prepared to weather the conflicts of business if it has created a shared sense of mission. As a family, make a conscious effort to create a mission statement describing where you want to go and how you plan to get there.

Farm Credit Service BAGs include increasing outstanding loan volume by 200 percent and increasing financial services income by 500 percent. They set a goal of becoming a "household name" and the "largest financial services provider" in the region in just eight years' time.

Thoughts to Take Away

- Successful business plans tend to demonstrate logical consistency throughout, rely on solid research and thinking rather than empty hyperbole, and emphasize the skills and strengths of the people behind the plan.

- Successful entrepreneurs seek insights and information from outsiders, recruiting advisory boards and joining business associations.

- Successful business owners learn to control costs, to focus on what is important, to encourage continual learning, and to integrate technology, among other success factors.

chapterNINE

Get Going

WHAT YOU WILL FIND IN THIS CHAPTER

- What drives the strategic objectives and financial projections of a well-developed business plan

- How to put an end to procrastination
- What character traits will support you in your success

Get going. Now. You are ready to prepare a plan for your business and to put it in writing.

Not so sure? Try doing what I just did—revisit the preceding eight chapters of this book, reading only the "Thoughts to Take Away" at the end of each chapter. As I did so, I felt a rising sense of anticipation. I believe that with these observations, techniques, and guidelines, a successful business plan—and a successful career as an entrepreneur—can be created by anyone who takes the time to master them. It's just a matter of developing your vision, then narrowing your focus.

When I coach clients through a business planning process, I like to compare it to passing through a funnel. They come with a very wide idea, and I help them narrow it down. Sometimes you have to say, "what am I *not* going to do?" in order to get a business concept to work.

The plan needs priorities. You need to think through "what do I do first?" and also, "what do I get rid of?" Drop the parts of the plan that aren't central to the operation, and seem likely to present headaches. For example, if you're planning to start a restaurant, you might decide not to include plans for home delivery at the start. Save that for the next phase, after you've mastered getting food from kitchen to table.

Look at your plans and think, "where can I narrow my focus?" Otherwise you are likely to find yourself spinning between priorities, not making real progress on any front. There's got to be time to do what needs to be done. Know what are the important priorities for you.

Hattie Bryant offered a piece of advice that might help you find your priorities:

The successful business owners' secret is that they love the "stuff" of what they do. Their definition of "stuff" may be subterranean. For example, the Graber people make bike racks to carry your bike someplace. They personally are not big bikers. It's not that they love the "stuff" of biking. If you dig down deep, though, they love "made in America." They love making a product that people appreciate. Small business owners who succeed over the long haul find something fabulous in their business to fall in love with. It could be the customers, the employees, the product, the processes. It could be just being able to say "I own a business." But they're in love. It's not work. Everybody's got huge problems. They've got crap they hate to deal with. But the "stuff" they love is bigger. It overrides.

Knowing what "stuff" you love in your business will help you find your priorities.

The planning process revisited

The business plan is the presentation of an argument, as well as an outline for your success. You analyze the business segment that you're in, taking a look at your history, at your external influences—your customers, competition, and industry. By deciding what to say no to, and where you will focus, you narrow the possibilities down to a business opportunity that you can pursue. With a start-up, it may be fairly lengthy list of strategic actions. With an existing business, it may be simpler—maintaining current product lines or service lines, or possibly adding one or two, or a plan to focus on reducing costs and building a more efficient operation.

The plan should present a linear argument, explaining what market opportunities you have chosen, and why. Then, after that argument is made, you're basically putting a plan of action together. You are saying, "These are the tactics we're going to be using, the resources that we need, and this is our financial expectation."

The argument creates the assumptions on which financial projections are based. Overall expectations are cast as annual projections, or quarterly projections, or even monthly projections. What are the nuances of comparable businesses in the industry? What might you expect in terms of seasonal effects on your revenue? Review the budget, and start looking at cash flow, specifically ending cash balances projected for each month.

By going through this process, you've accomplished two things: As a businessperson, you have a much better understanding of what your opportunities are, what strategies you need to pursue, how to implement those strategies, and what the financial implications are.

On top of that, you are able to communicate your financing needs to the outside world, in terms that relate to your business operations. At that point, you're able to take that information and go to financial institutions, in search of either equity or commercial debt, and present a plan.

That's the gist of the planning process—the trip through the narrow end of the funnel.

The writing process revisited

Every time you pick up a pencil or tap words on a keyboard, you're visualizing a reader for those words. If it's a note to a loved one, you don't leave out the "love ya" at the bottom, or you'll give the impression that you're angry. If you're writing a memo for your stuffy old banker, you don't leave out the "Dear Sir," because you know that's what he

expects to see. Like these simpler writing tasks, writing a business plan requires choosing an audience. Start by writing the version of the plan that is addressed to yourself. This first draft is a full and brutally honest version, for your eyes only. Subsequent drafts will be customized to specific audiences. For each version you produce, know your audience, and tailor what you say to what they should know or what they will be interested in.

An outline for the typical business plan has been included in chapters 4 through 9, as we discussed the executive summary, the business description, and plans for the marketing, personnel, and financial functions. A slightly different generic business plan outline that I have used in my counseling is included in appendix C.

Many writers find having an outline helps them start writing. But for many of us, procrastination is still a problem. Filling out Worksheet 9.1 may be just what you need to get you started.

Get Going!

Everybody procrastinates, and some procrastination is good. Sometimes, you're procrastinating on tasks that you shouldn't be doing in the first place. When the tasks seem overwhelming or unpleasant, or leading to unwanted consequences, you really need to think about why you are doing this. It may be that your gut is warning you to hold off for good reason.

Then there's the other type of procrastination—putting off something so vital that every day you delay is costing you in terms of opportunities lost. In my experience, figuring out how to *start* a difficult task is

Voices

Typically, business plans have two audiences. One is internal. The other external. The external tends to be financial. The plan is going to be used as a tool to raise equity, or to raise debt. And in this day and age, it's becoming more of a tool in strategic partnerships, mergers, and joint ventures.

—Tim Baye

usually the sticking point. Once started, it is relatively easy to get in the right frame of mind to continue.

With that in mind, I offer the following suggestions for getting going on your business plan. For each section you need to write, I will propose one task that, if you spent an hour or two on it, would get you off the proverbial dime.

An hour or two spent following these suggestions will get you off to a good start, but will not get you to a completed business plan. That process can take anywhere from 30 to 300 hours, depending on how much thought you're putting in and how complex your business is. An old Chinese proverb says, "A journey of a thousand miles starts with a single step." Consider these suggestions advice for putting on your running shoes.

Get going: front matter

You don't have to start by facing a blank page. I hope you've been working on your business plan as you've been reading this book, filling in the worksheets, and writing notes toward your own first draft. Now, take yourself to a pleasant location—your front porch or favorite coffee shop. Spend an hour or two reviewing the business descriptions in the plans included in this book, then go back and review your worksheets for chapter 4. Your business description, your vision statement, and your mission statement should not be difficult to write when you have examined the examples of others' business plans and completed chapter 4's worksheets for your own business.

Get going: marketing

The marketing function is so important to your business plan, it's hard for me to make just one suggestion to help you get started. So I'll give you two: one for start-up businesses, and one for ongoing businesses.

Start-up entrepreneurs. You're going to like this one, but it's going to take more than an hour. My advice to you: Get out of town. Go to a different city and talk to somebody who is in a business similar to the one you are planning to start. Call in advance, and explain that you are researching your idea. Visit their business during its hours of opera-

tion. Then take the owners out to dinner. People love an opportunity to talk about their businesses. They won't shut up—and they may even open their books to you. If you were planning a vacation, you would talk to people who'd visited your dream destination. This works on the same principle. It's a great way to find out more before you go.

Ongoing business owners. Try your hand at "story selling." Set aside an hour at a time of day when you tend to feel creative. Your goal is to uncover the great sales stories within your business, to guide you to the benefits most valued by your customers. The result will help you to be a better marketer and to write a better marketing plan.

Sit down with a pad of paper or a tape recorder, and tell a story about a customer and a sale you've made. Think of an outstanding success that didn't come easy. Be sure to include the difficulties along the way—reluctance you had to overcome, false steps, bad experiences you had to live down. Great stories have dramatic ups and downs. Now review what you've written. What compelled that customer to buy? What was it about your product, or your pitch, that gave this story a happy ending? Use those insights to strengthen your understanding of your customers and your selling process.

Get going: personnel

I can't stress enough the importance of people to the success of an enterprise. Many entrepreneurs find the "people" aspect of business one of the least attractive parts of management. Why? In part, because entrepreneurs tend to be very task-oriented, driven people. They're good at a lot of things, but often the skills of motivating and managing

Voices

One of the great strengths of an entrepreneur, which is also a weakness, is that they're highly motivated. They're so highly motivated that they don't want to take the time to plan. They just want to get into business and get it going. That's very risky to do.

—George Solomon

people are not high on that list. If it were, all the entrepreneurs would be happily employed as midlevel managers in large corporations, and nobody would be out there starting new businesses.

Where would an hour or two be best spent to get you going on personnel? I suggest you contact your professional or trade association, and explore their resources. You may find template job descriptions relevant to your operation. You may find salary surveys, giving you valuable real-world benchmarks. You may find upcoming events, such as seminars, workshops, or round-table discussions, that would help you improve your skills in this area.

Armed with information from your industry peers, you will find it easier to take the next steps—revisiting the worksheets for chapter 6, and starting to write your personnel plan.

Get going: financial

Venture capitalists told the Wisconsin Department of Commerce that the single most important factor in attracting their attention is the business plan. A soundly conceived and well-prepared financial section is obviously crucial to anyone seeking to secure investors or lenders.

There, that's enough pressure to keep anyone from starting! So let's find a way you can spend an hour that cuts this crucial task back down to a manageable size.

Three ideas come to mind. In chapter 4, Rodney Heller revealed that for him, preparing financial projections was easy once he found someone who knew standard ratios for his industry. "I've got a friend who's an accountant, and I sat down with him for an hour or two, and I said, 'How can I do this?' and he said, 'This is how I do it,'" said Heller. I suggest that, like Heller, you find a knowledgeable financial person and let him or her be your teacher.

Second, I suggest you make the first phone call, as Tim Baye described in chapter 7, to help you assess the market potential for your business. In an informational interview, you ask a potential client about the vendors they use, how much they buy from them, what they wish those vendors did differently or better. Baye suggests that, through a sufficient number of these phone calls, you will develop a good "feel" for your industry, your market-

place, and your share of the market. The full survey will take you more than an hour—he suggests you talk to three or four times the number of customers you hope to serve in a year—but in the first hour you spend on this task, you will learn a great deal.

And finally, try something so clerical it's no challenge at all. Prepare the formats for your financial projections. Review chapter 7's Worksheets 7.1 through 7.4, and decide whether you will use spreadsheet software or (ugh) pencil and graph paper for this task. Use any software that will perform calculations on rows and columns of numbers. Sophisticated chart-making capability may help you visualize your data, but it is not essential to the task. Spend one hour setting up the files in which you will enter your projections.

Any or all of these tips will help you write the financial section of your plan.

Final Touches

The final touches to your plan, including the all-important executive summary, are the last to come together. When you're ready for this stage, spend an hour preparing to write the executive summary. Print out every section of the plan you've written, and sit down with a highlighter and read through the draft. Highlight each statement that introduces or summarizes an argument, makes clear an assumption, or declares an intention to take a specific action. Write a first draft of the executive summary using these highlighted comments. Don't worry about making the wording flow—just get the thoughts on a page, in the same sequence they are presented in the plan. Further work sessions, revising and removing excess verbiage, will hone this into an effective executive summary.

The process of creating a business plan requires an investment of time. Some of my clients have reported spending as few as 30 hours, or as many as 300 hours, on the task. More is not necessarily better, but too little is definitely not enough. The quality of your thinking, the facts revealed by your research, the depth of your analysis, are all the result of the time you've invested. A complex business concept will take longer to think about and to write about. If a business has multiple owners, or key managers responsible for different functional areas, the business plan will be the result of a collaborative process. The management team must work together until all agree on the assumptions on which the plan is based—and that takes time.

The suggestions here, representing an hour or two spent on each area of the plan, are intended to give you a place to start. Work on the plan until you've worked out the flaws. Set aside time every week for this process until you're done.

Solicit Second Opinions

While you are writing your plan, share it with people all along the way. Talk to people who can help you honestly evaluate yourself, your attitudes and resources. Worksheet 9.1, "Self-Evaluation for Prospective Entrepreneurs," is a tool to help you. Answer as honestly as you can. If there are a number of areas where you rate yourself as No/Not Sure, ask another person to rate you as well. Others may see strengths and weaknesses that you yourself are unaware of. With their help, you'll learn where you need to strengthen your skills or re-evaluate your plans.

Some entrepreneurs gain additional experience by working for others in the industry. Others bring a partner into the business whose strengths balance

their weaknesses. But first, you must be aware of your weaknesses if you are to take corrective steps.

Parting Shots from My Colleagues

Throughout this book, I've been describing a unique game in which failure is often essential to success, and focus must be balanced with vision. I've saved a few of my favorite "bon mots" from my conversations with colleagues, to help you prepare for the challenge.

"Fail often and fail fast, because if you're not failing, you're not trying, " advised Fred Kiesner. "You're not stretching. The idea of safety in the future is totally going to change. Careers come and go very fast. Businesses, too. Nothing is safe anymore. But there is still enormous potential."

Don Kuratko observed, "The more flexible you are—I find those are the survivors. Adapt with and against your competition. Adapt to new technologies, new innovations, changes in the field. Adaptability is incredibly important."

David Zach shared this insight:

We always talk about managing our time better. But the real scarce resource is attention. Time is a linear concept, and attention is a nonlinear concept. While you are reading this book, you are noticing everything . . . the temperature of the environment you're sitting in, surrounding noises, other conversations. We can pay attention to a lot of different things at varying levels, at the same time. There is some research to suggest, in terms of gender differences, that men may be better at understanding the concept of linear time management. Women may be better at managing attention, doing a bunch of

---

Voices

When I teach the course for bankers, called "How to Read a Business Plan," I teach them to work backward from the sales estimate, to go back through the market analysis and identify how much market share, and how much market potential is available for this client.

—Tim Baye

things, coordinating them at the same time. That may be a very valuable advantage women have as entrepreneurs.

Brave enough to fail, flexible enough to try again, skilled in managing multiple priorities—that's you. You need to be the "Little Engine That Could," repeating the mantra, "I think I can. I think I can." I wear a watch with a little train on its face, to remind me "I can."

Conclusions

Writing a plan is not enough. You've got to move on it, to take action. Plan, write, line up the resources, then go. No holding back.

Don't let procrastination keep you from planning. Don't let planning keep you from acting—that's another form of procrastination.

Truly, in the planning stage, you need to gather support—support from your friends, from people whom you're currently working with. Announce that you're going to do it. Announcing something is really important. I get up in front of a group and I announce, "I'm going to lose 15 pounds." If you tell 300 people, you're much more likely to do it than if it's a secret.

Schedule this work—if you're a person who responds to schedules. Put it on a calendar. Put down dates by which you're going to have sections completed.

And design a reward system. When you finish a section, or finish a worksheet, think about something you love to do, and reward yourself. Stop waiting for the right time. There is no perfect time. Just start doing it. That's how this book got written.

Thoughts to Take Away

- The plan should present a linear argument, from which are drawn the assumptions on which strategic objectives and financial projections are based.

- Put an end to procrastination by spending one hour on a specific subtask that gets you started on the planning process.

- Be brave enough to fail, flexible enough to try again, and develop your skills in managing multiple priorities. Success will follow.

part**FOUR**

Real-World Business Plans

Gathered here are seven business plans and graphics (complete with grammar glitches and typos) prepared by real-world businesses facing real-world problems and opportunities. Most are reproduced in their entirety, just as they were presented to my colleagues and me.

Each plan reflects the approach of an individual or group of individuals to the challenges of planning, starting, and growing a business. Each plan has something to impart about business planning—and about preparing written plans for review.

Now it's your turn to be a business plan reviewer. Study the plans that follow.

business**PLAN**

Artful Fly

Presented to:

Applicants:

Tom Fisher, Jane Angler

Date:

Baye Introduction

In many ways, this is a classic story of a business start-up.

Three people, two of which are married to each other, discussing their collective love of a hobby decide to pursue this passion into the commercial arena. All three have "failed" in previous entrepreneurship efforts before. All three have dubious credit histories. All three are bright, inquisitive, excited about their business concept and willing to (initially) work hard to acquire the resources required to launch.

The three principals had varying backgrounds. One was a lawyer, who for some reason wouldn't/couldn't practice law anymore. One was a professor, who at the time and, I think by choice, couldn't/wouldn't teach. One was a carpenter, guide, farmer, painter, bartender, fly tier, lecturer . . . you get the picture. They each fell into the sociographic profile I've labeled: urban refugee. An urban refugee is most frequently someone who has reached their personal saturation level of metropolitan living and heads to the hills. After looking for employment in their field, and often spending more time commuting than they did in the "metropolis," the urban refugee commonly begins considering "owning a small business." This type of entrepreneur comprised most of my client base during my small business counseling years.

Based upon the strength of the plan and the strength of the partners' collective energy, intellect and persuasiveness, this project was funded by a commercial lender. However, the lender extended funding only after receiving a 90% loan guarantee from a state program.

In many ways, The Artful Fly is, tragically, a classic story of a business start-up. This is the story I was told.

Soon after funding was obtained problems began occurring between the partners. Squabbling about designs for promotional materials and lack of coordination with the printer resulted in "less than hoped for" initial brochures. Problems also developed in the areas of "work schedules" and spending authority. Deadlines for submitting advertisements to the major periodicals were missed. Turn-around in production of the frames was not sufficient. Fly inventories had been built in anticipation of orders, only to be mismatched with the inventory the customers wanted.

Tensions grew, both personally and with vendors. Although the product concept was well received by both the industry and the customers, the business failed to perform internally. Cash flow problems and the prevailing and growing distrust between the principals turned into an organizational malignant cancer. Within two years of launch, The Artful Fly was no more.

Thank goodness the bank obtained that loan guarantee.

- What are the strengths of this plan? What are the weaknesses?

- How does the market analysis assist in your understanding of the business?

- What do we know about their customers?

- What impact will the Internet have on this business?

- How could this business grow?

- What would you add to their promotional plans?

- Is this a family business? What problems or opportunities do you see?

TABLE OF CONTENTS

II. EXECUTIVE SUMMARY

The Artful Fly is a new business producing visually dramatic presentations of artificial fishing flies. The business is a corporation coequally owned and managed by Tom Fisher and Jane Angler. The Artful Fly obtains its fishing flies from four sources. These are: antique flies from fishermen who have gained historical prominence in the history of fly fishing, famous flies from fishermen who have recently received acclaim through their books about fly fishing and fly tying, professional flies from fishermen whose flies have demonstrated outstanding fly tying skills and standards, and finally customer flies from customers who forward their flies for framing. The Artful Fly mounts and frames these flies for sale to fly fishermen and their families.

The Artful Fly estimates sales of more than 1000 units during the first year of its operation. Gross sales are expected to be $187,421. On these sales the Artful Fly projects gross profits of 73% for its first year of operation. Net profits for the year are expected to be 18.6%. First year's return on equity is projected at 40.33%.

The Artful Fly projects a healthy profit in its first year of operation because it is the first national company whose business is mounting and framing fishing flies. Two companies compete with the Artful Fly for framing customer flies only. They do not, however, mount and frame customer flies, nor do they sell flies from other sources. The Artful Fly plans one special offering for Christmas. It is a combined offering of an autographed book by widely read fishing author Tim Troutman and four of his hand tied wet flies attractively framed. Arrangements have already been made with Mr. Troutman.

The Artful Fly plans to advertise its product through magazine display ads. It will run four ads per year in **Fly Fisherman, Fly Rod and Reel,** and **American Angler.**

The Artful Fly seeks debt funding of $44,000 at 11% annual interest for a term of five years. The funds are needed to purchase equipment, inventory, and advertising. Because of the high profitability of its products, the Artful Fly anticipates repayment within two years at the ordinary interest rates.

III DESCRIPTION OF BUSINESS

A. Nature of the Business

The Artful Fly is a start-up company which proposes to manufacture and retail visually dramatic presentations of fishing flies. The fishing flies are obtained from four sources:

Antique Flies: flies owned by fly fisherman who made historically significant contributions to fly fishing and fly tying,

Famous Flies: recently tied flies from well recognized and currently published fly tiers and fly fishermen writers,

Professional Flies: outstanding hand tied flies from professional fly tiers,

Customer Flies: from customers who desire to have their flies and photographs or mementoes dramatically framed.

Along with the frame are included professional documents authenticating the source of the fly or flies and a brass plate identifying the fly or flies and their source.

The Artful Fly will manufacture framed flies with its own framing and mounting process. The Artful Fly intends to promote its flies to the retail market through magazine advertising and mailed brochures. Purchases will be made by mail, telephone or fax. Distribution will be accomplished by mail or by private delivery service.

The Artful Fly is organized as a corporation with Tom Fisher and Jane Angler as co-equal owners The corporation and business will be located in Muskie County, Wisconsin. Ms. Angler has responsibility for marketing, finance and administrative operations Mr. Fisher directs procurement and manufacturing, and he is responsible for mounting flies, for identifying them, and for their visual appearance. Fisher and Angler will share equally all financial and personnel decision making.

B. History of The Artful Fly

The Artful Fly was formed to develop, promote and distribute framed flies similar to those currently available only through fund raising benefit auctions. The product, visually dramatic presentations of artificial flies, was developed over the last seven years with the Beaver Fly Fishers.

The Beaver Fly Fishers is a local fishing club of 250 members based in Capitalville, WI and affiliated nationally with the Federation of Fly Fishers. Once a year in the early Spring, the club holds a season opener and invites professional fly tiers and nationally recognized fly fishing experts to participate. The fly tiers hold demonstrations for the members, and the nationally recognized fly fishermen give talks and seminars on an aspect of fly fishing. The participation of fly tiers and speakers is commemorated by a tiers fly plate and a speakers fly plate. The tiers plate holds one fly from each of the professional fly tiers. The flies are mounted and then framed. Similarly for the speakers, each speaker is represented by one of his flies on the speakers plate. Both the tiers plate and the speakers plate are auctioned with the proceeds going to the club. On average tiers plates have sold for $600 but have gone for as high as $900. This year the tiers plate sold for $650. Speakers plates have sold on average for $500. This year the speakers plate sold for $675. Occasionally a prominent speaker will donate a fly to be auctioned for the club's benefit. This year Lefty Bass donated a single fly, a Lefty's Deceiver, which was mounted, framed and auctioned for $475. In the past salmon fly plates have sold for $1000.

Tom Fisher has done the mounting and framing of the tiers plate and speakers plate for the last seven year. Mr. Fisher a well known professional fly tier in his own right, has developed a national reputation for mounting and framing flies. He was a charter member of the Beaver Fly Fishers and has served since on its Board of Directors. This year Mr. Fisher was elected by the Federation of Fly Fishers, one of the largest fly fishing organizations in the county as Vice President of Conservation for the Great Rivers Council. Since 1977 he has run a trout fishing guide service in Wisconsin. Two years ago he was certified an Orvis approved trout guide

For more than 23 years Mr. Fisher has given fly tying demonstrations throughout the United States. These demonstrations have been sponsored by sports shops such as Gander Mountain and Orvis and fishing organizations such as Trout Unlimited and the Federation of Fly Fishers. Recently he was invited to join the fly tiers on the International Plate of the Federation of Fly Fishers, a distinct honor for any professional fly tier. He continues to mount and frame flies for the Beaver Fly Fishers as well as other fishing clubs in the Midwest. In January of this year, a noted journal published an article about Mr. Fisher and his accomplishments. (See Appendix A.)

C. Description of Artful Flies Product

1. Framed Flies: Retail

The Artful Fly offers framed fishing flies. The flies are either supplied by the Artful Fly or by the customer. The flies supplied by the Artful Fly fall into three categories:

Antique flies are supplied by the Artful Fly. Antique flies are flies which have been tied or used by fisherman who have achieved historical significance in the history of fly fishing. Examples of such flies are flies tied by the Polly Rosborough, Ray Bergman or Lee Wulff. A further example would be flies used by such persons as Robert Traver and Ernest Hemingway. Antique flies are limited in quantity and their value increases with each passing year.

Famous flies are tied by contemporary well known fly tiers and fisherman. These flies are tied by currently published fly fishing authors such as Arthur Whitefish, David Salmon, Charles Snapper, and Martha Minnow.

Professional flies offered by the Artful Fly are flies tied by outstanding fly tiers. These flies are tied with the finest materials, greatest care and highest skill. Often they are superb examples of recognized patterns, i.e. Coachman, Quill Gordon, Jock Scott, Grey Ghost, etc.

The Artful Fly plans to sell these three categories of flies pre-mounted in frames. For antique, famous, and professional flies, the prospective customer is given the choice of the fly or flies which he wants mounted by the Artful Fly. (See attached photographic example in Appendix B.) The variety of flies in the first two categories will always be limited. The Artful Fly will provide by brochure the list of flies which are available at any given time in the first two categories. The third category of flies allows for a greater range of choices. Customers will be able to choose any pattern in trout, bass, panfish, salmon, or steelhead flies. Because of the lower prices of these flies, the Artful Fly is able to offer sets of flies, i.e. Catskill flies, brook trout flies, the Ghost series, traditional salmon flies, deer hair bass bugs, the life cycle of the Mayfly, etc. New combinations of these flies offer unique marketing opportunities.

2. Special Products: Resale Retail

The Artful Fly plans to offer special, one time only products. One program which the Artful Fly plans for Christmas 1995 is a joint offering of an autographed copy of Tim Troutman's new book and the four flies which the book highlights, all attractively framed in a limited edition of only fifty units. Mr. Troutman is the most widely published of current fly fishing authors. He has 14 books in print and a busy schedule of appearances and seminars. Arrangements have already been finalized with Mr. Troutman.

3. Custom Framing Services: Retail

The fourth category of flies the Artful Fly will frame is flies from its customers. These flies may have been either tied or used by the customer. For some reason the customer wishes to dramatize his flies. (The Artful Fly refers to the customer as "he" because it is brief and because 84% of fly fishers are men. There are approximately 10,000 women fly fishers and these persons are included in the market.) He may want to commemorate a particularly memorable fishing trip, or he may be particularly proud of his own hand-tied creations and wish to exhibit them. The flies may even be mounted with photographs or other mementoes supplied by the customer.

In all categories of flies, the customer is given a choice of two styles of wood frames and these frames are offered in two finishes. In each style and finish, the customer is given the choice of two sizes of frames. The customer is also given four colors of matting from which to choose. Each framed fly unit will be double matted. Matting and frames are all of high quality materials and workmanship. The Artful Fly plans a fourteen day turn around on its orders. The assembly and mounting by the Artful Fly will be guaranteed for the life of the fly.

IV. MARKET ANALYSIS
A. The Industry

The fly fishing industry has undergone tremendous growth in the last ten years. The fly fishing market, conservatively estimated at $227,000,000, is expanding at the rate of 16.5% a year. (North American Fly Tackle Trade Assoc., 1993 survey) Fly fishing is the fastest growing participatory sport in America. More than 11 million people consider themselves avid fly fishermen, and 8.9 million people fly fish exclusively. (National Sports and Recreation Industry, 1990 study) The expansion of the fly fishing market is demonstrated by a number of developments. One sign of the growth in the fly fishing industry is the growth of the trade show for fly fishing tackle dealers. In 1987, fly tackle manufacturers and dealers first held a trade show. The show was sponsored and organized by the International Fly Tackle Dealer Association. At the original show, there were only 57 exhibitors. Last year the IFTD show had 325 exhibitors. IFTD's trade magazine, Fly Tackle Dealer, now goes to 11,000 dealers in fly fishing equipment and accessories. There has been a dramatic increase in the numbers of fly fishermen. These numbers are documented in the increase in sales in such essential items as fly rods, reels, lines, and leaders and in the increase in sales of trout and salmon stamps.

A central product in the industry is the artificial fly. It goes without saying that without artificial flies, there would be no fly fishing. As a further example of the growth in the fly fishing industry is the demand for artificial flies. Demand is well ahead of supplies. Last year the industry was short 200,000 dozen artificial fishing flies. The LL. Bean Company alone was short 100,000 dozen artificial flies. At the average retail price of flies nationally this shortage represents $3,000,000 in lost sales. There is no let up in the demand this year. (International Fly Tackle Dealers Association, 1994 show report)

Within the industry some fly tiers are recognized to be more skilled and to be more creative than others. Often these tiers are authors whose books describe the new patterns which they have created and the entomological basis for the success of their fly patterns. These tiers can demand up to $100 per fly. Highly skilled tiers produce few flies. They do exert, however, great influence on other fly tiers. Within the fly fishing community, their names are recognized, and their books are sought after. A fly from one of these "name" tiers is an heirloom on the order of a baseball autographed by a Hall of Famer. There is no national retail source for the purchase of flies from the "name" tiers at the present.

The numbers of dealers in fly tying equipment and fly tying products have increased dramatically. As with other areas of the fly fishing market, synthetic materials have been the subject of great experimentation. Fly tying vises, tool and hooks, the heart of fly tying, all have undergone tremendous growth in the numbers of manufacturers and retail outlets. Approximately 76% of all fly tying materials are purchased by mail order. The market for fly tying items has broadened so that vises are now available in prices ranging from $35 to $1000. Choices in tying materials, at one time only among natural materials, have become almost unlimited in type and quality. Synthetic dubbing, for instance, is available in ounce packets in a price range, depending on manufacturer and material, from $.95 to $3.95. Hooks have gone from a fairly stable market to a highly competitive one with Japanese and English imports at double the price of comparable domestic products now gaining in market share. Dealers who have marketed fly fishing equipment for years are constantly amazed at the sustained and growing demand for fly fishing products and gadgets embracing the newest technology

B. Fly Fishing Consumer

1. Demographics and Lifestyle
The market which the Artful Fly has targeted is the fly fisherman. The economic demographics for

fly fishing are second only to polo and are ahead of skiing and golf. The average fly fisherman is a white male who is married, a college graduate, and 40 years of age. His average income is $84,600. His average household income is $113,000. Most fly fishermen hold an administrative or management position. The majority have at least two major credit cards. (National Sports and Recreation Industry, 1990 study)

Traditionally the fly fishing market has been unique in several respects First the fly fisherman is print oriented. He owns an average of 35 books on angling and plans to purchase more. Fly fishing has produced the oldest and most extensive body of sport literature. The first references to fly fishing are found in texts from Roman times. A long line of English language fishing texts goes back 400 years into British history.

The fly fisherman is a traditionalist. Museums of fly fishing history have been started to commemorate the history of the sport and its founders and innovators. Fly fishermen have and will purchase historically significant flies and artifacts to form a connection with this fly fishing tradition. Artifacts from fly fishing history are collected and sold in a large underground market. Some items such as flies tied by Theodore Gordon are priceless. A select group of fly tiers have been innovators over the last century and a half. These tiers have published their thoughts and fly patterns, and their flies are rare and are sought by fly fisherman who have a strong sense of the fly fishing tradition. Yearly their books increase in value.

2. Market Segments
The profile of the consumer of flies, fly fishing equipment and accessories has been well defined through numerous trade surveys. (1993 North American Fly Tackle Trade Association survey, 1993 American Sports Fishing Association survey, 1994 *Trout Magazine* survey, 1990 National Sports and Recreation Industry survey) The composite demographic profile from these sources stands now as follows:

Age	30 to 50 years
	(median age - 46.6)
Income	$84,600 average individual
	$113,000 average
	household
Sex	84% male
Employment	Professional, managerial
	and administrative
Education	82.% attended/graduated
	college (72% graduated)
	41% attended/graduated
	post-graduate program
Family Status	Married (78.1%)
No. in Household	2 9
No. Fly Fishers	1.6
Race	White (99%)

The majority of fly fishermen tie their own flies and plan to purchase fly tying equipment each year.

3. Geography

The fly fishing market is international. At present international sales are 5% of all sales by fly fishing manufacturers. Most of these sales are European, but many originate in Japan, Australia, and New Zealand. The national market is evenly distributed throughout the United States. The national fly fishing market breaks down regionally as follows:

Northeast	25.5%
Midwest	17.6%
South	17.6%
West	40.3%

These regional percentages are fairly constant for the subscribers of major fly fishing magazines and the membership of national fly fishing organizations. The fastest growing part of the fly fishing industry is saltwater fly fishing. A new magazine dedicated solely to saltwater fly fishing begins publication this summer. Its name is **Saltwater Fly Fishing** and is being published by Abenaki Publishers, Bennington, VT.

4. Publication and Organization

Of the organizations dedicated to fly fishing, the two largest are Trout Unlimited and Federation of Fly Fishers. Trout Unlimited has 75,000 members dedicated to the broader objective of bettering the sport of trout fishing. The majority of its members, 66%, are exclusively fly fisherman. Almost the same percentage of members tie their own flies. Trout Unlimited has an official publication, **Trout**, which is a quarterly magazine mailed to all Trout Unlimited members. Federation of Fly Fishers has 17,000 members dedicated to the sport of fly fishing for all species of fish, both saltwater and fresh water. Federation of Fly Fishers publishes the quarterly magazine, **The Quill**, which is mailed to all its members. Both organizations have local chapters which meet regularly, usually monthly. Once a year they each hold national conventions.

C. Profile of Competition

No company in the fly fishing market offers framed flies Two companies, however, do advertise frames in kit form with single precut matting so that customers can mount their own flies. They are; Mountain Shadow Box Company and Shadowcraft Ltd..

Mountain Shadowbox, a three year old company located in Glide, Oregon, offers three different size shadowbox kits with precut matting. The shadow boxes are rectangular. The kits are pre-assembled with all parts in place except that the customer need glue in his flies. The mats offered are limited to two colors. The shadow boxes do not allow for photographs. The business is run out of the owner's house. The prices for the three sizes of shadow boxes are: 12" × 15" ($65.00), 13" × 17" ($79.00), and 17" × 21" ($94.00).

Shadowcraft Limited is a two year old company located in Medford, Massachusetts near Boston. Its owner is a retired advertising executive. Shadowcraft focuses its sales efforts on marketing pre-assembled frames and precut mats for flies and photographs from fishing trips. It is a one man operation run out of the owner's garage. With the pre-assembled frames, it also offers kits for mounting flies and photographs. The frames and frame kits are done by jobbers. Shadowcraft markets solely through fly fishing magazines and local trade shows. These kits are priced between $29.00 and $99.00. Finished frames ready for mounting flies run from $59.00 to $179.00.

Mountain Shadowbox Company and Shadowcraft Ltd. are both profitable and their sales are increasing.

The Artful Fly anticipates that neither Mountain Shadowbox Company nor Shadowcraft will enter the market of framed flies. Shadowcraft's owner has already indicated to us during an interview that he does not intend to expand into framed flies. He is a retired executive who plans to limit the time which he need spend on his new business. His greatest interest is to sell pre-packaged kits. Mountain Shadowbox Company does not have the capital to enter the framed flies business.

V. MARKETING OPPORTUNITIES AND BUSINESS STRATEGY

A. Opportunity

The Artful Fly is the first company to provide mounted and framed flies nationally. The Artful Fly will immediately capture the major share of the framed fly market and can hold the greatest share of its market because it will be the first national company to achieve name recognition and also because it has the flexibility to offer innovative and attractive programs for the future. The Artful Fly has made arrangements for purchasing large quantities of flies from the best known and respected fly tiers. The Artful Fly is confident it will continue to secure sufficient numbers of the finest examples of flies produced by the "name" tiers. The Artful Flies principal competitors, Mountain Shadow Box and Shadowcraft Ltd., have only the single program for the customer to frame his own flies.

The framed flies offered by the Artful Fly can be marketed to the **fly fishing consumer directly** or to **fly fishing tackle and accessories dealers, to gift stores, to furniture stores, and to art galleries.**

1. Consumer Direct - Mail

Sales direct to the consumer can be accomplished through sales campaigns using mailing lists purchased from fly fishing magazines, fly fishing organizations, and/or fly fishing merchandisers. The Artful Fly would describe its programs and provide photographs of examples in a six page color brochure suitable for mailing.

2. Consumer Direct - Magazines

Sales direct to the consumer can also be accomplished through magazine advertising. Advertising purchased in magazines selected for their economic profile would highlight programs attractive to the interests of the subscribers. The great variety of fly patterns with endless combinations of shape and color and often with a lengthy history to match would lend itself to special programs for special magazine audiences.

3. Consumer Indirect - Retail

The Artful Fly can also market its framed flies to tackle dealers as well as galleries and gift shops. The programs for antique and famous flies lend themselves more to sales to tackle dealers. They supply fly tiers with hooks and fly tying materials, and they number among their customers fly tiers who would appreciate and purchase rare antique and famous flies. Galleries and gift shops would be interested in framed flies which are visually distinctive and work well with decorating schemes.

4. Consumer Indirect - Mail Order Merchandisers

Finally the Artful Fly can market its programs to large fly fishing tackle and accessories merchandisers like Cabela's, Bass Fisherman, Orvis, L.L. Bean, Gander Mountain, etc.. There is an additional avenue for similar marketing techniques by using the regular mailings from credit card companies. With the customer's monthly statement, credit card companies will send advertising notices for a variety of products. The customer returns his order with his monthly payment, and the order is then billed on the next statement.

B. Strengths and Weaknesses of the Artful Fly

The strengths of the framed flies offered by the Artful Fly are fivefold.

• The Artful Fly <u>does the mounting and framing</u> of the flies. Skill and experience is needed to mount flies properly. The average customer does not have the skill or experience to mount large bass bugs, salmon flies, steelhead flies and saltwater flies.

• The Artful Fly <u>offers a large selection of frame shapes and finishes</u>. We offer oval and rectangular wood frames in light and dark finishes.

• The Artful Fly <u>offers a large variety of mat colors</u> allowing it to match the finish of the frame with the color of the flies.

• The Artful Fly <u>provides double cut matting with the openings customized</u> to the flies, photographs and memorabilia being framed.

• The Artful Fly offers <u>rare and distinctive flies</u> ranging from antique and famous to professional flies which the customer may either desire to collect or display.

The Artful Fly's direct competitors, Mountain Shadow Box and Shadowcraft Ltd., provide kits and pre-assembled frames for customers. They do not provide flies. The kits are attractive to the craft-oriented customer who wish to mount the flies himself. Neither the kits nor the pre-assembled frames, however, offer the variety of frame shapes, finishes and mat colors which the Artful Fly provides. Additionally Mountain Shadow Box and Shadowcraft Ltd. do not offer any programs which provide the customer with flies already framed. The Artful Fly alone will be offering in the national market antique, famous, and professional flies as well as its special programs such as the Troutman book and four flies.

C. Opportunity The Artful Fly Will Pursue - Position

The Artful Fly plans to market initially though magazine ads in **Fly Fisherman, American Angler,** and **Fly Rod and Reel.** These magazines have circulations of 145,418, 41,000, and 57,014 respectively. The Artful Fly's display ads are ⅙ page size and will run four times a year in the three magazines selected. The ad will inform the reader generally about the Artful Fly's products and then offer a brochure to anyone interested in looking more closely into purchasing framed flies.

After our telephone survey of advertisers in the three magazines selected, the Artful Fly expects conservatively 1½% of the readership to request the brochure and 6% of those requesting the brochure to purchase one of our products. These are the rates reported by the two frame companies

for their initial advertising campaigns. These are fairly standard returns throughout the industry. After publication of several issues of advertising, the Artful Angler expects its rate of request to grow to 2%. The 6% order rate could be increased to 15% through the use of an 800 number and follow up telephone calls.

Based on these rates, the Artful Fly projects more than 1000 sales during its first year of operation. Its operations begin when its national advertising campaign begins. The Artful Fly expects its orders to be distributed among its programs as follows:

Antique Flies	25
Famous Flies	150
Professional Flies	150
Customer Flies	557
Specials	150

With these sales, the Artful Fly estimates its gross sales for the first year of operations to be $187,421. The sales for each category break down as follows:

Antique Flies	$9,713
Famous Flies	$36,285
Professional Flies	$34,780
Customer Flies	$50,125
Specials	$56,518

VI. MARKETING PLAN
A. Introduction

The target for Artful Fly sales is fishermen who fly fish for trout, pike, bass, bluegills, saltwater species, salmon, steelhead, etc.. All these fishermen have purchased and studied artificial flies. Some tie them, and indeed many of these fishermen have purchased books and read articles about fly tying and the proper selection of flies. They are predisposed to consider flies seriously and to recognize that some flies are tied better than others.

Given its chosen market position, the Artful Fly perceives its products must fulfill four customer needs.

• The first need is <u>to commemorate a fond fishing memory</u>. The flies framed are the customer's and may include photographs or other memorabilia. Fly fishermen are encouraged to practice catch-

and-release. Thus the mounting of the "big" fish which was common in years past is now frowned upon as a way of preserving a trophy. The trophy becomes the picture of the "big" fish with the flies and other memorabilia related to catching it.

• The second need met by the framed flies produced by the Artful Fly is the need to stake out and own a part of fly fishing tradition. It is the need to collect historically significant objects. This need is found in every sport. For example Polly Rosborough innovated a series of flies using fur in creative ways as a body dubbing and wing material. This work is described in his book Tying and Fishing the Fuzzy Nymphs first published in 1965. His flies will increase in value over the years. They are being collected now by fly fishermen and tiers.

• The third need met by Artful Fly's framed flies is to identify the owner as a serious and knowledgeable fly fisherman. The buyer communicates to other fly fishermen that he has linked himself to the most historical elements of the fly fishing tradition. He is part of gentlemanly tradition going back hundreds of year to Isaac Walton and the English chalk streams.

• The fourth need met by Artful Flies framed flies is to provide unique and beautiful wall hangings. Artificial flies, especially salmon and steelhead flies, are often produced from rare and exotic materials which run the gamut from Polar Bear hair to Cockatoo tail feathers. The resulting fly becomes a work of art.

The following marketing plan seeks to meet these needs.

B. The Artful Fly's Product

The Artful Fly has selected the following products to best fulfill the markets needs and reinforce the Artful Fly's selected market position.

1. Pre-framed Flies

• **Antique** are framed flies of fishermen who have achieved historical significance in the history of fly fishing. The flies of Sylvester Nemes and Polly Rosborough are now available.

• **Famous** are framed flies from fishing authors who have achieved contemporary recognition by fly fishermen and fly tiers. The flies of Arthur Whitefish, David Salmon, Charles Snapper, and Martha Minnow are available and arrangements have been made with all of them.

• **Professional** are framed flies from outstanding professional fly tiers. These flies are tied with the finest materials and with the highest skill.

• **Customer** are framed flies which have been supplied by the customer.

2. Special Products

The Artful Fly has made arrangements with Tim Troutman and Arthur Whitefish for the simultaneous offering of their framed flies in conjunction with the publication of their new books. The Artful Fly continues to explore similar offerings with other prominent fly fishermen.

3. Custom Framing

The Artful Fly offers customers a large selection of frames, finishes, and matting colors and will mount flies and mementoes to the customers specifications.

4. New Products

The Artful Fly plans to offer framed flies with a theme. The new lines will offer professionally tied flies around a single subject such as the life cycle of the Mayfly, brook trout flies, etc.

The Artful Fly offers as part of its promotion of its product a lifetime warranty on the mounting of its flies. No other company provides this protection. Warranties have worked well in other areas of the fly fishing industry such as rods and reels. Orvis, for example, offers lifetime warranties on its fly rods and reels.

C. Pricing

The prices of flies mounted and framed by the Artful Fly varies with the programs offered. Prices will range between $76 and $325. For the five programs the prices average as follows:

Antique Flies	$325
Famous	$245
Professional	$200
Customer	$89
Special	$325

The prices for Professional and Customer programs are determined on a cost basis. The prices for the remaining programs are based on what customers in the market have paid in the past. Previous similar offerings at auction brought prices which support the ranges set out above. Fifteen years ago Lee Wulff offered twelve of his hand tied flies framed in a limited edition of 100 for $1000 each. They were all sold through magazine advertising in several months. Twenty five years ago Sylvester Nemes offered an autographed copy of one of his books and four of his hand tied flies framed for $125 in a limited edition of 100. They were sold within a year. This year Davy Wotton, a fly tier from Scotland, offered single framed flies in unlimited numbers for prices ranging between $175 and $225. Some have been sold but it is too early to determine the result.

D. Promotion

The Artful Fly plans to market its framed flies through selective magazine advertising. After careful analysis, the Artful Fly believes it can successfully market its product through display ads of one-sixth page size in Fly Fisherman, American Angler, and Fly Rod and Reel. These three magazines are read by fly fishermen in large numbers, and their advertisers have experienced solid rates of response. The Artful Fly has targeted the September issues of these magazines as its initial entry into the market. The Artful Fly believes this is the most cost effective way to first enter the market. The cost of printing and mailing brochures or promotion materials directly to consumers is more expensive than taking out multiple ads in fly fishing magazines. Also the ads will, in a years time, give name recognition for the Artful Fly. Marketing through gift shops, galleries, tackle dealers, and mail order merchandisers would come later after the Artful

Fly develops a track record for its prices and is, therefore, in a better position to negotiate dealer discounts.

E. Distribution

Initially the distribution of framed flies purchased from the Artful Fly will be through parcel post or private delivery services. The choice of the manner of delivery will be left to the customer at the time of purchases. Purchases will be either through an order form provided with the Artful Fly's brochure, or by fax or by telephone. The cost of delivery will be borne by the customer.

Finally the Artful Fly offers a turn around of 14 days or less on all orders. During the Christmas period the turn around time will be shortened if the customer agrees to use private delivery services

VI. LOCATION

The Artful Fly will be located in two places. The office will be in the residence of Ms. Angler on County Hwy. M in Swale Township. The production facilities will be in the residence of Mr. Fisher on Muddy Road approximately two miles from Ms. residence. Mr. Fisher has 300 square feet available for storage and for mounting flies and assembling frames. Also Mr. Fisher has access to several large farm storage facilities.

The Artful Fly's rural location does not impair its ability to advertise its products, to communicate with potential customers, or to ship its products to customers. Local postal service is speedy and reliable. UPS provides very good service, and many local businesses rely on it for daily deliveries. Further, deliveries of frames, matting, glass, etc. can be accomplished by commercial trucking service. In many instances where local manufacturers are involved the Artful Fly will be able to pick up the items needed.

Shipping costs will be borne by the Artful Fly's customers.

VII. BUSINESS OPERATION PLAN

A. Equipment Needs
The Artful Fly needs the following equipment:

1. One fax machine from Hawthorne Sales & Service for purchase $250
2. One Hewlett Packard fax machine from Hawthorne for purchase (HP 700) $550
3. One Packard Bell Computer from Hawthorne for purchase (DX2-66) $1100
4. One Hewlett Packard color scanner from Digicolor for purchase (2CX with word scan) . .$1175
5. One Canon color bubble jet printer (BJ 600 E) $500
6. One Syquest Drive for purchase (200 MB) $775

TOTAL $4350

B. Facility Needs

The space needs for the Artful Fly are easily satisfied. Ms. Angler has in her residence three rooms on average 12' × 10' available for office and storage space. Additionally a single room shed 25' × 20' is available on her property for storage. In his residence Mr. Fisher has several rooms available for production. They total approximately 300 square feet. The Artful Fly does not foresee any serious problems with storage. The flies themselves occupy very little space. The numerous frames and matting needed are easily stored in a limited space. Further, the quick turn around on orders for frames and mats should alleviate the need to keep large amounts of inventory on hand.

C. Labor

Initially the Artful Fly anticipates the need for creating three and one-third new jobs. Three positions are managerial. One is Tom Fisher who will manufacture the framed flies. He will train and supervise during the Christmas season one additional employee. Ms. Angler administers the Artful Fly office and directs marketing and finance. A third managerial employee will divide his or her time between administration and manufacture. All managerial employees will work at the same hourly rate. Subordinate seasonal employees will receive a lower hourly rate.

D. Inventory

The Artful Fly plans to build an inventory of five hundred units prior to the appearance of its first magazine ad. Fifty units of the special offering will be on hand before the Artful Fly's first display ads appear in September. The Artful Fly has already produced a prototype of the Hughes offering for advertising purposes. Also the Artful Fly will have the stock to produce twenty of the antique flies and seventy five of the famous flies. The remaining programs could be easily filled during August, just after the September magazine issues are mailed out.

The materials for assembling the projected five hundred units include fourteen separate items. These items and their start up cost are listed as follows:

Frames	
Oval	$3165.00
Square	5312.50
Glass	
Oval	935.00
Square	238.00
Matting	960.00
Craft Paper	48.90
Foam Core	50.00
Hangers	22.60
Glue	40.00
Glass Cleaner	21.10
Cleaning Towels	11.30
Boxes	504.00
Shipping Tape	15.00
Blister Packs	65.00
Flies	
Antique	2700.00
Famous	3375.00
Professional	1600.00
Troutman	2000.00
TOTAL	$ 21,063.40

E. Proprietary Information

The Artful Fly does not anticipate any need to license or to use intellectual properties. Very few flies have been copyrighted, and the Artful Fly has no intention of reproducing the ones which have been. Most flies have too long a history for any legal protections. Also no fly tiers who innovate new patterns seek any type of legal protection for them. Instead they publish their patterns and explain their use without any claim of protection.

One legal issue may arise. This issue attaches to the authentication of antique and famous flies. The Artful Fly has resolved this issue by requiring of all persons from whom they obtain these flies an affidavit attesting to its origin if the tier or owner is dead or a signed card from tiers or owners who are living. The original of these affidavits and cards will be maintained in the Artful Fly's files. In certain instances we will forward to the customer the original of the signed card.

VIII. ORGANIZATIONAL STRUCTURE, OWNERSHIP, AND MANAGEMENT

A. Organization and Ownership

The Artful Fly is organized as a Wisconsin corporation. The two stockholders of common stock are Tom Fisher and Jane Angler. They each own 50% of the common stock issued.

Responsibility for decision making at the Artful Fly is equally divided between Fisher and Angler. For the present they will administer the Artful Fly as a partnership. Ms. Angler will be assisted by her husband, and Mr. Fisher will be assisted by his son. Although both Mr. Fisher and Ms. Angler share decision making equally, they will concentrate their efforts in separate areas of the Artful Fly operations. Ms. Angler will take special responsibility for marketing, customer relations, record keeping and reporting, and the shipping of finished product to the consumer. Mr. Fisher will take special responsibility for relations with fly tiers, ordering supplies, assembly of frames, mounting of flies, artistic quality of product, quality control, and the boxing of the final product. They will share personnel decisions and financial decisions.

Management Team

The resumes of Ms. Angler and Mr. Fisher are attached. Their resumes are found in Appendices C and D. They are contributing office supplies, office machines, space, production tools, and cash valued at approximately $12,355.00.

IX. KEY RISKS

A. Low Sales

Although sales estimates are based on the sales history of comparable products and club auctions, the rate of sales may be lower than anticipated. Lower sales would be problematic because some important costs are fixed. These are magazine advertising costs, brochure printing costs, and the cost of startup inventory. The costs of brochures can be reduced by purchase of a scanner and laser printer.

B. High Sales

If sales are at a greater rate than anticipated then the Artful Fly would need to purchase inventory and train new personnel earlier than anticipated. The manufacturing process has been analyzed and reduced to 25 steps which can be easily communicated to prospective low skilled employees. The turn around for inventory orders varies. For framing and matting materials it is four weeks.

C. Weather

Distribution can be affected by severe winter weather. In the past snow storms have shut Muskie County down for a day or two. Although office and manufacturing operations would continue, the movement of the purchased product to the customer would be interrupted. One solution once the roads are clear is to transport product immediately to Capitalville, WI which would provide some catch up.

Financial Projections

The Artful Fly has made sales estimates and financial projections for its first year of operation. Based on these estimates and projections, it has been able to formulate a financing plan.

The Artful Fly estimates that its gross sales for the first year of its operations will be $187,421. These gross sales eventuate from a 1.5% response to its magazine advertising. The response rate of 1.5% used by the Artful Fly is the rate experienced by start up companies for comparable products. The greater percentage of sales will occur in the fall and early winter months.

Gross profits on average for all programs is 73%. The most profitable programs are the famous and professional flies which are 84% and 75.1% respectively. Net profits are estimated to be 18.6% for one years operation. Return on equity is projected to reach 40.33%.

Following its first year of operation, the Artful Fly estimates its ending cash balance to be $32,048. The Artful Fly plans to pay back in full its $44,000 loan within the first two years. The economic and financial worksheets and projected balance sheet for the Artful Fly are attached. (See appendix E)

Financial Statements for Artful Fly

(referred to as appendix E)

Total Sales Estimation & Analysis Report: Artful Fly

PRODUCT/SERVICE	Business-to-Business Annual Demand Estimates		Total Weighted Demand Estimate	Bus.-to-Bus. Sales Estimate	Retail Annual Demand Estimates		Retail Sales Estimate	Estimated Total Sales
Item 1: Antique	A. Maximum	0	0	0	A. Maximum:	15,000	9,713	9,713
	B. Most Likely:	0			B. Most Likely:	9,375		
	C. Minimum	0			C. Minimum:	7,125		
Item 2. Professional	A. Maximum	0	0	0	A. Maximum:	48,400	34,780	34,780
	B. Most Likely:	0			B. Most Likely:	30,000		
	C. Minimum	0			C. Minimum:	22,600		
Item 3: Famous	A. Maximum	0	0	0	A. Maximum:	59,290	36,285	36,285
	B. Most Likely:	0			B. Most Likely:	36,750		
	C. Minimum	0			C. Minimum:	27,685		
Item 4: Customer	A. Maximum	0	0	0	A. Maximum:	79,833	50,125	50,125
	B. Most Likely:	0			B. Most Likely:	49,573		
	C. Minimum	0			C. Minimum:	37,202		
Item 5: Specials	A. Maximum	0	0	0	A. Maximum:	59,290	56,518	56,518
	B. Most Likely:	0			B. Most Likely:	48,750		
	C. Minimum	0			C. Minimum:	36,725		
Item 6: _____	A. Maximum	0	0	0	A. Maximum:	0	0	0
	B. Most Likely:	0			B. Most Likely:	0		
	C. Minimum	0			C. Minimum:	0		
Item 7: _____	A. Maximum	0	0	0	A. Maximum:	0	0	0
	B. Most Likely:	0			B. Most Likely:	0		
	C. Minimum	0			C. Minimum:	0		
TOTALS	A. Maximum	0	0	0	A. Maximum:	281,173	187,419	187,419
	B. Most Likely:	0			B. Most Likely:	174,448		
	C. Minimum	0			C. Minimum:	131,337		

Projected Balance Sheet: Artful Fly

Period:	Jul-95 Beginning	Jun-96 Ending
ASSETS		
Cash	14,450	39,492
Receivables	0	0
Inventory	400	30,485
Total Current Assets:	14,850	69,977
Equipment	9,200	9,866
Facilities/Bldgs	0	0
Deprec. Intangibles	0	0
Land & non-deprec.	0	0
TOTAL ASSETS:	24,050	79,843
LIABILITIES		
Previous Debt	0	0
New Debt:	29,225	26,339
Short-term	25,000	22,532
Medium-term	4,225	3,808
Long-term	0	0
TOTAL LIABILITIES	29,225	26,339
EQUITY	(5,175)	53,504
TOTAL LIAB. & EQUITY:	24,050	79,843
LEVERAGE RATIOS		
Debt/Asset:	1.22	0.33
Debt/Equity:	-5.65	0.49
Fixed Charge Coverage:	NA	19.78
LIQUIDITY RATIOS		
Current Ratio:	NA	3.11
Quick Ratio:	NA	1.75
New Investment in Budget Period		
Depreciable Equipment	43,675	13,675
Depreciable Building	0	0
Depreciable Intangibles	0	0
Land & Non-Depreciable Assets	0	0
Working Capital/Inventory		30,000

OTHER FINANCIAL INFORMATION

Total Sales:	187,421
Gross Profit	137,056
Taxable Profit:	60,323
Net Profit:	45,476
Cash flow from Operations:	14,326
Sales Breakeven Point:	99,723
PROFITABILITY RATIOS	
Gross Margin:	73,13%
Taxable Profit Margin:	32.19%
Net Profit Margin:	24.26%
Cash flow from Operations/Sales:	7.64%
YEAR-END RETURN RATIOS (based upon cash flow)	
Return on Total Assets:	17.94%
Return on Dep. Assets:	104.76%
Return on Begin. Equity:	-276.82%
Financing Required	
Short-Term Debt	25,000
Medium-Term Debt	4,225
Long-Term Debt	0
Total	29,225

Notes:
1) Accounts payable estimates are not developed by the model. New (acquired within the planning period) short-term debt is assumed to be the only current liability.

PRO FORMA INCOME STATEMENT for Artful Fly

This document produced on: 08-Aug-95

	Jul-95	Aug-95	Sep-95	Oct 95	Nov-95	Dec-95	Jan-96	Feb-96	Mar-96	Apr-96	May-96	Jun-96	YEAR	% of Sales
Expected Monthly Sales	0	0	33,736	33,736	18,742	37,484	14,994	7,497	7,497	9,371	14,994	9,371	187,421	100.0%
Cost of Goods Sold	0	0	9,066	9,066	5,036	10,073	4,029	2,015	2,015	2,518	4,029	2,518	50,365	26.9%
Gross Profit	0	0	24,670	24,670	13,706	27,411	10,965	5,482	5,482	6,853	10,965	6,853	137,056	73.1%
Overhead Expenses														
Labor	0	0	0	4,478	7,464	7,464	4,478	4,478	4,478	4,478	4,478	4,478	46,275	24.7%
Utilities & Telephone	275	276	276	277	278	278	279	280	281	281	282	283	3,346	1.8%
Insurance	0	0	0	0	0	0	0	0	0	0	0	0	0	0.0%
Advertising & Promotion	2,050	0	5,060	76	2,071	0	0	2,010	0	77	77	0	11,420	6.1%
Travel & Entertainment	150	150	151	151	152	152	152	153	153	153	154	154	1,825	1.0%
Repairs & Maintenance	0	0	0	0	0	101	0	0	0	0	103	0	204	0.1%
Shipping & Postage	180	281	181	282	182	284	183	336	184	286	185	288	2,850	1.5%
Office Supplies	150	50	50	252	51	51	634	51	51	639	154	51	2,184	1.2%
Other (inc. rents & leases)	0	0	0	0	0	0	0	0	0	0	0	0	0	0.0%
Property & Other Taxes	134	134	134	134	134	134	134	134	134	134	134	134	1,609	0.9%
Total Overhead Expenses	2,939	891	5,853	5,650	10,330	8,464	5,861	7,441	5,281	6,049	5,566	5,388	69,713	37.2%
Depreciation														
Machinery & Equipment	296	296	296	323	323	323	326	326	326	326	326	326	3,809	2.0%
Building & Intangibles	0	0	0	0	0	0	0	0	0	0	0	0	0	0.0%
Operating Income (EBIT)	(3,235)	(1,187)	18,522	18,697	3,053	18,625	4,778	(2,285)	(124)	478	5,073	1,139	63,535	33.9%
Interest Expense	280	278	276	273	271	269	267	264	262	260	257	255	3,212	1.7%
Taxable Income (EBT)	(3,515)	(1,465)	18,246	18,424	2,782	18,356	4,511	(2,549)	(386)	218	4,816	884	60,323	32.2%
Est. Income Tax Obligation **	NA	0	4,491	4,534	685	4,518	1,110	0	0	54	1,185	218	14,846	7.9%
Tax Credits	NA	NA	NA	NA	NA	NA	NA	NA	NA	NA	NA	NA	0	0.0%
Estimated Income Taxes **	0	0	4,491	4,534	685	4,518	1,110	0	0	54	1,185	218	14,846	
Net Profit	(3,515)	(1,465)	13,755	13,890	2,097	13,838	3,401	(2,549)	(386)	165	3,631	666	45,476	

SUMMARY OF SELECTED YEAR END DATA:

Total Variable Costs (CGS)	=	50,365
Total Fixed Costs	=	72,925
(Overhead + Interest)		
Total Net Profit	=	45,476
Total Net Operations	=	
Cash Flow	=	14,326

SELECTED FINANCIAL RATIOS:

Variable Costs/Sales	=	26.87%
Fixed Costs/Sales	=	38.91%
Gross Margin/Sales	=	73.13%
Operating Profit/Sales	=	33.90%
After Tax Profit/Sales	=	24.26%
Cash Flow From Operations/Sales	=	7.64%
(internally generated cash flow)		
Sales Break Even Point ($'s)	=	99.723
Return on Beginning Current Assets	=	96.47%*
Return on Depreciable Assets	=	104.76%*
Return on Total Fixed Assets	=	32.50%*
Return on Beginning Equity	=	-276.82%*

NOTES:

(1) Assumes 11.5% cost of capital and 83% debt financing, with a 7 year loan for working capital & inventory.

(2) Assumes 11.5% cost of capital and 31% debt financing, with a 7 year loan for equipment and furnishings.

(3) Assumes 9.5% cost of capital and 0% debt financing, with a 20 year loan for land and structures.

(4) 3.0% inflation rate is applied to overhead expenses.

(5) Depreciation method chosen for equipt. is: double declining balance.
Depreciation method chosen for buildings is: straight-line.
Depreciation life determined by Federal tax definitions.

(6) The enterprise simulated is assumed to be a regular corporation.
Taxes are estimated based on this legal structure and the previous year's tax rates (federal, state, local & FICA).
Sole proprietor taxes include Self-Employment taxes. All other forms include only Fed. & State income taxes.

**(7) For monthly cashflow modeling all taxes are assumed to be withheld by the firm as monthly income is earned. This may cause monthly cashflows to be under-estimated in an one year forecast which has any one or more months of net income loss. The yearly total does reflect the actual expected amount of taxes owed for the forecasted year.

(8) Total sales are assumed to grow at an NA average annual rate.

(9) Cash flow projections assume that the total amount of debt financing needed is received as a lump sum in first month the firm requires financing, by category.

(10) Operations are assumed to begin -30 days from the current date: Aug-95

(11) Sales breakeven point are sales necessary to cover CGS, overhead & interest expenses.

(12) All return ratios based upon cash flows from operations, not profit.

PRO FORMA CASH FLOW FROM OPERATIONS STATEMENT for Artful Fly

	Jun 95	Jul-95	Aug-95	Sep-95	Oct-95	Nov-95	Dec-95	Jan-96	Feb-96	Mar-96	Apr-96	May-96	Jun-96	13 Month
Cash Sales	0	0	0	33,736	33,736	18,742	37,484	14,994	7,497	7,497	9,371	14,994	9,371	187,421
Collected Receivables	0	0	0	0	0	0	0	0	0	0	0	0	0	0
Other Income	0	0	0	0	0	0	0	0	0	0	0	0	0	0
Total Operation Cash Inflow	0	0	0	33,736	33,736	18,742	37,484	14,994	7,497	7,497	9,371	14,994	9,371	187,421
Operation/Overhead Costs	4,875	2,939	891	5,853	5,650	10,330	8,464	5,861	7,441	5,281	6,049	5,566	5,388	74,588
Direct/Raw Material Costs	0	21,060	0	0	23,676	0	0	23,809	0	0	0	0	11,905	80,450
Interest Expense	0	280	278	276	273	271	269	267	264	262	260	257	255	3,212
Income Taxes Paid**	0	0	0	4,491	4,534	685	4,518	1,110	0	0	54	1,185	218	14,846
Total Operation Cash Outflow	4,875	24,279	1,169	10,619	34,134	11,286	13,250	31,047	7,706	5,543	6,363	7,008	17,765	173,095
Total Cash Flow From Operations	(4,875)	(24,297)	(1,169)	23,117	(398)	7,456	24,234	(16,053)	(209)	1,954	3,008	7,985	(8,394)	14,326

NOTES:
(1) Direct/raw material purchases for each month represents the expected cost of goods to be sold in the following month, esculated by the CGS average inflation rate (Sales & CGS worksheet): 5.00%
(2) Direct/raw material purchases for the last month are assumed to be either a standard increase over the previous month or a repeat of the CGS number from 12 months prior to the last month. (adjusted by inflation)

PRO FORMA CONSOLIDATED STATEMENT OF CHANGES IN FINANCIAL POSITIONS: SOURCES AND USES OF FUNDS for Artful Fly

	Jun 95	Jul-95	Aug-95	Sep-95	Oct-95	Nov-95	Dec-95	Jan-96	Feb-96	Mar-96	Apr-96	May-96	Jun-96	13 Month
Sources of Funds														
Cash Flow from Operations	0	0	0	23,117	0	7,456	24,234	0	0	1,954	3,008	7,985	0	67,755
Increase in Short-Term Debt	25,000	0	0	0	0	0	0	0	0	0	0	0	0	25,000
Increase in Medium-Term Debt	4,225	0	0	0	0	0	0	0	0	0	0	0	0	4,225
Increase in Long-Term Debt	0	0	0	0	0	0	0	0	0	0	0	0	0	0
Increase in Payables/Accrual	0	0	0	0	0	0	0	0	0	0	0	0	0	0
Sale of Assets/Investments	0	0	0	0	0	0	0	0	0	0	0	0	0	0
Cash (Equity) Contribution	$14,450	0	0	0	0	0	0	0	0	0	0	0	0	14,450
Total Sources:	43,675	0	0	23,117	0	7,456	24,234	0	0	1,954	3,008	7,985	0	111,430
Uses of Funds														
Short-Term Debt Retirement	0	195	197	199	201	203	205	207	209	211	213	215	217	2,468
Medium-Term Debt Retirement	0	33	33	34	34	34	35	35	35	36	36	36	37	417
Long-Term Debt Retirement	0	0	0	0	0	0	0	0	0	0	0	0	0	0
To Purchase Equipment	9,200	2,900	125	200	0	1,000	125	0	0	125	0	0	0	13,675
To Purchase Bldg/Land/Intang	0	0	0	0	0	0	0	0	0	0	0	0	0	0
Other (includes Oper. Exps.)	4,875	24,279	1,169	0	398	0	0	16,053	209	0	0	0	8,394	55,378
Total Uses:	14,075	27,407	1,524	432	633	1,237	364	16,295	453	371	248	251	8,648	71,938
Changes in Financial Position:	29,600	(27,407)	(1,524)	22,684	(633)	6,219	23,870	(16,295)	(453)	1,583	2,760	7,734	(8,648)	98,648
Estimated Ending Cash Balance:	29,600	2,193	669	23,353	22,720	28,940	52,809	36,515	36,062	37,645	40,405	48,140	39,492	39,492
Changes in Inventory (2)	0	21,060	14,610	(9,066)	(5,036)	(10,073)	19,780	(2,015)	(2,015)	(2,518)	(4,029)	9,386	0	30,085
Changes in Receivables (3):	0	0	0	0	0	0	0	0	0	0	0	0	0	0

NOTES:

(1) Operation expense use of funds includes any negative operating cash flow. This assumption is intended to reflect realistic behavior to cash needs.

(2) Inventory changes affecting sources and uses of funds are reflected in cash flow from operations (direct material purchases). This line summarizes the monthly magnitude of change (Direct Material Purchases - Cost of Goods Sold).

(3) Changes in receivables affecting sources and uses of funds are reflected in cash flow from operations (credit sale collections). This line summarizes the monthly magnitude of changes in receivables.

PROJECTED BALANCE SHEET: Artful Fly

Period:	Jul-96 Beginning	Jun-97 Ending
ASSETS		
Cash	39,492	72,838
Receivables	0	0
Inventory	30,485	32,424
Total Current Assets:	69,977	105,262
Equipment	9,866	10,957
Facilities/Bldgs	0	0
Deprec. Intangibles	0	0
Land & non-deprec.	0	0
TOTAL ASSETS:	79,843	116,219
LIABILITIES		
Previous Debt	26,339	23,116
New Debt:		
Short-term	0	0
Medium-term	0	0
Long-term	0	0
TOTAL LIABILITIES	26,339	23,116
EQUITY	53,504	93,103
TOTAL LIAB. & EQUITY:	79,843	116,219
LEVERAGE RATIOS		
Debt/Asset:	0.33	0.20
Debt/Equity:	0.49	0.25
Fixed Charge Coverage:	NA	9.93
LIQUIDITY RATIOS		
Current Ratio:	NA	NA
Quick Ratio:	NA	NA
New Investment in Budget Period		
Depreciable Equipment	39,492	
Depreciable Building	3,500	
Depreciable Intangibles	0	
Land & Non-Depreciable Assets	0	
Working Capital/Inventory	35,992	

OTHER FINANCIAL INFORMATION

Total Sales:	206,163
Gross Profit	150,762
Taxable Profit:	53,729
Net Profit:	41,052
Cash flow from Operations:	41,522
Sales Breakeven Point:	129,396
PROFITABILITY RATIOS	
Gross Margin:	73.13%
Taxable Profit Margin:	26.06%
Net Profit Margin:	19.91%
Cash flow from Operations/Sales:	20.14%
YEAR-END RETURN RATIOS (based upon cash flow)	
Return on Total Assets:	35.73%
Return on Dep. Assets:	310.66%
Return on Begin. Equity:	-77.61%
Financing Required	
Short-Term Debt	0
Medium-Term Debt	0
Long-Term Debt	0
Total	0

Notes:

1) Accounts payable estimates are not developed by the model. New (acquired within the planning period) short-term debt is assumed to be the only current liability.

PRO FORMA INCOME STATEMENT for Artful Fly This document produced on: 08-Aug-95

	Jul-96	Aug-96	Sep-96	Oct-96	Nov-96	Dec-96	Jan-97	Feb-97	Mar-97	Apr-97	May-97	Jun-97	YEAR	% of Sales
Expected Monthly Sales	12,370	16,493	32,986	26,801	16,493	30,924	14,493	8,247	8,247	10,308	14,493	10,308	204,163	100.0%
Cost of Goods Sold	3,324	4,432	8,864	7,202	4,432	8,310	4,432	2,216	2,216	2,770	4,432	2,770	55,401	26.9%
Gross Profit	9,046	12,061	24,122	19,599	12,061	22,614	12,061	6,030	6,030	7,558	12,061	7,538	150,762	73.1%
Overhead Expenses														
Labor	4,478	4,478	4,478	4,478	7,464	7,464	4,478	4,478	4,478	4,478	4,478	4,478	59,710	29.0%
Utilities & Telephone	325	326	327	327	328	329	330	331	332	332	333	334	3,954	1.9%
Insurance	800	0	0	0	0	0	0	0	0	0	0	0	800	0.4%
Advertising & Promotion	5,500	100	5,528	101	2,323	101	102	2,341	102	102	103	103	16,505	8.0%
Travel & Entertainment	150	150	151	151	152	152	152	153	153	153	154	154	1,825	.9%
Repairs & Maintenance	0	0	0	0	0	152	0	0	0	0	154	0	306	0.1%
Shipping & Postage	205	331	206	332	207	334	208	387	209	337	210	339	3,306	1.6%
Office Supplies	100	100	101	101	101	101	102	102	102	102	103	103	1,217	0.6%
Other (inc. rents & leases)	400	150	151	151	152	152	152	153	153	153	154	154	2,075	1.0%
Property & Other Taxes	173	173	173	173	173	173	173	173	173	173	173	173	2,077	1.0%
Total Overhead Expenses	12,131	5,809	11,113	5,815	10,899	8,958	5,697	8,116	5,702	5,833	5,861	5,838	91,774	44.5%
Depreciation														
Machinery & Equipment	201	201	201	201	201	201	201	201	201	201	201	201	2,409	1.2%**
Buildings & Intangibles	0	0	0	0	0	0	0	0	0	0	0	0	0	0.0%
Operating Income (EBIT)	(3,286)	6,051	12,808	13,583	961	13,455	6,163	(2,207)	128	1,505	5,999	1,499	56,579	27.4%
Interest Expense	251	249	246	244	242	239	237	233	231	229	226	223	2,850	1.4%
Taxable Income (EBT)	(3,537)	5,802	12,562	13,339	219	13,216	5,926	(2,520)	(103)	1,276	5,773	1,276	53,729	26.1%
Est. Income Tax Obligation**	0	1,369	2,964	3,147	170	3,118	1,398	0	0	301	1,362	301	12,677	6.1%
Tax Credits	NA	NA	NA	NA	NA	NA	NA	NA	NA	NA	NA	NA	0	0.0%
Estimated Income Taxes**	0	1,369	2,964	3,147	170	3,118	1,398	0	0	301	1,362	301	12,677	6.1%
Net Profit	(3,537)	4,433	9,598	10,192	549	10,098	4,528	(2,520)	(153)	975	4,411	975	41,052	19.9%

SUMMARY OF SELECTED YEAR END DATA:

Total Variable Costs (CGS)	=	55,401
Total Fixed Costs	=	94,624
(Overhead + Interest)		
Total Net Profit	=	41,052
Total Net Operations Cash Flow	=	41,522

SELECTED FINANCIAL RATIOS:

Variable Costs/Sales	=	26.87%
Fixed Costs/Sales	=	45.90%
Gross Margin/Sales	=	73.13%
Operating Profit/Sales	=	27.44%
After Tax Profit/Sales	=	19.91%
Cash Flow From Operations/Sales	=	20.14%
(internally generated cash flow)		
Sales Break Even Point ($'s)	=	129,396
Return on Beginning Current Assets	=	59.34%*
Return on Depreciable Assets	=	310.66%*
Return on Total Fixed Assets	=	52.01%*
Return on Beginning Equity	=	77.61%*

NOTES:

(1) Assumes 11.5% cost of capital and 83% debt financing, with a 7 year loan for working capital & inventory.

(2) Assumes 11.5% cost of capital and 31% debt financing, with a 7 year loan for equipment and furnishings.

(3) Assumes 9.5% cost of capital and 0% debt financing, with a 20 year loan for land and structures.

(4) 3.0% inflation rate is applied to overhead expenses.

(5) Depreciation method chosen for equipt. is: double declining balance.
 Depreciation method chosen for buildings is: straight-line.
 Depreciation life determined by Federal tax definitions.

(6) The enterprise simulated is assumed to be a regular corporation.
 Taxes are estimated based on this legal structure and the previous year's tax rates (federal, state, local & FICA).
 Sole proprietor taxes include Self-Employment taxes. All other forms include only Fed. & State income taxes.

**(7) For monthly cashflow modeling all taxes are assumed to be withheld by the firm as monthly income is earned.
 This may cause monthly cashflows to be under-estimated in an one year forecast which has any one or more months of net income loss.
 The yearly total does reflect the actual expected amount of taxes owed for the forecasted year.

(8) Total sales are assumed to grow at an NA average annual rate.

(9) Cash flow projections assume that the total amount of debt financing needed is received as a lump sum in first month the firm requires financing, by category.

(10) Operations are assumed to begin 335 days from the current date: Aug-95

(11) Sales breakeven point are sales necessary to cover CGS, overhead & interest expenses.

(12) All return ratios based upon cash flows from operations, not profit.

PRO FORMA CASH FLOW FROM OPERATIONS STATEMENT for Artful Fly

	Jun 96	Jul-96	Aug-96	Sep-96	Oct-96	Nov-96	Dec-96	Jan-97	Feb-97	Mar-97	Apr-97	May-97	Jun-97	13 Month
Cash Sales	0	12,370	16,493	32,986	26,801	16,493	30,924	16,493	8,247	8,247	10,308	16,493	10,308	206,163
Collected Receivables	0	0	0	0	0	0	0	0	0	0	0	0	0	
Other Income	0	0	0	0	0	0	0	0	0	0	0	0	0	
Total Operation Cash Inflow	0	12,370	16,493	32,986	26,801	16,493	30,924	16,493	8,247	8,247	10,308	16,493	10,308	206,163
Operation/Overhead Costs	12,131	5,809	11,113	5,815	10,899	8,458	5,697	8,116	5,702	5,833	5,861	5,838	3,440	91,774
Direct/Raw Material Costs	4,587	9,174	7,454	4,587	8,601	4,587	8,601	4,587	2,294	2,294	2,867	4,587	2,867	57,340
Interest Expense	0	251	249	246	244	242	239	237	233	231	229	226	223	2,850
Income Taxes Paid**	0	1,369	2,564	3,147	170	3,118	1,398	0	0	301	1,362	301		12,677
Total Operation Cash Outflow	0	16,970	16,602	21,226	13,793	19,912	16,903	9,626	10,643	8,800	10,950	10,316	9,803	164,641
Total Cash Flow From Operations		(4,600)	(108)	11,204	13,008	(3,419)	14,022	6,867	(2,396)	(554)	(642)	6,177	505	41,522

NOTES:
(1) Direct/raw material purchases for each month represents the expected cost of goods to be sold in the following month, esculated by the CGS average inflation rate (Sales & CGS worksheet): 3.50%

(2) Direct/raw material purchases for the last month are assumed to be either a standard increase over the previous month or a repeat of the CGS number from 12 months prior to the last month. (adjusted by inflation)

PRO FORMA CONSOLIDATED STATEMENT OF CHANGES IN FINANCIAL POSITIONS: SOURCES AND USES OF FUNDS for Artful Fly

	Jun 96	Jul-96	Aug-96	Sep-96	Oct-96	Nov-96	Dec-96	Jan-97	Feb-97	Mar-97	Apr-97	May-97	Jun-97	13 Month
Sources of Funds														
Cash Flow from Operations	0	0	0	11,209	13,008	0	14,022	6,867	0	0	0	6,177	505	51,788
Increase in Short-Term Debt	0	0	0	0	0	0	0	0	0	0	0	0	0	0
Increase in Medium-Term Debt	0	0	0	0	0	0	0	0	0	0	0	0	0	0
Increase in Long-Term Debt	0	0	0	0	0	0	0	0	0	0	0	0	0	0
Increase in Payables/Accrual	0	0	0	0	0	0	0	0	0	0	0	0	0	0
Sale of Assets/Investments	0	0	0	0	0	0	0	0	0	0	0	0	0	0
Cash (Equity) Contribution	$ 39,492	0	0	0	0	0	0	0	0	0	0	0	0	39,492
Total Sources:	39,492	0	0	11,209	13,008	0	14,022	6,867	0	0	0	6,177	505	91,280
Uses of Funds														
Short-Term Debt Retirement	0	0	0	0	0	0	0	0	0	0	0	0	0	0
Medium-Term Debt Retirement	0	0	0	0	0	0	0	0	0	0	0	0	0	0
Long-Term Debt Retirement	0	0	0	0	0	0	0	0	0	0	0	0	0	0
To Purchase Equipment	0	0	3,500	0	0	0	0	0	0	0	0	0	0	3,500
To Purchase Bldg/Land/Intang	0	0	0	0	0	0	0	0	0	0	0	0	0	0
Other (includes Oper. Exps.)	4,854	4,854	365	259	263	3,684	267	270	2,668	829	920	280	283	14,942
Total Uses:	4,854	4,854	3,865	259	263	3,684	267	270	2,668	829	920	280	283	18,442
Changes in Financial Position:	39,492	(4,854)	(3,865)	10,950	12,745	(3,684)	13,755	6,597	(2,668)	(829)	(920)	5,897	222	72,838
Estimated Ending Cash Balance:	39,492	34,638	30,773	41,722	54,467	50,783	64,538	71,135	68,467	67,638	66,719	72,616	72,838	72,838
Changes in Inventory (2)	0	1,263	4,742	(1,410)	(2,615)	4,169	(3,723)	(2,138)	78	651	1,817	(1,565)	670	1,939
Changes in Receivables (3):	0	0	0	0	0	0	0	0	0	0	0	0	0	0

NOTES:

(1) Operation expense use of funds includes any negative operating cash flow. This assumption is intended to reflect realistic behavior to cash needs.

(2) Inventory changes affecting sources and uses of funds are reflected in cash flow from operations (direct material purchases). This line summarizes the monthly magnitude of change (Direct Material Purchases - Cost of Goods Sold).

(3) Changes in receivables affecting sources and uses of funds are reflected in cash flow from operations (credit sale collections). This line summarizes the monthly magnitude of changes in receivables.

PROJECTED BALANCE SHEET: Artful Fly

Period:	Jul-97 Beginning	Jun-98 Ending
ASSETS		
Cash	72,838	81,192
Receivables	0	0
Inventory	32,424	34,460
Total Current Assets:	105,262	115,652
Equipment	10,957	18,320
Facilities/Bldgs	0	0
Deprec. Intangibles	0	0
Land & non-deprec.	0	0
TOTAL ASSETS:	116,219	133,973
LIABILITIES		
Previous Debt	23,116	19,500
New Debt:		
Short-term	0	0
Medium-term	0	0
Long-term	0	0
TOTAL LIABILITIES	23,116	19,500
EQUITY	93,103	114,473
TOTAL LIAB. & EQUITY:	116,219	133,973
LEVERAGE RATIOS		
Debt/Asset:	0.20	0.15
Debt/Equity:	0.25	0.17
Fixed Charge Coverage:	NA	7.05
LIQUIDITY RATIOS		
Current Ratio:	NA	NA
Quick Ratio:	NA	NA
New Investment in Budget Period		
Depreciable Equipment	72,838	
Depreciable Building	12,500	
Depreciable Intangibles	0	
Land & Non-Depreciable Assets	0	
Working Capital/Inventory	60,338	

OTHER FINANCIAL INFORMATION

Total Sales:	216,471
Gross Profit	158,300
Taxable Profit:	32,203
Net Profit:	24,828
Cash flow from Operations:	27,929
Sales Breakeven Point:	165,410
PROFITABILITY RATIOS	
Gross Margin:	73.13%
Taxable Profit Margin:	14.88%
Net Profit Margin:	11.47%
Cash flow from Operations/Sales:	12.90%
YEAR-END RETURN RATIOS (based upon cash flow)	
Return on Total Assets:	20.85%
Return on Dep. Assets:	119.07%
Return on Begin. Equity:	30.00%
Financing Required	
Short-Term Debt	0
Medium-Term Debt	0
Long-Term Debt	0
Total	0

Notes:
1) Accounts payable estimates are not developed by the model. New (acquired within the planning period) short-term debt is assumed to be the only current liability.

PRO FORMA INCOME STATEMENT for Artful Fly This document produced on: 08-Aug-95

	Jul-97	Aug-97	Sep-97	Oct-97	Nov-97	Dec-97	Jan-98	Feb-98	Mar-98	Apr-98	May-98	Jun-98	YEAR	% of Sales
Expected Monthly Sales	12,988	17,318	34,635	28,141	17,318	32,471	17,318	8,659	8,659	10,824	17,318	10,824	216,471	100.0%
Cost of Goods Sold	3,490	4,654	9,307	7,562	4,654	8,726	4,654	2,327	2,327	2,909	4,654	2,909	58,171	
Gross Profit	9,498	12,664	25,328	20,579	12,664	23,745	12,664	6,332	6,332	7,915	12,444	7,915	158,300	73.1%
Overhead Expenses														
Labor	4,478	4,478	4,478	4,478	7,464	7,464	4,478	4,478	4,478	4,478	4,478	4,478	59,710	29.0%
Utilities & Telephone	400	401	402	403	404	405	406	407	408	409	410	411	4,867	2.2%
Insurance	900	0	0	0	0	0	0	0	0	0	0	0	900	0.4%
Advertising & Promotion	5,450	150	5,678	151	2,475	152	152	5,037	153	153	154	154	20,040	9.3%
Travel & Entertainment	150	150	151	151	152	152	152	153	2,040	153	154	154	3,712	1.7%
Repairs & Maintenance	0	0	0	0	0	152	0	0	0	0	154	0	306	0.1%
Shipping & Postage	230	256	256	408	258	410	259	412	260	414	261	416	3,991	1.8%
Office Supplies	125	126	126	126	126	127	127	127	128	128	128	128	1,521	.7%
Other (inc. rents & leases)	500	251	251	252	253	253	254	254	255	256	256	257	3,292	1.5%
Property & Other Taxes	186	186	186	186	186	186	186	186	186	186	186	186	2,232	1.0%
Total Overhead Expenses	13,739	8,760	14,141	8,768	12,436	10,420	7,134	12,175	9,028	7,297	7,301	7,305	118,503	54.7%
Depreciation														
Machinery & Equipment	428	428	428	428	428	428	428	428	428	428	428	428	5,137	2.4%**
Buildings & Intangibles	0	0	0	0	0	0	0	0	0	0	0	0	0	0.0%
Operating Income (EBIT)	(4,669)	3,476	10,759	11,383	(200)	12,897	5,102	(6,271)	(3,124)	189	4,935	182	34,660	16.0%
Interest Expense	221	218	215	212	209	206	203	201	197	195	191	189	2,457	1.1%
Taxable Income (EBT)	(4,890)	3,258	10,544	11,171	(409)	12,691	4,899	(6,472)	(3,321)	(6)	4,744	(7)	32,203	14.9%
Est. Income Tax Obligation**	0	746	2,415	2,558	0	2,906	1,122	0	0	0	1,086	0	7,374	3.4%
Tax Credits	NA	NA	NA	NA	NA	NA	NA	NA	NA	NA	NA	NA	0	0.0%
Estimated Income Taxes**	0	746	2,415	2,558	0	2,906	1,122	0	0	0	1,086	0	7,374	3.4%
Net Profit	(4,890)	2,512	8,130	8,613	(409)	9,785	3,777	(6,472)	(3,321)	(6)	3,657	(7)	24,828	11.5%

SUMMARY OF SELECTED YEAR END DATA:

Total Variable Costs (CGS)	=	58,171
Total Fixed Costs	=	120,960
(Overhead + Interest)		
Total Net Profit	=	24,828
Total Net Operations Cash Flow	=	27,929

SELECTED FINANCIAL RATIOS:

Variable Costs/Sales	=	26.87%
Fixed Costs/Sales	=	55.88%
Gross Margin/Sales	=	73.13%
Operating Profit/Sales	=	16.01%
After Tax Profit/Sales	=	11.47%
Cash Flow From Operations/Sales	=	12.90%
(internally generated cash flow)		
Sales Break Even Point ($'s)	=	165,410
Return on Beginning Current Assets	=	26.53%*
Return on Depreciable Assets	=	119.07%*
Return on Total Fixed Assets	=	24.03%*
Return on Beginning Equity	=	30.00%*

NOTES:

(1) Assumes 11.5% cost of capital and 0% debt financing, with a 7 year loan for working capital & inventory.

(2) Assumes 11.5% cost of capital and 0% debt financing, with a 7 year loan for equipment and furnishings.

(3) Assumes 9.5% cost of capital and 0% debt financing, with a 20 year loan for land and structures.

(4) 3.0% inflation rate is applied to overhead expenses.

(5) Depreciation method chosen for equipt. is: double declining balance.
Depreciation method chosen for buildings is: straight-line.
Depreciation life determined by Federal tax definitions.

(6) The enterprise simulated is assumed to be a regular corporation.
Taxes are estimated based on this legal structure and the previous year's tax rates (federal, state, local & FICA).
Sole proprietor taxes include Self-Employment taxes. All other forms include only Fed. & State income taxes.

**(7) For monthly cashflow modeling all taxes are assumed to be withheld by the firm as monthly income is earned.
This may cause monthly cashflows to be under-estimated in an one year forecast which has any one or more months of net income loss.
The yearly total does reflect the actual expected amount of taxes owed for the forecasted year.

(8) Total sales are assumed to grow at an NA average annual rate.

(9) Cash flow projections assume that the total amount of debt financing needed is received as a lump sum in first month the firm requires financing, by category.

(10) Operations are assumed to begin 700 days from the current date: Aug-95

(11) Sales breakeven point are sales necessary to cover CGS, overhead & interest expenses.

(12) All return ratios based upon cash flows from operations, not profit.

PRO FORMA CASH FLOW FROM OPERATIONS STATEMENT for Artful Fly

	Jun 97	Jul-97	Aug-97	Sep-97	Oct-97	Nov-97	Dec-97	Jan-98	Feb-98	Mar-98	Apr-98	May-98	Jun-98	13 Month
Cash Sales	0	12,988	17,318	34,635	28,141	17,318	32,471	17,318	8,659	8,659	10,824	17,318	10,824	216,471
Collected Receivables	0	0	0	0	0	0	0	0	0	0	0	0	0	
Other Income	0	0	0	0	0	0	0	0	0	0	0	0	0	
Total Operation Cash Inflow	0	12,988	17,318	34,635	28,141	17,318	32,471	17,318	8,659	8,659	10,824	17,318	10,824	216,471
Operation/Overhead Costs	0	13,739	8,760	14,141	8,768	12,436	10,420	7,134	12,175	9,028	7,297	7,301	7,305	118,503
Direct/Raw Material Costs	4,817	9,633	7,827	4,817	9,031	4,817	2,408	2,408	3,010	4,817	3,010	3,612	60,207	
Interest Expense	0	221	218	215	212	209	206	203	201	197	195	191	189	2,457
Income Taxes Paid**	0	0	746	2,415	2,558	0	2,906	1,122	0	0	0	1,086	0	7,374
Total Operation Cash Outflow	0	16,970	16,602	21,226	13,793	19,912	16,903	9,626	10,643	8,800	10,950	10,316	9,803	164,641
Total Cash Flow From Operations	0	18,776	19,357	24,597	16,355	21,676	18,349	10,867	14,784	12,235	12,309	11,589	11,106	188,542

NOTES:

(1) Direct/raw material purchases for each month represents the expected cost of goods to be sold in the following month, esculated by the CGS average inflation rate (Sales & CGS worksheet): 3.50%

(2) Direct/raw material purchases for the last month are assumed to be either a standard increase over the previous month or a repeat of the CGS number from 12 months prior to the last month. (adjusted by inflation)

PRO FORMA CONSOLIDATED STATEMENT OF CHANGES IN FINANCIAL POSITIONS: SOURCES AND USES OF FUNDS for Artful Fly

	Jun 97	Jul-97	Aug-97	Sep-97	Oct-97	Nov-97	Dec-97	Jan-98	Feb-98	Mar-98	Apr-98	May-98	Jun-98	13 Month
Sources of Funds														
Cash Flow from Operations	0	0	0	10,038	11,787	0	14,122	6,451	0	0	0	5,729	0	48,126
Increase in Short-Term Debt	0	0	0	0	0	0	0	0	0	0	0	0	0	0
Increase in Medium-Term Debt	0	0	0	0	0	0	0	0	0	0	0	0	0	
Increase in Long-Term Debt	0	0	0	0	0	0	0	0	0	0	0	0	0	
Increase in Payables/Accrual	0	0	0	0	0	0	0	0	0	0	0	0	0	
Sale of Assets/Investments		0	0	0	0	0	0	0	0	0	0	0	0	
Cash (Equity) Contribution	$ 72,838	0	0	0	0	0	0	0	0	0	0	0	0	72,838
Total Sources:	72,838	0	0	10,038	11,787	0	14,122	6,451	0	0	0	5,729	0	120,964
Uses of Funds														
Short-Term Debt Retirement	0	0	0	0	0	0	0	0	0	0	0	0	0	0
Medium-Term Debt Retirement	0	0	0	0	0	0	0	0	0	0	0	0	0	0
Long-Term Debt Retirement	0	0	0	0	0	0	0	0	0	0	0	0	0	0
To Purchase Equipment	0	0	12,500	0	0	0	0	0	0	0	0	0	0	12,500
To Purchase Bldg/Land/Intang	0	0	0	0	0	0	0	0	0	0	0	0	0	0
Other (includes Oper. Exps.)	0	6,074	2,328	291	294	4,655	300	302	6,431	3,885	1,797	314	601	27,272
Total Uses:	0	6,074	14,828	291	294	4,655	300	302	6,431	3,885	1,797	314	601	39,772
Changes in Financial Position:	72,838	(6,074)	(14,828)	9,747	11,493	(4,655)	13,822	6,149	(6,431)	(3,885)	(1,797)	5,415	(601)	81,192
Estimated Ending Cash Balance:	72,838	66,764	51,936	61,683	73,176	68,521	82,343	88,491	82,060	78,176	76,378	81,793	81,192	81,192
Changes in Inventory (2):	0	1,326	4,979	(1,480)	(2,746)	1,377	(3,909)	(2,245)	81	684	1,908	(1,643)	704	2,036
Changes in Receivables (3):	0	0	0	0	0	0	0	0	0	0	0	0	0	0

NOTES:

(1) Operation expense use of funds includes any negative operating cash flow. This assumption is intended to reflect realistic behavior to cash needs.

(2) Inventory changes affecting sources and uses of funds are reflected in cash flow from operations (direct material purchases).
This line summarizes the monthly magnitude of change (Direct Material Purchases - Cost of Goods Sold).

(3) Changes in receivables affecting sources and uses of funds are reflected in cash flow from operations (credit sale collections).
This line summarizes the monthly magnitude of changes in receivables.

business**PLAN**

BizCopy

Quality Printing Served Here

Bill Gaytes

General Manager / Owner

Business Plan

12/7/98

Table of Contents

Section I. Executive Summary

This purpose of preparing this document was to provide BizCopy inc. with a plan and vision to grow sales past the 1 million dollar level to 2 million in sales while remaining profitable. In preparing this plan the financial make up of BizCopy, the market place, products, pricing and promotion were examined. The purpose of the plan is to discover what activities and products are contributing to growth and to leverage these to accelerate growth.

The physical make up of BizCopy and the financial aspects of this were addressed first. Financial models of consolidating into one store were created keeping all current staff members (12) or dropping down to 10. The results of this showed that while total sales at the Profitville store are not large it is an important contributor to overhead and profit. Even with moving $16000.00 in monthly sales to store 1 and no new employees, profitability of the company suffered. Therefore we conclude that the satellite operation and concept is viable and should be continued.

If the one satellite store model was desirable then how about a second satellite operation? We next developed a model income statement opening a third store. The figures used to project monthly sales were the Profitville stores opening sales numbers.

This model showed that in the first 12 months of operation BizCopy inc. could expect to lose $60000.00 before the store would operate at break even. Conclusions from this model showed that this cost along with the $50000.00 to open a store could be better spent on an acquisition of an existing facility. This facility would of course need to be in a geographically desirable location for BizCopy.

When BizCopy's overall sales and individual client accounts are examined, we see a trend became apparent that needs repeated and accelerated. Managed accounts are up 38% while overall sales remain flat. BizCopy's outside sales efforts with the help of SHN marketing group are achieving results. The objective is to increase this type of activity through assigning accounts to managers and eventually hiring an additional account manager. An additional account manager can not be hired at this time because it would be in conflict with BizCopy's goal to achieve $41.17 per hour worked. The addition of another corporate account manager will happen when the output is up enough to allow BizCopy to comfortably add this position.

Mailing services has been a powerful addition to BizCopy's service offering. Marketing plans are being developed to better leverage this service.

- Does the personnel section illustrate the owner and staff competencies?

- Do you get a good mental picture of the business and how it will operate, the role location will play?

- How did they use research to learn about their customers?

- How are they using employee-based goals to move their company forward?

- How do they use financial rations to manage their business?

- What role does an advisory board play in the company's credibility and success?

- This company is not looking at financing, how is this plan different as they look at the company's management? Different audience?

- What is their competition like? Is this a highly competitive industry?

Overall BizCopy is a healthy company with financial ratios at average or above the industry. The printing industry is competitive and BizCopy is a contender in the Boise market. With attention to the above mentioned attributes BizCopy will hit the 2 million dollar level in 5 or less years.

Section II. Mission, Goals, and Objectives

Statement of Purpose

The purpose of BizCopy's business plan is to outline a strategy for growth in the commercial printing industry. This plan will examine several operational options to increase both market share and profit. Two fundamental questions will be answered; where are we right now? And how can we get where we want to go? We will analyze these two issues in detail. Please refer to the following questions that will be answered by this business plan.

1. What is BizCopy's market share and does BizCopy have the capacity to expand in this market?
2. If BizCopy is capable of growing, what are the ramifications in implementing this possible growth? How will this growth take place? In Appendix D are "what if" pro-forma financial statements and relevant growth potential material to assist you.
   a. Should BizCopy open a new store in a new location?
   b. What geographic area should BizCopy open a 3rd store in?
   c. What Geographic areas can BizCopy cover with two stores?
   d. Are there acquisition opportunities? Is this an option over starting a new store?
   e. Should BizCopy consolidate the two existing stores into one?
   f. Could the territories be covered with outside sales people?

A financial plan will mathematically analyze the questions above. Financial projections, sales forecasts, store analyses, and industry ratio analysis will be used as the foundation to explain our positions and conclusions. From these conclusions we will create a strategic plan for reaching the company goals and objectives.

General Description of the Business

BizCopy is in the communication business, helping businesses grow and profit by providing service and products to meet their needs. BizCopy provides free pick up and delivery, design services, color copies, high speed/volume black and white copies, offset printing both spot and process color, and mailing services. BizCopy has a corporate account manager to develop new business as well as service larger clients.

Stage of Development

BizCopy is 8.5 years old and is currently in the early stages of maturity in relation to the business cycle. The market for commercial printing is stable, and is between the mature and stagnant stages of the business cycle. Printing needs and overall demand for printing jobs are adequate for profitability. The industry is changing with the introduction of digital printing devices. BizCopy is preparing itself for these changes.

General Growth Plan

BizCopy wants to grow so that it may increase its market share. The dilemma facing BizCopy is how to promote this desired growth. Should BizCopy increase the number of its storefront, or should BizCopy consolidate into one location while increasing its sales force? One thing is for certain, BizCopy must exploit new areas in this industry while it continues to provide superior service to its long-term customers—as our customers are the key to future growth.

Mission Statement

At BizCopy, our mission is to provide superior, knowledgeable service and innovative solutions to businesses and professionals in the Success Valley at competitive rates. To accomplish this, we will wok harder to improve all facets of our trade. We will be vigilant in finding new ways to exceed the rising expectations of our clients and prospects. By doing these things, we expect our business to grow and prosper, while we achieve a higher level of job satisfaction.

Goals and Objectives

The goals for BizCopy are represented by customer based goals, employee based goals, and financial based goals. Accompanying objectives are presented to explain necessary steps in accomplishing these goals.

Customer Based Goals

1. BizCopy would like to be noted for having superior customer service.
   Related Objectives: Continuous improvement starting immediately.
   - Developing life long relationships with customers.
   - Providing knowledgeable and innovative solutions for customers' needs.
2. Increase Market Share.
   Related Objectives: Continuous improvement starting immediately.
   - Increase customer base.
   - Sell more services to current customers.
   - Offer more than printing services to customers.
   - Promote involvement in communications, other document needs, CD burning, etc...

Employee Based Goals:

1. BizCopy would like to provide more than just a job to employees.
   Related Objectives: Continuous improvement starting immediately.
   - Provide a good work environment. Fast paced and fun with a variety of job duties.
   - Promote teamwork.
   - Business growth allowing employees job rotation and promotions.
   - Growth enhanced by store expansion and by increasing services currently offered.
2. Sales per employee to exceed industry averages.
   Related Objectives: All goals to be met by end of second quarter 1999.
   - BizCopy plans to exceed the current industry average of $85,000.00 in annual sales per employee ($41.13 per hour).

- Replace inefficient equipment with newer faster models—thus increasing productivity.
- Cross-train staff to be able to assist in overloaded areas.
- Reduce turnaround time to under three days. NO EXCEPTIONS!

Financial Based Goals

1. Reduce costs to below industry average costs by the second quarter of 1999.
   Related objectives: All goals to be met by end of second quarter 1999.
   - Reduce labor costs to 27% of sales.
   - Reduce paper costs to 13% of sales.
   - Reduce material costs to 3% of sales.
     1. Exceed trade association averages in sales volumes. Related Objectives:
   - Enter the top $2 \leq h$ percentile in sales volume by the end of the first quarter, 1999.
   - Push for annual sales of $1,080,000.00 by the end of fiscal year 1999.
2. Exceed industry average owners' compensation.
   Related Objectives: Goal to be met by the end of fiscal year 1999.
   - Owners' compensation to increase into the top 25th percentile of industry's average owners' compensation.

Section III. Background Information

The Industry

BizCopy competes in the continually changing small commercial quick print industry. While the industry is currently in the mature stage of the business cycle, new technologies constantly provide areas to grow and/or gain a competitive advantage. Presently the quick print customer base is shrinking due to the fact businesses are increasingly meeting their documentation needs internally.

The small commercial printing industry as a whole has remained stable over the last 10 years, as illustrated by the following chart. BizCopy's ratios can be found on page 21 of the appendix.

TRENDS IN SELECTED RATIOS AND FACTORS, 1989-1998

YEAR:	1989	1990	1991	1992	1993	1994	1995	1996	1997	1998
CATEGORY										
COST OF OPERATIONS (%)	61.3	60.8	62.9	63.2	63.1	60.8	61.1	62	62.2	61.7	62.3
OPERATING MARGIN (%)	3.8	3.7	3.6	3.9	3.5	3.7	4.1	3.8	4.6	4	4.4
AVERAGE NET RCBLS. ($)	263	334	297	363	351	334	417	354	381	458	445
AVERAGE INVENTORIES ($)	112	145	143	150	148	145	174	148	146	152	163
AVERAGE NET WORTH ($)	441	574	521	633	618	574	735	619	641	681	668
CURRENT RATIO (xl)	2	1.8	1.7	1.8	1.9	1.8	1.8	1.8	1.6	1.4	1.5
QUICK RATIO (xl)	1.4	1.3	1.2	1.2	1.3	1.3	1.3	1.2	1.1	1	1
COVERAGE RATIO (xl)	4.4	3.9	4.3	4.5	3.7	3.9	4	3.7	4.5	4.2	4.3
ASSET TURNOVER (xl)	1.9	1.8	1.7	1.8	1.8	1.8	1.7	1.7	1.7	1.5	1.6
OPERATING LEVERAGE	1.1	1	1	1.1	0.9	1	1.2	0.9	1.2	0.9	1.1
FINANCIAL LEVERAGE	1	1	1.2	1.1	1	1	1	1	1.2	1	
TOTAL LEVERAGE	1.1	.9	1.1	1.2	0.8	0.9	1.2	0.9	1.3	0.9	1.2

Source: the *Almanac of Business and Industrial Financial Ratios*, 1998 edition.

Current and Future Industry Trends

Two present trends are presently occurring in the highly saturated quick print industry. First, large quick print companies are blanketing the nation with full service locations, offering a quality product, low prices, and various services to the customer Secondly, smaller quick print firms are consolidating their operations into few locations in an effort to reduce costs so that they may compete against larger companies. Overall, the trend is toward high quality, low price, and making available several services to the customer.

Products on the horizon entail all forms of digital printing—printing from electronic files vs. the traditional hard copy. New techniques enhanced by technology fuel this industry's growth potential by offering higher productivity, more options, and reduced overall operations costs. Unfortunately, new technologies are also making it feasible for the present quick print customer to meet their own documentation needs by purchasing their own equipment—thus the quick print customer base is shrinking.

Although sales are increasing throughout the industry, profit margins are decreasing as competing firms continue to reduce prices in an effort to remain competitive. Presently the average Cost of Goods Sold in the industry is approximately 20%, while profit margins are 11.9%.

Government regulation has not had a significant impact on business.

The Business "Fit" in the Industry

Currently BizCopy possesses 5% of the local market share (Corporate, Fairmarket, and Victory communities). BizCopy offers a high quality product, competitive prices, and various services to its customers—all of which are necessary to make it in this highly competitive industry. The long run key to success for BizCopy is to offer its customers the latest technology and the most innovative services in meeting customer needs. Recently BizCopy has successfully established a mailing service to broaden its services to the customer. Page 171 displays how BizCopy's prices compare to the market.

As indicated above, growth is based on the utilization of innovative processes. Integration of printing services and computers is essential to the future success of BizCopy. Therefore, BizCopy must make the following steps to insure its survival in the quick print industry:

- Digital printing and copying services.
- Increase process printing capabilities.
- Continued growth of mailing department.
- Become electronically compatible with customer by accepting files both in person and electronically.
- Quicker turnaround via E-mail and website ordering.

Section IV. Organizational Matters

A. Business Structure Management and Personnel

Business Structure

The two owners *(50% each)* of BizCopy, Bill and Carol Gaytes, chose to operate their business as an S-Corporation. Upon consulting their attorney and accountant they decided that the S-Corporation would be the most beneficial legal structure from a tax standpoint. This entity has, and continues to be the optimal legal structure for BitPrint.

Organizational Structure

- The current BizCopy team includes a president, two managers, and 10 employees.
- Our main divisions are administration, sales, marketing, customer service, manufacturing, design, and layout.

The Management "Team"

- Bill Gaytes is the President, General Manager, and one of two owners of BizCopy. Purchased QuickPrint 1989, later changed the name of the business to BizCopy.
- Carol Gaytes is the Secretary, Treasurer and one of two owners of BizCopy.
- Don Trumph is the Manager—oversees the day to day operations—of Store 1 (downtown). Don has bee with BizCopy since July of 1990.
- Andrew Peters is the Manager—oversees the day to day operations—of Store 2 (Profitville). Larry has been with BizCopy since February of 1993.
- Carl Schecter is BizCopy's Production Facilitator. Carl has been with BizCopy since February of 1991.

Outside Services

Various consultants BizCopy consults with.

Milton Greely: accountant.	$800.00 /mo.
Bert Arbor: attorney.	As needed
Valejo DiFuentes: banker- US Bank.	As needed
Jill Pagels: insurance broker.	$450.00 /mo.
Steve Nelson: marketing.	$1500.00 /mo.
Various for cleaning and maintenance.	As needed

Advisory Board

The advisory board meets bi-annually.

- Milton Greely: accountant.
- Bert Arbor: attorney.
- Valejo DiFuentes: banker.
- Matt McDonald: Documax in Atlanta.
- Robbie Perault: Quickprint in Topeka.
- Mars Feldman: Printquik in Elko.

Map Group

Meets monthly. Each participant hosts the meeting twice a year to discuss what is on the agenda.

- Karl Reese—owner of Corporate Interiors of Idaho.
- Jan Blueberry—owner of local TCBYs.
- Amber Anderson—owner of Anderson Architects.
- Kevin Forno—owner of Imazng.
- Don LeGrave—owner of Zero Products.

B. Operating Controls

Record Keeping Functions

Record keeping functions are shared amongst the owner, managers, and BizCopy's accountant. All financial activities—sales, accounts receivable, accounts payable, orders, inventory, payroll, etc.—are kept track of by BizCopy's current computer system. Transactions are adjusted electronically at the point of sale, when inventories are adjusted, etc. BizCopy's owners, managers, and accountant then utilize this information when necessary in preparing financial statements, evaluation cost control, preparing the payroll, ordering, etc.

Other Operations Controls

BizCopy keeps track of the following areas using information gathered from various sources.

- Paper costs as a percent of sales.
- Overall material costs as a percent of sales.
- Labor costs as a percent of sales.
- Sales per hour worked.
- Printing sales by day and by month.
- Copy counts—both color and black & white by day and by month.
- Typesetting sales by day and by month.
- Mailing services by month.
- Average turnaround time.
- Percentage of on time deliveries.

Section V. The Marketing Plan
A. Products and Services

Descriptions of Products and Services

BizCopy is a "full service" printing company—pick up and delivery, design of documents, printing of documents, and finally the mailing or delivery of such documents. Below is a list of products BizCopy provides. Following the product list is a chart with a percentage of sales breakdown (figure 1).

- Marketing Material: Brochures, invitations, announcements, newsletters, postcards, direct mail fliers, posters, news release, menus, etc.
- Business Communications: Handbooks, manuals, reports, directories, catalogs, surveys, bulletins, price books, overheads, transparencies, resumes, tickets, business reply mail, bulk mailing, etc.
- Business Stationary: Business cards, letterhead, envelopes, note pads, Rolodex cards, labels, etc.
- Office Forms: Invoices, purchase orders, statements, multi-pan carbon-less forms and snapset, message pads, work orders, price lists, inventory lists, large envelopes, business reply envelopes, continuously numbered forms, etc.

- Design: Typesetting, layout, scanning, high-resolution output to film or paper, file conversion, graphics, color copies from your disk, etc.
- Copying: High-speed, high-volume, full-color, black & white, multi-page, color overhead transparencies, self-service or full-service, etc.
- Mailing: Computerized sorting, CASS certifying, list maintenance, inkjet addressing—bar coding-Zip + 4, inserting, bulk mailing, lists for purchase, mail-merge letters, direct mail advertising, etc.
- Finishing: Binding—Comb, Plasticoil, Velo, and Saddle Stitch—, collating, folding, numbering, perforation, lamination, hole drilling, etc.

Features and Benefits Unique to BizCopy

The quick-print industry is highly saturated with cutthroat competitors. All quick-printers must offer competitive pricing, quality products, extensive product lines, expedient turn-around, and all around good service if they wish to succeed in the quick-print industry. Often times meeting these requirements is not enough. In these circumstances, a quick-printer must find a market niche by pro-

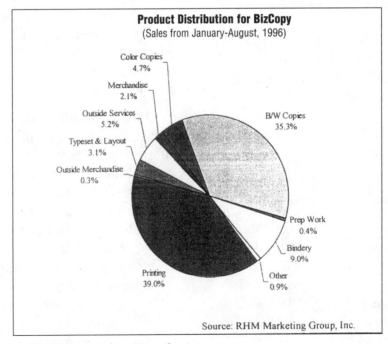

FIGURE 1: Product Distribution

viding additional features and services. BizCopy is building a niche by providing mailing services. BizCopy can design, print, and mail individual various jobs—alleviating several steps the customer once had the burden of doing themselves.

BizCopy offers a quality product at a competitive price, custom document design and layout, knowledgeable employees, and free pick-up and delivery. BizCopy has distinguished itself from other quick-printers by catering to businesses rather than the general public—thus filling a market niche.

Product Life Cycles and Seasonality

Product Life Cycles

BizCopy's products and services are scattered among the growth and maturity stages of the Product Life Cycle.

- Products in the Growth Stage: Color copies, printing from disk, and mailing are products and services with a lot of potential.
- Products in the Maturity Stage: Printing, B/W copies, bindery, and typesetting are products that have already witnessed the majority of their growth.

*Note: The products in the maturity stage are products that companies are increasingly producing internally. If this current trend continues, BizCopy will need to fill this void with new products and services, or by finding a new market niche.

Seasonality

All of BizCopy's products seem to fluctuate together, as their products are vertically integrated. Figure 2 illustrates BizCopy's seasonality.

Historical data suggest that March, May, August and September arc seasonally higher in sales than the remaining eight months. Because BizCopy's sales are seasonal, special attention needs to be paid to cash flows and budgeting.

Products/Services Growth Description

A relatively new product in the quick-print market is the use of digital printing. Digital printing allows a customer to bring their projects in on disk, instead of hard copies, to be produced.

As the world becomes more digital, so must everything in it—including BizCopy. If BizCopy does not keep up with digital technology, or technology in general, its competitors who do will gain a competitive advantage.

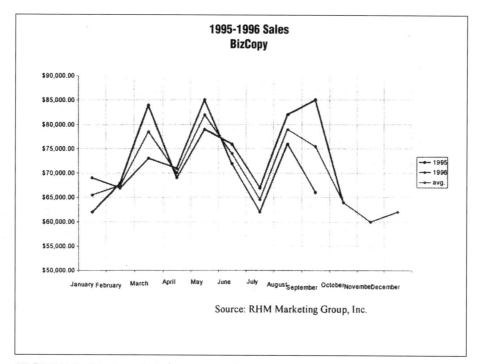

Source: RHM Marketing Group, Inc.

FIGURE 2: BizCopy's Sales Seasonality

B. Market Analysis

Customer Analysis

BizCopy's customers are both male and female professional representatives of local businesses. BizCopy's customers shop for their documentation needs during normal business hours—generally Monday through Friday: 8:00a.m to 6:00p.m. The main reason for purchase is business necessity. Quick-print customers weigh quality, price, convenience, and other factors when choosing a quick-printer (as indicated by our customer survey found on pages 50 - 58 in the appendix).

Competitive Analysis

There are several key competitors in this highly saturated market. Three such competitors are Kinko's, American Graphics, and Alphaprint. As indicated before, all competitors in the quick-print industry must provide a quality product at a reasonable price, in addition to being quick and convenient to be successful. All three of these companies have met these criteria. Pages 28 & 29 of the appendix detail the results of a competitive price survey we conducted.

In an effort to distinguish itself from the rest of the pack, a quick-printer must offer additional features or services aside from quality, price, and speed. In doing so, a quick-printer creates a niche for itself within the market. Some of BizCopy's competitors have distinguished themselves by:

- Kinko's—Caters to the walk-in customer by providing convenient locations, quality customer service, providing several copy machines/services, and by being open 24-hours a day. The key to Kinko's success is convenience and strong brand awareness.
- American Graphics—Offers cheap prices and has a good location. The key to American Graphic's success is pricing.
- Alphaprint—Offers competitive pricing with multiple locations for convenience. The key to Alphaprint's success is quality at a competitive price.
- BizCopy—Caters to businesses by providing competent sales representatives to business people who have less time in their day to go out for copies. BizCopy has taken the "one-stop shopping" approach by providing all documentation needs under one roof. Aside from providing "full service" to its target market, BizCopy offers a knowledgeable and courteous staff, quality, and competitive pricing. The key to BizCopy's success is that they have catered to a particular business market, or niche.

Market Potential

Current Trade Area

In saturated markets, the trade territory for quick-printers has traditionally been local. Because there are a large number of quick-printers in the valley—each with comparable quality and pricing—customers tend to go to the closest quick-printer to get their documents printed. However, if free pick-up and delivery are offered, the trade territory has the potential to increase in size. **The key to increasing the quick-print trade territory is to offer a quality sales staff who can convince outlying customers that location is not as important as quality and price when choosing a quick-printer.

- BizCopy's Downtown store services approximately one-half of Corporate (see appendix page 35). The downtown Corporate area is the most concentrated area of firms BizCopy has targeted as most likely to purchase in the region.
- BizCopy's Profitville store services the remainder of Corporate, Falcon, Perimeter, Fairmarket, and Victory.

Market Size and Trends

BizCopy's market size, 15,221 registered businesses and professionals in the valley (Corporate, Fairmarket, Victory), is larger than the industry average of approximately 5,000 (SHN Marketing Group). In addition to the vast size of the market, the valley is growing at a much higher rate than the national average.

While the market is relatively large—and growing—compared to the industry, BizCopy has captured only 4.6% of its target market (see figure 4).

C. The Marketing Plan

Location/Distribution

Location

BizCopy has two locations, one downtown Corporate on Major Street, the other on Profitville Avenue. Both locations are located in concentrated business areas in an effort to maximize convenience for BizCopy's target customers—business people. Both locations are ideal for attracting new business customers, as the stores are in high-traffic/convenient areas.

Distribution

Both locations serve as store fronts for walk-in customers who need to make photocopies, or are placing a printing order. Both stores are equipped with photocopiers, and are staffed with a sales staff. The Profitville location's responsibilities stop here—as it is just a storefront. All operations are based, and all printing jobs are done at the Major Street location.

All orders are collected at the Major Street store for processing and distribution— as this method is much more cost effective than equipping both locations with the necessary equipment to be self sufficient.

As the business grows, and more equipment becomes necessary to fill customer orders, there will become physical limitations as to how much equipment can efficiently fit at the Profitville Avenue location. While extra floor space has been allocated for, future growth may necessitate relocating the printing part of the business to a separate location.

Price/Quality Relationship

All quick-printers fit in the low price/high quality position in the price/quality relationship. As indicated before, to be successful a quick-printer must offer a quality product at a competitive price. Various firms gain market share by offering additional features and services.

BizCopy has positioned itself as a provider of a high quality product at a relatively high price. BizCopy can do this because they offer a combination of additional features and services that the competition does not match. Business communications expertise, quality employees, long-term relationships with customers, consistent and quality product, free pick-up and delivery, and quick turnaround times are a few of the features that distinguish BizCopy from the competition.

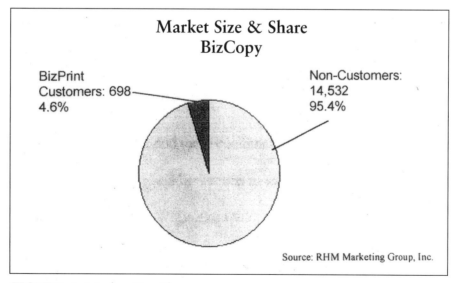

FIGURE 4: Market Size/Share

Promotional Strategies

Packaging

BizCopy has created a professional image by providing courteous, knowledgeable, and well-groomed employees. Further, both locations and delivery trucks are clean and professional looking. BizCopy's products are of high quality and are delivered quickly and on time.

Networking:

Networking is done through the Rotary Club, various leads, etc.

Advertising:

BizCopy's advertising budget is currently 2.41% of sales, which is higher than the industry average of 2.19%. This budget has been effective in the past, thus the future advertising budget will remain the same percentage of sales.

The current advertising budget is distributed amongst Yellow Pages ads, direct mailing, and various other advertising methods. Although BizCopy is currently advertised on television, through sponsoring the Fireman's Fund, BizCopy has established that the use of television and radio are not efficient means of advertising. Rather, the most effective method of advertising is through continued direct sales efforts—both personal sales attention, and direct mailing to current and potential customers.

Section VI. The Financial Plan

Sales Forecasts

Sales projections for 1999 were conducted, based on data collected over the last six years. Monthly sales percentages from these past years based on total sales for that current year were calculated. Then these percentages over the past six years were averaged by month. This final calculation was allocated on a monthly basis to a total sales forecast for 1999. Finally this allocation was used to develop final sales forecasts by month for 1999. The following represents these forecasts for 1999 by month.

Jan	$75,405.00	July	$73,525.00
Feb	$79,245.00	Aug	$79,140.00
March	$89,535.00	Sept	$83,080.00
April	$78,770.00	Oct	$84,180.00
May	$88,245.00	Nov	$76,195.00
June	$76,825.00	Dec	$70,965.00

Projected sales for 1999 are $955,110.00.

Cash Flow Projections

After these sales forecasts were developed, monthly cash flow projections for 1999 were calculated. The following assumptions were made in developing these projections.

1. Receivables are collected on a monthly basis after the sale.
2. Collections occur four months after the initial sale.
3. Monthly percentages of collections for receivable are as follows:
   - Eighty percent of sales are collected the first month following the sale.
   - Fifteen percent of sales are collected the second month following the sale.
   - Four percent of sales are collected the third month following the sale.
   - One percent of sales are collected the fourth month following the sale.
4. Other expense allocations are calculated as a percentage of sales.
5. Raw materials are 20% of sales.
6. Labor is 29% of sales.
7. G & A is 35% of sales.
8. Principal payments of $3,284.00 are incurred monthly.
9. The owner's salary is approximately $3,900.00 monthly.

A copy of BizCopy's financial statement can be found on pages 28 - 36 of the appendix. Financial ratios are presented on page 189.

Comparative Financial Ratios

BizCopy (Combined) vs. Industry Average
Multiple Shops: Sales Under $1,000,000

	BizCopy (Combined)	Industry Average
Solvency Rations		
Current	2.35	1.74
Quick	2.08	1.21
Safety Ratio		
Debt to Equity	0.83	1.69
Profitability Ratios		
Gross Profit Margin	81.33%	73.89%
Net Profit Margin	13.64%	16.95%
Asset Management Ratios		
Sales to Assets	3.45	3.28
Return on Assets (%)	47.12%	55.52%
Return on Investment (%)	86.08%	149.51%
Inventory Turnover (x)	9.48	11.77
Inventory (days)	38.52	31.00
A/R Turnover (x)	10.70	13.10
Collection Period (days)	34.12	27.87
A/P Turnover (x)	4.40	8.03
A/P (days)	83.04	45.45

Competitor Pricing Analysis

	BizCopy (Profitville)	The Printery	American Graphics	Budget Press	Uptown Printing	Kinko's
Letterhead—1000	$192.83	181.00	110.59	161.00	123.90	$181
Letterhead—2000	273.27	225.00	157.18	235.00	186.80	$276
Envelopes—1000	255.60	212.00	148.49	?	?	$216.45
Envelopes—2000	385.43	289.00	228.29	?	?	$354.03
Business Cards—500	75.95	157.00	68.32	75.95	90.00	?
Business Cards—1000	103.95	146.00	77.86	83.95	135.00	$186.69
Color Copies	n/a	n/a	1.80	n/a	0.99	1.00
Notes	n/a	n/a	>5	n/a	<1000	<1000
Special Fees	$150 setup	n/a	n/a	n/a	n/a	$35 color wash

Comparative Balance Sheet—12/31/98
BizCopy (Combined) vs. Industry Average
Multiple Shops: Total Sales Under $1000000

	BizCopy (Combined)		Industry Average	
	$	%	$	%
ASSETS				
Current Assets				
Cash	$ 42,622.97	15.45%	$ 28,031.00	12.86%
Accounts Receivable	$ 89,080.50	32.30%	$ 54,522.00	25.01%
Inventory	$ 18,769.12	6.80%	$ 15,836.00	7.26%
Other Current Assets	$ (1,601.17)	-0.58%	$ 19,882.00	9.12%
TOTAL CURRENT ASSETS	**$ 148,871.42**	**53.97%**	**$ 118,271.00**	**54.25%**
Non-Current Assets				
Equipment, Furniture, etc.	$ 321,165.30	116.44%	$ 258,424.00	118.54%
(Less Depreciation)	$ (212,307.60)	-76.97%	$(191,234.00)	-87.72%
Net Equipment	$ 108,857.70	39.47%	$ 67,190.00	30.82%
Real Estate	$ 15,606.73	5.66%	$ 6,766.00	3.10%
(Less Depreciation)	$ (1,727.35)	-0.63%	$ (751.00)	-0.34%
Net Real Estate	$ 13,879.38	5.03%	$ 6,015.00	2.76%
Other Non-Current Assets	$ 4,211.44	1.53%	$ 26,530.00	12.17%
TOTAL NON-CURRENT ASSETS	**$ 126,948.52**	**46.03%**	**$ 99,735.00**	**45.75%**
TOTAL ASSETS	**$ 275,819.94**	**100.00%**	**$ 218,006.00**	**100.00%**
LIABILITIES AND OWNER'S EQUITY				
Current Liabilities				
Accounts Payable	$ 40,463.29	14.67%	$ 23,219.00	10.65%
Notes Payable Within 1 Year	$ -	0.00%	$ 14,948.00	6.86%
Other Current Liabilities	$ 22,868.39	8.29%	$ 29,991.00	13.76%
TOTAL CURRENT LIABILITIES	**$ 63,331.68**	**22.96%**	**$ 68,158.00**	**31.26%**
Long-Term Liabilities				
Notes Payable Over 1 Year	$ 61,508.02	22.30%	$ 51,749.00	23.74%
Other Long-Term Liabilities	$ -	0.00%	$ 17,150.00	7.87%
TOTAL LONG-TERM LIABILITIES	**$ 61,508.02**	**22.30%**	**$ 68,899.00**	**31.60%**
TOTAL LIABILITIES	**$ 124,839.70**	**45.26%**	**$ 137,057.00**	**62.87%**
TOTAL OWNER'S EQUITY	**$ 150,980.24**	**54.74%**	**$ 80,949.00**	**37.13%**
TOTAL LIABILITIES & EQUITY	**$ 275,819.94**	**100.00%**	**$ 218,006.00**	**100.00%**

Comparative Income Statement (1997)

BizCopy (Combined) vs. Industry Averages
Multiple Shops: Total Gross Sales Under $1000000
Top Quartile

	BizCopy (Combined)		Industry Average	
	$	% of Sales	$	% of Sales
SALES				
Regular Printing	$ 429,775.72	45.11%	$ 427,479.00	59.87%
Copying	$ 307,373.91	32.26%	$ 158,750.00	22.23%
Color Copying	$ 58,523.99	6.14%	$ 34,204.00	4.79%
Brokered Sales	$ 22,854.55	2.40%	$ 73,036.00	10.23%
Other	$ 134,288.95	14.09%	$ 20,583.00	2.88%
TOTAL GROSS SALES	$ 952,817.12	100.00%	$ 714,052.00	100.00%
COST OF SALES				
Paper	$ 119,772.05	12.57%	$ 104,990.00	14.70%
Other Materials	$ 34,696.45	3.64%	$ 24,508.00	3.43%
Outside Services	$ 23,625.02	2.48%	$ 9,999.00	1.40%
Outside Purchases	$ (242.29)	-0.03%	$ 46,958.00	6.58%
TOTAL COST OF SALES	$ 177,851.23	18.67%	$ 186,455.00	26.11%
GROSS PROFIT	$ 774,965.89	81.33%	$ 527,597.00	73.89%
PAYROLL	$ 305,733.69	32.09%	$ 202,205.00	28.32%
OVERHEAD				
Building Rent	$ 48,703.35	5.11%	$ 34,820.00	4.88%
Depreciation	$ 55,830.78	5.86%	$ 20,839.00	2.92%
Copier Equipment Rental	$ 91,709.98	9.63%	$ 29,115.00	4.08%
Other Equipment Rental	$ 905.50	0.10%	$ 15,459.00	2.16%
Repairs & Maintenance	$ 4,030.16	0.42%	$ 7,581.00	1.06%
Advertising	$ 22,994.33	2.41%	$ 15,613.00	2.19%
Utilities	$ 15,240.61	1.60%	$ 12,374.00	1.73%
Property & Liability Insurance	$ 3,141.22	0.33%	$ 6,616.00	0.93%
Interest	$ 6,749.18	0.71%	$ 3,221.00	0.45%
Franchise Fees	$ -	0.00%	$ 23,562.00	3.30%
Accounting & Legal Fees	$ 15,160.69	1.59%	$ 5,606.00	0.79%
Travel & Entertainment	$ 10,788.05	1.13%	$ 3,804.00	0.53%
Auto Operating Expense	$ 11,028.63	1.16%	$ 6,907.00	0.97%
Auto Lease and/or Depr Pmts.	$ 2,759.90	0.29%	$ 3,614.00	0.51%
Office Supplies	$ 25,829.33	2.71%	$ 4,592.00	0.64%
Other Overhead	$ 47,522.03	4.99%	$ 10,642.00	1.49%
TOTAL OVERHEAD	$ 362,393.74	38.03%	$ 204,365.00	28.62%
TOTAL COSTS	$ 845,978.66	88.79%	$ 593,025.00	83.05%
OTHER INCOME / EXPENSES	$ 23,131.31	2.43%	$ 0	0.00%
NET OWNER'S COMPENSATION	$ 129,969.77	13.64%	$ 121,027.00	16.95%

Comparative Income Statement (1997)

BizCopy (Downtown) vs. Industry Averages
Multiple Shops: Total Gross Sales Under $1000000
Top Quartile

	BizCopy (Downtown)		Industry Average	
	$	% of Sales	$	% of Sales
SALES				
Regular Printing	$ 271,273.49	42.70%	$ 427,479.00	59.87%
Copying	$ 204,288.39	32.15%	$ 158,750.00	22.23%
Color Copying	$ 47,770.23	7.52%	$ 34,204.00	4.79%
Brokered Sales	$ 17,332.13	2.73%	$ 73,036.00	10.23%
Other	$ 94,688.56	14.90%	$ 20,583.00	2.88%
TOTAL GROSS SALES	**$ 635,352.80**	**100.00%**	**$ 714,052.00**	**100.00%**
COST OF SALES				
Paper	$ 78,194.24	12.31%	$ 104,990.00	14.70%
Other Materials	$ 21,277.33	3.35%	$ 24,508.00	3.43%
Outside Services	$ 14,778.96	2.33%	$ 9,999.00	1.40%
Outside Purchases	$ (242.29)	-0.04%	$ 46,958.00	6.58%
TOTAL COST OF SALES	**$ 114,008.24**	**17.94%**	**$ 186,455.00**	**26.11%**
GROSS PROFIT	**$ 521,344.56**	**82.06%**	**$ 527,597.00**	**73.89%**
PAYROLL	**$ 198,514.12**	**31.24%**	**$ 202,205.00**	**28.32%**
OVERHEAD				
Building Rent	$ 34,172.29	5.38%	$ 34,820.00	4.88%
Depreciation	$ 50,462.76	7.94%	$ 20,839.00	2.92%
Copier Equipment Rental	$ 59,679.91	9.39%	$ 29,115.00	4.08%
Other Equipment Rental	$ 623.10	0.10%	$ 15,459.00	2.16%
Repairs & Maintenance	$ 2,431.46	0.38%	$ 7,581.00	1.06%
Advertising	$ 13,367.16	2.10%	$ 15,613.00	2.19%
Utilities	$ 9,696.87	1.53%	$ 12,374.00	1.73%
Property & Liability Insurance	$ 2,061.32	0.32%	$ 6,616.00	0.93%
Interest	$ 5,698.31	0.90%	$ 3,221.00	0.45%
Franchise Fees	$ -	0.00%	$ 23,562.00	3.30%
Accounting & Legal Fees	$ 8,004.84	1.26%	$ 5,606.00	0.79%
Travel & Entertainment	$ 6,232.14	0.98%	$ 3,804.00	0.53%
Auto Operating Expense	$ 4,714.63	0.74%	$ 6,907.00	0.97%
Auto Lease and/or Depr Pmts.	$ 1,509.30	0.24%	$ 3,614.00	0.51%
Office Supplies	$ 18,973.68	2.99%	$ 4,592.00	0.64%
Other Overhead	$ 30,379.87	4.78%	$ 10,642.00	1.49%
TOTAL OVERHEAD	**$ 248,007.64**	**39.03%**	**$ 204,365.00**	**28.62%**
TOTAL COSTS	**$ 560,530.00**	**88.22%**	**$ 593,025.00**	**83.05%**
OTHER INCOME / EXPENSES	**$ 22,786.57**	**3.59%**	**$ -**	**0.00%**
NET OWNER'S COMPENSATION	**$ 97,609.37**	**15.36%**	**$ 121,027.00**	**16.95%**

Comparative Income Statement (1997)

BizCopy (Downtown) vs. BizCopy (Combined)

	BizCopy (Downtown)		BizCopy (Combined)	
	$	% of Sales	$	% of Sales
SALES				
Regular Printing	$ 271,273.49	42.70%	$ 429,775.72	45.11%
Copying	$ 204,288.39	32.15%	$ 307,373.91	32.26%
Color Copying	$ 47,770.23	7.52%	$ 58,523.99	6.14%
Brokered Sales	$ 17,332.13	2.73%	$ 22,854.55	2.40%
Other	$ 94,688.56	14.90%	$ 134,288.95	14.09%
TOTAL GROSS SALES	**$ 635,352.80**	**100.00%**	**$ 952,817.12**	**100.00%**
COST OF SALES				
Paper	$ 78,194.24	12.31%	$ 119,772.05	12.57%
Other Materials	$ 21,277.33	3.35%	$ 34,696.45	3.64%
Outside Services	$ 14,778.96	2.33%	$ 23,625.02	2.48%
Outside Purchases	$ (242.29)	-0.04%	$ (242.29)	-0.03%
TOTAL COST OF SALES	**$ 114,008.24**	**17.94%**	**$ 177,851.23**	**18.67%**
GROSS PROFIT	**$ 521,344.56**	**82.06%**	**$ 774,965.89**	**81.33%**
PAYROLL	**$ 198,514.12**	**31.24%**	**$ 305,733.69**	**32.09%**
OVERHEAD				
Building Rent	$ 34,172.29	5.38%	$ 48,703.35	5.11%
Depreciation	$ 50,462.76	7.94%	$ 55,830.78	5.86%
Copier Equipment Rental	$ 59,679.91	9.39%	$ 91,709.98	9.63%
Other Equipment Rental	$ 623.10	0.10%	$ 905.50	0.10%
Repairs & Maintenance	$ 2,431.46	0.38%	$ 4,030.16	0.42%
Advertising	$ 13,367.16	2.10%	$ 22,994.33	2.41%
Utilities	$ 9,696.87	1.53%	$ 15,240.61	1.60%
Property & Liability Insurance	$ 2,061.32	0.32%	$ 3,141.22	0.33%
Interest	$ 5,698.31	0.90%	$ 6,749.18	0.71%
Franchise Fees	$ -	0.00%	$ -	0.00%
Accounting & Legal Fees	$ 8,004.84	1.26%	$ 15,160.69	1.59%
Travel & Entertainment	$ 6,232.14	0.98%	$ 10,788.05	1.13%
Auto Operating Expense	$ 4,714.63	0.74%	$ 11,028.63	1.16%
Auto Lease and/or Depr Pmts.	$ 1,509.30	0.24%	$ 2,759.90	0.29%
Office Supplies	$ 18,973.68	2.99%	$ 25,829.33	2.71%
Other Overhead	$ 30,379.87	4.78%	$ 47,522.03	4.99%
TOTAL OVERHEAD	**$ 248,007.64**	**39.03%**	**$ 362,393.74**	**38.03%**
TOTAL COSTS	**$ 560,530.00**	**88.22%**	**$ 845,978.66**	**88.79%**
OTHER INCOME / EXPENSES	**$ 22,786.57**	**3.59%**	**$ 23,131.31**	**2.43%**
NET OWNER'S COMPENSATION	**$ 97,609.37**	**15.36%**	**$ 129,969.77**	**13.64%**

Comparative Income Statement (1997)

BizCopy (Profitville) vs. Industry Averages
Multiple Shops: Total Gross Sales Under $1,000,000
Top Quartile

	BizCopy (Profitville)		Industry Average	
	$	% of Sales	$	% of Sales
SALES				
Regular Printing	$ 158,502.23	49.93%	$ 427,479.00	59.87%
Copying	$ 103,085.52	32.47%	$ 158,750.00	22.23%
Color Copying	$ 10,753.76	3.39%	$ 34,204.00	4.79%
Brokered Sales	$ 5,522.42	1.74%	$ 73,036.00	10.23%
Other	$ 39,600.39	12.47%	$ 20,583.00	2.88%
TOTAL GROSS SALES	**$ 317,464.32**	**100.00%**	**$ 714,052.00**	**100.00%**
COST OF SALES				
Paper	$ 41,577.81	13.10%	$ 104,990.00	14.70%
Other Materials	$ 13,419.12	4.23%	$ 24,508.00	3.43%
Outside Services	$ 8,846.06	2.79%	$ 9,999.00	1.40%
Outside Purchases	$ -	0.00%	$ 46,958.00	6.58%
TOTAL COST OF SALES	**$ 63,842.99**	**20.11%**	**$ 186,455.00**	**26.11%**
GROSS PROFIT	**$ 253,621.33**	**79.89%**	**$ 527,597.00**	**73.89%**
PAYROLL	**$ 107,219.57**	**33.77%**	**$ 202,205.00**	**28.32%**
OVERHEAD				
Building Rent	$ 14,531.06	4.58%	$ 34,820.00	4.88%
Depreciation	$ 5,368.02	1.69%	$ 20,839.00	2.92%
Copier Equipment Rental	$ 32,030.07	10.09%	$ 29,115.00	4.08%
Other Equipment Rental	$ 282.40	0.09%	$ 15,459.00	2.16%
Repairs & Maintenance	$ 1,598.70	0.50%	$ 7,581.00	1.06%
Advertising	$ 9,627.17	3.03%	$ 15,613.00	2.19%
Utilities	$ 5,543.74	1.75%	$ 12,374.00	1.73%
Property & Liability Insurance	$ 1,079.90	0.34%	$ 6,616.00	0.93%
Interest	$ 1,050.87	0.33%	$ 3,221.00	0.45%
Franchise Fees	$ -	0.00%	$ 23,562.00	3.30%
Accounting & Legal Fees	$ 7,155.85	2.25%	$ 5,606.00	0.79%
Travel & Entertainment	$ 4,555.91	1.44%	$ 3,804.00	0.53%
Auto Operating Expense	$ 6,314.00	1.99%	$ 6,907.00	0.97%
Auto Lease and/or Depr Pmts.	$ 1,250.60	0.39%	$ 3,614.00	0.51%
Office Supplies	$ 6,855.65	2.16%	$ 4,592.00	0.64%
Other Overhead	$ 17,142.16	5.40%	$ 10,642.00	1.49%
TOTAL OVERHEAD	**$ 114,386.10**	**36.03%**	**$ 204,365.00**	**28.62%**
TOTAL COSTS	**$ 285,448.66**	**89.92%**	**$ 593,025.00**	**83.05%**
OTHER INCOME / EXPENSES	**$ 344.74**	**0.11%**	**$ -**	**0.00%**
NET OWNER'S COMPENSATION	**$ 32,360.40**	**10.19%**	**$ 121,027.00**	**16.95%**

Comparative Income Statement (1997)

BizCopy (Profitville) vs. BizCopy (Combined)

	BizCopy (Profitville)		BizCopy (Combined)	
	$	**% of Sales**	**$**	**% of Sales**
SALES				
Regular Printing	$ 158,502.23	49.93%	$ 429,775.72	45.11%
Copying	$ 103,085.52	32.47%	$ 307,373.91	32.26%
Color Copying	$ 10,753.76	3.39%	$ 58,523.99	6.14%
Brokered Sales	$ 5,522.42	1.74%	$ 22,854.55	2.40%
Other	$ 39,600.39	12.47%	$ 134,288.95	14.09%
TOTAL GROSS SALES	**$ 317,464.32**	**100.00%**	**$ 952,817.12**	**100.00%**
COST OF SALES				
Paper	$ 41,577.81	13.10%	$ 119,772.05	12.57%
Other Materials	$ 13,419.12	4.23%	$ 34,696.45	3.64%
Outside Services	$ 8,846.06	2.79%	$ 23,625.02	2.48%
Outside Purchases	$ -	0.00%	$ (242.29)	-0.03%
TOTAL COST OF SALES	**$ 63,842.99**	**20.11%**	**$ 177,851.23**	**18.67%**
GROSS PROFIT	**$ 253,621.33**	**79.89%**	**$ 774,965.89**	**81.33%**
PAYROLL	**$ 107,219.57**	**33.77%**	**$ 305,733.69**	**32.09%**
OVERHEAD				
Building Rent	$ 14,531.06	4.58%	$ 48,703.35	5.11%
Depreciation	$ 5,368.02	1.69%	$ 55,830.78	5.86%
Copier Equipment Rental	$ 32,030.07	10.09%	$ 91,709.98	9.63%
Other Equipment Rental	$ 282.40	0.09%	$ 905.50	0.10%
Repairs & Maintenance	$ 1,598.70	0.50%	$ 4,030.16	0.42%
Advertising	$ 9,627.17	3.03%	$ 22,994.33	2.41%
Utilities	$ 5,543.74	1.75%	$ 15,240.61	1.60%
Property & Liability Insurance	$ 1,079.90	0.34%	$ 3,141.22	0.33%
Interest	$ 1,050.87	0.33%	$ 6,749.18	0.71%
Franchise Fees	$ -	0.00%	$ -	0.00%
Accounting & Legal Fees	$ 7,155.85	2.25%	$ 15,160.69	1.59%
Travel & Entertainment	$ 4,555.91	1.44%	$ 10,788.05	1.13%
Auto Operating Expense	$ 6,314.00	1.99%	$ 11,028.63	1.16%
Auto Lease and/or Depr Pmts.	$ 1,250.60	0.39%	$ 2,759.90	0.29%
Office Supplies	$ 6,855.65	2.16%	$ 25,829.33	2.71%
Other Overhead	$ 17,142.16	5.40%	$ 47,522.03	4.99%
TOTAL OVERHEAD	**$ 114,386.10**	**36.03%**	**$ 362,393.74**	**38.03%**
TOTAL COSTS	**$ 285,448.66**	**89.92%**	**$ 845,978.66**	**88.79%**
OTHER INCOME / EXPENSES	**$ 344.74**	**0.11%**	**$ 23,131.31**	**2.43%**
NET OWNER'S COMPENSATION	**$ 32,360.40**	**10.19%**	**$ 129,969.77**	**13.64%**

BIZ COPY, INC. : PROJECTED INCOME

Third Store Option by Month

month 1

	Current Month		MAIN ST		PROFITVILLE		OTHER	
	Amount	Ratio	$ AMT	%	$ AMT	%	$ AMT	%
Sales:								
Printing sales	0.00		22,461.00	0.0%	11,342.00	0.0%	0.00	0.0%
Copy sales	0.00		15693.00	0.0%	7,755.00	0.0%	0.00	0.0%
Color copying	0.00		3,924.00	0.0%	1,120.00	0.0%	0.00	0.0%
Typesetting sales	0.00		1,661.00	0.0%	833.00	0.0%	0.00	0.0%
Bindery sales	0.00		6,204.00	0.0%	2,533.00	0.0%	0.00	0.0%
Subcontract & outside services	0.00		2,570.00	0.0%	1,267.00	0.0%	0.00	0.0%
Mailing services	0.00		3,919.00	0.0%	407.00	0.0%	0.00	0.0%
Fax sales	0.00		507.00	0.0%	263.00	0.0%	0.00	0.0%
Other sales	0.00		102.00	0.0%	0.00	0.0%	0.00	0.0%
Discounts on sale	0.00		-3,856.00	0.0%	397.00	0.0%	0.00	0.0%
Net sales	0.00		53,185.00	#DIV/0!	25,123.00	#DIV/0!	2,000.00	#DIV/0!
Cost of sales:								
Paper products expense	0.00		6,834.27	12.9%	3,620.22	14.4%	270.00	13.5%
Other materials & supplies	0.00		2,180.59	4.1%	1,004.92	4.0%	80.00	4.0%
Subcontract	0.00		1,398.77	2.6%	819.01	3.3%	60.00	3.0%
Waste disposal cost	0.00		53.19	0.1%	62.81	0.3%	20.00	1.0%
Freight	0.00		53.19	0.1%	0.00	0.0%	20.00	1.0%
Purchase discounts	0.00		0.00	0.0%	0.00	0.0%	0.00	0.0%
Mailing supplies	0.00		0.00	0.0%	0.00	0.0%	0.00	0.0%
Cost of sales	0.00		10,519.99	19.8%	5,506.96	21.9%	450.00	22.5%
Gross profit	0.00		42,665.01	#DIV/0!	19,616.04	#DIV/0!	1,550.00	#DIV/0!
Payroll costs:								
Management salaries & bonuses	0.00		3,089.00	0.0%	2,162.00	0.0%	1,760.00	0.0%
Sales salaries	0.00		0.00	0.0%	0.00	0.0%	1,320.00	0.0%
Direct labor cost	0.00		8,709.00	0.0%	4,249.00	0.0%	1,829.00	0.0%
Payroll taxes	0.00		1,400.00	0.0%	705.00	0.0%	550.00	0.0%
Employee benefits	0.00		0.00	0.0%	0.00	0.0%	0.00	0.0%
Employee leasing	0.00		55.00	0.0%	0.00	0.0%	0.00	0.0%
Mailing labor	0.00		0.00	0.0%	0.00	0.0%	0.00	0.0%
Mailing employee leasing	0.00		23.00	0.0%	0.00	0.0%	0.00	0.0%
Total payroll costs	0.00		13,276.00	25.0%	7,116.00	28.3%	5,459.00	273.0%
Operating expenses:								
Equipment rental—copiers/typeset	0.00		4,505.00	0.0%	2,000.00	10.0%	2,000.00	10.0%
Equipment rental—mailing equip.	0.00		156.00	0.0%	75.00	0.0%	50.00	0.0%
Rent0.00	3,676.00		0.0%	1,251.00	0.0%	1,300.00	0.0%	
Interest expense	0.00		273.00	0.0%	200.00	0.0%	0.00	0.0%

Third Store Option by Month

Page 2 of 6
month 1

	Current Month		MAIN ST		PROFITVILLE		OTHER	
	Amount	Ratio	$ AMT	%	$ AMT	%	$ AMT	%
Utilities	0.00		476.00	0.0%	200.00	0.0%	200.00	0.0%
Telephone	0.00		417.00	0.0%	300.00	0.0%	300.00	0.0%
Operating supplies	0.00		435.00	0.0%	50.00	0.0%	50.00	0.0%
Advertising	0.00		887.00	0.0%	531.00	0.0%	354.00	0.0%
Office	0.00		393.00	0.0%	50.00	0.0%	50.00	0.0%
Postage	0.00		100.00	0.0%	25.00	0.0%	25.00	0.0%
Dues & subscriptions	0.00		188.00	0.0%	113.00	0.0%	75.00	0.0%
Travel	0.00		334.00	0.0%	200.00	0.0%	134.00	0.0%
Meals & entertainment	0.00		200.00	0.0%	100.00	0.0%	100.00	0.0%
Auto expenses	0.00		135.00	0.0%	135.00	0.0%	135.00	0.0%
Auto rental / lease	0.00		0.00	0.0%	0.00	0.0%	275.00	0.0%
Insurance	0.00		275.00	0.0%	225.00	0.0%	225.00	0.0%
Janitorial & trash	0.00		180.00	0.0%	0.00	0.0%	0.00	0.0%
Legal & accounting	0.00		500.00	0.0%	250.00	0.0%	208.00	0.0%
Consulting / training	0.00		750.00	0.0%	450.00	0.0%	300.00	0.0%
Bad debts	0.00		265.00	0.0%	160.00	0.0%	100.00	0.0%
Fees, licenses, taxes, bank charges	0.00		125.00	0.0%	100.00	0.0%	100.00	0.0%
Uniform rental & laundry	0.00		25.00	0.0%	15.00	0.0%	15.00	0.0%
Repairs equipment	0.00		125.00	0.0%	100.00	0.0%	100.00	0.0%
Small parts	0.00		415.00	0.0%	250.00	0.0%	165.00	0.0%
Miscellaneous	0.00		340.00	0.0%	200.00	0.0%	136.00	0.0%
Contributions	0.00		0.00	0.0%	0.00	0.0%	0.00	0.0%
Computer expense	0.00		340.00	0.0%	200.00	0.0%	136.00	0.0%
Cash over & short	0.00		0.00	0.0%	0.00	0.0%	0.00	0.0%
Depreciation	0.00		2,700.00	0.0%	300.00	0.0%	300.00	0.0%
Total operating expenses	-		18,215.00	34.2%	7,480.0	29.8%	6,833.00	341.7%
								1500
Income from operations	-		11,174.01	21.0%	5,020.04	#DIV/0!	(10.742.00)	#DIV/0!
Other income & expenses:								
Interest income	0.00		0.00	0.0%	0.00	0.0%	0.00	0.0%
Sale of assets	0.00		0.00	0.0%	0.00	0.0%	0.00	0.0%
Postage profit	0.00		0.00	0.0%	0.00	0.0%	0.00	0.0%
Total other income & expense	-		-	#DIV/0!	-	#DIV/0!	-	#DIV/0!
Income before officer's compensation	-		11,174.01	21.0%	5,020.04	20.0%	(10,742.00)	-537.1%
Officer's compensation								
Officer's salary	3,000.00	#DIV/0!	1,500.00	50.0%	900.00	30.0%	600.00	20.0%
Payroll taxes	230.00	#DIV/0!	115.00	50.0%	69.00	30.0%	46.00	20.0%
Officer's benefits	390.00	#DIV/0!	195.00	50.0%	117.00	30.0%	78.00	20.0%
Officer's life insurance	238.00	#DIV/0!	119.00	50.0%	71.40	30.0%	47.60	20.0%
Total officer's compensation	3858.00	#DIV/0!	1,929.00	3.6%	1,157.40	4.6%	771.60	38.6%
Net income	$ (3858.00)	#DIV/0!	$ 9,245.01	17.4%	$ 3,862.64	-100.1%	$ (11,513.60)	-575.7%

Third Store Option by Month

month 2 OTHER $ AMT	%	month 3 OTHER $ AMT	%	month 4 OTHER $ AMT	%	month 5 OTHER $ AMT	%	month 6 OTHER $ AMT	%	month 7 OTHER $ AMT	%
0.00	0.0%	0.00	0.0%	0.00	0.0%	0.00	0.0%	0.00	0.0%	0.00	0.0%
0.00	0.0%	0.00	0.0%	0.00	0.0%	0.00	0.0%	0.00	0.0%	0.00	0.0%
0.00	0.0%	0.00	0.0%	0.00	0.0%	0.00	0.0%	0.00	0.0%	0.00	0.0%
0.00	0.0%	0.00	0.0%	0.00	0.0%	0.00	0.0%	0.00	0.0%	0.00	0.0%
0.00	0.0%	0.00	0.0%	0.00	0.0%	0.00	0.0%	0.00	0.0%	0.00	0.0%
0.00	0.0%	0.00	0.0%	0.00	0.0%	0.00	0.0%	0.00	0.0%	0.00	0.0%
0.00	0.0%	0.00	0.0%	0.00	0.0%	0.00	0.0%	0.00	0.0%	0.00	0.0%
0.00	0.0%	0.00	0.0%	0.00	0.0%	0.00	0.0%	0.00	0.0%	0.00	0.0%
0.00	0.0%	0.00	0.0%	0.00	0.0%	0.00	0.0%	0.00	0.0%	0.00	0.0%
3,500.00	#DIV/0!	8,100.00	#DIV/0!	8,600.00	#DIV/0!	13,900.00	#DIV/0!	13,500.00	#DIV/0!	7,600.00	#DIV/0!
472.50	13.5%	1,093.50	13.5%	1,161.00	13.5%	1,876.50	13.5%	1,822.50	13.5%	1,026.00	13.5%
140.00	4.0%	324.00	4.0%	344.00	4.0%	556.00	4.0%	540.00	4.0%	304.00	4.0%
105.00	3.0%	243.00	3.0%	258.00	3.0%	417.00	3.0%	405.00	3.0%	228.00	3.0%
35.00	1.0%	81.00	1.0%	86.00	1.0%	139.00	1.0%	135.00	1.0%	76.00	1.0%
35.00	1.0%	81.00	1.0%	86.00	1.0%	139.00	1.0%	135.00	1.0%	76.00	1.0%
0.00	0.0%	0.00	0.0%	0.00	0.0%	0.00	0.0%	0.00	0.0%	0.00	0.0%
0.00	0.0%	0.00	0.0%	0.00	0.0%	0.00	0.0%	0.00	0.0%	0.00	0.0%
787.50	22.5%	1,822.50	22.5%	1,935.00	22.5%	3,127.50	22.5%	3,037.50	22.5%	1,710.00	22.5%
2,712.50	#DIV/0!	6,277.50	#DIV/0!	6,665.00	#DIV/0!	10,772.50	#DIV/0!	10,462.50	#DIV/0!	5,890.00	#DIV/0!
1,760.00	0.0%	1,760.00	0.0%	1,760.00	0.0%	1,760.00	0.0%	1,760.00	0.0%	1,760.00	0.0%
1,320.00	0.0%	1,320.00	0.0%	1,320.00	0.0%	1320.00	0.0%	1,320.00	0.0%	1,320.00	0.0%
1,829.00	0.0%	1,829.00	0.0%	1,829.00	0.0%	1,829.00	0.0%	1,829.00	0.0%	1,829.00	0.0%
550.00	0.0%	550.00	0.0%	550.00	0.0%	550.00	0.0%	550.00	0.0%	550.00	0.0%
0.00	0.0%	0.00	0.0%	0.00	0.0%	0.00	0.0%	0.00	0.0%	0.00	0.0%
0.00	0.0%	0.00	0.0%	0.00	0.0%	0.00	0.0%	0.00	0.0%	0.00	0.0%
0.00	0.0%	0.00	0.0%	0.00	0.0%	0.00	0.0%	0.00	0.0%	0.00	0.0%
5,459.00	156.0%	5,459.00	67.4%	5,459.00	63.5%	5,459.00	39.3%	5,459.00	40.4%	5,459.00	71.8%
2,000.00	10.0%	2,000.00	10.0%	2,000.00	10.0%	2,000.00	10.0%	2,000.00	10.0%	2,000.00	10.0%
50.00	0.0%	50.00	0.0%	50.00	0.0%	50.00	0.0%	50.00	0.0%	50.00	0.0%
1,300.00	0.0%	1,300.00	0.0%	1,300.00	0.0%	1,300.00	0.0%	1,300.00	0.0%	1,300.00	0.0%
0.00	0.0%	0.00	0.0%	0.00	0.0%	0.00	0.0%	0.00	0.0%	0.00	0.0%

	month 2 OTHER $ AMT	%	month 3 OTHER $ AMT	%	month 4 OTHER $ AMT	%	month 5 OTHER $ AMT	%	month 6 OTHER $ AMT	%	month 7 OTHER $ AMT	%
	200.00	0.0%	200.00	0.0%	200.00	0.0%	200.00	0.0%	200.00	0.0%	200.00	0.0%
	300.00	0.0%	300.00	0.0%	300.00	0.0%	300.00	0.0%	300.00	0.0%	300.00	0.0%
	50.00	0.0%	50.00	0.0%	50.00	0.0%	50.00	0.0%	50.00	0.0%	50.00	0.0%
	354.00	0.0%	354.00	0.0%	354.00	0.0%	354.00	0.0%	354.00	0.0%	354.00	0.0%
	50.00	0.0%	50.00	0.0%	50.00	0.0%	50.00	0.0%	50.00	0.0%	50.00	0.0%
	25.00	0.0%	25.00	0.0%	25.00	0.0%	25.00	0.0%	25.00	0.0%	25.00	0.0%
	75.00	0.0%	75.00	0.0%	75.00	0.0%	75.00	0.0%	75.00	0.0%	75.00	0.0%
	134.00	0.0%	134.00	0.0%	134.00	0.0%	134.00	0.0%	134.00	0.0%	134.00	0.0%
	100.00	0.0%	100.00	0.0%	100.00	0.0%	100.00	0.0%	100.00	0.0%	100.00	0.0%
	135.00	0.0%	135.00	0.0%	135.00	0.0%	135.00	0.0%	135.00	0.0%	135.00	0.0%
	275.00	0.0%	275.00	0.0%	275.00	0.0%	275.00	0.0%	275.00	0.0%	275.00	0.0%
	225.00	0.0%	225.00	0.0%	225.00	0.0%	225.00	0.0%	225.00	0.0%	225.00	0.0%
	0.00	0.0%	0.00	0.0%	0.00	0.0%	0.00	0.0%	0.00	0.0%	0.00	0.0%
	208.00	0.0%	208.00	0.0%	208.00	0.0%	208.00	0.0%	208.00	0.0%	208.00	0.0%
	300.00	0.0%	300.00	0.0%	300.00	0.0%	300.00	0.0%	300.00	0.0%	300.00	0.0%
	100.00	0.0%	100.00	0.0%	100.00	0.0%	100.00	0.0%	100.00	0.0%	100.00	0.0%
	100.00	0.0%	100.00	0.0%	100.00	0.0%	100.00	0.0%	100.00	0.0%	100.00	0.0%
	15.00	0.0%	15.00	0.0%	15.00	0.0%	15.00	0.0%	15.00	0.0%	15.00	0.0%
	100.00	0.0%	100.00	0.0%	100.00	0.0%	100.00	0.0%	100.00	0.0%	100.00	0.0%
	165.00	0.0%	165.00	0.0%	165.00	0.0%	165.00	0.0%	165.00	0.0%	165.00	0.0%
	136.00	0.0%	136.00	0.0%	136.00	0.0%	136.00	0.0%	136.00	0.0%	136.00	0.0%
	0.00	0.0%	0.00	0.0%	0.00	0.0%	0.00	0.0%	0.00	0.0%	0.00	0.0%
	136.00	0.0%	136.00	0.0%	136.00	0.0%	136.00	0.0%	136.00	0.0%	136.00	0.0%
	0.00	0.0%	0.00	0.0%	0.00	0.0%	0.00	0.0%	0.00	0.0%	0.00	0.0%
	300.00	0.0%	300.00	0.0%	300.00	0.0%	300.00	0.0%	300.00	0.0%	300.00	0.0%
	6,833.00	195.2%	6,833.00	84.4%	6,833.00	79.5%	6,833.00	49.2%	6,833.00	50.6%	6833.00	89.9%
	1500		1500		1500		1500		1500		1500	
	(9,579.50)	#DIV/0!	(6,014.50)	#DIV/0!	(5,627.00)	#DIV/0!	(1,519.50)	#DIV/0!	(1,829.50)	#DIV/0!	(6,402.00)	#DIV/0!
	0.00	0.0%	0.00	0.0%	0.00	0.0%	0.00	0.0%	0.00	0.0%	0.00	0.0%
	0.00	0.0%	0.00	0.0%	0.00	0.0%	0.00	0.0%	0.00	0.0%	0.00	0.0%
	-	#DIV/0!	-	#DIV/0!	-	#DIV/0!	-	#DIV/0!	-	#DIV/0!	-	#DIV/0!
	(9,579.50)	-479.0%	(6,014.50)	-300.7%	(5,627.00)	-281.4%	(1,519.50)	-76.0%	(1,829.50)	-91.5%	(6,402.00)	-320.1%
	0.00	20.0%	0.10	20.0%	0.06	20.0%	0.04	20.0%	0.04	20.0%	0.04	20.0%
	0.00	20.0%	0.10	20.0%	0.06	20.0%	0.04	20.0%	0.04	20.0%	0.04	20.0%
	0.00	20.0%	0.10	20.0%	0.06	20.0%	0.04	20.0%	0.04	20.0%	0.04	20.0%
	0.00	20.0%	0.10	20.0%	0.06	20.0%	0.04	20.0%	0.04	20.0%	0.04	20.0%
	771.60	38.6%	771.60	38.6%	771.60	38.6%	771.60	38.6%	771.60	38.6%	771.60	38.6%
	(10,351.10)	-295.7%	(6,786.10)	-83.8%	(6,398.60)	-74.4%	(2,291.10)	-16.5%	(2,601.10)	-19.3%	(7,173.60)	-94.4%

Third Store Option by Month

	month 8 OTHER $ AMT	%	month 9 OTHER $ AMT	%	month 10 OTHER $ AMT	%	month 11 OTHER $ AMT	%	month 12 OTHER $ AMT	%	year 2 OTHER $ AMT	%
	0.00	0.0%	0.00	0.0%	0.00	0.0%	0.00	0.0%	0.00	0.0%	0.00	0.0%
	0.00	0.0%	0.00	0.0%	0.00	0.0%	0.00	0.0%	0.00	0.0%	0.00	0.0%
	0.00	0.0%	0.00	0.0%	0.00	0.0%	0.00	0.0%	0.00	0.0%	0.00	0.0%
	0.00	0.0%	0.00	0.0%	0.00	0.0%	0.00	0.0%	0.00	0.0%	0.00	0.0%
	0.00	0.0%	0.00	0.0%	0.00	0.0%	0.00	0.0%	0.00	0.0%	0.00	0.0%
	0.00	0.0%	0.00	0.0%	0.00	0.0%	0.00	0.0%	0.00	0.0%	0.00	0.0%
	0.00	0.0%	0.00	0.0%	0.00	0.0%	0.00	0.0%	0.00	0.0%	0.00	0.0%
	0.00	0.0%	0.00	0.0%	0.00	0.0%	0.00	0.0%	0.00	0.0%	0.00	0.0%
	0.00	0.0%	0.00	0.0%	0.00	0.0%	0.00	0.0%	0.00	0.0%	0.00	0.0%
	13,200.00	#DIV/0!	12,500.00	#DIV/0!	16,100.00	#DIV/0!	18,750.00	#DIV/0!	18,800.00	#DIV/0!	240,000.00	#DIV/0!
	1,782.00	13.5%	1,687.50	13.5%	2,173.50	13.5%	2,531.25	13.5%	2,538.00	13.5%	32,400.00	13.5%
	528.00	4.0%	500.00	4.0%	644.00	4.0%	750.00	4.0%	752.00	4.0%	9,600.00	4.0%
	396.00	3.0%	375.00	3.0%	483.00	3.0%	562.50	3.0%	564.00	3.0%	7,200.00	3.0%
	132.00	1.0%	125.00	1.0%	161.00	1.0%	187.50	1.0%	188.00	1.0%	2,400.00	1.0%
	132.00	1.0%	125.00	1.0%	161.00	1.0%	187.50	1.0%	188.00	1.0%	2,400.00	1.0%
	0.00	0.0%	0.00	0.0%	0.00	0.0%	0.00	0.0%	0.00	0.0%	0.00	0.0%
	0.00	0.0%	0.00	0.0%	0.00	0.0%	0.00	0.0%	0.00	0.0%	0.00	0.0%
	2,970.00	22.5%	2,812.50	22.5%	3,622.50	22.5%	4,218.75	22.5%	4,230.00	22.5%	54,000.00	22.5%
	10,230.00	#DIV/0!	9,687.50	#DIV/0!	12,477.50	#DIV/0!	14,531.25	DIV/0!	14,570.00	#DIV/0!	186,000.00	#DIV/0!
	1,760.00	0.0%	1,760.00	0.0%	1,760.00	0.0%	1,760.00	0.0%	1,760.00	0.0%	1,760.00	0.0%
	1,320.00	0.0%	1,320.00	0.0%	1,320.00	0.0%	1,320.00	0.0%	1,320.00	0.0%	1,320.00	0.0%
	1,829.00	0.0%	1,829.00	0.0%	1,829.00	0.0%	1,829.00	0.0%	1,829.00	0.0%	1,829.00	0.0%
	550.00	0.0%	550.00	0.0%	550.00	0.0%	550.00	0.0%	550.00	0.0%	550.00	0.0%
	0.00	0.0%	0.00	0.0%	0.00	0.0%	0.00	0.0%	0.00	0.0%	0.00	0.0%
	0.00	0.0%	0.00	0.0%	0.00	0.0%	0.00	0.0%	0.00	0.0%	0.00	0.0%
	0.00	0.0%	0.00	0.0%	0.00	0.0%	0.00	0.0%	0.00	0.0%	0.00	0.0%
	0.00	0.0%	0.00	0.0%	0.00	0.0%	0.00	0.0%	0.00	0.0%	0.00	0.0%
	5,459.00	41.4%	5,459.00	43.7%	5,459.00	33.9%	5,459.00	29.1%	5,459.00	29.0%	66,000.00	27.5%
							81996					
	2,000.00	10.0%	2,000.00	10.0%	2,000.00	10.0%	2,000.00	10.0%	2,000.00	10.0%	2,000.00	10.0%
	50.00	0.0%	50.00	0.0%	50.00	0.0%	50.00	0.0%	50.00	0.0%	50.00	0.0%
	1,300.00	0.0%	1,300.00	0.0%	1,300.00	0.0%	1,300.00	0.0%	1,300.00	0.0%	1,300.00	0.0%
	0.00	0.0%	0.00	0.0%	0.00	0.0%	0.00	0.0%	0.00	0.0%	0.00	0.0%

Third Store Option by Month

Page 6 of 6

month 2 OTHER $ AMT	%	month 3 OTHER $ AMT	%	month 4 OTHER $ AMT	%	month 5 OTHER $ AMT	%	month 6 OTHER $ AMT	%	month 7 OTHER $ AMT	%
200.00	0.0%	200.00	0.0%	200.00	0.0%	200.00	0.0%	200.00	0.0%	200.00	0.0%
300.00	0.0%	300.00	0.0%	300.00	0.0%	300.00	0.0%	300.00	0.0%	300.00	0.0%
50.00	0.0%	50.00	0.0%	50.00	0.0%	50.00	0.0%	50.00	0.0%	50.00	0.0%
354.00	0.0%	354.00	0.0%	354.00	0.0%	354.00	0.0%	354.00	0.0%	354.00	0.0%
50.00	0.0%	50.00	0.0%	50.00	0.0%	50.00	0.0%	50.00	0.0%	50.00	0.0%
25.00	0.0%	25.00	0.0%	25.00	0.0%	25.00	0.0%	25.00	0.0%	25.00	0.0%
75.00	0.0%	75.00	0.0%	75.00	0.0%	75.00	0.0%	75.00	0.0%	75.00	0.0%
134.00	0.0%	134.00	0.0%	134.00	0.0%	134.00	0.0%	134.00	0.0%	134.00	0.0%
100.00	0.0%	100.00	0.0%	100.00	0.0%	100.00	0.0%	100.00	0.0%	100.00	0.0%
135.00	0.0%	135.00	0.0%	135.00	0.0%	135.00	0.0%	135.00	0.0%	135.00	0.0%
275.00	0.0%	275.00	0.0%	275.00	0.0%	275.00	0.0%	275.00	0.0%	275.00	0.0%
225.00	0.0%	225.00	0.0%	225.00	0.0%	225.00	0.0%	225.00	0.0%	225.00	0.0%
0.00	0.0%	0.00	0.0%	0.00	0.0%	0.00	0.0%	0.00	0.0%	0.00	0.0%
208.00	0.0%	208.00	0.0%	208.00	0.0%	208.00	0.0%	208.00	0.0%	208.00	0.0%
300.00	0.0%	300.00	0.0%	300.00	0.0%	300.00	0.0%	300.00	0.0%	300.00	0.0%
100.00	0.0%	100.00	0.0%	100.00	0.0%	100.00	0.0%	100.00	0.0%	100.00	0.0%
100.00	0.0%	100.00	0.0%	100.00	0.0%	100.00	0.0%	100.00	0.0%	100.00	0.0%
15.00	0.0%	15.00	0.0%	15.00	0.0%	15.00	0.0%	15.00	0.0%	15.00	0.0%
100.00	0.0%	100.00	0.0%	100.00	0.0%	100.00	0.0%	100.00	0.0%	100.00	0.0%
165.00	0.0%	165.00	0.0%	165.00	0.0%	165.00	0.0%	165.00	0.0%	165.00	0.0%
136.00	0.0%	136.00	0.0%	136.00	0.0%	136.00	0.0%	136.00	0.0%	136.00	0.0%
0.00	0.0%	0.00	0.0%	0.00	0.0%	0.00	0.0%	0.00	0.0%	0.00	0.0%
136.00	0.0%	136.00	0.0%	136.00	0.0%	136.00	0.0%	136.00	0.0%	136.00	0.0%
0.00	0.0%	0.00	0.0%	0.00	0.0%	0.00	0.0%	0.00	0.0%	0.00	0.0%
300.00	0.0%	300.00	0.0%	300.00	0.0%	300.00	0.0%	300.00	0.0%	300.00	0.0%
6,833.00	51.8%	6,833.00	54.7%	6,833.00	42.4%	6,833.00	36.4%	6,833.00	36.3%	6833.00	34.2%
	1500		1500		1500		1500		1500		1500
(2,062.00)	#DIV/0!	(2,604.50)	#DIV/0!	185.50	#DIV/0!	2,239.25	#DIV/0%	2,278.00	#DIV/0!	38,004.00	#DIV/0!
0.00	0.0%	0.00	0.0%	0.00	0.0%	0.00	0.0%	0.00	0.0%	0.00	0.0%
0.00	0.0%	0.00	0.0%	0.00	0.0%	0.00	0.0%	0.00	0.0%	0.00	0.0%
0.00	0.0%	0.00	0.0%	0.00	0.0%	0.00	0.0%	0.00	0.0%	0.00	0.0%
-	#DIV/0!	-	#DIV/0!	-	#DIV/0!	-	#DIV/0!	-	#DIV/0!	-	#DIV/0!
(2,062.00)	-103.1%	(2,604.50)	-130.2%	185.50	9.3%	2,239.25	112.0%	2,278.00	113.9%	38,004.00	15.8%
0.04	20.0%	0.04	20.0%	0.04	20.0%	0.04	20.0%	0.04	20.0%	0.04	20.0%
0.04	20.0%	0.04	20.0%	0.04	20.0%	0.04	20.0%	0.04	20.0%	0.04	20.0%
0.04	20.0%	0.04	20.0%	0.04	20.0%	0.04	20.0%	0.04	20.0%	0.04	20.0%
0.04	20.0%	0.04	20.0%	0.04	20.0%	0.04	20.0%	0.04	20.0%	0.04	20.0%
771.60	38.6%	771.60	38.6%	771.60	38.6%	771.60	38.6%	771.60	38.6%	9,260.00	3.9%
$(2,833.60)	-21.5%	$(3,376.10)	-27.0%	$(586.10)	-3.6%	$1,467.65	7.8%	$1,506.40	8.0%	$28,744.00	12.0%

BIZ COPY, INC. PROJECTED INCOME
same employees

	Current Month Amount	Ratio	Major St. $ AMT.	%	Profitville $ AMT.	%	Other $ AMT.	%
Sales:								
Printing sales	29,955.00	42.84%	0.00	0.0%	0.00	0.0%	0.00	0.0%
Copy sales	20,743.00	29.66%	0.00	0.0%	0.00	0.0%	0.00	0.0%
Color copying	4,657.00	6.66%	0.00	0.0%	0.00	0.0%	0.00	0.0%
Typesetting sales	2,199.00	3.14%	0.00	0.0%	0.00	0.0%	0.00	0.0%
Bindery sales	7,869.00	11.25%	0.00	0.0%	0.00	0.0%	0.00	0.0%
Subcontract & outside services	3,402.00	4.87%	0.00	0.0%	0.00	0.0%	0.00	0.0%
Mailing services	4,187.00	5.99%	0.00	0.0%	0.00	0.0%	0.00	0.0%
Fax sales	668.00	0.96%	0.00	0.0%	0.00	0.0%	0.00	0.0%
Other sales	102.00	0.15%	0.00	0.0%	0.00	0.0%	0.00	0.0%
Discounts on sale	-3,856.00	-5.51%	0.00	0.0%	0.00	0.0%	0.00	0.0%
Net sales	69,926.00	100.00%	-	0.0%	-	0.0%	-	0.0%
Cost of sales:								
Paper products expense	8,985.49	12.85%	0.00	0.0%	0.00	0.0%	0.00	0.0%
Other materials & supplies	2,797.04	4.00%	0.00	0.0%	0.00	0.0%	0.00	0.0%
Subcontract	1,839.05	2.63%	0.00	0.0%	0.00	0.0%	0.00	0.0%
Waste disposal cost	0.00	-	0.00	0.0%	0.00	0.0%	0.00	0.0%
Freight	0.00	-						
Purchase discounts	0.00	-	0.00	0.0%	0.00	0.0%	0.00	0.0%
Mailing supplies	0.00	-	0.00	0.0%	0.00	0.0%	0.00	0.0%
Cost of sales	13,621.58	19.48%	-	0.0%	-	0.0%	-	0.0%
Gross profit	56,304.42	80.52%	-	0.0%	-	0.0%	-	0.0%
Payroll costs:								
Management salaries & bonuses	3,706.08	5.30%	0.00	0.0%	0.00	0.0%	0.00	0.0%
Sales salaries	2,097.78	3.00%	0.00	0.0%	0.00	0.0%	0.00	0.0%
Direct labor cost	11,340.00	16.20%	0.00	0.0%	0.00	0.0%	0.00	0.0%
Payroll taxes	1,657.25	2.37%	0.00	0.0%	0.00	0.0%	0.00	0.0%
Employee benefits	699.26	1.00%	0.00	0.0%	0.00	0.0%	0.00	0.0%
Employee leasing	153.84	0.22%	0.00	0.0%	0.00	0.0%	0.00	0.0%
Mailing labor	3,111.71	4.45%	0.00	0.0%	0.00	0.0%	0.00	0.0%
Mailing- employee leasing	349.63	0.50%	0.00	0.0%	0.00	0.0%	0.00	0.0%
Total payroll costs	23,115.54	33.04%	-	0.0%	-	0.0%	-	0.0%

Operating expenses:

	Current Month Amount	Ratio	Major St. $ AMT.	%	Profitville $ AMT.	%	Other $ AMT.	%
Equipment rental copiers/typeset	5,700.00	8.15%	0.00	0.0%	470.00	10.0%	570.00	10.0%
Equipment rental mailing equip.	300.00	0.43%	0.00	0.0%	0.00	0.0%	0.00	0.0%
Rent	3,800.00	5.43%	0.00	0.0%	0.00	0.0%	0.00	0.0%
Interest expense	501.00	0.72%	0.00	0.0%	0.00	0.0%	0.00	0.0%
Utilities	750.00	1.07%	0.00	0.0%	0.00	0.0%	0.00	0.0%
Telephone	610.00	0.87%	0.00	0.0%	0.00	0.0%	0.00	0.0%
Operating supplies	475.00	0.68%	0.00	0.0%	0.00	0.0%	0.00	0.0%
Advertising	1,780.00	2.55%	0.00	0.0%	0.00	0.0%	0.00	0.0%
Office	450.00	0.64%	0.00	0.0%	0.00	0.0%	0.00	0.0%
Postage	150.00	0.21%	0.00	0.0%	0.00	0.0%	0.00	0.0%
Dues & subscriptions	300.00	0.43%	0.00	0.0%	0.00	0.0%	0.00	0.0%
Travel	750.00	1.07%	0.00	0.0%	0.00	0.0%	0.00	0.0%
Meals & entertainment	300.00	0.43%	0.00	0.0%	0.00	0.0%	0.00	0.0%
Auto expenses	750.00	1.07%	0.00	0.0%	0.00	0.0%	0.00	0.0%
Auto rental / lease	0.00	-	0.00	0.0%	0.00	0.0%	0.00	0.0%
Insurance	500.00	0.72%	0.00	0.0%	0.00	0.0%	0.00	0.0%
Janitorial & trash	180.00	0.26%	0.00	0.0%	0.00	0.0%	0.00	0.0%
Legal & accounting	960.00	1.37%	0.00	0.0%	0.00	0.0%	0.00	0.0%
Consulting / training	1,500.00	2.15%	0.00	0.0%	0.00	0.0%	0.00	0.0%
Bad debts	0.00	-	0.00	0.0%	0.00	0.0%	0.00	0.0%
Fees, licenses, taxes, bank charges	300.00	0.43%	0.00	0.0%	0.00	0.0%	0.00	0.0%
Uniform rental & laundry	50.00	0.07%	0.00	0.0%	0.00	0.0%	0.00	0.0%
Repairs equipment	300.00	0.43%	0.00	0.0%	0.00	0.0%	0.00	0.0%
Small parts	825.00	1.18%	0.00	0.0%	0.00	0.0%	0.00	0.0%
Miscellaneous	650.00	0.93%	0.00	0.0%	0.00	0.0%	0.00	0.0%
Contributions	0.00	-	0.00	0.0%	0.00	0.0%	0.00	0.0%
Computer expense	750.00	1.07%	0.00	0.0%	0.00	0.0%	0.00	0.0%
Cash over & short	0.00	-	0.00	0.0%	0.00	0.0%	0.00	0.0%
Depreciation	3,100.00	4.43%	0.00	0.0%	0.00	0.0%	0.00	0.0%
Total operating expenses	25,731.00	36.80%	-	0.0%	570.00	2.2%	570.00	2.2%
Income from operations	7,457.88	10.67%	-	0.0%	(570.00)	-7.6%	(570.00)	-7.6%

Current Month	Major St. Amount	Ratio	Profitville $ AMT.	%	Other $ AMT.	%	$ AMT.	%
Other income & expenses:								
Interest income	0.00	-	0.00	0.0%	0.00	0.0%	0.00	0.0%
Sale of assets	0.00	-	0.00	0.0%	0.00	0.0%	0.00	0.0%
Postage profit	0.00	-	0.00	0.0%	0.00	0.0%	0.00	0.0%
Total other income & expense	0.00	--	0.00	#DIV/0!	0.00	#DIV/0!	0.00	#DIV/0!
Income before officer's compensation	7,457.88	10.67%		-0.0%	(570.00)	-7.6%	(570.00)	-7.6%
Officer's compensation								
Officer's salary	3,000.00	4.29%	0.00	0.0%	0.00	0.0%	0.00	0.0%
Payroll taxes	230.00	0.33%	0.00	0.0%	0.00	0.0%	0.00	0.0%
Officer's benefits	390.00	0.56%	0.00	0.0%	0.00	0.0%	0.00	0.0%
Officer's life insurance	239.00	0.34%	0.00	0.0%	0.00	0.0%	0.00	0.0%
Total officer's compensation	3,859.00	5.52%	-	0.0%	-	0.0%	-	0.0%
Net income	3,598.88	5.15%	$-	0.0%	$ (570.00)	-15.8%	$(570.00)	-15.8%

Single Store Option: 10 Employees

BIZ COPY, INC.
PROJECTED INCOME
same employees

	Current Month Amount	Ratio	MAJOR ST $ AMT.	%	PROFITVILLE $ AMT.	%	OTHER $ AMT.	%
Sales:								
Printing sales	28,955.00	43.26%	0.00	0.0%	0.00	0.0%	0.00	0.0%
Copy sales	18,743.00	28.01%	0.00	0.0%	0.00	0.0%	0.00	0.0%
Color copying	4,657.00	6.96%	0.00	0.0%	0.00	0.0%	0.00	0.0%
Typesetting sales	2,199.00	3.29%	0.00	0.0%	0.00	0.0%	0.00	0.0%
Bindery sales	7,869.00	11.76%	0.00	0.0%	0.00	0.0%	0.00	0.0%
Subcontract & outside services	3,402.00	5.08%	0.00	0.0%	0.00	0.0%	0.00	0.0%
Mailing services	4,187.00	6.26%	0.00	0.0%	0.00	0.0%	0.00	0.0%
Fax sales	668.00	1.00%	0.00	0.0%	0.00	0.0%	0.00	0.0%
Other sales	102.00	0.15%	0.00	0.0%	0.00	0.0%	0.00	0.0%
Discounts on sale	3,856.00	.5.76%	0.00	0.0%	0.00	0.0%	0.00	0.0%
Net sales	66,926.00	######	-	0.0%	-	0.0%	-	0.0%
Cost of sales:								
Paper products expense	8,599.99	12.85%	0.00	0.0%	0.00	0.0%	0.00	0.0%
Other materials & supplies	2,677.04	4.00%	0.00	0.0%	0.00	0.0%	0.00	0.0%
Subcontract	1,760.15	2.63%	0.00	0.0%	0.00	0.0%	0.00	0.0%
Waste disposal cost	0.00	-	0.00	0.0%	0.00	0.0%	0.00	0.0%
Freight	0.00	-						
Purchase discounts	0.00	-	0.00	0.0%	0.00	0.0%	0.00	0.0%
Mailing supplies	0.00	-	0.00	0.0%	0.00	0.0%	0.00	0.0%
Cost of sales	13,037.18	19.48%	-	0.0%	-	0.0%	-	0.0%
Gross profit	53,888.82	80.52%	-	0.0%	-	0.0%	-	0.0%
Payroll costs:								
Management salaries & bonuses	3,547.08	5.30%	0.00	0.0%	0.00	0.0%	0.00	0.0%
Sales salaries	2,007.78	3.00%	0.00	0.0%	0.00	0.0%	0.00	0.0%
Direct labor cost	9,000.00	13.50%	0.00	0.0%	0.00	0.0%	0.00	0.0%
Payroll taxes	1,586.15	2.37%	0.00	0.0%	0.00	0.0%	0.00	0.0%
Employee benefits	669.26	1.00%	0.00	0.0%	0.00	0.0%	0.00	0.0%
Employee leasing	147.24	0.22%	0.00	0.0%	0.00	0.0%	0.00	0.0%
Mailing labor	2,978.21	4.45%	0.00	0.0%	0.00	0.0%	0.00	0.0%
Mailing-employee leasing	334.63	0.50%	0.00	0.0%	0.00	0.0%	0.00	0.0%
Total payroll costs	20,270.34	30.34%	-	0.0%	-	0.0%	-	0.0%

Single Store Option: 12 Employees

Other income & expenses:								
Interest income	0.00	0.0%	0.00	0.0%	0.00	0.0%	—	—
Sale of assets	0.00	0.0%	0.00	0.0%	0.00	0.0%	—	—
Postage profit	0.00	0.0%	0.00	0.0%	0.00	0.0%	—	—
Total other income & expense	0.00	#DIV/0!	0.00	#DIV/0!	0.00	#DIV/0!	––	––
Income before officer's compensation	(570.00)	-7.6%	(570.00)	-7.6%	—	0.0%	7,457.88	10.67%
Officer's compensation								
Officer's salary	0.00	0.0%	0.00	0.0%	0.00	0.0%	3,000.00	4.29%
Payroll taxes	0.00	0.0%	0.00	0.0%	0.00	0.0%	230.00	0.33%
Officer's benefits	0.00	0.0%	0.00	0.0%	0.00	0.0%	390.00	0.56%
Officer's life insurance	0.00	0.0%	0.00	0.0%	0.00	0.0%	239.00	0.34%
Total officer's compensation	-	0.0%	-	0.0%	-	0.0%	3,859.00	5.52%
Net income	$ (570.00)	-15.8%	$ (570.00)	-15.8%	$-	0.0%	3,598.88	5.15%
Other income & expenses:								
Interest income	0.00	0.0%	0.00	0.0%	0.00	0.0%	—	—
Sale of assets	0.00	0.0%	0.00	0.0%	0.00	0.0%	—	—
Postage profit	0.00	0.0%	0.00	0.0%	0.00	0.0%	—	—
Total other income & expense	-	#DIV/0!	-	#DIV/0!	-	#DIV/0!	-	-
Income before officer's compensation	(570.00)	7.2%	(570.00)	-7.2%	—	0.0%	7,887.48	11.79%
Officer's compensation								
Officer's salary	0.00	0.0%	0.00	0.0%	0.00	0.0%	3,000.00	4.48%
Payroll taxes	0.00	0.0%	0.00	0.0%	0.00	0.0%	230.00	0.34%
Officer's benefits	0.00	0.0%	0.00	0.0%	0.00	0.0%	390.00	0.58%
Officer's life insurance	0.00	0.0%	0.00	0.0%	0.00	0.0%	239.00	0.36%
Total officer's compensation	-	0.0%	-	0.0%	-	0.0%	3,859.00	5.77%
Net income	$ (570.00)	-14.1%	$ (570.00)	-14.1%	$-	0.0%	4,028.48	6.02%

BIZCOPY

PRO FORMA INCOME STATEMENT
MONTHLY FOR YEAR ENDING DEC 31, 1999

	% OF SALES (DECIMAL)	JAN	FEB	MAR	APR	MAY	JUN	JLY	AUG	SEPT	OCT	NOV	DEC	TOTAL
SALES FORECASTS														
REGULAR PRINTING	0.4511	$34,015.20	$35,747.42	$40,389.24	$35,533.15	$39807.32	$34,655.76	$33,167.13	$35,700.05	$37,477.39	$37,973.60	$34,371.56	$32,012.31	$430,850.12
COPYING	0.3226	$24325.65	$25,564.44	$28,883.99	$25,411.20	$28,467.84	$24,783.75	$23,719.17	$25530.56	$26,801.61	$27,156.47	$24,580.51	$22,893.31	$308,118.49
COLOR COPYING	0.0614	$4,629.87	$4,865.64	$5,497.45	$4,836.48	$5,418.24	$4,717.06	$4,514.44	$4,859.20	$5,101.11	$5,168.65	$4,678.37	$4,357.25	$58,643.75
BROKERED SALES	0.024	$1,809.72	$1,901.88	$2,148.84	$1,890.48	$2,117.88	$1,843.80	$1,764.60	$1,899.36	$1,993.92	$2,020.32	$1,828.68	$1,703.16	$22,922.64
OTHER	0.1409	$10,624.56	$31,165.62	$12,615.48	$11,098.69	$12,433.72	$10,824.64	$10,359.67	$11150.83	$11,705.97	$11,860.96	$10,735.88	$9,998.97	$134,575.00
TOTAL GROSS SALES	1	$75,405	$79,245	$89,535	$78,770	$88,245	$76,825	$73,525	$79,140	$83,080	$84,180	$76,195	$70,965	$955,110
COST OF SALES														
PAPER	0.1257	$9,478.41	$9,961.10	$11,254.55	$9,901 39	$11,092.40	$9,656.90	$9242.09	$9,947.90	$10,443.16	$10,581.43	$9,577.71	$8920.30	$120,057.33
OTHER MATERIALS	0.0364	$2,744.74	$2,884.52	$3,259.07	$2,867 23	$3,212.12	$2,796.43	$2,676.31	$2,880.70	$3,024.11	$3,064.15	$2,773.50	$2583.13	$34,766.00
OUTSIDE SERVICES	0.0248	$1,870.04	$1,965.23	$2,220.47	$1,953.50	$2,188.48	$1,905.26	$1,823.42	$1,962.67	$2,060.38	$2,087.66	$1,889.64	$1,759.93	$23,686.73
OUTSIDE PURCHASES	-0.0003	($22.62)	($23.77)	($26.86)	($23.63)	($26.47)	($23.05)	($22.06)	($23.74)	($24.92)	($25.25)	($22.86)	($21.29)	($286.53)
TOTAL COST OF SALES	0.1866	$14,070.57	$14,787.12	$16,707.23	$14,698.48	$16,466.52	$14,335.55	$13,719.77	$14,767.52	$15,502.73	$15,707.99	$14,217.99	$13,242.07	$178,223.53
GROSS PROFIT		$61,334.43	$64,457.88	$72,827.77	$64,071.52	$71,778.48	$62,489.46	$59,805.24	$64,372.48	$67,577.27	$68,472.01	$61,977.01	$57,722.93	$776,886.47
PAYROLL	0.3209	$24,197.46	$25,429.72	$28,731.78	$25,277.29	$28,317.82	$24,653.14	$23,594.17	$25,396.03	$26,660.37	$27,013.36	$24,450.98	$22,772.67	$306,494.80
OVERHEAD														
BUILDING RENT	0.0511	$3,853.20	$4,049.42	$4,575.24	$4,025.15	$4,509.32	$3,925.76	$3,757.13	$4,044.05	$4,245.39	$4,301.60	$3,893.56	$3,626.31	$48,806.12
DEPRECIATION	0.0586	$4,418.73	$4,643.76	$5,246.75	$4,615.92	$5,171.16	$4,501.95	$4,308.57	$4,637.60	$4,868.49	$4,932.95	$4,465.03	$4,158.55	$55,969.45
COPIER EQUIP. RENTAL	0.0963	$7,261.50	$7,631.29	$8,622.22	$7,585.55	$8,497.99	$7,398.25	$7,080.46	$7,621.18	$8,000.60	$8,106.53	$7,337.58	$6,833.93	$91,977.09
OTHER EQUIP. RENTAL	0.001	$75.41	$79.25	$89.54	$78.77	$88.25	$76.83	$73.53	$79.14	$83.08	$84.18	$76.20	$70.97	$955.11
REPAIRS & MAINTENANCE	0.0042	$316.70	$332.83	$376.05	$330.83	$370.63	$322.67	$308.81	$332.39	$348.94	$353.56	$320.02	$298.05	$4,011.46
ADVERTISING	0.0241	$1,817.26	$1,909.80	$2,157.79	$1,898.36	$2,126.70	$1,851.48	$1,771.95	$1,907.27	$2,002.23	$2,028.74	$1,836.30	$1,710.26	$23,018.15
UTILITIES	0.016	$1206.48	$1,267.92	$1,432.56	$1,260.32	$1,411.92	$1,229.20	$1,176.40	$1,266.24	$1,329.28	$1346.88	$1,219.12	$1,135.44	$15,281.76
PROPERTY & LIAB. INS.	0.0033	$248.84	$261.51	$295.47	$259.94	$291.21	$253.52	$242.63	$261.16	$274.16	$277.79	$251.44	$234.18	$3,151.86
INTEREST	0.0071	$535.38	$562.64	$635.70	$559.27	$626.54	$545.46	$522.03	$561.89	$589.87	$597.68	$540.98	$503.85	$6,781.28
ACCOUNTING & LEGAL FEES	0.0159	$1,198.94	$1,260.00	$1,423.61	$1,252.44	$1,403.10	$1,221.52	$1,169.05	$1,258 33	$1,320.97	$1,338.46	$1,211.50	$1,128.34	$15,186.25
TRAVEL & ENTERTAINMENT	0.0113	$852.08	$895.47	$1,011.75	$890.10	$997.17	$868.12	$830.83	$894.28	$938.80	$951.23	$861.00	$801.90	$10,792.74
AUTO OPERATING EXPENSE	0.0116	$874.70	$919.24	$1,038.61	$913.73	$1,023.64	$891.17	$852.89	$918.02	$963.73	$976.49	$883.86	$823.19	$11,079.28
AUTO LEASE AND/OR DEPR. PMTS.	0.0029	$218.67	$229.81	$259.65	$228.43	$255.91	$222.79	$213.22	$229.51	$240.93	$244.12	$220.97	$205.80	$2,769.82
OFFICE SUPPLIES	0.0271	$2,043.48	$2,147.54	$2,426.40	$2,134.67	$2,391.44	$2,081.96	$1,992.53	$2,144.69	$2,251.47	$2,281.28	$2064.88	$1,923.15	$25,883.48
OTHER OVERHEAD	0.0499	$3,762.71	$3,954.33	$4,467.80	$3,930.62	$4,403.43	$3,833.57	$3,668.90	$3,949.09	$4,415.69	$4,200.58	$3,802.13	$3,541.15	$47,659.99
TOTAL OVERHEAD	0.3804	$28,684.06	$30,144.80	$34,059.11	$29,964.11	$33,568.40	$29,224.23	$27,968.91	$30,104.86	$31,603.63	$32,022.07	$28,984.58	$26,995.09	$363,323.84
OTHER EXPENSES	0.0011	$82.95	$87.17	$98.49	$86.65	$97.07	$84.51	$80.88	$87.05	$91.39	$92.60	$83.81	$78.06	$1050.62
TOTAL COSTS		$67,035.05	$70,448.81	$79,596.62	$70,026.53	$78,449.81	$68,297.43	$65,363.73	$70,355.46	$73,858.12	$74,836.02	$67,737.36	$63,087.89	$849,092.79
NET OWNER'S COMPENSATION		$8,369.95	$8,796.19	$9,938.38	$8,743.47	$9,795.19	$8,527.57	$8,161.27	$8,784.54	$9,221.88	$9,343.98	$8,457.65	$7,877.12	$106,017.21

Customer & Non-User Survey

Copyright 1998, SHN

Firm:
SIC:

Please record all respondee side comments and explanations in the margins. This input is an extremely valuable part of the survey.

---

1. *What items does your firm have printed or copied, or what services do you use?*
   (Prompt with choices if necessary. Check all that apply.)

   ___ Desktop publishing (A)
   ___ Stationary, envelopes, or letterhead (B)
   ___ Business cards (C)
   ___ Forms: invoices, prescription pads, statements, order forms, inventory sheets (D)
   ___ Marketing materials: brochures, newsletters, flyers, promotional pieces (E)
   ___ Labels (F)
   ___ Manuals: training materials, specification books, instructions (G)
   ___ Color copies (H)
   ___ Copies: black & white (including high-speed) (I)
   ___ Bindery or finishing (J)
   ___ OTHER:_____ (K)

2. I am going to list certain factors that might affect your choice of a printing and copying service. For each factor I read, please tell me if it is very, somewhat, or not important to you.

   (Repeat the 3 choices, as necessary. The "Other" column is for coding purposes, only.)

	IMPORTANCE			
	Very	Somewhat	Not	Other
Take original from disk (L-2)	___ (3)	___ (2)	___ (1)	___ (0)
Typesetting (M-3)	___ (3)	___ (2)	___ (1)	___ (0)
Pick-up & delivery (N-4)	___ (3)	___ (2)	___ (1)	___ (0)
Location (0-5)	___ (3)	___ (2)	___ (1)	___ (0)
Friendly/Courteous staff (P-6)	___ (3)	___ (2)	___ (1)	___ (0)
Knowledgeable employees (Q-7)	___ (3)	___ (2)	___ (1)	___ (0)
Graphic design (R-8)	___ (3)	___ (2)	___ (1)	___ (0)
Full color copies (S-9)	___ (3)	___ (2)	___ (1)	___ (0)
Output to color (T-10)	___ (3)	___ (2)	___ (1)	___ (0)
Output to black/white (U-11)	___ (3)	___ (2)	___ (1)	___ (0)
Copying turnaround same/next day (V-12)	___ (3)	___ (2)	___ (1)	___ (0)
Printing turnaround under 3 days (W-13)	___ (3)	___ (2)	___ (1)	___ (0)
Carbonless forms (X-14)	___ (3)	___ (2)	___ (1)	___ (0)
1 or 2 color printing (Y-15)	___ (3)	___ (2)	___ (1)	___ (0)
4 color process printing (Z-16)	___ (3)	___ (2)	___ (1)	___ (0)
Mailing services (AA- 17)	___ (3)	___ (2)	___ (1)	___ (0)
Binding services (AB- 18)	___ (3)	___ (2)	___ (1)	___ (0)
Superior quality (AC-19)	___ (3)	___ (2)	___ (1)	___ (0)
Competitive price (AD-20)	___ (3)	___ (2)	___ (1)	___ (0)

2.1. Ask only if "Competitive Price" is rated VERY important. [If "price" is not rated VERY important, go to next page.]

Of the factors you rated "VERY important" from above, which one is your highest priority?
(If necessary, restate choices rated "Very important".)
[Record a 1 in the left margin above, next to the highest priority]

Which one would you say is your 2nd highest priority?
[Record a 2 in the left margin above next to the 2nd highest priority]

Is there a 3rd highest priority?
[Record a 3 in the left margin above next to the 3rd highest priority]

3. *What printing and copying service did you use most often during the past 6 months?*
   (Select only one. Have respondees indicate which is their <u>primary</u> or <u>main</u> printer.)

   ___ Not willing to divulge (AE- 17)
   ___ BizCopy (AE-16)
   ___ BizCopy as main, among multiple printers * (AE-15)
   ___ Alphaprint-Northwood (AE-14)
   ___ Alphaprint-Western(AE-13)
   ___ Grays (AE-12)
   ___ Eastpark (AE-I 1)
   ___ Kinko's (AE-10)
   ___ National Press (AE-9)
   ___ The Printery (AE-8)
   ___ American Graphics (AE-7)
   ___ Sunwalk Printers (AE-6)
   ___ Profitville Printers (AE-5)
   ___ Capital Graphics(AE-4)
   ___ Other: _____ (AE-3)
   ___ Multiple printers (AE-2)
   ___ Don't know or won't say (AL-1)

   *   Names of multiple printers, if provided: _____

NON BizCopy users—Continue to next page.

BizCopy USERS—Skip the next page. Go on to question 5.

NON BizCopy only!!

4. *Your response indicates that you do not use BizCopy most often for printing and copying services.* Can you tell me the most important reason why not?

   ___ Response reveals he/she does use BizCopy.
         or
   ___ Not open convenient hours (AF-12)
   ___ Use a friend/relative/neighbor/client (AF-11)
   ___ Not in a convenient location (AF-10)
   ___ Prices too high (AF-9)
   ___ Not familiar with BizCopy (AF-8)
   ___ Never been approached (AF-7)
   ___ Satisfied with present printer (AF-6)
   ___ BizCopy has given unsatisfactory service (AF-5)
   ___ Do printing/copying in-house (AF-4)
   ___ BizCopy is not a commercial printer (AF-3)
   ___ Decision is made at another location (AF-2)
   ___ Other: _____ (AF-1)
   ___ Don't know (AF-0)

Skip to page 6 from here (omit section below)

4.1. *What percent of your printing and copying would you say is done 4 with BizCopy?*

   ___ 50% or more [Code as "customer" (AE-15) then go on to next page]
   ___ Under 50% [Code as "multiple" (AE-2)] **then ask:**
What is the most important reason why you don 't use BizCopy for more than 50% of your outside printing and copying? [Record response at the top of this page]

Skip to page 6

5. For the services you use, please rate your primary printing and copying service as <u>better than expected</u>, <u>about as expected</u>, or <u>worse than expected</u>.

(Repeat the ratings as necessary. Be prepared to code for "Don't Use" but don't offer it as a response option.)

	Importance			
	Better than expected	About as expected	Worse than expected	don't use this service
Take original from disk (AG)	___ (3)	___ (2)	___ (1)	___ (0)
Typesetting (AII)	___ (3)	___ (2)	___ (1)	___ (0)
Pick-up & delivery (AI)	___ (3)	___ (2)	___ (1)	___ (0)
Location (AJ)	___ (3)	___ (2)	___ (1)	___ (0)
Friendly/Courteous staff (AK)	___ (3)	___ (2)	___ (1)	___ (0)
Knowledgeable employees (AL)	___ (3)	___ (2)	___ (1)	___ (0)
Graphic design (AM)	___ (3)	___ (2)	___ (1)	___ (0)
Full color copies (AN)	___ (3)	___ (2)	___ (1)	___ (0)
Output to color (AO)	___ (3)	___ (2)	___ (1)	___ (0)
Output to black/white (AP)	___ (3)	___ (2)	___ (1)	___ (0)
Copying turnaround same/next day (AQ)	___ (3)	___ (2)	___ (1)	___ (0)
Priming turnaround under 3 days (AR)	___ (3)	___ (2)	___ (1)	___ (0)
Carbonless forms (AS)	___ (3)	___ (2)	___ (1)	___ (0)
I or 2 color printing (AT)	___ (3)	___ (2)	___ (1)	___ (0)
4 color process printing (AU)	___ (3)	___ (2)	___ (1)	___ (0)
Mailing services (AV)	___ (3)	___ (2)	___ (1)	___ (0)
Binding services (AW)	___ (3)	___ (2)	___ (1)	___ (0)
Superior quality (AX)	___ (3)	___ (2)	___ (1)	___ (0)
Competitive price (AY)	___ (3)	___ (2)	___ (1)	___ (0)

6. If you could make suggestions to the management of your primary printer for improving their products or services, what is the single most important change you would recommend?

___ Deliver when promised (AZ-9)
___ Improve work quality (AZ-8)
___ Faster turnaround (AZ-7)
___ Lower prices (AZ-6)
___ Improve employee knowledge (AZ-5)
___ Friendlier staff (AZ-4)
___ Offer pick-up and delivery (AZ-3)
___ Increased communication (AZ-2)
___ Other: _____ (AZ-1)
___ No changes (AZ-0)

All Respondees

7. How did you first hear about the printer you use?

___ Inherited the relationship (BA-11)
___ Have done business with them for years (BA-10)
___ Use a friend/relative/client (BA-9)

___ Located nearby (BA-8)
___ Yellow Pages ad (BA-7)
___ Recommendation/word-of-mouth/referral (BA-6)
___ Sales person (BA-5)
___ Sign on building (BA-4)
___ Brochure/newsletter (BA-3)
___ Direct-mail (BA-2)
___ Other: _____ (BA-1)
___ Don't know (BA-0)

8.*What department makes the ultimate decision about which printing or copying service to use?*
___ Multiple departments (BB-10)
___ Administration (BB-9)
___ Human Resources/Personnel (BB-8)
___ Purchasing (BB-7)
___ Marketing/Sales (BB-6)
___ Production (BB-5)
___ Office Manager (BB-4)
___ Senior Management/Owner (BB-3)
___ Secretary of Receptionist (BB-2)
___ Other: _____ (BB-1)
___ Don't know (BB-0)

9.*How frequently does you firm use outside printing and copying services?*
___ 12 or more times per year (BC-6)
___ 7–11 times per year (BC-5)
___ 4–6 times per year (BC-4)
___ 3 times per year (BC-3)
___ Less than one time per year (BC-2)
___ Other: _____ (BC-1)
___ Don't know (BC-0)

10. *What does your firm typically spend monthly for outside printing and copying services?*
___ Over $1,000 (BD-6)
___ $501 -$1,000 (BD-5)
___ $301 - $500 (BD-4)
___ $151-$300 (BD-3)
___ $75 - $150 (BD-2)
___ under $75 (BD- 1)
___ Don't know (BD-0)

11 .*About how many people does your firm employ at your location?*
___ 5,000 and above (BE-10)
___ 1,000–4,999 (BE-9)
___ 500–999 (BE-8)
___ 250–499 (BE-7)
___ 100–249 (BE-6)
___ 50–99 (BE-5)
___ 25–49 (BE-4)
___ 10–24 (BE-3)
___ 5–9 (BE-2)
___ 1–4 (BE-1)
___ Don't know (BE-0)

RESPONDEE INFO [Try, but do not force]

12. *Last question. Please give me your name and position.*

Name: _____
Position: _____
Name of firm's business: _____
Interviewer's name: _____
Date: _____

business**PLAN**

Blue Sky Travel

Business Plan for Blue Sky Travel

Plan Years: 1995–1999

Confidential

CONFIDENTIALITY STATEMENT

The information, data and drawings embodied in this business plan are strictly confidential and are supplied on the understanding that they will be held confidentially and not disclosed to third parties without the prior written consent of Blue Sky Travel Incorporated.

BUSINESS PLAN PURPOSE STATEMENT

The purpose of this document is for internal company use. It is intended to assist the owners of Blue Sky Travel, Inc. to productively and efficiently plan, measure, and manage the growth of this small business.

- What do you think of this plan? Do you like the organization?
- What is the strategy for distribution for their product?
- What are the risks they face?
- Where are they? Do you have a good idea of how the company runs?
- What is their system for distribution?
- How do they relate to their customers?
- Who are their customers?
- Are they profitable?
- Example of a start-up plan
- How did the writer prove his/her competence to own and manage the agency in the personnel section?
- How were the promotional goals and plans spelled out?
- How would you explain the impact of the Internet on Blue Sky?
- Is this business viable in today's market with the airlines cutting commissions to travel agents?
- Did they explain their working relationship? What if the partnership dissolves?
- Will location have an impact on this business?
- Do you understand their niche markets from what you have read?

Business Plan for Blue Sky Travel
Plan Years: 1995–1999
Confidential

EXECUTIVE SUMMARY

Company Name: Blue Sky Travel, Incorporated
Contact: Cecilia Cielo, Nadine Nuvole
Address: 1234 Overlook Drive
Paris, FL
Telephone: (987) 654-3219

Company Overview

Blue Sky Travel, Incorporated is a startup travel agency located in one of the fastest growing areas of the country, as well as within the state of Florida. The travel agency is owned and managed by two partners, Cecilia Cielo and Nadine Nuvole, whose previous experience in marketing and highly successful small business ownership/operation has been extremely useful in the early start-up months. The partners' ties to the community and previous business relationships have given the business a strong client base from which to grow into the future.

Blue Sky Travel plans to utilize an outside, independent sales force to keep overhead expenses down and return on sales as high as possible. The owners see this method of travel agency sales to be the "wave of the future", as well as the surest way to maintain profitability in a highly competitive industry. However, the owners will have to quickly build business relationships with tour and consortium travel brokers to insure this profitability, as well. The business must also employ an experienced travel agency business manager to run to the day-to-day operations and to bolster the travel industry inexperience of the ownership.

Blue Sky Travel has identified three customer groups to target for their travel-related services. They are: 1) The corporate conference traveler, 2) The senior citizen/retiree traveler, and 3) The university (student, staff, and faculty) traveler from the area universities.

Vision

The owners envision expansion of the company resulting from three primary areas within the next five year period. First, the owners foresee continued growth in travel services to corporate and business conference attendees at specialized training workshops. Secondly, continued expansion is also envisioned in senior citizen,

retiree travel-related services. The owners envision the agency being the preferred provider of travel services to this growing population in the greater Paris, Florida area. Finally, continued expansion of the student and faculty related travel business is expected to grow as the two area universities grow.

Relating to this vision, the owners have five agreed upon objectives for the company. One is to become profitable within the first 12 months of operation and then achieve at least a 5% pre-tax profit within the next 4 years. Another objective is to be the predominant travel agency-of-choice for the senior citizen/retiree traveler. Thirdly, to increase corporate sales to at least $10,000 per month by the second year of operation. Fourthly, expand university sales to approximately 10% of all the agency's sales by the second year of operation. And finally, hire an experienced travel agency manager, as well as four additional outside contract travel agents.

Financial Summary

Projected Income Statement Summary

($ 000s)	Estimates				
	1995	1996	1997	1998	1999
Net Sales	$496	$862	$1,353	$2,194	$3,286
Cost of Sales	$445	$754	$1,184	$1,919	$2,876
Gross Profit	$51	$108	$169	$275	$410
S G.& A. Expense	$73	$103	$130	$191	$241
Other Expense					
Other Income	$0	$0	$0	$0	$0
Net Income (Before Tax)	($22)	$5	$39	$84	$169

COMPANY DATA

Business Description

The two partners began the travel agency in January of 1995 as a sub-Chapter S corporation and now employ two full-time inside agents and one independent outside agent. Blue Sky Travel (BST) offers a full line of travel planning and other travel related services. The organization has a strong commitment to service, value, and the specialized needs of its target customers that sets it apart from the other travel agencies in the area. As mentioned above, the agency will be focusing on corporate travel with an emphasis on the business conference traveler, the senior citizen/retiree vacation traveler, and various university student groups. faculty, and staff travelers from the area universities.

BST is located in an office complex near the University of Florida/Paris Campus. With the growth of the campus and the east areas, Paris is the fastest growing city in the state of Florida, coupled with the continuing growth of the senior citizen population, the area universities, and area businesses, the agency is offering a set of unique travel services that have not been emphasized by other area agencies. The agency is one of two travel agencies in Paris and the only local agency known to cater directly to senior citizens.

Current Position And Future Outlook

The business is situated in period of expansion within the travel industry, as well as within an area of the country that is exhibiting a strong expansion trend. As of 1993, the travel industry in the southern U.S. and Paris has shown a 15% annual growth in sales revenue compared to 9% for the rest of the U S The total market represents $93.5 billion in sales.

One of the primary goals of this company is to achieve a profit within 12 months and then achieve a pre-tax profit level of at least 5% of sales within 4 years. This will be attained through providing cost-effective service and meeting the unique travel needs of the core customer groups, as well as through the use of outside sales and tour/consortium brokers. In addition, as a startup business, the partners' immediate concerns focus on increases in sales and obtaining break-even as quickly as possible. The primary issues facing the business are marketing and selling to the core customers they have labeled as their target market and to build cost-effective business relationships with tour/consortium brokers.

Management And Ownership

The travel agency is currently owned and operated by Cecilia Cielo and Nadine Nuvole. Cielo owns approximately 70% of the agency and Nuvole's ownership constitutes the remaining 30%. Neither owner has any direct experience in the travel agency industry.

Therefore, the need for an experienced travel agency business manager is quite apparent. However, what the two owners do possess is an immediate client listing, referral source, and basis of cashflow.

Cecilia Cielo, through a previous business ownership relationship, has a guaranteed book of business through a local training organization for the vocational rehabilitation industry. Cielo is the sole provider of travel-related services for the booking of all airline flights, hotel, and auto rental arrangements needed for these corporate training conferences and the attendees. Cielo also has over ten years of previous, and very successful, business ownership and marketing/sales experience.

Likewise, Nadine Nuvole, through personal contacts at the University of Florida/Paris, has been able to attain the rights for the travel arrangements for many of the sports teams on the campus, as well as other campus groups travel needs Nuvole also has personal contact and involvement with many senior citizen groups in the area from which travel business has already been established.

Objectives Delineated

1) Reach a profitable status within 12 months, then achieve a pre-tax profit of 5% as sales are expanded to $3 million over the next four years.
2) Garner 60% of the senior citizen/retiree travel business in the Paris-area adult communities within five years.
3) Expand corporate sales to $10,000 per month by the second year of operation.
4) Increase vacation package sales to the area universities to approximately 10% of total agency sales by the second year.
5) Hire a fill-time Business Manager by the third year of operation and contract with four additional independent, outside sales agents by the second year of operation.

Business Plan for Blue Sky Travel
Plan Years: 1995–1999
Confidential

Strategies To Attain Objectives

Objective: Reach a pre-tax profit of 5% with sales approaching $3 million.

Strategies:
- Concentrate bookings in outside tour packages as the margins associated with tour packages are much higher than the regulated CRS bookings.
- Build business relationships with high income producing tour providers/consortiums through direct contact and frequent use.
- Hire outside sales personnel and stress community contact. Outside sales agents allow the company to keep overhead expenses down that are associated with employees.
- Increase exposure and presence through increased marketing to the university, business, and retiree community.
- Increase service capability and response time to the corporate workshop traveler.

Objective: Become the major provider of travel services to the retiree community of Paris.

Strategies:
- Provide travel workshops and seminars in local area retiree communities,
- Increase advertising in retiree related media and community newspapers.
- Offer travel promotions directly to the senior-aged, retiree age group.
- Develop relationships with tour providers to meet the special needs of the senior traveler and promote this service.

Objective: Expand corporate sales to $10,000 per month by the second year of operation.

Strategies:
- Increase marketing presentations to area businesses to two per week.
- Increase exposure of the travel agency and its services to local business groups through participation in business group functions.

- Promote a "one-stop shopping" approach to the business conference traveler that entails detailed conference pre-planning services and arrangement of all conference needs from lodging, meal planning, and airline travel to conference amenities.
- Offer attractive pricing schemes and discount plans to the corporate travel coordinator or business owner for repeat usage of the agency's travel services.

Objective: Increase vacation package sales to the area universities to approximately 10% of total agency sales by the second year.

Strategies:
- Increase advertising on the university campuses through advertising placed in the university student newspapers, posters at campus bookstores and other high traffic areas on the campuses, and through brochures and fliers provided directly to students, faculty, and staff
- Increase marketing presentations to student and faculty affairs personnel to offer travel services for special events and activities.
- Offer special pricing for vacation and travel packages during the peak travel seasons for the students and faculty. The seasons would include the annual spring break and Christmas break,

Objective: Hire a full-time Business Manager by the third year of operation and contract with four additional independent, outside sales agents by the second year of operation.

Strategies:
- Through networking and conversations with other travel agents and agencies at industry functions, locate and hire a business manager with strong travel agency management and sales experience.
- Through networking with other agents and advertising in the newspaper, recruit independent, toutside sales agents.

Business Plan for Blue Sky Travel
Plan Years: 1995–1999
Confidential

INDUSTRY DATA

Industry Overview And Size

The travel industry, as it is known today, had its beginnings with the advent of the airline industry. Travel agencies have grown as the airlines and air travel have grown. In fact, as of 1993, travel agencies realized approximately 60% of their total revenues as coming from airline and air travel sales. Despite the large sales base resulting from the airlines, the growth of the travel industry ebbed during the recent recession. However, it has shown revitalized growth as people are now traveling in record numbers. To emphasize this fact, the total volume of agency sales was $93.5 billion dollars as of 1993. This represented a 9% annual increase in business since 1991. Total bookings today approximate $100 billion dollars. In addition, travel agencies in all regions of the U.S. saw their revenues increase since 1991. But the most pronounced growth was in the South which saw an annual growth rate of 15% (Travel Weekly Focus - Trade Newspaper; 1994 U.S. Travel Agency Survey; August 1994 edition)

Pricing And Value

Pricing in the travel agency industry is strongly dictated by the Central Reservation System (CRS) which acts as a clearing house for airline reservations and ticketing, as well as many other travel services. Consequently, any margin on sales processed through the CRS is built into this reservation delivery system. The pre-determined margin within the CRS is 10% with a $50 cap on all reservations. An additional service fee is being considered for some travel services to offset the cap imposed by the CRS and some of the airline carriers.

However, pricing and margins related to travel services outside of the CRS are more flexible and profitable. By using group negotiated pricing with tour package vendors, wholesalers, and consortium or cooperative travel brokers margins are expected to be 15% on the average. Because competition is able to obtain similar, if not identical, pricing through the CRS, strong business relationships with several outside tour vendors will be emphasized. Tour vendors

and wholesalers will be found that offer travel destinations, pricing, and services relating directly to the core customers identified by this agency. These relationships will be established through researching available travel brokers, direct contact with likely candidates, and through frequent and varied use of these travel brokers to ascertain their quality and to establish a usage and commission history.

By developing and utilizing these tour vendor relationships, BST will be able to maximize margins, obtain pricing flexibility and value, and differentiate itself from the competition by offering travel destinations and tour packages that cater to the special needs of the senior citizen, the desires of the university student and faculty member, and the necessities of the business traveler. This specialized travel planning service will allow for uniqueness of pricing and value to the customer, as well as to differentiate services from the competition.

MARKET DATA

Customer Profile

As competition has intensified within the travel industry, the impetus to better understand different customers and customer groups has become more important. The partners of the agency have identified the core customer types that best suit business goals. These customers are senior citizen/retired couples. university students, faculty, and staff, and corporate travelers with an emphasis on the business conference traveler. These three types of travelers will be focused on because of their availability to travel and, especially in the case of the senior citizen and business traveler, their monetary capability to travel. This group of customers have been identified as the predominate growth groups in the east Paris area. In addition, readily available and guaranteed customers are already in existence within these identified groups.

Competition

Competition within the travel industry can be broken down into three categories:

Business Plan for Blue Sky Travel
Plan Years: 1995–1999
Confidential

1) National Companies: National companies have attained national exposure, size, and recognition. Companies such as AAA (American Automobile Association) and American Express would be examples of national competitors.
2) University Specific Companies: University specific companies are those that have exclusive contract with the state of Florida or a specific university to provide defined travel services to various segments of the university population. Collegiate Travel is one such company in the east Paris area which has this exclusive arrangement.
3) Local Companies. Local companies are of the same basic size and makeup of Blue Sky Travel and are located in east Paris area All local companies sales are dictated by the same price structures by the airlines and the CRS. There are 14 local travel agencies within the east Paris area that have been identified.

Most recently, the national companies have grown the fastest due to their size, name recognition, and advertising ability. However, the local company growth and financial condition has remained steady with new firms entering the market and very few firms exiting the market. This is attributed to the ability of the small, local firms providing a higher level of personalized service that the national companies haven't been able to accomplish.

Marketing Strategies

Blue Sky Travel has chosen to cater to the retired senior citizen, the corporate traveler emphasizing the business conference traveler, and the university population in the central Paris area Emphasis will be placed on value, personalized service and the customization of travel requirements, and ease of accessibility of travel related services. The last emphasis entails meeting arid exceeding the customers travel needs from the first contact by providing travel pre-planning services to providing all travel arrangements. Promotion of these travel services will be done through participation in community events, special travel seminars for senior citizens, direct advertising in area newspapers and other media, sales presentations to businesses and business groups, and direct mail, posters, and brochures on the area university campuses. In addition, continuous contact will be maintained with area university officials to procure the travel services and arrangements for specific student, faculty, and staff events and activities. Similarly, Blue Sky Travel will differentiate itself from the other local travel agencies by marketing and promoting its travel arrangement expertise to the business community.

The travel agency will utilize an outside and inside sales force to capture potential travel bookings or sales. The inside sales force will be responsible for the final processing of all bookings. Payment and bookings will be processed at the agency itself. Credit cards, checks, and cash will be accepted as payment for all travel services provided. The outside agents will continue their personal marketing efforts within the leisure travel business with an emphasis on the BST core customer groups.

OPERATIONAL PLANS

Sales Forecasts

The sales plan for the travel agency is targeting $496,000 by the end of 1995 and $862,000 in 1996. The plan is based on increasing travel service arrangements with employers and employer groups, increasing sales to the senior citizen vacation traveler, and increased sales to students, faculty, and assorted student groups from area universities, The forecasted sales breakdown by market in 1996 is:

	% OF SALES	SALES
Corporate Sales (including conference travel)	60	$517,200
Senior Citizen Vacation Sales	30	$258,600
University Sales	10	$ 86,200

Business Plan for Blue Sky Travel
Plan Years: 1995–1999
Confidential

Product Description

The primary travel products and services that will be sold will include, but are not limited to, airline tickets, train tickets, hotel arrangements, rental car arrangements, cruises, tours and charter services, vacation packages, business conference/meeting planning and arrangement services, and student and faculty activity travel services. The grouping of these individual services and products will be emphasized through tour, vacation, and conference packages in order to optimize sales and profitability. If the service or product is sold through the Central Reservation System (CR5), the margin on sales will be around 10%. If the service or product is sold through a tour vendor or wholesaler, margins can be expected to be 15%.

The forecasted sales by product or service for 1996 are:

Autie Ticketing	$382,000
Other Ticketing	$19,000
Motel Arrangements	$75,000
Auto Rental	$25,000
Cruises	$30,000
Tours/Packages	$86,000
Conference Travel	$135,000
Student/Faculty Activities	$110,000

Advertising And Promotion

The promotional activities of the travel agency will focus on the following;

- Space advertising in local, university, and senior citizen community newspapers and publications will be used to promote the range of travel products and unique travel services offered by the agency, starting in October 1995.
- Four color, one-page brochures and posters emphasizing the unique products and services of the agency will be developed and tailored to the specific customer groups identified, beginning January 1996.

- Road-side marquee advertising will be utilized and modified on a monthly basis to promote a different travel product or service.
- Yellow page advertising will begin in October of 1995.

The partners will become more prominent in the local chamber of commerce and other community associations. They will take part in and sponsor local community, university, and business events beginning in January 1996.

Selling Methods

Selling plans for the travel agency are:

- Recruit two independent, outside sales agents by August 1995, with selling experience and an existing customer base, to expand coverage in the greater Paris area.
- Increase the sales calls by the partners to three per week.
- Recruit two additional independent, outside sales agents by February 1996.
- Inside agents will increase service efforts through ticket delivery and telephone follow-up upon return to garner repeat business and sales.
- Inside agents will increase telemarketing efforts of area businesses and senior citizen communities to qualify prospective clients and presentations.
- The two partners will continue to increase exposure of the agency through involvement and coordination of community events and functions.
- The two partners will initially perform all sales management and coordination duties until the agency business manager is hired.

The outside sales agents will be charged with maintaining their previously established client base. However, all sales to this client base and any new client sales will now be processed through BST. As independent contractors, these outside travel agents will not be directly supervised by any BST owners or employees. However, the ongoing coordination and followup with these individuals will be initially performed by the owners of the company. The agency business manager will take over this function upon hire.

Salary and Commission Structure

The two inside travel agents are compensated on a salary plus commission basis. Commissions for the inside travel agents are currently capped at 1% of sales made. The owners plan to begin drawing a salary in the second year of operation. An employee benefits package has not been implemented nor planned for at this time. This position may be considered at a later date if sales and profits permit,

The outside travel agents are compensated on a commission only basis. The commission structure for these individuals is on a negotiated basis. They generally fall between 2% to 7% of all sales made and processed through BST.

Facility Plans

The agency is currently situated in a second floor suite at 1234 Overlook Drive, Paris, Florida. The office is part of the Overlook commercial office complex In east Paris. A move from this site is anticipated by mid-1996 to allow for easier accessibility, visibility, and parking by the agency clientele. New site locations will be determined beginning in March 1996 from available office space situated in the greater Paris area. No more than 1200 square feet of space will be needed as outside sales will be the emphasis of this agency.

FINANCIAL PLANS

Assumptions

The sales data were developed by the two partners using brief startup sales numbers at the inception of the business, customer projections, and industry derived sales figures for startup travel agen-

cies. Cost information was developed from internally generated data with assistance from the agency's retained accounting firm. Operating expenses were developed through a pro-forma budget process. The income statement is cash accounting based. Long-term debt will not be used as means of financing the business. Income taxes were estimated on a conservative approach utilizing the maximum tax rate of 34%.

Other key assumptions: The partners will forego salaries at the onset of the planning period and until the business shows a consistent sales base to support the taking of salaries. A target date the partners have set to begin drawing salaries from the business is January 1996. Salary increases for the inside sales agents will be capped at 4%/year through the planning period. All other adjustments to earning potential will be realized through the commission structure of the business.

As a part of the financial plans, three case scenarios were developed for the Summary Income Statement for Blue Sky Travel, Incorporated. The first case represents the most likely case to occur. The second or low case scenario assumes that the expansion into the travel services market is slower than forecast. Sales in the low case are 85% of the most likely case (plan). The third case or high case assumes rapid access into the travel services market with sales forecast at 10% over plan.

Definitions

The definitions below correspond to each line item found on the Income Statement for

Sales: The revenue realized from selling travel related services.

Cost of Sales: The cost associated with the sale of travel related services. Generally, the payment to the CRS/ARC system.

Gross Profit: The revenue remaining for company use alter the cost of sales are deducted from total sales.

General & Administration Line Items

Payroll & Payroll Related Expense: Salaries and wages and any associated costs involved in the payment of the salaries or wages to BST employees.

Payroll Taxes: Any Federal, state, local income taxes, as well as the social security and medicare expenses that the company is responsible for paying for the benefit of the company's employees.

Travel & Entertainment: Costs associated with the travel and entertainment of the owners not related to marketing of a potential customer.

Rent/Utilities/Telephone: Costs associated with the payment of rent, electricity, and telephone in relation to the office location.

Insurance/Legal/Accounting: Costs of business insurance (general liability, workers compensation, etc.), attornies fees, and outside accounting fees.

Office & Supplies: The costs associated with keeping the office stocked with office supplies and other necessary items to operate the day-to-day business,

Equipment Expense: Costs associated with the maintenance or lease of office equipment.

Auto, Truck Expense: Costs associated with the lease and maintenance of company owned vehicles.

Other: Any other miscellaneous costs that result from the operation of the business.

Sales & Marketing Line Items

Commissions: The payment to travel agents for the sales they make. Generally, based on a set percentage of the sale amount.

Advertising: Costs associated with the promotion of the company to the general public or target customers to increase sales.

Travel & Entertainment: Costs associated with the travel and entertainment of perspective customers intended to increase sales.

SUMMARY INCOME STATEMENT

Most Likely Case:
($s)

	1995	1996	Estimates 1997	1998	1999
SALES	$495,835	$862,075	$1,353,088	$2,193,566	$3,286,348
COST OF SALES:	$444,812	$754,316	$1,183,952	$1,919,370	$2,875,555
GROSS PROFIT	$51,024	$107,759	$169,136	$274,196	$410,794
OPERATING EXPENSES:					
Total General & Administration	$65,468	$91,850	$112,687	$141,702	$169,294
Total Sales & Marketing	$7,397	$11,121	$17,531	$48,871	$71,727
OTHER INCOME	$0	$0	$0	$0	$0
PROFIT (LOSS)	($21,842)	$4,789	$38,918	$83,622	$169,773
INCOME TAXES	($7,426)	$1,628	$13,232	$28,432	$57,723
NET PROFIT (LOSS)	($14,416)	$3,160	$25,686	$55,191	$112,050

Low Case:
($'s)

	1995	1996	Estimates 1997	1998	1999
SALES	$421,460	$732,764	$1,150,124	$1,864,531	$2,793,396
COST OF SALES:	$378,090	$641,168	$1,006,359	$1,631,464	$2,444,222
GROSS PROFIT	$43,370	$91,595	$143,766	$233,066	$349,175
OPERATING EXPENSES:					
Total General & Administration	65,468	$91,850	$112,687	$141,702	$169,294
Total Sales & Marketing	$7,397	$11,121	$17,531	$48,871	$71,727
OTHER INCOME	$0	$0	$0	$0	$0
PROFIT (LOSS)	($29,496)	($11,375)	$13,548	$42,493	$108,154
INCOME TAXES	($10,028)	($3,868)	$4,606	$14,448	$36,772
NET PROFIT (LOSS)	($19,467)	($7,508)	$8,941	$28,045	$71,381

High Case:
($'s)

	1995	1996	Estimates 1997	1998	1999
SALES	$545,419	$948,283	$1,488,396	$2,412,922	$3,614,983
COST OF SALES:	$489,293	$829,747	$1,302,347	$2,111,307	$3,163,110
GROSS PROFIT	$56,126	$118,535	$186,050	$301,615	$451,873
OPERATING EXPENSES:					
Total General & Administration	$65,468	$91,850	$112,687	$141,702	$169,294
Total Sales & Marketing	$7,397	$11,121	$17,531	$48,871	$71,727
OTHER INCOME	$0	$0	$0	$0	$0
PROFIT (LOSS)	($16,740)	$15,565	$55,832	$111,042	$210,852
INCOME TAXES	($5,691)	$5,292	$18,983	$37,754	$71,690
NET PROFIT (LOSS)	($11,048)	$10,273	$36,849	$73,288	$139,162

The following pages show a detailed Income Statement and Balance Sheet.
For brevity, only the most likely case scenario is shown.

INCOME STATEMENT

($s)

	Forecast Jan 95	Forecast Feb 95	Forecast Mar 95	Forecast Apr 95	Forecast May 95	Forecast Jun 95
SALES	$1,600	$20,050	$23,960	$37,775	$36,000	$41,150
COST OF SALES						
Total Cost of Sales	$0	$18,045	$21,564	$33,998	$32,400	$37,035
GROSS PROFIT	$1,600	$2,005	$2,396	$3,778	$3,600	$4,115
GENERAL & ADMINISTRATION						
Payroll & Payroll Related Exp.	$1,951	$2,707	$3,600	$2,448	$2,278	$2,450
Payroll Taxes	$149	$207	$275	$450	$421	$453
Travel & Entertainment	$0	$0	$0	$0	$0	$0
Rent/Utilities/Telephone	$1,290	$982	$1,094	$1,393	$1,328	$1,400
Insurance/Legal/Accounting	$1,293	$0	$695	$200	$200	$200
Office & Supplies	$1,220	$525	$730	$600	$625	$200
Equipment Expense	$185	$0	$60	$0	$0	$240
Auto, Truck Expense	$0	$0	$0	$0	$0	$0
Other	$435	$705	$980	$395	$400	$250
Total General & Administration	$6,523	$5,126	$7,434	$5,436	$5,252	$5,193
SALES & MARKETING:						
Commissions	$16	$201	$240	$378	$360	$412
Advertising	$135	$0	$174	$130	$150	$200
Travel & Entertainment	$0	$0	$0	$0	$0	$0
Auto	$0	$0	$0	$0	$0	$0
Total Sales & Marketing	$151	$201	$414	$508	$510	$612
PROFIT (LOSS)	($5,074)	($3,322)	($5,452)	($2,216)	($2,162)	($1,690)
INCOME TAXES	($1,725)	($1,129)	($1,854)	($754)	($735)	($575)
NET PROFIT (LOSS)	($3,349)	($2,192)	($3,598)	($1,463)	($1,427)	($1,115)

INCOME STATEMENT

($s)

	Forecast Jul 95	Forecast Aug 95	Forecast Sep 95	Forecast Oct 95	Forecast Nov 95	Forecast Dec 95
SALES	$46,150	$48,550	$53,800	$56,900	$62,300	$67,600
COST OF SALES:	$41,535	$43,695	$48,420	$51,210	$56,070	$60,840
Total Cost of Sales	$4,615	$4,855	$5,380	$5,690	$6,230	$6,760
GROSS PROFIT						
GENERAL & ADMINISTRATION						
Payroll & Payroll Related Exp.	$2,450	$2,450	$2,450	$2,450	$2,450	$2,450
Payroll Taxes	$453	$453	$453	$453	$453	$453
Travel & Entertainment	$0	$0	$0	$0	$0	$0
Rent/Utilities/Telephone	$1,497	$1,444	$1,400	$1,395	$1,395	$1,463
Insurance/Legal/Accounting	$200	$200	$200	$200	$200	$200
Office & Supplies	$200	$200	$200	$200	$200	$200
Equipment Expense	$0	$0	$240	$0	$0	$300
Auto, Truck Expense	$0	$0	$0	$0	$0	$0
Other	$250	$250	$250	$250	$250	$250
Total General & Administration	$5,050	$4,997	$5,193	$4,948	$4,948	$5,316
SALES & MARKETING						
Commissions	$462	$486	$538	$569	$623	$676
Advertising	$250	$250	$250	$300	$300	$300
Travel & Entertainment	$0	$0	$0	$0	$0	$0
Auto	$0	$0	$0	$0	$0	$0
Total Sales & Marketing	$712	$736	$788	$869	$923	$976
PROFiT (LOSS)	($1,147)	($878)	($601)	($127)	$359	$468
INCOME TAXES	($390)	($298)	($204)	($43)	$122	$159
NET PROFIT (LOSS)	($757)	($579)	($397)	($84)	$237	$309

INCOME STATEMENT

($s)

	Total 1995	Forecast 1996	Forecast 1997	Forecast 1998	Forecast 19999
SALES	$495,835	$862,075	$1,353,088	$2,193,566	$3,286,348
COST OF SALES:					
Total Cost of Sales	$444,812	$754,316	$1,183,952	$1,919,370	$2,875,555
GROSS PROFIT	$51,024	$107,759	$169,136	$274,196	$410,794
GENERAL & ADMINISTRATION					
Payroll & Payroll Related Exp.	$30,134	$50,000	$60,000	$75,000	$90,000
Payroll Taxes	$4,675	$9,250	$11,100	$13,875	$16,650
Travel & Entertainment	$0	$0	$0	$0	$0
Rent/Utilities/Telephone	$16,081	$18,000	$23,000	$31,250	$39,000
Insurance/Legal/Accounting	$3,788	$4,100	$4,900	$5,800	$6,900
Office & Supplies	$5,100	$5,000	$5,700	$6,100	$6,500
Equipment Expense	$1,025	$1,000	$2,587	$3,877	$4,044
Auto, Truck Expense	$0	$0	$0	$0	$0
Other	$4,665	$4,500	$5,400	$5,800	$6,200
Total General & Administration	$65,468	$91,850	$112,687	$141,702	$169,294
SALES & MARKETING					
Commissions	$4,958	$8,621	$13,531	$43,871	$65,727
Advertising	$2,439	$2,500	$4,000	$5,000	$6,000
Travel & Entertainment	$0	$0	$0	$0	$0
Auto	$0	$0	$0	$0	$0
Total Sales & Marketing	$7,397	$11,121	$17,531	$48,871	$71,727
PROFiT (LOSS)	($21,842)	$4,789	$38,918	$83,622	$169,773
INCOME TAXES	($7,426)	$1,628	$13,232	$28,432	$57,723
NET PROFIT (LOSS)	($14,416)	$3,160	$25,686	$55,191	$112,050

BALANCE SHEET

($s)

	Forecast Month end Dec 95	Forecast Month end Dec 96	Forecast Month end Dec 97	Forecast Month end Dec 98	Forecast Month end Dec 99
ASSETS					
Current:					
Cash & Equivalents	$8,000	$29,500	$45,000	$100,000	$230,000
Accounts Receivable	$0	$0	$0	$0	$0
Inventory	$0	$0	$0	$0	$0
Notes Receivable	$0	$0	$0	$0	$0
All other Current	$0	$0	$0	$0	$0
Total Current Assets	$8,000	$29,500	$45,000	$100,000	$230,000
Fixed Assets:					
Buildings	$0	$0	$0	$0	$0
Land	$0	$0	$0	$0	$0
Equipment	$3,000	$5,000	$5,000	$5,000	$5,000
Automobiles	$0	$0	$0	$0	$0
Less Accumulated Depreciation	($3,000)	($5,000)	($5,000)	($5,000)	($5,000)
Other Assets	$600	$600	$1,000	$1,000	$1,000
TOTAL ASSETS	$8,600	$30,100	$46,000	$101,000	$231,000
LIABILITIES & NET WORTH					
Current;					
Short term notes payable & debt	$4,000	$3,000	$2,000	$1,000	$0
Long term debt due	$0	$0	$0	$0	$0
Accounts Payable	$150	$300	$1,000	$1,000	$2,000
Accrued Interest	$0	$0	$0	$0	$2,000
Income Taxes Payable	($7,400)	$1,600	$13,000	$28,000	$58,000
Total Current Liabilities	($3,250)	$4,900	$16,000	$30,000	$62,000
Long Term Debt	$0	$0	$0	$0	$0
Deferred Taxes	$0	$0	$0	$0	$0
All Other Non Current	$28,000	$21,000	$14,000	$7,000	$0
Less Accumulated Loss	($17,150)	$0	$0	$0	$0
TOTAL LIABILITIES	$7,600	$25,900	$30,000	$37,000	$62,000
NET WORTH/Equity	$1,000	$4,200	$16,000	$64,000	$169,000
TOTAL LIABILITIES & NET WORTH	$8,600	$30,100	$46,000	$101,000	$231,000

business**PLAN**

O'Toole's Machining, Inc.

Business Plan, 1997-1999

Strictly Confidential

O'Toole's Machining, Inc.

1234 Pleasant Valley Rd.

P.O. Box 123

Driver, Wisconsin

Distributed Copy # ___ of ___ Published and Distributed Copies

O'Toole's—Introductory letter from Tim Baye

The business plan of O'Toole's Machining represents the wisdom of a very good manager and owner. Although the owner could have prepared minimal loan application materials for the lender, he chose to recognize the watershed event occurring with his company and took time to manage it well. The story:

O'Toole's had grown from a small tool & die shop to a production machining shop in a period of only eight years. Now (1997) the owner had just the opportunity he'd been working so very hard to get: first tier supplier status with a major OEM. Sales would double, maybe even triple or quadruple. Staff would need to be hired. Management? Supervisory? Are these necessary or just added overhead and would these types of people change our "family" culture?

The facility we're in—no way. We've either got to move or add onto this building. New machines, which ones? What about my existing customers? While this new client will in a large way dictate our future, what about those who have been with us through the years? Systems? I know what this means, in theory! How do these concepts apply to us.

As a result of his initial meeting with the bank, the owner was referred to my office. Bank referrals continue to be my program's largest source of new clients. The owner indicated he wanted the deluxe version of Business Planning 101. After listening to him for nearly one hour (in retrospect that was probably the longest speech ever given by this introvert) I knew what this gentleman wanted: to re-invent his company, and to re-invent himself—as a cutting edge manager.

While part of the focus of the business planning effort remained to raise funding for expansion, the overall effort reflected a greater ideal—to chart a course. Therefore, the planning process, and the document generated as a result, were relatively comprehensive and detailed.

The written plan was completed, funding secured (conventional) but in reduced amounts. Most expansion has been funded by internal resources. Then tragedy struck—the owner died in an accident.

The plan has now taken on a new audience, and role. The owner's widow has stepped into the role of company president. She has used the plan as a text, a guide of her husband's thoughts and goals. She's also used the plan as a training manual for a general manager he's recently hired.

We are currently updating the document and continuing to hold regular planning sessions.

- What are the strengths of this plan? How is it arranged?

- Is this business too reliant on a single customer? What could they do to change that?

- How are they using technology to their advantage?

- What are their plans for expansion?

- What would happen if the owner died? What plans are there for succession?

- Is the SWOT analysis realistic? Honest and Open? Do you know the threats to this business's success?

- Do the manuals and organization chart add to the credibility of the plan?

Table of Contents

Appendices

*Not Included in this book.

Executive Summary

O'Toole's Machining, Inc. (O'Toole's) is a precision production machining company serving both original equipment manufacturers and other Midwestern machining companies. O'Toole's is an S corporation owned 100% by Mike O'Toole. The machining operation is located in Driver, WI, in what is currently a 15,000 square foot facility.

Established in 1989, O'Toole's has grown from 1989 sales of $82,000 and a staff of one, to sales projected to exceed $4,000,000 and a staff of 50 full-time-equivalents in 1997-98. Though much of this latest growth can be attributed to serving one major client, John Deere, Inc.-Dubuque, O'Toole's has experienced sales and profit growth in almost every year of existence. O'Toole's net profit has ranged between 6.4% to 9.8% of revenue during the past 30 months. O'Toole's return on assets has ranged from 7.0% to 11.1% during the same period.

O'Toole's latest client relationship John Deere, Inc. and its Dubuque, IA, plant will increase O'Toole's sales by better than three times over 1996 levels. With this growth comes additional concerns related to building and machine capacities. O'Toole's will now bear responsibilities for purchasing the raw materials and maintain significant raw material inventories. Prior to serving John Deere, O'Toole's services and customer mix had not required O'Toole's to maintain any significant amount of raw material inventory.

O'Toole's has been producing flywheels for John Deere throughout most of 1997, has upgraded its machining centers and prepared its staff for this expansion. O'Toole's has been selected by John Deere- Dubuque to be the dedicated supplier of its flywheels for a five year time-frame.

O'Toole's has continued to serve its historic customers as a machining service subcontractor. O'Toole's plans to use both the John Deere contract, and its relationships with both vendors and other machining companies, as a platform for continued expansion into the original equipment manufacturer market, throughout the Upper Midwestern states. O'Toole's 1 is projecting sales of $5.2 million in 1997-98, $6.8 million in 1998-99 and $8.2 million in 1999-2000. O'Toole's is projecting net profits of 7.9%, 6.7% and 5.0% for each of these respective periods.

In order to implement its planned growth, O'Toole's requires an addition to its facility, addition of one new machining center each year from 1997 to 2000, and an initial build-up of its raw material and fixed goods inventory during 1997. For 1997 O'Toole's is seeking commercial debt funding of: 1) $302,000 for real estate/facility development; 2) $130,000 for machining equipment; and 3) $190,000 for inventory buildup. O'Toole's seeks market rates for each loan. O'Toole's seeks a 20 mortgage for the facility expansion and 5 year amortization for the equipment and inventory loans.

O'Toole's is also pursuing additional commercial debt financing to support its planned acquisition of one new machining center for years 1998 and 1999.

Description and History of O'Toole's Machining, Inc.

General Description

O'Toole's Machining, Incorporated (O'Toole's) is a precision machining company producing machined industrial parts and components, primarily for original equipment manufacturers and other Midwestern machining companies. O'Toole's is an S corporation solely owned by Mike and Erin O'Toole.

O'Toole's has served the needs of industrial customers since 1989. Current major customers include: John Deere Dubuque Works (Dubuque, IA), Precision Machining, Inc. (Madison, WI), Iowa State Stamping (Dubuque, IA), Performance Combustion, Inc. (Monroe, WI), along with numerous smaller accounts. O'Toole's has recently produced specific tolerance, industrial components, including flywheels for John Deere diesel engines, plates for Caterpillar heavy equipment, and rings and drive shafts for food processing equipment. O'Toole's also provides both partial (sub-assembly) and complete assembly operations for its customers. Recent assembly services included, units assembled for Bluebird Industrial Glass (Spring Green, WI) and for Precision Machining, Inc. (Madison, WI)

O'Toole's generated approximately $1.1 million in sales for calender years 1996 and 1995. From this revenue, O'Toole's earned net operating income of approximately 6.5% and 8.9% respectively.

O'Toole's serves its markets through the work of 50 technical, production, administrative and management staff. O'Toole's utilizes more than $1 million in production assets. Machining is performed at O'Toole's eight computerized numeric controlled (CNC) turning centers (lathes) and three CNC machining centers. Quality assurance begins at each work order's quoting stage and is supported with a dedicated quality assurance and inspection facility located within the production floor. Product design is conducted through CAD and CAM systems.

O'Toole's relies upon its close relationships with both raw material and service vendors for serving its customers. Primary raw material vendors include: Waupaca Foundry, Waupaca, WI (castings), Iroquois Foundry, Browntown, WI (castings) and Midwest Manufacturing, Inc. Kellogg, IA (flywheel rings). Accounting support is provided by Honkamp, Krueger & Co., Platteville, WI. Legal counsel is provided by Kopp, McKichan, Geyer & Skemp, also of Platteville. To date, banking services have been provided by First National Bank, Platteville.

O'Toole's operates from a 15,000 sq.ft. facility located in Driver, Wisconsin, a community of 10,000 people and home to the University of Wisconsin-Driver.

History of O'Toole's

O'Toole's began as O'Toole's Tool & Die Company (O'Toole's T&D) on January 1, 1989. O'Toole's was established through an $18,000 equity investment by Mike O'Toole, leveraged with a $50,000 equipment loan and a $10,000 line of credit from First National Bank, Driver. O'Toole's T&D was located in an 900 sq.ft. facility, employed one person and generated $82,000 in revenue during this first year of operation. Customers included Precision Machining, Inc., Performance Combustion, Inc., Coleman Motor Products, Inc., and Bluebird Industrial Glass.

In 1990 O'Toole's T&D expanded its facility to 2,500 sq.ft., added equipment (totaling $84,161) and built its customer base. During the calender year, O'Toole's T&D generated revenues of $232,000, and had built its asset holdings to $245,817.

In 1992, due to rent increases and production plans, O'Toole's T&D moved to its existing site.

The 6,000 sq ft. facility and improved production capabilities allowed the company to generate $369,000 in sales and solidify its customer base. The real estate and facility occupied by O'Toole's T&D is owned by the family of Mike O'Toole's and is leased to O'Toole's .

O'Toole's T&D incorporated in 1993 and was renamed O'Toole's Machining, Inc. (O'Toole's). O'Toole's acquired its first CNC turning center. Up to 1993 O'Toole's had primarily produced tooling, principally designed by Mike O'Toole. O'Toole's principal customer base remained: Performance Combustion, Precision Machining, Coleman Motor Products, and Bluebird 1G. O'Toole's now employed 6 staff, generated nearly $500,000 in sales, earned an annual profit of 10%, on a total investment of $300,000.

In 1994 O'Toole's began to move its product line toward industrial component machining. O'Toole's ' s initial CNC machining contracts were with other machining companies, Precision Machining, Inc. (PMI) and Performance Combustion (PCI). Through these customers O'Toole's made parts for Oscar Mayer, APV Crepaco, Caterpillar, John Deere, and many others. Sales in 1994 increased by over 60% from 1993, to $834,000.

O'Toole's started production machining for Iowa State Stamping Co in 1995. As volume increased, more equipment was added and the rear building was upgraded. Sales grew again by over 25% to $1,102,000. By the end of 1995 O'Toole's was employing 30 staff and held assets with an original purchase value of $1,183,998.

1996 was a pivotal year for O'Toole's . The company began producing flywheels for John Deere Dubuque Works through PCI. John Deere's demand had exceeded PCI's capacity and PCI was unwilling to expand to meet John Deere's needs. John Deere was aware of Dlviii's subcontracting support for PCI. John Deere approached O'Toole's with an offer to discuss a much expanded role as a primary machined component vender. O'Toole's also completed a major expansion to its facility to 15,000 sq.ft. In 1996, O'Toole's employed 35 staff and generated revenue of $1,065,000.

Product Lines

As evidenced in the history of the company, O'Toole's has expanded its product and service lines. O'Toole's earliest products were primarily tooling and die services. Over the past few years O'Toole's has repositioned its production capabilities toward both job-shop/short run and production (long-run) precision machining. Recently, O'Toole's has added parts assembly services and materials inventory capabilities, in response to customer demand. Following represents O'Toole's major product lines:

Short-run Precision Machining Services

1. O'Toole's quotes job based upon customers bid request and engineering drawings OR quote based upon on-going/historic production of part for customer.
2. Castings and other raw materials purchased by customer and direct shipped to O'Toole's for machining.
3. Production run volumes range from single to 100 parts.
4. Most short-run machining and finishing services performed on both CNC turning and milling centers.
5. Parts shipped either directly to customer or to third party manufacturer.
6. Examples of O'Toole's short-run customers and parts include:
   a) Machining for food processing equipment via Performance Combustion of Monroe, WI.
   b) Parts machining for Caterpillar Company via Iowa State Stamping and Precision Machining.
   c) Parts machining for lawn and garden equipment via Bluebird Components. Bluebird Components actually serves in a brokerage capacity in selling these parts.

Long-run Production Machining of Industrial Components

1. O'Toole's quotes job based upon customers bid request and engineering drawings OR quote based upon on-going/historic production of part for customer.

2. Castings and other raw materials are purchased and held in inventory by O'Toole's until scheduled machining.
3. Production run volumes range from 100 to 40,000/units.
4. Most long-run machining and finishing services performed on both CNC turning and milling centers. Most sales of long-run production services also incorporate shorterrun services within the overall production/machining process.
5. Parts shipped directly to customer.
6. Examples of O'Toole's long-run customers and parts include:
   a) Flywheels being produced for John Deere, Inc.-Dubuque Engine Works
   b) Most of the examples included in the short-run service-line description.

Industrial Component, Equipment and Machine Assembly Services

1. O'Toole's quotes job based upon customers bid request and engineering drawings OR quote based upon on-going/historic production of part for customer.
2. Components to be assembled either machined by O'Toole's or shipped via customer to O'Toole's for assembly. Machine assembly involves processing unit from the casting stage to frill assembly, packaging and shipping.
3. Assembly production run volumes range from 5 parts to 400/units.
4. Assembled units shipped directly to customer.
6. Examples of O'Toole's unit assembly customers include:
   a) Assembly aids for Bluebird Insulated Glass.
   b) Auxiliary drive units for John Deere, Inc.

Market Analysis

O'Toole's current and near-term future overall market is best defined as transportation/agricultural! industrial machinery original equipment manufacturers (OEM) located in the Upper-Midwestern United States. O'Toole's perceives that it can best compete in these industrial segments within a five state region, including: Illinois, Indiana, Iowa, Minnesota and Wisconsin.

A secondary market for O'Toole's is to continue to serve as a subcontracted machining service provider for other Upper-Midwestern machining firms whose capacity and/or capabilities are not adequate to meet the needs of their own customers. However, O'Toole's believes that future prosperity resides in targeting the OEM market, rather than the machining subcontracting market.

Profiles O'Toole's Primary Existing/Historic Customers

1. **John Deere Dubuque Works**
   a) Customer Since: August, 1996
   b) Products/Services: Flywheels, sub-assembly
   c) Sales History: 1997 (to-date) $2~IQ00, 1996 ~iJA.Q, 1995 $0.
   d) Primary Contact Person: Laura Doves, Purchasing, Gunnar Malvo
   e) Key to Business Relationships: Quality, Delivery, Contacts
   f) Expectations for near-term: Contract to be signed, letter-of-intent has been received indicating future plans (See Appendix A) Expected orders in next twelve months: 50,000 flywheels ($4,000,000) revenue.
   Expected orders:
   1998, 60-70,000 flywheels ($4.8-5.6 million);
   1999, 80-100,000 flywheels ($6.4-8.0 million);
   2000, 100-150,000 flywheels ($8.0-12.0 million).

2. **Precision Machining, Inc.**
   a) Customer Since: Inception (1989)
   b) Products/Services: Sub-contract machining of Caterpillar production parts, OEM parts, APV Crepaco
   c) Sales History: 1997 (to-date) $101,000, 1996 $198,000, 1995 $171,000
   d) Contact Person: Steve Fossen, Steve O'Toole
   e) Key to Business Relationship: Family relationship, quality and delivery
   f) Expectations for near-term: Stable—could increase. Expected orders in next twelve months: $300-400,000. Sales volume expected to increase at an annual average of 10-20% over prior year. O'Toole's expects to extend highest priority to maintaining this account, until such time that O'Toole's is able to replace revenue from direct sales to OEMs.

3. **Iowa State Stamping, Inc.**
   a) Customer Since: 1995
   b) Products/Services: Subcontract, Caterpillar parts machining
   c) Sales History: 1997 (to-date) $92,000, 1996 $225,000, 1995 $154,000
   d) Contact Person; Tom Brilson
   e) Key to Business Relationship: Quality, delivery
   f) Expectations for near-term: Stable. Expected orders in next twelve months: $300-400,000. O'Toole's expects to extend highest priority to maintaining this account, until such time that O'Toole's is able to replace revenue from direct sales to OEMs.

4. **Performance Combustion, Inc.**
   a) Customer Since: 1989
   b) Products/Services: Subcontract, John Deere and other OEM parts machining
   c) Sales History: 1997 (to-date) $370,000 1996 $338,000, 1995 $172,000
   d) Contact Person: Bill Goodren
   e) Key to Business Relationship: Quality, delivery
   f) Expectations for near-term: Declining, volatile. Expected orders in next twelve months: $250,000. Rumored to be moving entire division to southern U.S.

5. **Bluebird Components**
   a) Customer Since: 1991
   b) Products/Services: Brokerage for various manufacturers
   c) Sales History: 1997 (to-date) $49,000, 1996 $77,000, 1995 $124,000
   d) Contact Person: Clark Murray
   e) Key to Business Relationship: Price and quality
   f) Expectations for near-term: Stable. Expected orders in next twelve months: $150,000

Prospective Customers/Markets

O'Toole's recognizes that relying too heavily upon a single customer (John Deere-Dubuque) for a majority of sales is a risky strategy for an extended period of time. While O'Toole's is excited about and has high expectations regarding its John Deere relationship, O'Toole's expects to use this relationship as a springboard to pursue similar long-run production contracts from similar original equipment manufacturers (OEM). Some of O'Toole's prospective (OEM) customers include:

1. Caterpillar - direct; without the lead being generated by O'Toole's or Iowa State Stamping.
2. J.I. Case.
3. International Harvester.
4. John Deere Mexico (all purchasing currently administered through John Deere -Dubuque)

Average expenditure for machined parts from third party vendors for construction and agricultural implement OEMs is estimated to be between 3% and 7% of gross revenues, 5% ave. (Source: PMI) Based upon Dun & Bradstreet profiles on the above prospects, market potential for machined parts for each of these prospects is as follows:

	U.S. Market	Market Potential	O'Toole's Market Share	O'Toole's Sales
1. Caterpillar	8,384,000	419,200	1.5% - 2.5%	$4.2 - 10,500
2. JI. Case.	2,809,000	140,450	2.5% - 3.5%	$3.5 - 4,900
3. International Harvester	Unknown	I-H assumed to have similar sales and outsourcing practices as Caterpillar, J.I. Case and John Deere.		
4. John Deere Torreon, Mexico	Unknown	Market potential and O'Toole's sales performance assumed to be similar to John Deere-Dubuque, 50,000 units/year, sales potential $4 million/year.		

Note: Within O'Toole's 1997-2000 planning period, no more than one OEM customer is expected to be added to O'Toole's customer base. O'Toole's would not have the production and management capacity to effectively manage growth inherent with serving two or more of the above prospects.

Competition

O'Toole's Machining faces competition from a number of sources. It is the intent of management to thwart competitive threats with a high quality product and timely delivery. Following are competitors located in the Driver/Dubuque area:

1. Weaver Metal Products, Cascade, IA and Driver, WI.
   a) Product-line: Large cast parts milled for printing industry.
   b) Staff/Employees: ~100
   c) Known Customers: Rockwell International
   d) Strengths: Established customer base. Long-term employees.
   e) Weaknesses:
   f) Competitive Strategy:

2. JMI - 3 , Driver, WI.
   a) Product-line: Small - medium sized parts turned and milled for printing industry. Low volume, prototypes
   b) StafUEmployees: ~22
   c) Known Customers: Rockwell International
   d) Strengths: Credit: Good, Sales ~$1.2 million. Horizontal and vertical milling capabilities.
   e) Weaknesses: Limited size and capacity
   f) Competitive Strategy: to pursue complex low volume work.

3. Peruville Machine, Peruville, WI.
   a) Product-line: Medium sized machine parts for military/government.
   b) Staff/Employees: ~64
   c) Known Customers: Accudine, Wauzeka Valve

d) Strengths: Credit: Good. Sales ~$3.5 million. Good equipment.

e) Weaknesses: Micro-management, poor labor relations

f) Competitive Strategy: High tech machining, reduction of labor costs.

O'Toole's does not believe that any of these local competitors can actually produce the quality of flywheels currently demanded by John Deere-Dubuque. However, the following firms have the capability, capacity and, to a lesser extent, the track record to compete within the same product-lines and target markets as O'Toole's .

4. Lincoln State Machine and Tool Works, Inc., North Milkin, IL
   a) Product-line: CNC Milling/Machining
   b) Staff/Employees: —110
   c) Known Customers: John Deere
   d) Strengths: Sales $5-10 million, large established company. 40K sq. ft. facility
   e) Weaknesses: High labor costs, costly process(es)
   f) Competitive Strategy: Unknown at this time. Privately held company. Owner, Claude Kudovich; Controller, Diane Banker; Buyer, Sherri Manson.

5. Wazit Manufacturing, Mucwonego, WI.
   a) Product-line: CNC milling/machining
   b) Staff/Employees: ~100±
   c) Known Customers: John Deere
   d) Strengths: Credit: Good. Sales $5-10 million. Established 1997
   e) Weaknesses: Wazit's process has already been analyzed and rejected by John Deere.
   f) Competitive Strategy: ?

Industry Trends

This is an exciting time in the machining industry. Many changes are currently taking place. Most of these changes revolve around automation. Fortunately O'Toole's is well ahead of many in the industry in utilizing these advancing technologies. Robert O'Toole, Quality Assurance Manager is responsible for implementing technological improvements.

Some of the major trends affecting this industry today include:

1.) ISO 9000 Certification for quality purposes.
2.) OSHA Requirements/Environmental Issues.
3.) EDI instant invoicing, information exchange.
4.) Bar Coding, UPC Coding.
5.) Electronic time scanning.

O'Toole's recognizes the significance of each of these trends both upon its internal operations and upon its ability to manage its own business strategy. Appendix B contains an summary of the nature of each trend issue and O'Toole's response.

O'Toole's will not depend upon its proficiency in addressing these industry trends as a core competitive strategy, but will seek to neutralize any negative impact the trend may have upon its overall business strategy. O'Toole's will meet all key customer requirements in quality assurance and planning, and will adopt industry standards in communication technology. However, most of the above issues represent neither fatal threats, nor emerging technological opportunities. Therefore, O'Toole's does not view these changes as either positively or negatively impacting its overall business strategy.

Business Strategy and Competitive Position

Strengths & Weaknesses of O'Toole's
O'Toole's Strengths:

1. Relationships with key vendors (e.g. Waupaca Foundry).
2. General quality of assets and workforce.
3. Track record of meeting delivery dates.
4. Comparative labor and overhead cost (lower).
5. Relationships with existing customers and financial strength of these customers.
6. Access to U.W. Driver graduates and technical support.
7. Track record of generating repeat and expanded business with customers.
8. Current business strategy focus on pursuing OEM production contracts.

O'Toole's Weaknesses

1. Anticipated growth from John Deere account implies a four fold increase in revenues, requirements of purchasing and carrying inventories of raw materials, and staffing challenges—all representing significant risks for O'Toole's management team.

2. Current size of O'Toole's facility—negative influence on production capacity and efficiency.

3. O'Toole's's facility is not currently accessible by rail, nor by interstate highway. Although, interstate highway connection planned within existing Wisconsin Dept. Of Transportation construction schedule,~date of completion 2009.

4. O'Toole's is currently leveraged above industry average.

5. O'Toole's is a closely held, family corporation. Little additional equity can be expected from current stockholders to fund new business development/expansion.

Market Opportunities

1. **Capitalize on recently developed John Deere-Dubuque relationships.** With a letter of intent in hand, negotiations proceeding on a 5 year purchasing contract with potential to generate between $3.0 to $9.0 million in revenue, and with gross profit margins averaging between 37-44%, this opportunity represents the single best growth option for O'Toole's . The potential for serving other John Deere plants, both domestic and foreign, within the next 2-5 years enhances this opportunity.

Exploiting the John Deere opportunity creates a serious set of management and production challenges for O'Toole's . The expected significant increase in inventory carrying costs, direct labor costs and interest/lease payments for the necessary facility expansion, new equipment and other related production investments will all seriously challenge O'Toole's operation, administrative and financial management capabilities.

However, since April, 1997 O'Toole's has been machining nearly all of the John Deere Dubuque's flywheels, as a subcontractor for Performance Combustion, Inc. Scrap rates, set-up times and production runs have steadily improved. These improvements have been greatly enhanced by sourc-

ing a new vender of castings, Waupaca Foundry. O'Toole's past vender, Iroquois Foundry, could not maintain consistent product quality necessary to meet both O'Toole's and John Deere's requirements. The relationship with Waupaca Foundry tremendously enhances the attractiveness of the John Deere opportunity because Waupaca's castings improve O'Toole's scrap rates, run times and most importantly (to-date) have enabled O'Toole's to maintain its margins and ability to meet delivery times.

2. **Maintain and expand sales to Precision Machining, Inc., and Iowa State Stamping, Inc.** Both PMI and DSI are firmly established as Caterpillar Corp. vendors. Both PMI and DSI offer O'Toole's a wide variety of opportunities to subcontract work. Serving these two customers allows O'Toole's to diversify its service line, without the requirement to build and carry inventories. This subcontracting work allows O'Toole's to gain experience in serving a significant OEM (Caterpillar) and provides a relationship/platform from which to pursue direct sales to Caterpillar in the future.

3. **Pursue long-run production contracts with original equipment manufacturers (OEM) similar to John Deere, within a five state region in the Upper Midwestern U.S.** If O'Toole's can successfully serve John Deere-Dubuque for the upcoming year as an independent vender (without Performance Combustion serving as the primary vender and O'Toole's as subcontractor), O'Toole's can exploit this experience to pursue additional primary vender contracts with other OEM's within O'Toole's geographic market.

4. **Reintroduce a tooling and die making operation.** This opportunity would reduce O'Toole's market and sales potential and not take advantage of the market relationships it has developed over the past 24 months.

5. **Commit resources to aggressively expand O'Toole's service line into assembly services, both for existing/historic customers and for other potential customers.** If O'Toole's is able to secure a long-term flywheel production contract with John DeereDubuque beyond the next 3-6 months, O'Toole's will likely be able to generate additional revenue from unit assembly services of $1.0-1.5 million/year, with gross profit margins equal to or exceeding that received for O'Toole's subcontracting services to PMI and DSI.

O'Toole's Overall Marketing and Business Strategy

Vision: To be a primary vender of production machining and component assembly services to industrial, construction, transportation and agricultural OEMs located within the Upper Midwestern U.S.

Mission: O'Toole's will compete as a primary vender of production machining and component assembly services with OEMs through its commitment to total quality, on-time delivery, production efficiency and low overall cost of servicing the client.

Goals: To retain and expand O'Toole's relationship with John Deere-Dubuque, through the production of engine flywheels for a minimum of a five year period. To generate a minimum of $4.0 million/year of revenue and to earn gross profits of at least $1.6 million/year from production of John Deere-Dubuque flywheels (35-45% gross profit margin excluding direct labor costs).

To retain and expand O'Toole's relationship with PMI and DSI as a subcontracting machining service provider. To increase revenues for the next three years from both of these customers by 10-30%/year, while maintaining a gross profit margin of 78-82% (excluding direct labor costs).

To capture John Deere-Dubuque's outsourced parts/component assembly contracts (specifically for its engine flywheels) in 1997-98, and to generate between $ 1.0-1.5 million/year, while maintaining gross profits margins equal to or exceeding those generated through O'Toole's machining subcontracting services (78-82%).

To secure primary vender status with an additional OEM (other than John Deere) by the end of 1998.

Marketing Position/Competitive Strategy

O'Toole's intends to achieve its goals by managing its market position as a comparable low cost, on-time delivery provider of production machined and assembled industrial components. Product quality will also meet or exceed customers requirements.

O'Toole's believes that its vender relationships, comparative cost advantage in labor and overhead and existing customer relationships will enable it to achieve and sustain this market position.

O'Toole's intends to exploit its relationship as a subcontractor with PMI and DSI to gain experience serving other OEMs (e.g. Caterpillar). O'Toole's intends to use this experience to eventually achieve primary vender status with OEMs (other than John Deere), while not jeopardizing O'Toole's relationship with PMI and DSI.

Marketing Plan

Pricing Policies

1. **Quote development**
   a) when raw material inventory carried
   O'Toole's 1 utilizes a standardized production quoting system based upon estimated/historic machine set-up aid operation times (currently $52/hour) and upon special tooling design and development times (currently $42/hour). Materials required for production are priced though a simple cost-plus process, 10-15% O'Toole's cost of material. See Appendix C for sample quote development/pricing form.
   b) when raw material provided by customer See above.

2. **Gross Profit Margin targets**
   a) when raw material inventory carried 35-45%, excluding direct labor costs.
   b) when raw material provided by customer

3. **Credits and Terms of Payment**
   Net 30 days

Promotion and Selling Practices

Overall, O'Toole's selling and sales management activities are conducted by Mike O'Toole, O'Toole's CEO. The following outline summarizes key account responsibilities:

Account/Customer	Day-to-day	Account Executive
John Deere	Bill Minton	Mike O'Toole
Precision Machining	Bill Minton	Mike O'Toole
	Robert O'Toole	
Iowa State Stamp	Bill Minton	Mike O'Toole

O'Toole's intends to build its marketing staff and support functions within the next 12-24 months. A dedicated sales staff person (engineering/technical sales background), and/or collaboration with an established manufacturer's representative may be necessary in order for O'Toole's to implement its plans to build its OEM customer base.

Operational Plan

Facility Requirements

Existing

O'Toole's currently operates in a 15,000 sq.ft. steel frame and construction, poured concrete floor facility. The facility is heated with natural gas, cooled by central air, and has a mist collection system for air quality control. The facility has 208-3 phase electrical service, both 800 and 600 amp. This facility has a climate controlled office section. The facility is leased to O'Toole's by Mike and Erin O'Toole.

O'Toole's initial occupancy of this facility began as a 6000 sq.ft. converted auto repair building. In 1996, the facility was expanded to its current size.

See Appendix D for a floor plan diagram of the current facility.

Planned

In order to address the inventory carrying and storage requirements inherent with O'Toole's decision to pursue the John Deere-Dubuque flywheel production project, an expansion of facility/warehouse space is necessary. O'Toole's has explored three options to meet the materials storage and handling issues: 1) Lease warehousing space within the Driver Trade Area; 2) Relocate O'Toole's entire production operations to a newer, larger facility, AND either retain the lease on the current facility for warehousing and some non-John Deere machining services OR let the lease expire and centralize all O'Toole's operations in a new facility; 3) Sponsor an expansion on O'Toole's existing facility.

Analysis of the operational effectiveness and cost of each option, along with consideration of the impact each option would have upon the personal financial well-being of Mike and Erin O'Toole, prompted O'Toole's to pursue the third option: 3) Sponsor an expansion on O'Toole's existing facility.

Based upon O'Toole's own designs, material resource planning and construction quotes, this facility expansion will include the following:

1. 11,000 sq.ft., steel frame and construction, addition, attached to the existing facility's western wall (see diagram in Appendix D);
2. Areas for raw material, work-in-progress, assembly components and finished goods inventory.

This facility will enable O'Toole's to better serve its long-run production customers through improved inventory practices and quality control. The facility will also enable O'Toole's to pursue more favorable receivables turnover (quicker payment) with major customers, due to O'Toole's improved ability to implement a just-in-time order shipment response system.

Equipment Requirements

Existing

O'Toole's utilizes more than $1.25 million in production assets, some leased and some owned. Machining is performed at O'Toole's eight computerized numeric controlled (CNC) turning centers (lathes) and three CNC machining centers. O'Toole's recently acquired additional equipment to support its production machining operations, including a Daewoo H-5O, horizontal machining center. This machining center is currently being fitted with fixtures and tooling for the John Deere-Dubuque flywheel production process. Approximate machine cost/investment: $300,000. Equipment is leased from vendor.

Planned

To maintain production efficiency and meet the requirements of implementing O'Toole's marketing strategy and plan the following equipment is expected to be acquired during this plan's timeframe:

PLAN'S TIMEFRAME		
1998:	One additional workcell:	One horizontal CNC machining center, (~$300K) Two CNC turning centers (lathes), (~$300K)
1999:	One additional workcell:	One horizontal CNC machining center, (~$300K) Two CNC turning centers (lathes), (~$300K)
2000:	One additional workcell:	One horizontal CNC machining center, (~$300K) Two CNC turning centers (lathes), (~$300K)

Total expected new equipment acquisitions during the 1997-2000 planning period are expected to require $1.8 million in funding. Funding expected to be provided via retained earnings (cash flow from operations), equipment leases and commercial debt.

Vendors of this equipment are expected to include: Midland Machinery (Pewaukee, WI); Yarnazen Machinery (Milwaukee, WI) and Precision Machine (Milwaukee, WI).

Staffing Requirements
Existing

Appendix E contains O'Toole's current organizational chart and a listing of all O'Toole's staff members (and compensation rates), as of June 10, 1997. O'Toole's operates three daily work shifts. Each shift is supervised by a production supervisor and department group leaders. The shift supervisors, group leaders and quality assurance manager are responsible for staff training, job scheduling, production supervision and troubleshooting. Job descriptions for managers and supervisors are also included in Appendix E.

O'Toole's is currently managed by Mike O'Toole, Chief Executive Officer/President, Robert O'Toole, Quality Assurance Manager. Production management is provided by Bill Minton.

Administrative support is provided by Amy Kalke and Cathy Wegner.

O'Toole's developed a comprehensive Quality Manual in August, 1996 to support its production processes and as an internal staff communication document. This manual outlines in detail most aspects of O'Toole's production, quality assurance and production documentation policies. See Appendix F for a copy of O'Toole's Quality Manual.

O'Toole's rate of hourly compensation ranges from $5.00- $14.00/hour. Insurance and vacation benefits are extended to all full-time employees.

O'Toole's has recently adopted a number of workplace conduct and environment policies, including safety and sexual conduct policies (See Appendix E). O'Toole's expects to continuously review its work environment and adopt/change policies which promotes the most efficient, safe and rewarding workplace for its staff.

Planned

O'Toole's expects to maintain this current organizational structure, staffing levels through the end of the 1997 calender year. If production demands from John Deere-Dubuque, PMI and DSI continue to grow as expected the following staffing additions are expected:

STAFFING ADDITIONS	
1998:	No additional full-time staff additions. Some job restructuring, shift transfers and stepped-up training expected.
1999:	6 - 8 additional production staff, $9.00/hour average starting hourly wage. Plus benefits.
2000:	8 - 10 additional production staff, $9.00/hour average starting hourly wage. Plus benefits

Management staff additions, if necessary, are expected to be filled through internal advancement and promotion.

Vender/Supplier Requirements
Existing

O'Toole's current network of material and service vendors appears adequate to support its overall business strategy and marketing plan.

Planned
No new additions.

Quality Assurance and Control Practices
Existing

Quality assurance practices and policies are addressed in O'Toole's Quality Manual (Appendix F). Robert O'Toole, Quality Assurance manager is primarily responsible for implementation and administration of all quality assurance issues, however, all O'Toole's staff are held responsible for quality: production, performance and work place behavior. John Klein is first shift inspector. Joshua Wenzle is second shift inspector.

Scrap Ratios and Production Performance. The acquisition of the John Deere-Dubuque flywheel account presented significant challenges to O'Toole's production staff. Up to this time O'Toole's had primarily provided short- to medium-run machining services to its customers. The John Deere account requires significant production runs in the 1000's of parts, and poses serious material supply and handling requirements.

Until June, 1997, the flywheel castings were being supplied by Iroqious Foundry. These castings proved to be generally inadequate for the tolerances demanded by both O'Toole's and John Deere. Scrap rates over 5% were a regular occurrence.

O'Toole's and John Deere jointly approached Waupaca Foundry, Waupaca, Wisconsin as a potential replacement vendor of the flywheel castings. A purchase agreement was developed and Waupaca began shipping castings in June, 1997. These castings proved to be vastly superior to the Iroqious. The benefits of this improved vendor relationship have been realized in a number of areas, including:

1. More consistent casting quality, resulting in less tool wear, fewer calibration/fixture/clamp adjustments and higher production rates (shorter run times);
2. Increased overall production volume, result of longer production runs, fewer changeovers, less scrap from setup;
3. Less experienced operators allowed to have longer periods of uninterrupted machine time and operation—leads to improved training opportunities and increased operator self-confidence.

O'Toole's projects scrap rates for John Deere-Dubuque flywheels between 1-2% during the next 18-36 months.

Planned

Updating Quality Manual. Integration of John Deere-Dubuque industrial engineering support and consultation into O'Toole's production processes. Addition of two production inspectors: 1 roving inspector, first shift; 1 third shift inspector.

Organizational Structure, Management Plan and Advisors

O'Toole's Legal Form & Ownership

O'Toole's is an S corporation registered in the state of Wisconsin. O'Toole's 100 shares of stock are owned entirely by Mike and Erin O'Toole, Driver, Wisconsin:

Organization of the Corporation

See Organizational Chart in Appendix E.

Management Staff

Chief Executive Officer and President	Mike O'Toole
Quality Assurance Manager	Robert O'Toole
Production Manager	Bill Minton
Office Manager	Amy Kalke

Corporate Advisors

Accountant	Honnig, Kreiger & Co., Driver, WI.
Attorney	Kopf, McEegan, & Grempler, Driver, WI
Insurance	Allied Insurance. Driver, WI.
Banking	First National Bank, Driver.
Business Development	Timothy M. Baye, Associate Professor, UWExtension, Business Outreach
Process & Waste Engineering	Wisconsin Manufacturing Extension Partnership, SW

Key Risks and Risk Management

All firms face risks as a normal part of conducting business. Given O'Toole's aggressive sales growth and working asset expansion plans, the consequences of effectively anticipating and managing potential risks are critical to O'Toole's success. The following highlights some potential risks/issues O'Toole's may face within the next three years, and outlines O'Toole's expected response to these events:

1. General economic slowdown, especially in durable good orders.

O'Toole's response: Commit more resources to marketing. Evaluate cost reduction alternatives. Evaluate approaches to restructure/reduce direct labor costs. Refine production processes.

O'Toole's strategy of aggressively pursuing sales to John Deere, whereby revenue from Deere will represent more than 75% of O'Toole's sales, may at first glance represent a very risky and potentially devastating marketing approach. However, the nature of how the John Deere flywheels are utilized within Deere's multiple and diverse operations alleviates some of this concern. O'Toole's flywheels are assembled into Deere agricultural equipment, construction equipment, electrical generators, industrial machinery and tug boats. While a few of these products will be impacted by changes in the economy, Deere (and thereby O'Toole's) assumes that not all divisions will be adversely impacted equally.

2. Entry of large employer into Driver labor market.

O'Toole's response: Diversify service lines to utilize staff in alternative production areas (e.g. promote sales of assembly work in addition to machining services). Step up staff training programs. Offer additional benefits and revise wage scale. Refine production processes.

3. Threat of union/labor organizing.

O'Toole's response: Retain services of professional negotiator. Refine production processes. Automate production processes where possible. Evaluate approaches to restructure/reduce direct labor costs.

Financial Analysis, Projections and Funding Plan

Analysis of O'Toole's Current Financial Situation and Recent History

Appendix G contains O'Toole's June, 1997 balance sheet & income, along with 1996, 1995 and 1994 calender year-end reports of the same.

Sales History: O'Toole's has grown from generating gross revenues of $82,000 (1989) to sales ranging between $2-3.3 million by the end of the 1997 calender year. For the past four calender years (1993-96), O'Toole's has experienced annual average revenue growth of 13.3%. This growth has allowed O'Toole's 1 to strengthen its operational efficiency, financial position, while it solidified its customer base and expanded its product line into more production (long-run) machining services.

Analysis of O'Toole's Current Financial Condition

The following table highlights some of O'Toole's key financial data and ratios:

($OOOs)	June, 1997	Dec., 1996	Dec., 1995
Current Assets	729	208	145
Fixed Assets	779	620	729
Current Liabilities	617	174	189
Long Term Liabilities	610	466	478
Equity	318	216	207
Sales	1,098	1,065	1,102
Gross Profit (incl. direct labor)	291 (26%)	286 (27%)	314 (28%)
Net Profit	108 (9.8%)	68 (6.4%)	97 (9%)
Current Ratio	1.18	1.2	0.8
Liabilities/Asset	0.79	0.77	0.76
Liabilities/Equity	3.86	2.96	3.22
Net Profit/Asset	7.0%	8.2%	11.1%
Net Profit/Equity	34.1%	31.5%	46.9%

O'Toole's financial performance from December, 1996 to June, 1997 provides insight into how it will likely perform in pursuing the John Deere-Dubuque flywheel opportunity. Since, April, 1997 until July, 1997 O'Toole's has produced most of John Deere's flywheels, as a subcontractor for Performance Combustion, Inc.(ICI) As of July, 1997 PCI is no longer John Deere's flywheel vendor. O'Toole's is now the primary vendor of these parts. O'Toole's receivables and payables both reflect this development. O'Toole's is currently producing approximately 200 flywheels/day for John Deere. O'Toole's has begun receiving flywheel casting shipments directly from Waupaca Foundry. O'Toole's has begun building both flywheel raw material inventory and finished goods inventory to serve John Deere's shipping/due date requirements.

O'Toole's current net profit, both in absolute terms and as a percentage of sales, are up substantially from December, 1996, and are equivalent to 1995 numbers. This trend has occurred in spite of the fact that the flywheel sales (long-run production) generate nearly one-half the gross profit (per sales $) as do short-run sales. Flywheels generate ~40% gross profit margin (excluding direct labor), as compared to gross profit margins of ~0% (excluding direct labor) for short-run machining (PMI, DSI, Bluebird, etc.).

Because O'Toole's has taken advantage of production efficiencies gained with longer runs of parts, while controlling its overhead expenses (except for related increases in equipment lease payments), profitability numbers (net profit, net/equity) have improved since December, 1996. Likewise, O'Toole's has not experienced an erosion of its current ratio or its liability/asset ratio during this transition period.

O'Toole's has experienced some reduction in profitability and leverage ratios. Its net profit/asset ratio has dropped slightly, 7% as compared to 8.2%. This is large part is due to the lower gross profit margins for flywheels, as compared to short-run (jobber) machining services, and the increased proportion of sales the flywheels now represent. The key leverage ratio, liabilities/equity has also increased (i.e. worsened). This is in part due to O'Toole's recent additions of lease hold improvements, machinery and inventory, most financed with either trade terms, vendor financing, line-of-credit and a Wisconsin Department of Commerce loan.

Nevertheless, O'Toole's has not experienced any serious cashflow difficulties during the last few months. O'Toole's expects its overall cash position to improve with continued sales to John Deere, PMI and DSI, along with constrained and planned minimal growth of overhead expenditures.

Sales Assumptions

O'Toole's expects to maintain sales to its historic customers (QM1, DSI, PCI, Bluebird) while concurrently expanding sales of long-run production services to John Deere, and other large OEMs. However, for this planning period (1997-1999) O'Toole's does not anticipate adding another large OEM to its customer base, until it has frilly explored all expansion opportunities with John Deere (Waterloo, IA; Torreon, Mexico; etc.). contracts, while not introducing too large of a strategic risk by becoming totally dependent upon a single customer. O'Toole's flywheels represent components for agricultural equipment, construction equipment, tug boats, and electrical generation equipment.

While strategically not as preferred as having a much wider customer base, John Deere's internal business strategy and diversification provides small vendors such as O'Toole's significant benefits. O'Toole's is able to better understand the needs and motivations of a only few John Deere purchasing agents (as compared with managing relationships with purchasing agents from numerous customers). O'Toole's also benefits from serving a multi-national, diversified OEM whose own efforts to manage negative impacts of economic changes is passed onto its supplier network. In O'Toole's case, John Deere utilizes O'Toole's flywheels in a wide variety of products, all targeted at different markets.

O'Toole's projects sales to John Deere of $4.5 million of both flywheels and assembly services during the period of Oct/Dec., 1997 to September, 1998. O'Toole's expects that sales to John Deere will remain flat with respect to Dubuque shipments, but will increase by ~$1.5 million by 1998 due to sales to John Deere-Torreon, Mexico. Both Dubuque and Torreon sales are assumed to again increase in 1999-2000, by approximately 25-40%.

O'Toole's projects sales of approximately $1.04 million in sales for subcontracted machining services (e.g. PMI, DSI, Bluebird and PCI).

Contracts with a new OEM is assumed to have been obtained by the 1999-2000 budget year. Sales to this new customer are assumed to begin at $500,000 during this budget period, with average gross profit margins of 40%.

See Appendix H for a more complete summary of O'Toole's 1997-1998 sales estimate.

Profitability Assumptions

O'Toole's assumes that within the 1997-1999 planning period it will be able to maintain, or improve upon, its historic gross and net profit ratios. O'Toole's assumes that it will be able to produce the John Deere-Dubuque flywheels with an average 42% gross profit ratio (excluding direct labor costs).

O'Toole's assumes that it will continue to produce short-run, sub-contracted machining services for O'Toole's , DSI, PCI and Bluebird with an average 82% gross profit ratio (excluding direct labor costs).

Sales and Financial Projections (Pro Forma Budgets)

See Appendix I

O'Toole's Funding Requirements

Funding Required 1997-1998:

$190,000 term loan for inventory buildup and working capital.
Requesting market rates (—9.25%) with a 5 year amortization.
Funding needed by September, 1997.
$130,000 term loan for CNC, CMM work cell.
Requesting market rates (~9.25%) with a 5 year amortization.
Funding needed by October, 1997
$302,000 term loan for 11,000 square foot facility expansion and land acquisition. Requesting market rates (—9.00%) with a 20 year amortization. Approval of funding needed by August, 1997 in order to commission construction and real estate contracts.

All funding requested during 1997-1998 represents 100% of total funds required for working capital, equipment acquisition and facility expansion.

Funding Required 1998-1999:

$400,000 term loan for CNC horizontal lathes and machining centers. Requesting market rates (~.25%) with a 5 year amortization. Funding needed by October, 1998. O'Toole's will contribute 33% down ($200,000) of the total investment package ($600,000)

Funding Required 1999-2000:

$500,000 term loan for CNC horizontal lathes and machining centers. Requesting market rates (~.25%) with a 5 year amortization. Funding needed by October, 1999. O'Toole's will contribute 16.5% down ($100,000) of the total investment package ($600,000)

Appendices

Appendix A: Letter of Intent to O'Toole's , and Historic Flywheel Purchases by John Deere-Dubuque Engine Works

Appendix B: Summary of Major Industrial Trends and O'Toole's responses.

Appendix C: Sample of O'Toole's Quote Development Worksheet

Appendix D: Facility Plan and Diagram

Appendix E: O'Toole's Organizational Chart, Staff Compensation Schedule, Key Job Descriptions and Safety/Harassment Policy

Appendix F: O'Toole's Quality Manual

Appendix G: O'Toole's Current and Historic Financial Reports (Balance Sheet and Income Statements: YTD, 1996, 1995 & 1994)

Appendix H: O'Toole's Sales Estimate Spreadsheet, FY: 1997-98

Appendix I: O'TOOLE's Pro Forma Balance Sheets, Income Statements, Cash Flows From Operations and Sources & Uses of Funds, FY: 1997-98, 1998-99, 1999-2000

Appendix H: O'Toole's Sales Estimate Spreadsheet
FY: 1997-98

Customer Sales

Customer	1997 YTD	Jan-97	Feb-97	Mar-97	Apr-97	May-97	Jun-97
Bluebird Components	4.8%	14.5%	1.8%	6.7%	0.6%	2.9%	6.2%
Iowa State Stamping & Mfg	9.2%	27.4%	12.3%	6.9%	6.2%	9.8%	4.0%
Performance Combustion	36.8%	15.6%	32.2%	47.8%	38.6%	65.2%	21.3%
John Deere Dubuque Works	28.2%	0.0%	6.9%	6.0%	35.3%	6.5%	63.5%
Precision Machining	10.0%	21.3%	20.7%	20.0%	7.1%	7.2%	2.9%
Other	11.0%	21.2%	26.1%	12.6%	12.2%	8.4%	2.1%

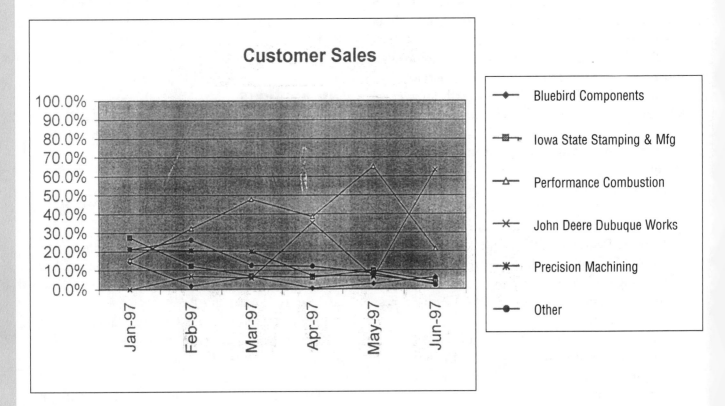

Appendix I: O'Toole's Pro Forma Balance Sheets, Income Statements, Cash Flows from Operations and Sources & Uses of Funds, FY: 1997-98, 1998-99, 1999-2000

Total Sales Estimation & Analysis Report: O'Toole's Machining, Inc.

	Business-to-Business Annual Demand Estimates	Total Weighted Demand Estimate	Bus.-to-Bus. Sales Estimate	Retail Annual Demand Estimates	Retail Sales Estimate	Estimated Total Sales
Item 1: Short-Run Mach.	A. Maximum: 1,225,000 B. Most Likely: 1,050,000 C. Minimum: 850,000	1,037,500	11,037,500	A. Maximum: 0 B. Most Likely: 0 C. Minimum: 0	0	1,037,500
Item 2: Long-Run Prod. Mach.	A. Maximum: 5,000,000 B. Most Likely: 4,000,000 C. Minimum: 3,000,000	4,000,000	4,000,000	A. Maximum: 0 B. Most Likely: 0 C. Minimum: 0	0	4,000,000
Item 3: Assembly Services	A. Maximum: 1,000,000 B. Most Likely: 500,000 C. Minimum: 0	500,000	500,000	A. Maximum: 0 B. Most Likely: 0 C. Minimum: 0	0	500,000
Item 4: _____	A. Maximum: 0 B. Most Likely: 0 C. Minimum: 0	0	0	A. Maximum: 0 B. Most Likely: 0 C. Minimum: 0	0	0
Item 5: _____	A. Maximum: 0 B. Most Likely: 0 C. Minimum: 0	0	0	A. Maximum: 0 B. Most Likely: 0 C. Minimum: 0	0	0
Item 6: _____	A. Maximum: 0 B. Most Likely: 0 C. Minimum: 0	0	0	A. Maximum: 0 B. Most Likely: 0 C. Minimum: 0	0	0
Item 7: _____	A. Maximum: 0 B. Most Likely: 0 C. Minimum: 0	0	0	A. Maximum: 0 B. Most Likely: 0 C. Minimum: 0	0	0
TOTALS:	A. Maximum: 7,225,000 B. Most Likely: 5,550,000 C. Minimum: 3,850,000	5,537,500	5,537,500	A. Maximum: 0 B. Most Likely: 0 C. Minimum: 0	0	5,537,500

BUSINESS-TO-BUSINESS ANNUAL SALES ESTIMATION WORKSHEET: O'Toole's Machining, Inc.

CUSTOMER/ SALES PROSPECT	ESTIMATED ANNUAL DEMAND ITEM 1: Short-Run Mach. (1)	(2) PROBABILITY OF DEMAND BEING REALIZED	(3) WEIGHTED DEMAND ESTIMATES: (1) & (2)	(4) TOTAL WEIGHTED DEMAND ESTIMATES: 3A+3B+3C	(5) PROBABILITY OF OBTAINING SALE	*REALISTIC SALES ESTIMATE* (4) & (5)	Comments
1. Precision Machining, Inc.	A. Maximum: 400,000	A. Maximum: 10%	A. Maximum: 40,000				
	B. Most Likely: 350,000	B. Most Likely: 80%	B. Most Likely: 280,000	350,000	100%	350,000	
	C. Minimum: 300,000	C. Minimum: 10%	C. Minimum: 30,000				
2. Iowa State Stamping	A. Maximum: 400,000	A. Maximum: 10%	A. Maximum: 40,000				
	B. Most Likely: 350,000	B. Most Likely: 80%	B. Most Likely: 280,000	350,000	100%	350,000	
	C. Minimum: 300,000	C. Minimum: 10%	C. Minimum: 30,000				
3. Performance Combustion	A. Maximum: 250,000	A. Maximum: 10%	A. Maximum: 25,000				
	B. Most Likely: 200,000	B. Most Likely: 60%	B. Most Likely: 120,000	190,000	100%	190,000	
	C. Minimum: 100,000	C. Minimum: 30%	C. Minimum: 45,000				
4. Bluebird Components	A. Maximum: 175,000	A. Maximum: 10%	A. Maximum: 17,500				
	B. Most Likely: 150,000	B. Most Likely: 80%	B. Most Likely: 120,000	147,500	100%	147,500	
	C. Minimum: 100,000	C. Minimum: 10%	C. Minimum: 10,000				
5. _____	A. Maximum: _____	A. Maximum: ___%	A. Maximum: 0				
	B. Most Likely: _____	B. Most Likely: ___%	B. Most Likely: 0	0	___%	0	
	C. Minimum: _____	C. Minimum: ___%	C. Minimum: 0				
6. _____	A. Maximum: _____	A. Maximum: ___%	A. Maximum: 0				
	B. Most Likely: _____	B. Most Likely: ___%	B. Most Likely: 0	0	___%	0	
	C. Minimum: _____	C. Minimum: ___%	C. Minimum: 0				
7. _____	A. Maximum: _____	A. Maximum: ___%	A. Maximum: 0				
	B. Most Likely: _____	B. Most Likely: ___%	B. Most Likely: 0	0	___%	0	
	C. Minimum: _____	C. Minimum: ___%	C. Minimum: 0				
8. _____	A. Maximum: _____	A. Maximum: ___%	A. Maximum: 0				
	B. Most Likely: _____	B. Most Likely: ___%	B. Most Likely: 0	0	___%	0	
	C. Minimum: _____	C. Minimum: ___%	C. Minimum: 0				
9. _____	A. Maximum: _____	A. Maximum: ___%	A. Maximum: 0				
	B. Most Likely: _____	B. Most Likely: ___%	B. Most Likely: 0	0	___%	0	
	C. Minimum: _____	C. Minimum: ___%	C. Minimum: 0				
10. _____	A. Maximum: _____	A. Maximum: ___%	A. Maximum: 0				
	B. Most Likely: _____	B. Most Likely: ___%	B. Most Likely: 0	0	___%	0	
	C. Minimum: _____	C. Minimum: ___%	C. Minimum: 0				
11. _____	A. Maximum: _____	A. Maximum: ___%	A. Maximum: 0				
	B. Most Likely: _____	B. Most Likely: ___%	B. Most Likely: 0	0	___%	0	
	C. Minimum: _____	C. Minimum: ___%	C. Minimum: 0				
12. _____	A. Maximum: _____	A. Maximum: ___%	A. Maximum: 0				
	B. Most Likely: _____	B. Most Likely: ___%	B. Most Likely: 0	0	___%	0	
	C. Minimum: _____	C. Minimum: ___%	C. Minimum: 0				
TOTALS:	A. Maximum: 1,225,000		A. Maximum: 122,500				
	B. Most Likely: 1,050,000		B. Most Likely: 800,000	1,037,500		1,037,500	
	C. Minimum: 850,000		C. Minimum: 115,000				

BUSINESS-TO-BUSINESS ANNUAL SALES ESTIMATION WORKSHEET: O'Toole's Machining, Inc.

CUSTOMER/SALES PROSPECT	ESTIMATED ANNUAL DEMAND — ITEM 1: Long-Run Prod. (1)	(2) PROBABILITY OF DEMAND BEING REALIZED	(3) ESTIMATES: (1) & (2)	(4) SALES PROSPECT ESTIMATES: 3A+3B+3C	(5) PROBABILITY OF OBTAINING SALE	*REALISTIC SALES ESTIMATE* (4) & (5)	Comments
1. John Deere-Dubuque	A. Maximum: 5,000,000 B. Most Likely: 4,000,000 C. Minimum: 300,000	A. Maximum: 10% B. Most Likely: 80% C. Minimum: 10%	A. Maximum: 500,000 B. Most Likely: 3,200,000 C. Minimum: 300,000	4,000,000	100%	4,000,000	
2. John Deere-Waterloo	A. Maximum: ___ B. Most Likely: ___ C. Minimum: ___	A. Maximum: ___% B. Most Likely: ___% C. Minimum: ___%	A. Maximum: 0 B. Most Likely: 0 C. Minimum: 0	350,000	___%	0	
3. John Deere-Mexico	A. Maximum: ___ B. Most Likely: ___ C. Minimum: ___	A. Maximum: ___% B. Most Likely: ___% C. Minimum: ___%	A. Maximum: 0 B. Most Likely: 0 C. Minimum: 0	0	___%	0	s
4. _____	A. Maximum: ___ B. Most Likely: ___ C. Minimum: ___	A. Maximum: ___% B. Most Likely: ___% C. Minimum: ___%	A. Maximum: 0 B. Most Likely: 0 C. Minimum: 0	0	___%	0	
5. _____	A. Maximum: ___ B. Most Likely: ___ C. Minimum: ___	A. Maximum: ___% B. Most Likely: ___% C. Minimum: ___%	A. Maximum: 0 B. Most Likely: 0 C. Minimum: 0	0	___%	0	
6. _____	A. Maximum: ___ B. Most Likely: ___ C. Minimum: ___	A. Maximum: ___% B. Most Likely: ___% C. Minimum: ___%	A. Maximum: 0 B. Most Likely: 0 C. Minimum: 0	0	___%	0	
7. _____	A. Maximum: ___ B. Most Likely: ___ C. Minimum: ___	A. Maximum: ___% B. Most Likely: ___% C. Minimum: ___%	A. Maximum: 0 B. Most Likely: 0 C. Minimum: 0	0	___%	0	
8. _____	A. Maximum: ___ B. Most Likely: ___ C. Minimum: ___	A. Maximum: ___% B. Most Likely: ___% C. Minimum: ___%	A. Maximum: 0 B. Most Likely: 0 C. Minimum: 0	0	___%	0	
9. _____	A. Maximum: ___ B. Most Likely: ___ C. Minimum: ___	A. Maximum: ___% B. Most Likely: ___% C. Minimum: ___%	A. Maximum: 0 B. Most Likely: 0 C. Minimum: 0	0	___%	0	
10. _____	A. Maximum: ___ B. Most Likely: ___ C. Minimum: ___	A. Maximum: ___% B. Most Likely: ___% C. Minimum: ___%	A. Maximum: 0 B. Most Likely: 0 C. Minimum: 0	0	___%	0	
11. _____	A. Maximum: ___ B. Most Likely: ___ C. Minimum: ___	A. Maximum: ___% B. Most Likely: ___% C. Minimum: ___%	A. Maximum: 0 B. Most Likely: 0 C. Minimum: 0	0	___%	0	
12. _____	A. Maximum: ___ B. Most Likely: ___ C. Minimum: ___	A. Maximum: ___% B. Most Likely: ___% C. Minimum: ___%	A. Maximum: 0 B. Most Likely: 0 C. Minimum: 0	0	___%	0	
TOTALS:	A. Maximum: 5,000,000 B. Most Likely: 4,000,000 C. Minimum: 3,000,000		A. Maximum: 5,000,000 B. Most Likely: 3,200,000 C. Minimum: 300,000	4,000,000	___%	4,000,000	

BUSINESS-TO-BUSINESS ANNUAL SALES ESTIMATION WORKSHEET: O'Toole's Machining, Inc.

CUSTOMER/ SALES PROSPECT	ESTIMATED ANNUAL DEMAND ITEM 3: Assembly Services	(2) PROBABILITY OF DEMAND BEING REALIZED	(3) WEIGHTED DEMAND ESTIMATES: (1) & (2)	(4) TOTAL WEIGHTED DEMAND ESTIMATES: 3A+3B+3C	(5) PROBABILITY OF OBTAINING SALE	*REALISTIC SALES ESTIMATE* (4)&(5)	Comments
1. John Deere-Dubuque	A. Maximum: 1,000,000	33%	A. Maximum: 33,333	500,000	100%	500,000	0
	B. Most Likely: 500,000	33%	B. Most Likely: 166,667				
	C. Minimum: 0	33%	C. Minimum: 0				
2. _____	A. Maximum: _____	___%	A. Maximum: 0	0	___%		0
	B. Most Likely: _____	___%	B. Most Likely: 0				
	C. Minimum: _____	___%	C. Minimum: 0				
3. _____	A. Maximum:	___%	A. Maximum: 0	0	___%		0
	B. Most Likely:	___%	B. Most Likely: 0				
	C. Minimum:	___%	C. Minimum: 0				
4. _____	A. Maximum:	___%	A. Maximum: 0	0	___%		0
	B. Most Likely:	___%	B. Most Likely: 0				
	C. Minimum:	___%	C. Minimum: 0				
5. _____	A. Maximum:	___%	A. Maximum: 0	0	___%		0
	B. Most Likely:	___%	B. Most Likely: 0				
	C. Minimum:	___%	C. Minimum: 0				
6. _____	A. Maximum:	___%	A. Maximum: 0	0	___%		0
	B. Most Likely:	___%	B. Most Likely: 0				
	C. Minimum:	___%	C. Minimum: 0				
7. _____	A. Maximum:	___%	A. Maximum: 0	0	___%		0
	B. Most Likely:	___%	B. Most Likely: 0				
	C. Minimum:	___%	C. Minimum: 0				
8. _____	A. Maximum:	___%	A. Maximum: 0	0	___%		0
	B. Most Likely:	___%	B. Most Likely: 0				
	C. Minimum:	___%	C. Minimum: 0				
9. _____	A. Maximum:	___%	A. Maximum: 0	0	___%		0
	B. Most Likely:	___%	B. Most Likely: 0				
	C. Minimum:	___%	C. Minimum: 0				
10. _____	A. Maximum:	___%	A. Maximum: 0	0	___%		0
	B. Most Likely:	___%	B. Most Likely: 0				
	C. Minimum:	___%	C. Minimum: 0				
11. _____	A. Maximum:	___%	A. Maximum: 0	0	___%		0
	B. Most Likely:	___%	B. Most Likely: 0				
	C. Minimum:	___%	C. Minimum: 0				
12. _____	A. Maximum:	___%	A. Maximum: 0	0	___%		0
	B. Most Likely:	___%	B. Most Likely: 0				
	C. Minimum:	___%	C. Minimum: 0				
TOTALS:	A. Maximum: 1,000,000		A. Maximum: 333,333	500,000	___%	500,000	
	B. Most Likely: 500,000		B. Most Likely: 166,667				
	C. Minimum: 0		C. Minimum: 0				

business**PLAN**

Red's Automotive Services, Inc.

Funding Proposal & Business Plan, 1999–2002

Strictly Confidential

Red's Automotive Service, Inc.

1234 Industrial Dr.

Bluetown, Wisconsin 51234

Red's Automotive— Introductory letter from Tim Baye

The owner of Red's Automotive Service Inc. (Red's) symbolizes America's concept of the "entrepreneur." After working as a service technician, and later as the service manager, for a Ford car dealership in a large metropolitan area, Red's founder realized that he wanted to return to his small town AND to establish his own business. Using accumulated savings and retirement monies, the expected proceeds of the sale of his house, and developing a business plan for his new venture (while still employed by the car dealership) Red's founder laid the groundwork for his venture.

Bank loan in hand, the building went up in a town near his boyhood home. Sales grew well beyond the initial business plan projections. Staff and market share also grew. However, the toll of growing this business did exact a stiff price — divorce. By the time of the founder's family difficulties, Red's commanded ~40-45% market share within its trade area.

Divorce complete, energies renewed, Red's founder faced his professional life with the following proposition:

Maintain existing business strategy and channel energies into other areas

vs.

Continue to pursue business growth and personal fulfillment through his vocation/profession

Red's founder chose the latter. Strapped by the financial burden of the divorce and by the remaining sales potential within his existing trade area, Red's business opportunities must be evaluated creatively—outside the box. New geographic markets and service lines were researched. Competition evaluated, along with a hard look into Red's management abilities, existing "market position" and availability to secure both financial and staffing resources.

End result:

1. New operation—in adjacent trade area to existing operation. Same media market.
2. Additional service lines—diesel/over-the-road truck service, along with an agricultural/commercial tire sales/delivery service.
3. Conduct initial "new operation" promotion through the investigation of market potential. Red's contacted every commercial fleet within both existing trade area and anticipated trade area to solicit historic purchase data, competitor profiles and comments regarding what he'd have to do in order to capture their business.
4. Acquire the competition—purchase real estate from an agricultural cooperative, negotiate the closure of the cooperative's auto service business and the purchase of their tire truck (while retaining the employment of the tire truck sales/delivery person).
5. Creatively use personal/business reputation, management consultant and knowledge of banking market changes to secure a "bidding war" between financial institutions for funding this project—even though all involved knew that Red's founder was cash poor and would barely meet guarantee institutions project participation (equity) requirements.

Occupation of the new facility is expected in Early 2000. Staff recruitment is underway. Management training is being implemented. Direct sales materials and promotional plan is in development.

- Who is the audience for this plan? What is the purpose of the plan?
- How did family issues affect the business?
- Is this a growth industry, a mature industry or a declining one?
- How should they grow? Expand existing location or acquire additional sites?
- What research was done for the new market?
- Who is their customer?
- What personal decisions enter into the decision?

Table of Contents

Page

* Only a small portion of these financial projections have been included in this book.

Funding Proposal & Business Plan: Red's Automotive Service, Inc.   [page 1]

Project/Executive Summary

Red's Automotive Service, Inc. (Red's) is a full service, automotive and truck repair business. Red's is closely held regular corporation, located and headquartered in Bluetown, Wisconsin. Red's began operations in October, 1995.

Since 1995, Red's has experienced growth in both revenue and profits. Currently, Red's commands approximately 45% of the Bluetown (15 mile radius) trade area market share. Sales during the past two fiscal years (Sept.) have averaged ~$708,000 to $698,000. Profits have averaged between $8,400 to $21,400 during the same period.

Red's currently operates in a 5,760 sq.ft. facility located in the Bluetown, Wisconsin industrial park. Red's currently pays $1,800/month rent to Todd Red for use of this facility. Red's working assets and equipment are tailored to serving the retail and small commercial fleet automotive and truck repair market. To date, Red's has purchased $117,000 in diagnostic, repair, service vehicles, computers and tools to support its services. Service work is also supported with an average parts and supplies inventory with an average cost value of $32,000.

Recent analysis of market conditions, potential and Red's market share (Appendix A) indicates that, while Red's sales will continue to grow, replication of sales growth rates of the previous three years is unlikely. Sales growth within the Bluetown trade area is likely to range between 8-17%, generating proportionate profit growth. This market environment prompts consideration of product-line expansion, establishment of operations in a different trade area, or both, to foster continued business growth and development. Given this scenario, Red is planning on establishing a new operation in the Teal City, Wisconsin trade area, targeting the retail, commercial and heavy duty truck repair market.

Analysis of both the customer and competitor characteristics of the Teal City trade area indicate significant market potential for all three market segments. In particular, the nearest heavy duty truck repair competitor is Gus's Truck and Tractor, Grayer, Wisconsin, located approximately twenty-five miles south of Teal City. A detailed customer analysis and sales forecast for both the Teal City and the existing Bluetown operation is contained in Appendix B. Careful consideration was given to possible sales erosion from the existing Bluetown operation, given the anticipated establishment of the Teal City operation within both the retail and commercial repair service lines.

Assuming the establishment of Red's Teal City operation, financial projections for Bluetown incorporate sales estimates of $622,700 (a 10% decrease from 1998-99 sales), gross profit of $377,475, after tax profit of $87,420 and cash flow from operations of $155,479. The Bluetown operation will require no new funding to support its operations during the 1999-2000 fiscal year.

The Teal City operation financial projections incorporate sales estimates of $631,050, with a retail component of' $271,250 (~44% of Bluetown's retail sales projection). The balance of the Teal City sales estimate, $359,800, is assumed to be derived from commercial and heavy duty truck repair services. Of this, only $47,000 of sales are anticipated to be generated from "off-the-highway" or from yet-to-be-identified prospects. Prospects who have already been contacted by Red's and qualified (in terms of dollars spent on repair services in the past year) represent the remaining $312,800 of Red's Teal City operation's sales estimate.

Red's Teal City operation is projected to generate gross profits of $350,552 (55.6% of sales), after tax profit of $2,059 and, cash flow from operations of $16,092 during its first fiscal year of operation. However, the Teal City operation is also absorbing all of Todd Red's salary ($60,000/yr.), even though Mr. Red is splitting his time between both operations. Second year operations are expected to generate $15,707 in after tax profits, and $49,496 in cash flow. Third year operations are projected to earn $22,128 in after tax profits and $55,711 in cash flow. See Appendix F 1 for three year financial projections for the existing Bluetown operation. See Appendix F2 for three year financial projections for the proposed Teal City operation.

In order to support the establishment of Red's Teal City operation, facility, site, equipment and staff development are required. Red's estimates that

Funding Proposal & Business Plan: Red's Automotive Service, Inc.   [page 2]

it can support it's sales potential via a 80'x160' steel pole building, with appropriate office and storage space (See Appendix H for engineering drawings). The planned site of this facility is located behind the existing COTSE/Community Oil facility located on Route 66, Teal City, Wisconsin. As of September 20, 1999, Red's has received approval from the City of Teal City for its planned facility and site development. Estimated cost of acquiring and developing this site and facility is $394,550.

Red's Teal City is also planning on acquiring $105,000 in automobile and truck repair and diagnostic equipment. See Appendix J for a detailed list of this equipment. Red's is expecting to support its initial operations with an acquisition of $10,000 of parts and supplies inventory. Red's is also planning on acquiring COTSE's existing tire service truck and on hiring the current COTSE employee to support tire sales and service. Acquisition of this truck is included in the previously mentioned equipment list. Red is planning on hiring five staff (including the current COTSE employee) to support the Teal City operations.

As of September 28, 1999, Todd Red submitted and had accepted an offer for purchase of the targeted real estate for the Teal City facility. The seller, Community Oil of Teal City, Wisconsin, accepted Red's offer of $41,350 for a 3.15 acre site. Red contributed $8,500 in cash and secured commercial debt in the amount of $32,750 at 8.50% annual interest, amortized over a 20 year period, to fund this acquisition.

To fund this business expansion, Red's is seeking an additional $483,300 in the form of commercial debt. Working capital debt needs are estimated at $25,000. Equipment debt funding needs are estimated at $105,000. Site development and facility construction debt funding needs amount to $353,300. The Teal City operations pro forma's assume all support of this debt, along with the previously mentioned real estate acquisition loan.

Description of Red's Automotive Service, Inc.

Red's Automotive Service, Inc. (Red's) is a regular corporation, established in 1995 and headquartered in Wisconsin. All stock of Red's is solely owned by Todd Red, of Teal City, Wisconsin.

Red's currently serves the Bluetown, Wisconsin trade area through the provision of complete automobile and light truck repair services via a facility located within the Bluetown industrial park. This facility is owned by Todd Red and leased to Red's at a current rate of $1,800/month.

Red's current business advisor's include:

Accounting:	Stan Schectyor, Grant County Accounting, Teal City, WI;
Legal:	Rob Pagano, Foote & Riordan, Teal City, WI
Banking:	Matthew Folletson, FMC Bank, Bluetown, WI
Management:	Timothy M. Baye, Associate Professor-Business Outreach, UW-Extension

Financial History of Red's Automotive Service, Inc.

Red's currently adheres to a September 30 fiscal year. Tax returns for years 1995-96, 1996-97, and 1997-98 are included in Appendix C. A summary of significant financial data is provided below:

Year	Revenue	Gross Profit	Taxable Profit	Assets
1995–96	$288,529	$193,379	$ 26,202	$ 71,968
1996–97	526,853	319,244	37,750	138,708
1997–98	708,376	399,849	53,752	194,667
1998–99	698,822	425,029	34,733	178,575

Funding Proposal & Business Plan: Red's Automotive Service, Inc.   [page 3]

Note: Operations were dramatically affected during the fiscal year of 1998-99 due to protracted divorce proceedings between Todd Red and Renee Red. In spite of these distractions, Red's was able to retain a significant portion of its market (Appendix A) and generate a respectable profit. This profit was impacted both by loss of gross revenue (due to Todd's absences) and by increased overhead expenditures (due to need to hire a shop manager).

Service/Product Lines
Red's Bluetown

Red's Bluetown

Red's Bluetown operation offers its customers three major types of automotive and light truck repair and maintenance services: routine maintenance and repair services; parts replacement and repair services; major diagnostic and system repair/replacement services.

Routine Maintenance and Repair Services

Services include: engine oil and chassis lubrication; transmission maintenance; heating and air conditioning system maintenance; brake system maintenance; and engine adjustments/tune-ups.

Parts Replacement and Repair Services

Services include: tire replacement and alignment; brake system upgrading; filter replacement; suspension system repair/replacement; electrical system repair/replacement; heating and cooling system repair/replacement; installation of audio equipment; exhaust system repair/replacement; and engine control and ignition (ROM computer system) repair/replacement.

Major Diagnostic and System Repair/Replacement Services

A competitive strength of Red's, these services address major engine, electronic and drive train systems. Most of these services result in average purchases over $500. Most of these services rely on computer aided diagnosis, along with analysis by technicians.

All of the above services are currently provided by Red's staff to both the privately owned vehicle market and the commercial fleet market within the Bluetown trade area.

Red's Teal City

Red's Teal City operation will offer all the above services for the Teal City trade area for both the privately owned vehicle and the commercial fleet market. In addition, the Teal City operation will also offer complete maintenance, repair and parts replacement services for the over-the-road and heavy duty truck market.

Over-the-Road/Heavy Duty Truck Services

Services will include: oil replacement and lubrication, suspension and alignment, electrical systems, exhaust systems, diesel controls and ignition, transmission, and heating/cooling system repair/replacement.

Bluetown & Teal City Trade Area Tire Service and Sales

Red's has agreed to acquire Neufeldt, Bluetown, tire service and sales operation. This component of Neufeldt business served the northern Green County, Wisconsin private vehicle, farm implement and truck market. Red's has agreed to purchase Neufeldt's tire service truck for $35,000, along with retaining the employment of Neufeldt tire technician, Clark Thomasson. This service will be coordinated through the Red's Teal City operation. See Appendix K for Red's purchase agreement with COTSE.

Market/Customer Profile

Much of the following market profile draws upon Red's initial 1995-97 business plan (See Appendix G). Given that Red's will continue to operate from its Bluetown facility, and given that this business plan and funding proposal is primarily focused upon the Teal City trade area, and the Green County over-the-road/heavy duty truck market, most of the following analysis is focused on the planned Teal City operation.

Funding Proposal & Business Plan: Red's Automotive Service, Inc.   [page 4]

Geographic Markets

Bluetown

See page 5, Red's 1995–97 business plan.

Teal City

The targeted geographic market for Red's Teal City operation is determined by customer type. The expected geographic market region for the privately owned vehicle and commercial/governmental fleet markets includes an area extending fifteen to twenty miles from the proposed Red's Teal City facility. This area includes the communities of Cities of Teal City and Purpleville; Villages of Flowerton, Poloski, Grayer and Alfredville, and, Townships of Mt. Faith, Mount Cena, Freedom, North Teal City, Little Green, Flowerton, Glen Ellen, Jadetown, South Teal City, Harborboro, Peru, Hamilton, Poloski, Purpleville and Charlemagne.

Total population residing in Red's Teal City trade area is estimated as 24,345. Bluetown' s trade area population is estimated as 11,574. Population in the geographic trade area shared by both Red's Teal City and Bluetown is estimated as 1,694. Total population targeted by Red's Teal City and Bluetown is estimated as 37,613. (Source: Wis. Applied Population Lab, see Appendix I)

Customer Profiles: Retail

Red's is planning on continuing to serve similar types of retail customers in both the Teal City and the Bluetown operations, as was described in Red's 1995-97 business plan:

1. **Turn-Key Customers.** Owners/lessors of privately held vehicles who require complete and comprehensive automotive repair services. These type of customers do not typically do any of their own repair or maintenance work. Quality, convenience and sense of "trust" are primary benefits sought. Value versus price is key to sale. Primary retail customer market for both Red's operations.

2. **Aspiring Mechanic.** Owners/lessors of privately held vehicles who perform some of their own repair and maintenance work. Bring vehicle to repair business when problem surpasses their ability to either diagnose or repair. Trust is key issue, along with price. This type of customers is price sensitive because they would prefer to have been able to perform the work themselves.

3. **Insurance Referrals.** Owners/lessors of privately held vehicles who have experienced a major vehicle failure, theft or damage. Price is primary concern for insurance referral. Request for service based upon lowest repair estimate.

4. **Association Membership Referrals.** Owners/lessors of privately held vehicles who have experienced a vehicle break-down or other major disfunction while traveling within the Teal City or Bluetown trade area. Referrals made from AAA or WATA. Quality of service, convenience and turn-around time primary benefit sought.

Customer Profiles: Commercial, etc.

5. **Commercial, Institutional and Government Fleets.** Customers are typically professional, technical or managerial persons whose responsibility includes purchasing maintenance and repair services for vehicles owned/leased by their organization. Customers typically have fleet automobiles, delivery vehicles or service vehicles. Customers often have a combination of each.

Key benefit sought by this type of customer is immediate service, prompt turn-around and ability to plan for routine maintenance. Value/Quality versus price is key issue.

6. **Other Vehicle Repair Businesses.** Repair service shops both within the Teal City/Bluetown trade area and in adjacent regions who experience an inability to service a specific technical problem. Benefit sought is solving the specific problem within a reasonable turn-around time. Price is usually not a major consideration.

Customer Profiles: Over-the-Road Transportation Vehicles (Semi-Tractors)

7. **Independent Owner/Operators.** Owns/leases semi-tractor for transport services. Immediate service and prompt turn-around time primary benefit sought for repair services. Ability to negotiate price and plan routine maintenance service also key.

Funding Proposal & Business Plan: Red's Automotive Service, Inc.   [page 5]

8. **Transportation Fleet Managers.** Manage and authorize on-the-road services for semi-tractors and other trucks. Seek immediate service and prompt repair turn-around. Typically require independent certification of repair/service qualifications, electronic invoicing and funds transfer, and/or terms of trade. Key to sale is driver's satisfaction, quality of service and convenience. Transportation firms located within the Teal City-Bluetown trade area, or those firms maintaining regular delivery schedules within this trade area will also seek negotiated, routine maintenance services.

Customer Profiles: Agricultural and Construction Vehicles

Customers will tend to be located within or adjacent to Teal City-Bluetown trade area. Customer behavior and expectations similar to over-the-road customers. Additional need of this customer segment includes "on-site" repair services for vehicles experiencing breakdown! malfunctions in the field.

Customer Profiles: Tire Service

COTSE's tire service has historically served three customer segments: Farmers; Municipal Vehicles; and, Commercial Fleet Vehicles. The tire service sells replacement tires and mounting services on-site. Average sales and gross profit margins are as follows:

Market	Average Monthly Sales	Average Gross Profit Margin
Farmers	$7,000	20%
Municipal	$1,000	50%
Commercial	$2,500	12%
Mounting Service (combined markets)	$ 500	100%

Refer to Appendix D for a listing of Red's Bluetown existing/historic commercial and industrial customers for 1997-98.

Competition

Red's operation in both Bluetown, and in the planned Teal City operation, faces competition in the retail markets from a number of sources including both independent vehicle service shops, and shops located within car dealerships. Red's 1995-98 business plan (Appendix G) provides a detailed analysis of most of the competitors Red's has faced during the past 3 years. This section updates some of the profiles found in the earlier plan. Red's Teal City over-the-road and heavy duty truck service line faces one primary regional competitor, located ~25 miles south of Teal City. Below is a summary of each competitor:

Over-the-Road/Heavy Duty Vehicles
A) **Gus's Truck & Tractor**
  1. Service Lines: Truck repair services. Agricultural equipment/vehicle services
  2. Locations: Grayer, WI
  3. Markets: U.S. Hwys 10/30/151
  4. Labor Rate: $34.00
  5. Strategy: Convenience, location dependent
  6. Strengths: Experience (staff) in serving heavy duty trucks. Established in market.
  7. Weaknesses: Average service quality

B) **Truck World**
  1. Service Lines: Truck repair services. Truck and trailer sales
  2. Locations: Dubuque, IA; Browntown, WI
  3. Markets: U.S. Hwys 10/30/151/20
  4. Labor Rate: $55.00
  5. Strategy: Convenience, quality, location dependent
  6. Strengths: Experience (staff) in serving heavy duty trucks. Established in market.
  7. Weaknesses: Distance from northern Green county, WI market

Funding Proposal & Business Plan: Red's Automotive Service, Inc.   [page 6]

Retail and Commercial Fleets
C) Larry's Mack (General Motors)

1. Service Lines:	New & used car dealership, including service department
2. Locations:	Teal City
3. Markets:	Teal City, Bluetown, Purpleville
4. Labor Rate:	$48-58
5. Strategy:	Leverage relationships with car sales customers
6. Strengths:	Staffs training by factory. Staffs knowledge of newer vehicles.
7. Weaknesses:	Staffs skills are average, to below average.

D) Settlers' Motors (General Motors)

1. Service Lines:	New & used car dealership, including service department
2. Locations:	Teal City
3. Markets:	Teal City, Bluetown, Purpleville
4. Labor Rate:	$47
5. Strategy:	Leverage relationships with car sales customers
6. Strengths:	Staffs training by factory. Staffs knowledge of newer vehicles.
7. Weaknesses:	Staffs skills are average, to below average.

E) Bucholz Automotive

1. Service Lines:	Automotive service and repair
2. Locations:	Teal City
3. Markets:	Teal City trade area
4. Labor Rate:	$~45
5. Strategy:	Unknown, may not have focused business strategy
6. Strengths:	Locally owned, well known within trade area.
7. Weaknesses:	Reputation for below average service quality. Below average capability in "high-tech" repair services.

F) Brown's 76

1. Service Lines:	Automotive service and repair
2. Locations:	Teal City
3. Markets:	Teal City trade area
4. Labor Rate	$47
5. Strategy:	Convenience to market, location dependent
6. Strengths:	Locally owned. Location on "square" and business Route 66
7. Weaknesses:	Reputation for good-to-average service quality. Below average capability in "high-tech" repair services.

Funding Proposal & Business Plan: Red's Automotive Service, Inc.   [page 7]

Market/Industry Trends

Major trends within Red's industry (vehicle repair services) and markets include:

- The era of the combined "gas/service station" has disappeared. Independent vehicle service firms must equal or exceed service quality and technical capabilities of dealerships (located within their market area).
- Basic services (non-electrical/computer) remain the primary general vehicle service demanded of independents (70-80%).
- High-tech services represent 20-30% of sales, yet most if not all of this work is on vehicles 3± years old. Work on newer cars remains covered by most factory warrantees.
- Appearances of both service staff and of the facility are crucial to the customer's perception of service quality and trustworthiness. Yearly expenditures on diagnostic equipment, software and staff training are increasing at an increasing rate, in order for independents to remain competitive to dealerships.

Market Potential

Bluetown/Teal City Trade Area

Total trade area expenditures for vehicle repair services for the Bluetown/Teal City geographic market are estimated to be between $3,009,040 and $2,764,944, with a mean estimate of $2,886,992. This market potential estimate is derived from both per capita expenditure estimates and per vehicle expenditure estimates.

Assuming population growth of 1.0%/year and expenditure growth of 2.0%/year, Bluetown/Teal City trade area market potential is expected to increase by ~$100,000/year.

A complete analysis of the Bluetown/Teal City market potential is included in Appendix A, along with an analysis of Red's Bluetown historic market share.

Complete profiles of trade area population estimates and vehicle registrations is included in Appendix I.

Additional commercial fleet market potential (based upon individual prospects historic purchases) is found in Appendix B.

Red's Business Strategies

Retail

Bluetown, Retail & Commercial: Quality of Service, Convenience

Red's Bluetown intends to maintain its focus of serving a relatively broad mix of retail and commercial repair and maintenance clients throughout the northern Green County/Bluetown trade area. Red's Bluetown will continue to focus on serving its existing market segments (retail and commercial) by maintaining a high standard of service quality, prompt repair turn-around, staff training (both technical and customer service) and through the continued management and leadership of the operation by Todd Red. Mr. Red plans to spend 40-50% of his "on-site" time at the Bluetown location.

Teal City, Retail: Quality of Service, Convenience, Name Recognition

Red's Teal City will focus on transferring its market success in Bluetown to the retail customers living and working in the Teal City trade area. The retail strategies of Teal City and Bluetown will mirror each other. Market communications can be leveraged. Both Teal City and Bluetown share essentially the same radio market, and both of the newspapers serving either community are owned by the same publisher. Mr. Red plans to spend 50-60% of his "on-site" time at the Teal City location.

Commercial/Over-the-Road/ Heavy Duty Vehicle

Teal City: Quality of Service, Proximity to Market, Relationships with Fleet Managers

Based upon Red's exploration of commercial fleet demand (via interviews with individual firms and organizations) a considerable market opportunity appears to exist within the central Green

Funding Proposal & Business Plan: Red's Automotive Service, Inc.   [page 8]

county area. Red's will attempt to capture and expand its market share in these segments through it's facility's Route 66 location, by improving its ability to direct its own marketing efforts and, by the strength of Red's staff skills. Key to this effort will be the adoption of a formal marketing function to the company, along with extensive sales and customer service training of all Red staff.

Marketing Plan
Pricing Policies:
Currently, Red's Bluetown charges a flat labor rate of $42.00/hour of billable service work. As of early 2000, both Bluetown and Teal City operations will charge $44.00/hour of billable service work. The over-the-road truck and heavy duty vehicle service work will be charged at a flat rate of $50.00/hour. Both of theses rate structures are slightly below or equal to that prevailing within the trade area.

Parts and tire prices will be based upon costs and gross profit margin targets.

Gross Profit Margin targets:
During the past two fiscal years Red's Bluetown has generated gross profit margins between 60.8% ('98-99) and 56.8%('97-98). Red's is targeting 60% average gross profit margins for both Bluetown and Teal City operations within the three year timeframe of this business plan.

Parts revenue and outsourced services is expected to generate an average gross profit margin of 35%. Service gross profit margins are by definition 100%, given that all internal/billable labor related expenses are viewed as overhead expenditures for the purposes of budgeting and planning.

Tire sales will be expected to generate ~15% gross profit. Mounting services are expected to generate 100% gross profit margins.

Credits and Terms of Payment:
Retail: Payment in cash, credit card or personal check upon delivery.
Commercial: Cash, credit card or invoiced, net 30 days for pre-qualified customers.

Truck: Cash, credit card, electronic funds transfer, or invoiced, net 30 days for prequalified customers
Tires: Payment in cash, credit card or personal check upon delivery.

Promotion and Selling Practices
Personal/direct selling, periodic advertisements in local weekly newspapers, and through active promotion of "word-of-mouth."

Distribution
All repair and maintenance services will be delivered through either Red's Bluetown or Red's Teal City facilities.

Tire sales and service will be distributed through both facilities and via the planned acquisition of the COTSE tire truck.

Operational Plan
Facility Requirements:
Bluetown
Continuation of lease for the 5,760 sq.ft. facility located at 1234 Industrial Dr., Bluetown, Wisconsin. No additional facility development required for this operation during the upcoming three year time frame.

Teal City
Land. Acquisition of 3.15 acre site located within the U. S. Route 66 corridor on the north side of the City of Teal City, Wisconsin. This site resides within the Teal City industrial park. See Appendix H for site map and development plans.

Building. Construction of a 80'x160' (12,800 sq.ft.) steel pole building, with poured concrete floor. 2,000 sq.ft. of this facility will be dedicated to office, administrative and storage space. 9,600 sq.ft. of facility will be dedicated to the repair and maintenance shop. 480 sq.ft. will be dedicated to a "quick lube" area. Cost of site acquisition, development and building construction is estimated as $394,550.

Funding Proposal & Business Plan: Red's Automotive Service, Inc.   [page 9]

Equipment Requirements
Bluetown
No additional equipment acquisitions are anticipated at the Bluetown operation during the next three years.

Teal City
Red's Teal City will require a complete mix of automobile, truck and heavy duty vehicle repair and diagnostic equipment. See Appendix J for a complete list. Office furniture and equipment will also be required. Additionally, Red's is planning on acquiring the COTSE tire service truck. Total estimated cost for planned equipment and other working asset acquisitions is $105,000.

Staffing Requirements
Overall Management: Todd Red will manage both operations, splitting his time 40-50% at the Bluetown operation, 50-60% at the Teal City operation. Mr. Red will be compensated with a $60,000/year salary for each of the upcoming three years, plus a $6,000/year benefit package (primarily insurance benefits).

Bluetown
Staffing will include four full time employees and one part time employee: a shop manager ($35,000/year salary, $3,500/year benefits); three repair technicians ($11.00, $11.50 & $12.00/hour, benefits at 10% of annual wage); and, an administrative assistant ($7.00/hour, no benefits). No additional staff is anticipated required at the Bluetown operation during the upcoming three years. Wage adjustments are expected to average 5% per year.

Teal City
Staffing will include five full time employees (all newly created jobs): four repair technicians — a heavy duty vehicle technician ($14.00/hour, 10% benefits); two automotive/commercial truck technicians ($11.00 & $10.00/hour, 10% benefits); one tire service technician ($9.50/hour, no benefits); and, one administrative assistant ($8.50/hour, no benefits).

This staffing plan is anticipated to meet service/sales needs during the first 12-18 months of operation. Addition of one heavy duty vehicle technician or one automotive/truck technician **OR** promotion of an existing staff member to shop manager of the Teal City operation, along with his/her replacement being hired is expected.

Vender/Supplier Requirements: No changes expected during the 1999-2002 time frame. Initial parts inventory required at Red's Teal City projected at $10,000.

Management Plan
All management functions are expected to be addressed by Todd Red. Marketing, administrative and supervision support will be provided by shop supervisor(s) and administrative assistants.

Management Structure
Todd Red	Sole stock holder, general manager.
Johnnie Vogt	Bluetown shop supervisor/manager
Melissa Gallagher	Administrative assistant

Ownership Structure
Red's Automotive Service, Inc. is a regular corporation headquartered in Bluetown, Wisconsin. All common/voting stock held by Todd Red, Teal City, Wisconsin.

Bluetown facility (real estate and building) privately held by Todd Red. Leased to Red's Automotive Service, Inc. at a monthly rate of $1,800.

Teal City facility (real estate and building) planned to be privately held by Todd Red **OR** held by Red's Automotive Service, Inc. Lease rate (in the case of private holding by Todd Red) expected to be established at monthly P.I.T.I. (principal, interest, taxes and insurance).

Financial Analysis, Projections and Funding Plan
Analysis of Reds's Current Financial Situation and Recent History
Since 1995, Red's has experienced grown in both revenue and profits. Currently, Red's commands approximately 45% of the Bluetown (15 mile radius)

Funding Proposal & Business Plan: Red's Automotive Service, Inc.   [page 10]

Year	Revenue	Gross Profit	Taxable Profit	Assets
1995-96	$ 288,529	$193,379	$ 26,202	$ 71,968
1996-97	526,853	319,244	37,750	138,708
1997-98	708,376	399,849	53,752	194,667
1998-99	698,822	425,029	34,733	178,575

trade area market share. Sales during the past two fiscal years (Sept.) have averaged ~$708,000 to $698,000. Profits have averaged between $8,400 to $34,700 during the same period.

Red's currently adheres to a September 30 fiscal year. A summary of significant financial data is provided in the boxed table above.

Appendix A contains an analysis of Red's Bluetown history sales and estimated market share.

Appendix C contains copies of Red's 1995-96, 1996-97 and 1997-98 federal tax returns and most recent financial statements.

Appendix E contains Todd Red's personal financial statements.

Appendix D contains a list of Red's Bluetown 1997-98 commercial fleet sales records.

Sales Projections and Assumptions

Bluetown

Reds' Bluetown expects to maintain sales similar to its recent history, except for a portion of both retail and commercial sales to be diverted to the Teal City operation. Red's sales averaged $703,000 during the period of 1996-1998. Red's Bluetown's initial annual sales estimate of $622,074 (1999–2000) is based upon this average, adjusting for erosion of sales due to the anticipated establishment of Red's Teal City operation.

Red's Bluetown retail sales for FY1999-00 are projected at $464,688. Commercial fleet sales are projected at $157,386. Commercial fleet sales projections are based upon sales generated within the Bluetown trade area to existing Red customers during FY1997-98. Red's Bluetown's monthly/seasonal sales estimates are also based upon its last three year monthly averages. See Appendix B for a sum-

mary of retail, private sector commercial and public sector commercial sales projections.

Service sales for FY1999-00 are projected at $238,255. Parts sales are projected at $382,241. Other revenue is projected at $2,208.

Sales forecasts for FY 2000-01, 2001-02 are based upon a continuation of monthly and semiannual sales trends, along with a nominal growth rate: 8.0% FY2000-01 and, 7.0% FY2001-02.

Teal City

Red's Teal City expects to generate gross sales of $613,050 during FY1999-2000. Retail sales are projected at $271,250. Commercial fleet and heavy duty vehicle sales are projected at $281,800. Tire sales are projected at $75,000. Other income is projected at $3,000.

Only $52,500 of the commercial fleet and heavy duty vehicle sales estimate is based upon "as needed/off-the-highway" market. Of this $25,000 is expected from miscellaneous public sector customers, $12,500 from agricultural service firms and, $15,000 from over-the-road semis. The balance of the fleet estimate ($229,300) is based upon interviews with individual prospective customers located within the Teal City trade area.

Red's Teal City's monthly/seasonal sales estimates are also based upon Red's Bluetown's last three year monthly averages. See Appendix B for a summary of retail, private sector commercial and public sector commercial sales projections.

Service sales for FY1999-00 are projected at $211,697. Parts sales are projected at $341,353.

Sales forecasts for FY 2000-01, 2001-02 are based upon a continuation of monthly and semiannual sales trends, along with a nominal growth rate: 12.0% FY2000-01 and, 10.0% FY2001-02.

Funding Proposal & Business Plan: Red's Automotive Service, Inc.   [page #]

Combined Market Share Analysis

Red's combined Bluetown and Teal City sales projections for FY1999-00 ($1,253,754) represents an anticipated market share of'—43 .4%. This market share estimate is equivalent to that experienced by Red's Teal City during the past two fiscal years. This market share estimate is based upon only estimated purchases by local population and owners of registered vehicles. This market share estimate is likely overstated, given that Red's sales estimates also include sales to vehicles not registered within the Bluetown/Teal City trade area (e.g. over-the-road semis).

Financial Analysis, Projections and Funding Plan

Financial Projections (Pro Forma Budgets) FY1999-00, 2000-01, 2001-02

Bluetown: See Appendix Fl
Teal City: See Appendix F2

Red's Funding Requirements

Bluetown

No funding, other than that generated internally, required during planning period of 1999-2002

Teal City

Funding Required 1999-2000: Real Estate: $32,750 term loan for acquisition of COTCE 3.15 acre site. Todd Red has already contributed $8,500 (20.6%) of purchase price of $41,350 and has secured commercial debt from FMC Bank, Bluetown, at 8.50% annual interest, 20 amortization for this acquisition.

Funding Required 1999-2000: Building. $353,300 term loan for site development and building construction. Requesting market rates (<9.00%) with a 20 year amortization. Funding needed by November 10, 1999.

Equipment. $105,000 term loan for acquisition of equipment. Requesting market rates (<9.00%) with a 7 year amortization. Funding needed by January 1, 2000.

Working Capital $25,000 term loan for acquisition of initial parts inventory and start-up costs for

Teal City operation. Requesting market rates (<9.50%) with a 7 year amortization. Funding needed by January 1, 2000.

Funding Required 2000-2001: No commercial debt anticipated. Internal sources of funds for asset acquisitions.

Funding Required 2001-2002: No commercial debt anticipated. Internal sources of funds for asset acquisitions.

Appendices

Appendix A: Analysis of Bluetown/Teal City Trade Area Automotive Repair Service Market and Red's Bluetown Historic Market Share

Appendix B: Sales Forecast for proposed Red's Teal City and Red's Bluetown.

Appendix C Red's Current Financial Statements and 1995-1998 Federal tax returns

Appendix D: Red's Historic/Existing Customer Lists

Appendix E: Todd Red's Personal Financial Statements

Appendix Fl: Red's Bluetown 1999-2002 Pro Forma Financial Statements

Appendix F2: Red's Teal City 1999-2002 Pro Forma Financial Statements

Appendix G: Red's 1995-97 Business Plan

Appendix H: Red's Teal City Site and Facility Plans, Building Construction Cost Estimates

Appendix I: Population Estimates and Vehicle Registrations for Bluetown and Teal City Trade Areas

Appendix J: Red's Teal City Equipment Requirements

Appendix K: Purchase Agreement for COTSE/Peoples Oil Tire Service & Equipment. Tire sales records of COTSE. Appendices

Red's—Appendices

Appendix A: Analysis of Bluetown/Teal City Trade Area Automotive Repair Service Market and Red's Bluetown Historic Market Share

Market Analysis: Red's Automotive, Inc.
Bluetown & Teal City Operations
Trade Area Definition

Bluetown Trade Area – 15 mile radius around City of Bluetown
Teal City Trade Area – 17 mile radius around Teal City

Bluetown Trade Area:	Population	11,574
	Registered Vehicles	8,363
Teal City Trade Area:	Population	24,345
	Registered Vehicles	17,201
Shared Trade Area:	Population	1,694
	Registered Vehicles	1,022
Total (joint) Trade Area:	Population:	37,613
	Registered Vehicles	26,586

Sources: 1998 Population Estimates, Wisconsin Applied Population Lab
1999 Vehicle Registration Analysis, Wisconsin Dept. of Transportation

Joint Market Potential Estimate
(Total Annual Trade Area Expenditures on Automotive Repair Services)
Average Expenditure/Capita: $80/person
(Source: U.S. Census, County Business Patterns)
Average Expenditures/Registered Vehicle: $104/vehicle
(Source, U.S. Census, County Business Patterns)
Population (per capita) based Red's Market Potential Estimate (19999)

Population	*	Per Capita Expenditure	=	Market Potential
37613	*	$80	=	$3,009,040

Registered Vehicle based Red's Market Potential Estimate (1999)

Registered Vehicles	*	Ave. Expenditures/ Vehicle (Green Co.)	=	Market Potential
26586	*	$104	=	$2764,944
Mean Estimated Market Potential, 1999		=	2,886,992	

Assuming Annual Population & Registered Vehicle Growth Rates of 1.0%/year ad
Average Expenditure Growth Rates of 2.0%/year, Revised Market Potential Estimates

Estimated Market Potential, 2000	=	2,974,179
Estimated Market Potential, 2001	=	3,063,999
Estimated Market Potential, 2002	=	3,156,532

Market Analysis: Red's Automotive, Inc.

Red's Automotive, Inc.'s Sales History

Year	Sales (Gross)	Market Potential Estimate (Bluetown Trade Area Only)	Market Share Estimate (Sales/Market Potential)
1995–96	$287,922	$1,509,504	19.07%
1996–97	$525,901	$1,555,091	33.82%
1997–98	$714,053	$1,602,055	44.57%
1998–99	$698,000	$1,650,437	42.29%

Note: Gross sales data from Red's Automotive, Inc. internal monthly reports, years 1995-99.

Appendix B: Sales Forecast for proposed Red's Teal City and Red's Bluetown Total Sales Estimation & Analysis Report: 1999-2000 Red's Automotive

	Business-to-Business Annual Demand Estimates	Total Weighted Demand Estimate	Bus.-to-Bus. Sales Estimate	Retail Annual Demand Estimates	Retail Sales Estimate	Estimated Total Sales
Item 1: Bluetn/Exist/Private. A. Maximum:	0			523,439		
B: Most Likely:	116,300	116,300	116,300	465,000	464,688	580,988
C. Minimum:	0			425,000		
Item 2: Bluetn/Exist/Private. A. Maximum:	0			0		
B: Most Likely:	33,478	33,478	33,478	0	0	33,478
C. Minimum:	0			0		
Item 3: Bluetn/Exist/Public A. Maximum:	0			0		
B: Most Likely:	7,967	7,967	7,967	0	0	7,967
C. Minimum:	0			0		
Item 4: Teal City/Private A. Maximum:	0			325,000		
B: Most Likely:	178,000	178,000	145,800	275,000	271,250	417,050
C. Minimum:	0			200,000		
Item 5: Teal City/Private A. Maximum:	0			0		
B: Most Likely:	66,500	66,500	53,400	0	0	53,400
C. Minimum:	0			0		
Item 6: Teal City/Public A. Maximum:	0			0		
B: Most Likely:	78,700	96,700	82,600	0	0	82,600
C. Minimum:	0			0		
Item 7: Teal City/Tires A. Maximum:	0			84,000		
B: Most Likely:	0	0	0	75,000	75,000	75,000
C. Minimum:	0			66,000		
TOTALS: A. Maximum:	0			932,439		
B: Most Likely:	480,945	498,945	439,545	815,000	810,938	1,250,483
C. Minimum:	0			691,000		

Sales Prospects: Red's Teal City

437-7777	AMPI: Bob Gilson	
	Sales Potential	"98-99" Expenditure $20,000
834-3578	Kovachik-Grayer: Corinne Dove	98-99 Expenditure $30,000
834-3701	Farm Coop: John Kramer	98-99 Expenditure $10,000
834-5272	Horizon	$?
459-6484	Southwest Mfr: Jack Johnson	98-99 Expenditure $60,000
834-3232	Riverview Electric Coop: Don Skearns: Manager:	
	Ron Kolby	98-99 Expenditure $15,000
834-8766	KH Woodworks: Mark Meyers	98-99 Expenditure $10,000
834-4900	Millworks: Rodney Boyle	$?
	Karstens: Bill	$?
834-5099	Culligan: George Knupp	98-99 Expenditure $3,000
834-5254	Teal City Care Center	98-99 Expenditure $1,000
834-3297	Morrow Electric: Bob Morrow	98-99 Expenditure $12,000
834-7900	Claas Body Shop: Jim Claas	98-99 Expenditure $2,000
834-5243	Teal City Auto Body: Mannie Perlberg	98-99 Expenditure $1,000
834-8769	DGM Feeds: Dan Maurer	98-99 Expenditure $4,000
	Combination of Feed Suppliers	98-99 Expenditure $12,500
	Combination of Cenex Land O'Lakes	98-99 Expenditure $20,000
	Don's Supermarket	98-99 Expenditure $10,000
933-5282:	Collision Repair Center: John Ferris	98-99 Expenditure $2,000
	Combination of all Fleet	98-99 Expenditure $15,000

Municipal Client: Annually

834-3648	Green Co. Highway Dept: Mark Bracht	95% of work in house
834-7224	Green Co. Commission on Aging: Rhonda	99 Expenditure $6,000
834-3268	Green Co. Sheriff Dept: Charles	99 Expenditure $8,500
446-4479	Green Co. DNR: 834-6574 Charles Pearson	99 $?
834-5357	City of Teal City: 65% in House	99 $18,000
834-3253	Green Regional Hospital: Anthony Perrine	99 Expenditure $5,000
834-7488	Land Conservation: (Est. $1,000/month)	99 Expenditure $12,000
834-4224	Meadow Manor	99 Expenditure $1,200
	Combination of Misc. Fleet	99 Expenditure $25,000

Appendix F1: Red's Bluetown 1999-2002 Pro Forma Financial Statements

PROJECTED BALANCE SHEET: Red's Automotive, Bluetown

Appendix F1 of this plan showed projections for the upcoming three years for the Bluetown location. Appendix F2 showed projections for the upcoming three years for the Teal City location.

Included here you will find only the first year's Balance Statement, Income Statement, Statement of Cash Flow from Operations, and sources and uses of funds, for the Bluetown location.

Period:	Dec-99 Beginning	Nov-00 Ending	OTHER FINANCIAL INFORMATION	
ASSETS				
Cash	33,466	147,846		
Receivables	62,796	15,546	Total Sales:	622,704
Inventory	31,745	32,971	Gross Profit:	377,475
Total Current Assets:	128,007	196,363	Taxable Profit:	132,749
Equipment	44,431	22,216	Net Profit:	87,240
Facilities/Bldgs	0	0	Cash flow from	
Deprec. Intangibles	0	0	Operations:	155,479
Land & non-deprec.	0	0	Sales Breakeven	
TOTAL ASSETS:	172,438	218,579	Point:	367,065
LIABILITIES			PROFITABILITY RATIOS	
Previous Debt	203,795	162,696	Gross Margin:	60.62%
New Debt:	0	0	Taxable Profit	
Short-term	0	0	Margin:	21.32%
Medium-term	0	0	Net Profit	
Long-term	0	0	Margin:	14.01%
TOTAL LIABILITIES:	203,795	162,696	Cash flow from	
			Operations/Sales:	24.97%
EQUITY	(31,357)	218,579		
TOTAL LIAB. & EQUITY:	928,692	1,602,306		
LEVERAGE RATIOS			YEAR-END RETURN RATIOS	
Debt/Asset:	1.18	0.74	(based upon cash flow)	
Debt/Equity:	-6.50	2.91		
Fixed Charge			Return on Total	
Coverage:	NA	2.17	Assets:	71.13%
			Return on Dep.	
LIQUIDITY RATIOS			Assets:	349.93%
Current Ratio:	NA	NA	Return on	
Quick Ratio:	NA	NA	Begin. Equity:	-495.83%
New Investment in Budget Period		33,466		Financing Required
Depreciable Equipment		0		
Depreciable Building		0	Short-Term Debt	0
Depreciable Intangibles		0	Medium-Term Debt	0
Land & Non-Depreciable Assets		0	Long-Term Debt	0
Working Capital/Inventory		33,466	Total	0

Notes:

1) Accounts payable estimates are not developed by the model. New (acquired within the planning period) short-term debt is assumed to be the only current liability.

RUN DATE: Oct-99

PRO FORMA INCOME STATEMENT for Red's Automotive, Bluetown

This document produced on: 15-Oct-99

	DEC-99	JAN-00	FEB-00	MAR-00	APR-00	MAY-00	JUN-00	JLY-00	AUG-00	SEPT-00	OCT-00	NOV-00	YEAR	% OF SALES
Expected Monthly Sales	44,860	53,547	48,480	49,824	556,649	50,444	44,860	49,824	55,408	59,131	60,993	51,685	622,704	100.0%
Cost of Goods Sold	17,657	21,090	17,902	19,618	22,316	19,864	17,657	19,618	2,126	23,297	24,033	20,354	245,230	39.4%
Gross Profit	27,203	32,457	27,576	30,205	34,333	30,581	27,203	30,205	33,583	35,834	36,960	31,331	337,475	60.6%
Overhead Expenses														
Labor	7,852	7,852	7,852	7,852	7,852	7,852	7,852	7,852	7,852	7,852	7,852	7,852	94,222	15.1%
Utilities & Telephone	600	602	603	605	606	608	609	611	612	614	615	617	7,300	1.2%
Insurance	1,175	1,178	1,181	1,184	1,187	1,190	1,193	1,196	1,199	1,202	1,205	1,208	14,295	2.3%
Advertising & Promotion	600	602	603	605	606	608	609	611	612	615	615	617	7,300	1.2%
Travel & Entertainment	330	331	332	332	333	334	335	336	337	337	338	339	4,015	0.6%
Repairs & Maintenance	510	511	513	514	515	516	518	519	520	522	523	524	6,205	1.0%
Shipping & Postage	200	201	201	202	202	203	203	204	204	205	205	206	2,433	0.4%
Office Supplies	610	611	613	615	616	618	619	621	622	624	625	627	7,420	1.2%
Other (inc. rents & leases)	4,795	4,807	4,819	4,831	4,843	4,855	4,867	4,880	4,892	4,904	4,916	4,929	58,338	9.4%
Property & Other Taxes	380	380	380	380	380	380	380	380	380	380	380	380	4,565	0.7%
Total Overhead Expenses	17,052	17,074	17,096	17,118	17,141	17,163	17,185	17,208	17,230	17,253	17,275	17,298	206,094	33.1%
Depreciation														
Machinery & Equipment	1,851	1,851	1,851	1,851	1,851	1,851	1,851	1,851	1,851	1,851	1,851	1,851	22,216	3.6%
Buildings & Intangibles	0	0	0	0	0	0	0	0	0	0	0	0	0	0.0%
Operating Income (EBIT)	8,300	13,531	8,631	11,236	15,341	11,566	8,167	11,146	14,501	16,730	17,834	12,182	149,165	24.0%
Interest Expense	1,368	1,368	1,368	1,368	1,368	1,368	1,368	1,368	1,368	1,368	1,368	1,368	16,416	2.6%
Taxable Income (EBT)	6,932	12,163	7,263	9,868	13,973	10,198	8,799	9,778	13,133	18,362	16,466	10,814	132,749	21.3%
Est. Income Tax Obligation **	2,376	4,170	2,490	3,383	4,790	3,496	2,331	3,352	4,502	5,267	5,645	3,707	45,509	7.3%
Tax Credits	NA	NA	NA	NA	NA	NA	NA	NA	NA	NA	NA	NA	0	0.0%
Estimated Income Taxes **	2,376	4,170	2,490	3,383	4,790	3,496	2,331	3,352	4,502	5,267	5,645	3,707	45,509	7.3%
Net Profit	4,555	7,994	4,773	6,485	9,183	6,702	4,468	8,426	8,631	10,096	10,821	7,107	87,240	14.0%

SUMMARY OF SELECTED YEAR END DATA:SELECTED FINANCIAL RATIOS:

Total Variable Costs (CGS)	=	245,230
Total Fixed Costs (Overhead + Interest)	=	222,510
Total Net Profit	=	87,240
Total Net Operations Cash Flow	=	155,479

Variable Costs/Sales	=	39.38%
Fixed Costs/Sales	=	35.73%
Gross Margin/Sales	=	60.62%
Operating Profit/Sales	=	23.95%
After Tax Profit/Sales	=	14.01%
Cash Flow From Operations/Sales (internally generated cash flow)	=	24.97%

Sales Break Even Point ($'s)	=	367,065
Return on Beginning Current Assets	=	121.46%*
Return on Depreciable Assets	=	349.93%*
Return on Total Fixed Assets	=	141.81%*
Return on Beginning Equity	=	-495.83%*

NOTES:

(1) Assumes 9.0% cost of capital and 70% 0% debt financing, with a 2 year loan for working capital & inventory.

(2) Assumes 9.0% cost of capital and 0% debt financing, with a 3 year loan for equipment and furnishings.

(3) Assumes 9.5% cost of capital and 0% debt financing, with a 20 year loan for land and structures.

(4) 3.0% inflation rate is applied to overhead expenses.

(5) Depreciation method chosen for equipt. of is: double declining balance. Depreciation method chosen for buildings of is: straight-line. Depreciable life determined by Federal tax definitions.

(6) The enterprise simulated is assumed to be a regular corporation. Taxes are estimated based on this legal structure and the previous year's tax rates (federal, state, local & FICA). Sole proprietor taxes include Self-Employment taxes. All other forms include only Fed. & State income taxes. See manual for other important notes.

** (7) For monthly cashflow modeling all taxes are assumed to be withheld by the firm as monthly income is earned. This may cause monthly cashflows to be under-estimated in an one year forecast which has any one or more months of net income loss. The yearly total does reflect the actual expected amount of taxes owed for the forecasted year.

(8) Total sales are assumed to grow at an 0% average annual rate.

(9) Cash flow projections assume that the total amount of debt financing needed is received as a lump sum in first month the firm requires financing, by category.

(10) Operations are assumed to begin 60 days from the current date: 15-Oct-99

(11) Sales breakeven point are sales necessary to cover CGS, overhead & interest expenses.

* (12) All return ratios based upon cash flows from operations, not profit.

PRO FORMA CASH FLOW FROM OPERATIONS STATEMENT for: Red's Automotive, Bluetown

	Nov-99	Dec-99	Jan-00	Feb-00	Mar-00	Apr-00	May-00	Jun-00	Jul-00	Aug-00	Sep-00	Oct-00	Nov-00	13 Month
Cash Sales	0	4,629	5,526	4,893	5,141	5,846	5,205	4,629	5,141	5,718	6,102	6,294	5,333	64,258
Collected Receivables	0	28,161	44,477	42,724	43,731	48,850	46,725	41,900	43,497	48,056	51,877	54,098	48,806	542,900
Other Income	0	56,516	8,280	0	0	0	0	0	0	0	0	0	0	62,796
	=======	=======	=======	=======	=======	=======	=======	=======	=======	=======	=======	=======	=======	=======
Total Operation Cash Inflow	0	89,307	86,282	47,417	48,872	54,696	51,930	46,529	48,638	53,772	57,879	60,392	54,139	669,954
Operation/Overhead Costs	0	17,052	17,074	17,096	17,118	17,141	17,163	17,185	17,208	17,230	17,253	17,275	17,298	206,094
Direct/Raw Material Costs	0	21,195	17,991	19,716	22,427	19,963	17,745	19,716	21,935	23,413	24,153	20,456	17,745	246,456
Interest Expense	0	1,368	1,368	1,368	1,368	1,368	1,368	1,368	1,368	1,368	1,368	1,368	1,368	16,416
Income Taxes Paid **	0	2,376	4,170	2,490	3,383	4,790	3,496	2,331	3,352	4,502	5,267	5,645	3,707	45,509
	=======	=======	=======	=======	=======	=======	=======	=======	=======	=======	=======	=======	=======	=======
Total Operation Cash Outflow	0	41,992	40,603	40,671	44,297	43,262	39,772	40,600	43,863	46,514	48,040	44,744	40,118	514,475
Total Cash Flow From Operations	0	47,315	15,679	6,746	4,575	11,434	12,158	5,929	4,776	7,258	9,939	15,648	14,021	155,479

PRO FORMA CONSOLIDATED STATEMENT OF CHANGES IN FINANCIAL POSITION: SOURCES AND USES OF FUNDS for: Red's Automotive, Bluetown

	Nov-99	Dec-99	Jan-00	Feb-00	Mar-00	Apr-00	May-00	Jun-00	Jul-00	Aug-00	Sep-00	Oct-00	Nov-00	13 Month
Sources of Funds														
Cash Flow from Operations	0	47,315	15,679	6,746	4,575	11,434	12,158	5,929	4,776	7,258	9,939	15,648	14,021	155,479
Increase in Short-Term Debt	0	0	0	0	0	0	0	0	0	0	0	0	0	0
Increase in Medium-Term Debt	0	0	0	0	0	0	0	0	0	0	0	0	0	0
Increase in Long-Term Debt	0	0	0	0	0	0	0	0	0	0	0	0	0	0
Increase in Payables/Accruals	0	0	0	0	0	0	0	0	0	0	0	0	0	0
Sale of Assets/Investments	0	0	0	0	0	0	0	0	0	0	0	0	0	0
Cash (Equity) Contribution $	33,466	0	0	0	0	0	0	0	0	0	0	0	0	33,466
Total Sources:	33,466	47,315	15,679	6,746	4,575	11,434	12,158	5,929	4,776	7,258	9,939	15,648	14,021	188,943
Uses of Funds														
Short-Term Debt Retirement	0	0	0	0	0	0	0	0	0	0	0	0	0	0
Medium-Term Debt Retirement	0	0	0	0	0	0	0	0	0	0	0	0	0	0
Long-Term Debt Retirement	0	0	0	0	0	0	0	0	0	0	0	0	0	0
To Purchase Equipment	0	0	0	0	0	0	0	0	0	0	0	0	0	0
To Purchase Bldg/Land/Intang.	0	0	0	0	0	0	0	0	0	0	0	0	0	0
Other (includes Oper.Exps.)	0	3,425	3,425	3,425	3,425	3,425	3,425	3,425	3,425	3,425	3,425	3,425	3,425	41,099
Total Uses:	0	3,425	3,425	3,425	3,425	3,425	3,425	3,425	3,425	3,425	3,425	3,425	3,425	41,099
Changes in Financial Position:	33,466	43,890	12,254	3,321	1,150	8,009	8,733	2,504	1,351	3,833	6,514	12,223	10,596	147,846
Estimated Ending Cash Balance:	33,466	77,356	89,610	92,931	94,082	102,091	110,824	113,328	114,679	118,512	125,027	137,249	147,846	147,846
Changes in Inventory (2):	0	3,539	(3,098)	1,815	2,809	(2,353)	(2,119)	2,060	2,316	1,588	856	(3,577)	(2,609)	1,226
Changes in Receivables (3):	0	12,069	3,544	(1,937)	952	1,953	(1,486)	(1,669)	1,185	1,636	1,152	601	(2,454)	15,346

NOTES:

(1) Direct/raw material purchases for each month represents the expected cost of goods to be sold in the following month, esculated by the CGS average inflation rate (Sales & CGS worksheet) 2.00%

(2) Direct/raw material purchases for the last month are assumed to be either a standard increase over the previous month or a repeat of the CGS number from 12 months prior to the last month. (adjusted by inflation)

NOTES:

(1) Operation expense use of funds includes any negative operating cash flow. This assumption is intended to reflect realistic behavior to cash needs.

(2) Inventory changes affecting sources and uses of funds are reflected in cash flow from operations (direct material purchases). This line summarizes the monthly magnitude of change (Direct Material Purchases Cost of Goods Sold).

(3) Changes in receivables affecting sources and uses of funds are reflected in cash flow from operations (credit sale collections). This line summarizes the monthly magnitude of changes in receivables.

Copyright: ReCon Associates, 1994

PROJECTED BALANCE SHEET: Red's Automotive, Bluetown

Period:	Dec-00 Beginning	Nov-01 Ending
ASSETS		
Cash	147,846	199,496
Receivables	15,546	16,790
Inventory	32,971	34,295
Total Current Assets:	196,363	250,581
Equipment	22,216	21,429
Facilities/Bldgs	0	0
Deprec. Intangibles	0	0
Land & non-deprec.	0	0
TOTAL ASSETS:	218,579	272,010
LIABILITIES		
Previous Debt	162,696	148,296
New Debt:		
Short-term	0	0
Medium-term	0	0
Long-term	0	0
TOTAL LIABILITIES:	162,696	148,296
EQUITY	55,883	123,714
TOTAL LIAB. & EQUITY:	218,579	272,010
LEVERAGE RATIOS		
Debt/Asset:	0.74	0.55
Debt/Equity:	2.91	1.20
Fixed Charge Coverage:	NA	1.57
LIQUIDITY RATIOS		
Current Ratio:	NA	NA
Quick Ratio:	NA	NA
New Investment in Budget Period		147,846
Depreciable Equipment		25,000
Depreciable Building		0
Depreciable Intangibles		0
Land & Non-Depreciable Assets		0
Working Capital/Inventory		122,846

OTHER FINANCIAL INFORMATION

Total Sales:	672,521
Gross Profit:	407,673
Taxable Profit:	96,524
Net Profit:	67,831
Cash flow from Operations:	91,050
Sales Breakeven Point:	470,748

PROFITABILITY RATIOS

Gross Margin:	60.62%
Taxable Profit Margin:	14.35%
Net Profit Margin:	10.09%
Cash flow from Operations/Sales:	13.54%

YEAR-END RETURN RATIOS (based upon cash flow)

Return on Total Assets:	33.47%
Return on Dep. Assets:	192.84%
Return on Begin. Equity:	162.93%

Financing Required

Short-Term Debt	0
Medium-Term Debt	0
Long-Term Debt	0
Total	0

Notes:

1) Accounts payable estimates are not developed by the model. New (acquired within the planning period) short-term debt is assumed to be the only current liability.

RUN DATE: Oct-99

PRO FORMA INCOME STATEMENT for: Red's Automotive, Bluetown
This document produced on: 15-Oct-99

	Dec-00	Jan-01	Feb-01	Mar-01	Apr-01	May-01	Jun-01	Jul-01	Aug-01	Sep-01	Oct-01	Nov-01	YEAR	% of Sales
Expected Monthly Sales	48,449	57,830	49,119	53,810	61,181	54,480	48,449	53,810	59,841	63,862	65,872	55,820	672,521	100.0%
Cost of Goods Sold	19,069	22,777	19,334	21,188	24,101	21,453	19,069	21,188	23,571	25,161	25,955	21,982	264,848	39.4%
Gross Profit	29,379	35,053	29,785	32,622	37,080	33,027	29,379	32,622	36,269	38,701	39,917	33,838	407,673	60.6%
Overhead Expenses Labor	12,489	12,489	12,489	12,489	12,489	12,489	12,489	12,489	12,489	12,489	12,489	12,489	149,870	22.3%
Utilities & Telephone	650	652	653	655	657	658	660	661	663	665	666	668	7,908	1.2%
Insurance	1,367	1,370	1,374	1,377	1,380	1,384	1,387	1,391	1,394	1,398	1,401	1,405	16,627	2.5%
Advertising & Promotion	600	602	603	605	606	608	609	611	612	614	615	617	7,300	1.1%
Travel & Entertainment	330	331	332	332	333	334	335	336	337	337	338	339	4,015	0.6%
Repairs & Maintenance	510	511	513	514	515	516	518	519	520	522	523	524	6,205	0.9%
Shipping & Postage	200	201	201	202	202	203	203	204	204	205	205	206	2,433	0.4%
Office Supplies	610	611	613	615	616	618	619	621	622	624	625	627	7,420	1.1%
Other (inc. rents & leases)	5,075	5,088	5,100	5,113	5,126	5,139	5,152	5,164	5,177	5,190	5,203	5,216	61,744	9.2%
Property & Other Taxes	452	452	452	452	452	452	452	452	452	452	452	452	5,422	0.8%
Total Overhead Expenses	22,283	22,306	22,329	22,353	22,376	22,400	22,424	22,447	22,471	22,495	22,519	22,543	268,945	40.0%
Depreciation														
Machinery & Equipment	2,149	2,149	2,149	2,149	2,149	2,149	2,149	2,149	2,149	2,149	2,149	2,149	25,787	3.8%
Buildings & Intangibles	0	0	0	0	0	0	0	0	0	0	0	0	0	0.0%
Operating Income (EBIT)	4,948	10,599	5,306	8,120	12,555	8,478	4,807	8,026	11,649	14,057	15,249	9,146	112,940	16.8%
Interest Expense	1,368	1,368	1,368	1,368	1,368	1,368	1,368	1,368	1,368	1,368	1,368	1,368	16,416	2.4%
Taxable Income (EBT)	3,580	9,231	3,938	6,752	11,187	7,110	3,439	6,658	10,281	12,689	13,881	7,778	96,524	14.4%
Est. Income Tax Obligation **1,064	2,744	1,171	2,007	3,325	2,114	1,022	1,979	3,056	3,772	4,126	2,312	28,694	4.3%
Tax Credits	NA	NA	NA	NA	NA	NA	NA	NA	NA	NA	NA	NA	0	0.0%
Estimated Income Taxes **	1,064	2,744	1,171	2,007	3,325	2,114	1,022	1,979	3,056	3,772	4,126	2,312	28,694	4.3%
Net Profit	2,516	6,487	2,768	4,745	7,861	4,997	2,417	4,678	7,225	8,917	9,755	5,466	67,831	10.1%

SUMMARY OF SELECTED YEAR END DATA:

Total Variable Costs (CGS)	=	264,848
Total Fixed Costs	=	285,361
(Overhead + Interest)		
Total Net Profit	=	67,831
Total Net Operations Cash Flow	=	91,050

SELECTED FINANCIAL RATIOS:

Variable Costs/Sales	=	39.38%
Fixed Costs/Sales	=	42.43%
Gross Margin/Sales	=	60.62%
Operating Profit/Sales	=	16.79%
After Tax Profit/Sales	=	10.09%
Cash Flow From Operations/Sales	=	13.54%
(internally generated cash flow)		
Sales Break Even Point ($s)	=	470,748
Return on Beginning Current Assets	=	46.37%*
Return on Depreciable Assets	=	192.84%*
Return on Total Fixed Assets	=	44.84%*
Return on Beginning Equity	=	162.93%*

NOTES:
(1) Assumes 9.0% cost of capital and 70% 0% debt financing, with a 2 year loan for working capital & inventory.
(2) Assumes 9.0% cost of capital and 0% debt financing, with a 3 year loan for equipment and furnishings.
(3) Assumes 9.5% cost of capital and 0% debt financing, with a 20 year loan for land and structures.
(4) 3.0% inflation rate is applied to overhead expenses.
(5) Depreciation method chosen for equipt. of is straight-line. Depreciation method chosen for buildings of is: straight-line. Depreciable life determined by Federal tax definitions.
(6) The enterprise simulated is assumed to be a regular corporation. Taxes are estimated based on this legal structure and the previous year's tax rates (federal, state, local & FICA). Sole proprietor taxes include Self-Employment taxes. All other forms include only Fed. & State income taxes. See manual for other important notes.
** (7) For monthly cashflow modeling all taxes are assumed to be withheld by the firm as monthly income is earned. This may cause monthly cashflows to be under- estimated in an one year forecast which has any one or more months of net income loss. The yearly total does reflect the actual expected amount of taxes owed for the forecasted year.
(8) Total sales are assumed to grow at an 0% average annual rate.
(9) Cash flow projections assume that the total amount of debt financing needed is received as a lump sum in first month the firm requires financing, by category.
(10) Operations are assumed to begin 425 days from the current date: 15-Oct-99
(11) Sales breakeven point are sales necessary to cover CGS, overhead, and interest expenses.
* (12) All return ratios based upon cash flows from operations, not profit.

Copyright: ReCon Associates, 1994

business**PLAN**

Resume.com

resume.com

A new venture proposal

Created by:

Alicia Hephner

David Wallace

Updated January 20, 2000

by David W. Wallace

Executive Summary

The Situation

Over the last 50 years unemployment rates have ranged from 4.4% to over 9.7% of the total U.S. Population, providing a market of 2.8 to 10.6 million job seekers at any given time. These individuals are in a constant state of turnover, almost half of those unemployed remain so for fewer than 5 weeks, the median duration of unemployment is 6 weeks. Finding a job is difficult and stressful, and 30% of new hires were considered "failures" in 1998 because they were paired with the wrong company.

There are many companies that attempt to serve as an intermediary between the employer and job seeker; aiming to connect the best potential candidates with the companies who are searching for employees. Several of these firms have taken to providing these services online, resulting in a fragmentation of the industry and a multitude of equal options available to the employer and job seeker. This fragmentation has defeated the purpose of these services, preventing them from providing every job to every candidate and vice-versa.

The Proposal

resume.com will use the internet to achieve its two primary goals:

1. Make it easier for job seekers to find an appropriate job.
2. Make it easier for employers to find appropriate employees.

This service will be based at an internet site located at http://www.resume.com. The site will have a distinct division into areas for resume input by job seekers and areas for use by employers to locate the candidates they need in today's business world.

The current niche in the industry is a small one due to the continual entrance of new competitors and the wide variety of different products available. This niche is for a large company with many large corporate customers and individual resume suppliers that provides a simple and quick to use database with a highly accurate search-engine that produces results for customers and suppliers, thereby consolidating the industry and expanding it to its full potential. This is the specific niche that resume.com aims to occupy. To do so, the company must have sufficient capital to aggressively market to buyers and suppliers.

The key success factors for resume.com are;

- the size of the database of employees and employers,
- the sophisticated search capabilities of the web site,
- the alliances to reduce costs and increase market share,
- the unique design targeted towards speed and ease of use,
- and the brand name/domain name that creates a strong internet presence.

- Who are the customers for this service?

- With .coms, how does one do market research? How do we learn about what is the competition?

- Who are they going to attract customers?

- How much money are they going to make? How will they make money?

- How will they establish links to large and small companies? What strategic alliances do they need to build?

- Did the writer present a plan that appeals to the reader?

- What expertise is needed to make this business a success and where are they finding it?

The largest barrier to this vision is the ability of resume.com to attract sufficient numbers of potential employees to provide value to the companies that are the customers of the web site. Without the supplies of resumes, the company will have difficulty maintaining subscriber numbers and generating revenue from subscription fees and advertising. Based upon the success of similar start-up companies in on-line businesses and the need for this product in the marketplace, the goals of resume.com are reasonable and attainable with an aggressive and intelligent marketing plan.

The new venture to create a comprehensive online resume referral service will have a positive return for the individuals who invest in it. The industry has a large number of fragmented competitors, but no individual company that dominates the business.

Industry Analysis

Overview – The Current Market Conditions

Over the last 50 years unemployment rates have ranged from 4.4% to over 9.7% of the total U.S. Population, providing a market of 2.8 to 10.6 million potential customers at any given time. These individuals are in a constant state of turnover, almost half of those unemployed remain so for fewer than 5 weeks, the median duration of unemployment is 6 weeks.

The federal "quit" rate, used by some economists to gauge labor market activity, is at its highest point in years. It rose to 14.7% in October and November 1999 after averaging just 11.8% a month in 1997/8. This rate measures the number of people each month who are not working because they voluntarily left their jobs without retiring.

Employees are looking for work more often, and the revolving marketplace maintains large numbers of potential new and repeat customers. The number of people seeking employment is immense, and the labor market remains tight with companies desperate for good employees.

While the employment services industry is large and diverse, the online employment services industry is moderately sized; it is an international market that is growing quickly. The market has numerous new entrants each year, which is resulting in increasing competition and fragmentation.

The majority of online business to consumer (B2C) services are unprofitable in their start-up phase of operation and suffer major losses. However, if a company survives its initial start-up period and progresses into its growth phase, it will generally yield a gross profit margin of 18% on advertising and sales revenue.

Revenues follow the demand for employees and the demand for employment; this demand fluctuates with the economy and the unemployment rate. Whether the economy is doing very well or if it is stagnant, there will always be people searching for employment and employers searching for employees.

When the economy is doing well, and employees are scarce, the currently employed will be looking for opportunities for advancement. When the economy is doing poorly and jobs are scarce, many will be looking for jobs and employers will be looking for the best candidates. Either scenario provides an on-line employment agency with both its supplies and its customers.

Internet technology and software designers are essential resources to creating a web site. Depending on provided services, entry into this industry can be achieved quickly and only moderate expenditures are required to furnish necessary software. As a result of these market conditions, competition in the online employment service firms is fierce.

Rivalry

Rivalry in the industry is a strong force. There are several companies that provide the majority of the same services. The competition is currently very strong in this industry with approximately eighty-seven online employment service providers listed under the Yahoo! employment page alone. Appendix 1 provides a list of the industry's major players and a brief description of the competition. Some of the larger companies are headhunter.net, careerpath.com, and monster.com; these are resume.com's main competition.

Headhunter.net

Headhunter.net is one of the largest, high-traffic sources of information on the Internet for job seekers, employers, and recruiters. On average, 120,000+

users visit Headhunter.net every business day. The site now has over 140,000 current jobs listings, with salary values ranging from entry level to over $500,000, and over 247,000 résumés.

Because it offers a $20 basic posting, Headhunter.net is a popular job site among companies of all sizes that place value on what they spend to attract high-quality candidates. Many global companies use Headhunter.net as an integral component of their strategic recruiting program. Jobs on Headhunter.net are all directly posted by registered users. (Registration is free.)

Jobs and résumés are drawn from all areas of the United States and from many foreign countries. Approximately 95% of jobs are based in the U.S., although some positions are for prospective employees who will be working abroad.

Headhunter.net has a powerful geographical search capability, based on a proprietary database of latitudinal and longitudinal data for 250,000 cities and towns anywhere in the world. A job-seeker can request specific positions within 30 miles of, say, Derry, NH, and Headhunter.net lists all suitable jobs in the order of proximity to that location.

Headhunter.net also enables recruiters and job candidates to search by any key word, such as "marketing research" or "JAVA programmer," as well as by occupation, travel requirements, and other criteria.

Headhunter.net allows recruiters to write and post detailed job listings directly on-line and then instantly modify them to correct job criteria, such as "salary." An automatic update feature ensures that Headhunter.net's job database is always current by purging listings that have not been updated within a month of when they were posted. It also protects recruiters and the confidentiality of companies by restricting access to critical private information.

Carreerpath.com

CareerPath.com provides one-stop shopping for the Web's largest number of the most current jobs listings. The listings come from two sources: they're pulled from the Help Wanted ads of the nation's leading newspapers, and from the Web sites of leading employers. In each case, no listing has remained on our database for more than two weeks, so all our jobs are the freshest

anywhere. The newspaper jobs database is searchable by geography, newspaper, job type and keyword. The employers' listing database is searchable by geography, employer, job type and keyword.

CareerPath.com was co-founded in October 1995 by six major newspapers: The Boston Globe, Chicago Tribune, Los Angeles Times, The New York Times, San Jose Mercury-News and The Washington Post. The five parent companies of these newspapers: Knight-Ridder Inc., New York Times Co., Times Mirror Co., Tribune Co., and The Washington Post Co., financially backed CareerPath.com with an additional investment from Cox Interactive Media, Gannett Co., and Hearst Corp.

Monster.com

Monster.com is the leading global online network for careers, connecting the most progressive companies with the most qualified career-minded individuals. Monster.com is committed to leading the market by offering innovative technology and superior services that give consumers and businesses more control over the recruiting process.

The Monster.com network consists of sites in the United States, Canada, United Kingdom, Netherlands, Belgium, Australia and France, with additional sites to launch soon in Germany and Singapore.

For Job Seekers: Monster.com is a lifelong career network job seekers can use to expand their careers, providing continuous access to the most progressive companies, as well as interactive, personalized tools to make the process effective and convenient. Features include: My Monster, resume management, a personal job search agent, a careers network, chats and message boards, privacy options, expert advice on job-seeking and career management and free newsletters.

For Employers: Monster.com offers employers cost-effective and efficient recruiting solutions, including real-time job postings, complete company profiles and resume screening, routing and searching. Features for members include resume skills screening, real-time recruiting, a comprehensive resume database with more than one million resumes, resume routing, and private label functionality

Substitutes

resume.com faces a moderate force from substitutes. Online employment services may offer the most convenience for the price, but there are several other options available to employees and employers. The industry's substitutes that provide essentially the same service without the convenience and ease that Internet servers provide include newspapers and listing agencies.

Offering the same features, but at a significantly higher cost are professional headhunters, in-house company recruiters, and employment agencies. These are as easy to use for the employee or employer, but cost significantly more than an on-line service.

Threat of New Entrants

There is a moderate to low threat of new entrants in the online employment server provider industry. As a result of increasing start-up expenditures for advertising and general marketing expenses, many new entrants can not manifest the capital necessary to successfully enter the market. Many may try, but they cannot penetrate the already saturated market without sufficient funding.

Additionally, existing competition is strong and abundant. Although there little to no web related regulations which appear to make the industry appealing, the previously mentioned barriers to entry are significant enough to greatly reduce the possible threat of new entrants.

Power of Buyers

Buyers are a strong force in the industry. Despite the size of the market, there are also a very large number of options and substitutes available as alternatives. Without the companies purchasing the resumes, an online employment company could not conduct business. Therefore the primary focus of marketing and advertising in this industry is to attract buyers and suppliers.

Power of Suppliers

Suppliers are a strong industry force. If a company does not have a large number of high quality employees in its database, employers will not search the company's database for job candidates. The reverse is also true for job seekers; if an online employment service does not have prestigious companies searching its database, job seekers will be more likely to search a competitor with a larger number of employers.

Industry Conclusions

Since the mid-ninety's, online commerce has been growing at an incredible rate. Like any industry, this growth will eventually slow. Although there are many potential customers, there are only so many sites that can maintain a substantial yet profitable market share. When market saturation occurs, it is likely that the larger companies will take a proactive strategic stance by distinguishing their sites as more user friendly and merging with competitors.

To penetrate this market successfully, a new entrant must be well capitalized and prepared to suffer losses to gain the users that will make it profitable in the long term. As the industry growth slows, a consolidation is inevitable when companies attempt to solidify their dominance in the market. A large market presence must be established now, during the growth phase of the industry to gain from this consolidation.

resume.com

Pricing Structure:

Like money of the other players in the industry, resume.com receives its revenues from two main sources. The majority of revenues come from the sales of services to employers. The remainder of revenues is the result of advertising sold on a company's web site to industry and service related providers.

Sales Revenues

In the industry there are two distinct groups that can be targeted as customers; the employees uploading resumes to a web site, and the employers searching that site for the resumes that fit their needs. The sites charging the employees have a posting fee from $5-$20 to upload a resume with certain premiums that can boost the price to $90 for advance placement or additional data inclusion. These sites generally offer this pool of users free to any company that wants to search their database. The sites that charge employers have two different fee structures; a per-period charge for unlimited access, or a per-contact charge that is incurred when information on how to contact an individual is released to them from the web site. The per-period charges are monthly, quarterly, or annually and range from $1300-$1700 per year. The fees per contact are in the range of $7-$12 per contact.

resume.com's revenue is generated by the subscriber's fee that companies will be charged to use our database system. resume.com will have a quarterly fee structure offering unlimited access to the site for corporations and offer resumes placement to employees free of charge. This fee structure will attract larger businesses that will have many positions to fill and expect to make continual usage of the service. These customers will have a pull effect on the suppliers by increasing the number of available positions and therefore the desirability of supplying resume.com with a resume.

The average competitor of resume.com charges companies approximately $1500 per year for unlimited access. On a quarterly basis, customers of resume.com will pay a fee of $300. These businesses will then have the ability to search our existing database for employees and review their resumes, and they will also be able to post the jobs that they have available.

Advertising Revenue

Advertising is a major source of revenue on the web, and resume services benefit from ads on their sites for other businesses. Current advertising is based on an agreement that guarantees a minimum percentage of display time for total site visits per month. These fees vary widely due to the differences in site visitation counts and holding time, in sites similar to resume.com the average fee was around $100-$250 per month for a typical banner ad that rotated between several advertisers and was anticipated to have more than 1000 hits per month.

resume.com's advertising income is based upon a $150/mo. fee to a rotating group of 10 initial advertisers. Increasing fees and members annually as allowed and guaranteeing minimum percentages of time per advertiser per month are built into the fee structure. resume.com will be highly competitive in the advertising arena because of the visibility to both

individual and corporate clients, as well as the ability to offer B2B and B2C specifically or together.

Space on resume.com's web site will be available for advertising. By selling both banner ads and links to other web sites, resume.com will be able to increase revenues. The initial advertisers on the site will be other on-line or high-tech companies that offer products complimentary to the resume placement services. This advertising space can be sold to companies like Barnes and Noble who offer literature on job hunting or resume building services. This will not only create additional revenue for resume.com, but it will also help to form alliances with companies providing services that are targeted at the same market. These alliances will be beneficial to resume.com's first years in the industry because they will not only aid in funding the basic business expenses incurred as the company begins to grow, but they may also provide links back to resume.com's web site.

Strategic Advantages

resume.com has several strategic advantages. These advantages include the domain name/brand name, image, niche, alliances, ease of use, speed, search capabilities, and company image. These advantages will allow resume.com to create a specific niche for itself in order to obtain the greatest percentage of market share possible.

Name

The company's name, resume.com, is one such advantage because it plays an essential part in creating an image for the company. The domain name on the World Wide Web was purchased by the company, which assures that no one else may use the name and tarnish the image associated with it.

One of the first steps most people take in attempting to find information on the web is to simply type the subject that he or she is looking for with the ".com" suffix as a destination web address. In the specific case of people seeking jobs and employees; often this key word will be "Resumes" with the ".com" ending. This will bring all of these potential suppliers and buyers to our site.

Image

resume.com's image is a crucial piece of their marketing and will serve as a strategic advantage. The company will be positioned as both the only place to find jobs and employees, as well as the best place to find jobs or employees.

The marketing strategy that will cultivate this image is detailed below.

Niche

The current niche in the industry is a small one due to the continual entrance of new competitors and the wide variety of different products available. This niche is for a large company with many customers and suppliers that provides a simple and quick to use database with a highly accurate search-engine that produces accurate results for customers and suppliers.

The current key factors for success in this industry lie in a service bundle, competitive rates, and database volume. In order to become a key player in this market it is necessary for new entrants to utilize every possible resource in order to be recognized as the best and most inexpensive. The easiest way to enter the small niche available is to make use of these key success factors and offer a promotional period that provides the product free of charge to future customers in hopes of gaining loyalty and build a database. The target customer in this niche is the large corporation with multiple hiring needs. Marketing to these customers is a unique approach in the market and has the advantage of creating large numbers of jobs available with relatively few customers, increasing desirability to suppliers. Once established with buyers and suppliers, the company will need to exploit the niche by emphasizing the service bundles that it offers and the speed and ease of use over other substitutes and competition. resume.com intends to move into this niche and grow to become the dominant force in the market by focusing on product differentiation and market specialization towards the large corporate customer.

This positioning will be a result of the company's tremendous size of their job and employer database that the company will have. The database will be compiled in a manner that will make it quick and easy to use. The online forms for both employers and seekers will be clear and informative. This ease of use will make resume.com's site more popular among busy employers and job seekers.

These forms will be designed so that a person can then be added to the database and retrieved through all relevant queries. Combined with the sheer size of the database and the advanced nature of the search engine resume.com will have a competitive advantage over the competition.

Human Resources

The value chain in appendix 2 shows the importance of human resources in the company. The human resources department of the company will play a major role in resume.com's success; much of this success will be a result of marketing personnel. Human resources will provide a sales staff whose goal will be to obtain companies to who will pay for the service. The sales staff will accomplish this goal through personal selling. This sales staff must be persuasive, friendly, and customer service oriented. If the sales force is not convincing and persuasive, the company will not establish the essential employer customer base. Additionally, if the sales force is not compiled of people who are friendly and helpful, they will have a much more difficult time building relationships with companies. Without numerous employers, job seekers will be less likely to post their resumes online with resume.com rather than with one of their numerous competitors. The reverse of this situation is also true; if the resume.com does not have enough job seekers in its database, employers will not be interested in buying resumes.

Marketing Strategies

resume.com will target college graduates as one prime source of resume providers. These potential suppliers will be targeted through career centers and career fairs on campus, advertisements in college newspapers and by posting flyers in classrooms and frequently visited establishments. It is key for the company to establish and maintain outstanding relationships with accredited universities and their career centers. Many students rely on their career centers for assistance in after graduation job placement. If resume.com can capitalize on this edge and gain a significant percentage of recent college graduates using their service, they will be more likely to attract many of the companies who are currently recruiting on college campuses. Presently, numerous companies spend thousands of dollars in recruiting on campuses. If resume.com can create and sustain a positive relationship with universities, they will have an incredible advantage in recruiting job seekers to add to their employee base.

At promotional events, like job fairs, resume.com will heavily recruit both employers and job hunters. This will be accomplished by using their excellent sales staff to persuade people to visit the site; perhaps, they may be able to set up portable workstations at which job hunters can input their resumes.

The company will additionally need to utilize the career section of major metropolitan newspapers. If resume.com places ads in the career section of newspapers, their advertisements will reach the target market and make that market aware of substitute products that are more efficient than searching the newspaper. These ads will target employment sections that have jobs available on the site, and be limited to areas likely to draw a response from someone with web access.

Using resume.com

The process for using resume.com is simple. The system itself is separated into two distinct areas for use. First, there is the area designed for the uploading of resumes on an individual basis. People can post their resumes online for companies and other potential employers to view. The company has made it faster and easier for anyone to upload a resume just by filling out the coded forms that are supplied online. In addition, these forms allow the employee to cut and paste from his or her resume directly into the form sheet.

Once customers have completed the on-line resume forms they have a few available options to choose from. Along with a database of on-line resumes, the company will offer a search engine that facilitates those actively searching for employment. This will be the second half of the system. Like the uploading side of the system, this is also a search-oriented resource.

After the job seeker has uploaded a resume into the system, resume.com will be an interactive service where people can actively search for jobs on-line.

For example, if you were to upload your resume, you would then have access to this area. Access to the job searching area will not be provided unless a person has uploaded his or her resume. After uploading a resume, job seekers will be issued an id number that will allow them to update resumes or search for job openings at a later date. This condition will help to increase the number of resumes that resume.com has in its database, which in turn will help build and support the company's image as being the largest resume provider. After access is established the user can search jobs in particular areas that match their skills, previous employment, or salary requirements. The user can also narrow the search by specifying desired geographic area, duration of employment, and industry types.

Internal Management and Operations

In order to effectively manage the tremendous number of resumes and job postings, resume.com will need to invest in a highly advanced search engine. Building the most advanced search engine will not be as difficult as it sounds. A key to success in this venture is to create a search engine that would be based on a number of questions contained in the query. By organizing resumes into as many possible fields as possible, the search engine will classify each document in thousands of ways. The search engine classifies information into fields or categories including job category, amount of experience, positions held, work periods or duration per position, level of education completed, willingness to relocate, desired salary range, and many others

For example, if AT&T Communications was a client of resume.com, and they wished to fill a certain position in computer resource management they would take the following steps. AT&T would fill out an information sheet that will be used by the search engine; the sheet would establish a set of criteria which is required of potential employees. Once activated, the search engine would scan the contents of the database and retrieve all files (or resumes) with matching criteria. AT&T also has the ability to select desired parameters, which do not need to be absolute. For example, one could search for 5-10 years of experience instead of just 5 years, or just 7 years of experience. Following the output, AT&T would then have the option of contacting that person via resume.com, or through another form of communication like fax or phone. Once contacted, further research and interviews can be conducted. Similarly, if a company wished to search our database for potential employees that fit a certain profile across the board instead of for a particular job position like experience, education, and ability to relocate to another country, they could. In the query they would input all of the required criteria and conduct the search. Due to the massive categorizing of information through the fields this is done very easily.

For job seekers using resume.com the search engine will work the same way. The available jobs that are posted on-line are also categorized in fields allowing the user to search in a similar fashion. They will be able to look at jobs paying a certain amount in a certain area or any combination of information that is needed. For example, a job seeker could look for a punch press operating job that pays $12/hr and enter the city of his or her choice, and the search engine will generate and display a list of all available jobs matching the specified criteria. In the end, usage of resume.com's services saves companies and job seekers time, as well as the high costs of headhunting and recruiting.

As previously discussed in the Pricing section, resume.com's revenue will be generated by the subscriber fee that companies will be charged to use our database system. The average competitor of resume.com charges companies approximately $1500 per year. On a quarterly basis, customers of resume.com will pay a fee of $300, and in return, they will be granted full access to the system. Additional revenues will be the result.

resume.com will offer, as a unique addition to their system, the option of informing employers of newly posted resumes that match previously designated criteria. This service will only be provided if the employer should so desire. This is a unique time saving feature that resume.com can use as a prime differentiation among competition and can be used to attract businesses. By eliminating the need to constantly conduct searches of our extensive database system, a company can create a virtual account on the system that is automated and customized for their needs. A business could have a profile in effect all the time and constantly receive feedback on potential employees, without having to continuously spend time searching the database.

Essential Alliances

In order for resume.com to establish itself as a key player in the industry, the company needs to enter in some essential alliances with software and hardware companies as well as major customers.

One such alliance would be an alliance with a server company. If resume.com could enter an alliance with a company such as IBM, the results could include lowered research and development costs as well as maintenance costs of the system itself. The lowered costs of a server and sheer size of IBM would be a beneficial asset to use in the future.

Another alliance would be with Oracle, a developer of database software. In return for employment services, resume.com could benefit from the assistance in creating the large, flexible database required to manage the employee and employer data.

Additionally, these alliances would increase the likelihood that these companies would use resume.com as an employment service, making the site more attractive to potential employees.

Key Success Factors

resume.com possesses key elements that make it superior to the competition. As noted earlier, the size of the database, strategic alliances, as well as the ease of use of the system will be key strategic advantages. Unlike the competition, resume.com's standardized information forms will make both the input of information and the output from the search engine work seamlessly together. By creating a standardized format the typical confusions caused by differing titles and other minor discrepancies in the information will be totally eliminated, allowing for a seamless and fast database upon which to search.

Along with the ease of use, the sheer size, and the advanced nature of the search engine resume.com has one other key advantage over the competition that is both sustainable and free of cost; its name. resume.com is not only the name of the company, but it is also the domain name of the World Wide Web site. This creates very high brand name recognition and makes the site easy to locate and remember for buyers and suppliers. Additionally, the majority of search engines will target searches for the key word, "resumes," toward the resume.com domain name. This is done because the search engine can find the key word, "resumes," in the actual domain name which is the first piece of information a search engine scans.

Starting up the Business

In the beginning, resume.com will face the most difficult part of creating and establishing its business because it needs to design and develop their database and search engine. The design and development of these tasks will most likely be outsourced due to the high level of skill that the company will require to ensure high quality.

Once the system is developed and implemented through outsourcing, there will be one position in the company that will need to be filled by a member of the team that helped to create the system. This person's duties would include the continuous maintenance of the existing system. Again, being of a technical nature, this is a position that must be filled by a member of the team that created the system either on a full time or contractual basis.

With the capital-intensive start-up costs out of the way, resume.com would need to take care of specific tasks. These tasks would include the procurement of a server, or a company that would post the site on the World Wide Web and allow the company to access to it at relatively low costs. In addition to these tasks, a staff would need to be hired and office facilities located.

Financial Projections and Discussion:

A profit & loss statement for resume.com for the first five years of the company's life is shown in appendix F-1. This statement shows that the business will yield an 18% net profit margin in the initial growth phase of its life. The company will begin its profitability in year two and steadily increase net income through its growth phase. Other positive trends shown in appendix F-1 include a steady reduction of the debt obligation and bearable interest expenses on that debt for the company. In other words, the company will be able to support the repayment of the debt required to begin operations. Appendix F-2 shows the allocation of the expenses for resume.com per year during the growth phase. This chart shows how the money spent to maintain the business every year will be allocated.

For the purposes of the projections used, numbers for expenses are driven by percentages of total revenues. This approach is based on the analysis of comparable web businesses such as Netscape, Excite, and Amazon.com that display similar percentage costs for their on-line operations.

No revenues are associated with the offering of one free year of service for 1000 employer users. This will result in a first year loss of 1.5 million dollars followed by slow growth of only 5% to year 2. It is believed that in the current web market a heavy advertising and marketing cost must be incurred in conjunction with a free promotional period to overcome the substantial competitive barrier to entry.

The initial loss will be covered by the start-up capital from long term debt financing. The initial debt requirement of $1.5 million will be distributed as follows; 60% 20 year bank note at 7%, 40% 20 year personal loans at 7% to be obtained from private investors close to the management of the firm. The business will be profitable beginning in year two with minimal sales revenue growth rates and continued costs of production.

Also included in the net income figure is other income. Other income is mainly advertising income that comes from selling space on the resume.com web site. The income figure is based upon a $150 per month fee charged to a rotating group of 10 initial advertisers. Fees per customer will increase in dollar amount as will the number of advertisers per year. These estimates of advertising revenue are based on comparable charges for business sites on-line in 1999, assuming no increase in fees to advertisers from current rates.

Direct labor includes labor costs associated with generating subscription revenue for the current period. Direct materials are the equipment purchased for the maintenance of the site and other materials directly associated with the cost of acquiring the subscription revenue for the current period. All other costs for the business are considered expenses in the income statement portion of the P&L and apportioned by category.

The P&L statement in appendix F-1 also calculates the historical coverage ratio that relates the ability of the debt to cover its current debt liability with the cash available for debt service. This is similarly reflected in the cash flow / current maturities of long-term debt ratio. Both show that the company will have sufficient funds to support the debt obligation in years to come. This is very important as the intention of the management is to finance the company entirely with debt to maintain a 100% management ownership interest and then relieve the company of its debt obligation as soon as possible.

The key assumption in the financial analysis is the number of subscribers. Pricing structure is based on industry averages; the annual fees are 10-20% below competition and the prices for advertising are at the approximate mean value of the industry. The only true question is the ability of resume.com to attract sufficient numbers of potential employees to provide value to the companies that are the customers of the web site. To maintain the current rate structure and break even in year 6 of operations an initial base of 1000 customers is needed, with a 10% growth rate in number of customers.

This situation demands that aggressive marketing and advertising be utilized in order to draw customers and suppliers to the site. A high level of process quality must be maintained to ensure supplier and customer satisfaction. These strategies and an implementation of a simple, thorough, and expedient web site will be the keys to resume.com's success.

Conclusions

The new venture to create an on-line resume referral service will have a positive return for the individuals who invest in it. The industry has a large number of competitors but no individual company that dominates the business to larger companies with the fee structure and features that resume.com will use. The key success factors for resume.com are the size of the database, the alliances to reduce costs and increase market share, the unique design targeted towards speed and ease of use, the sophisticated search capabilities of the web site for both customers and suppliers, and the brand name/domain name that creates a strong presence on the web.

After an loss in the first year of operations these factors of success will create a profitable business that can grow to control the market and target

specifically large businesses with expansive staffing requirements. Outsourcing technical needs to create the on-line hub of the business will be complimented by bringing on full time maintenance staff to continually ensure the quality of Resume.com's product.

To maintain the current rate structure and break even in year 6 of operations an initial base of 1000 customers is needed, with a 10% growth rate in number of customers. Based upon industry trends and the success of similar start-up companies in on-line businesses, these numbers are reasonable and attainable with an intelligent and aggressive marketing plan.

Appendix 1

- 1 Stop Job Service - opportunity to publish your resume nationally at no charge to you.
- 4hire Resume Service - view resumes of individuals from a target university, stated regional preference, and industry.
- A+ On-line Resumes - aggressive resume posting and marketing service for job seekers. Post your resume where it will be seen - show how innovative and resourceful you are!
- Appointments Page, The - Irish focused; new vacancies emailed nightly; search online and contact Irish job providers via the site.
- Atlanta Job Resource Center - employment candidates can locate contract, consulting, or permanent work and submit resumes.
- B.F. Services - For those individuals who are looking for a new career. You can browse through help wanted ads or you can find out how to place your resume on the Internet.
- BDH Resumes - helps customers put their resumes on the Web.
- Best Jobs in the USA Today - services for job seeker and employers: post or read resumes, employment ads from USA Today and other media, job fair listings, career store, recruitment advertising, healthcare employment and more!
- Best Resumes on the NET, The - offers resume examples, interview advice, and job search help.
- Bradley CVs & Career Services - Professional CV service & careers advice for individuals & companies. FREE CV, job searching & interview advice at our website.

- Canadian Resumé Centre - to give employed applicants a chance to be considered for alternative career opportunities while minimizing the risk to their present positions.
- CandidatePool - offers candidates to be hired without placement fees paid. Companies can receive unlimited resumes and have unlimited searches for 1 annual fee.
- Capital Region Employment Network - provides listings of resumes, jobs, company profiles, job fairs, and hosting services.
- Career & Resume Management for the 21st Century - professional career and resume services for job seekers, employers, recruiters and related personnel.
- Career Avenue - post your resume and search for a new job. Employers section for listing new jobs. Head Hunter Section for listing candidates.
- Career Magazine - comprehensive resource center featuring job openings, employer profiles, resumes, a forum, articles, and more.
- Career Shop - enroll your resume for free in a national databank.
- CareerCity - search the job database and submit your resume online. Also offers a career center, resume samples, and interview strategies.
- CareerExchange - provides US and Canada employment and resume information services to job candidates, employers, and recruitment firms.
- CareerFairs.com - up-to-date listing of national career fairs and job listings.
- Careerfile - free and confidential resume referral service for busy professionals and a low-cost efficient search option for employers; servicing New England.
- CareerMart - a bustling audiographic employment marketplace, advertising diversified jobs; employment ads; high-tech careers; job resumes, campus interviews; market research; employment advice; job career fairs.
- CareerNet - jobs, employers, and more.
- Careers OnLine - work, education and training opportunities.
- Christian Jobs Online - provides a location for Christian employers and Christian job seekers to find each other.
- Contractors Direct - free database of contractors, freelancers and self-employed people available for employment, contracts or jobs. Employers can search for the skills they need.
- DC's Resume Net - provides posting of resumes and searching through online job databases.
- Direct-Jobs
- Easynet Job-Centre - place a CV, peruse the jobs on offer and look for people to employ.
- EmploymentSkills - submit or view resumes.
- Employnet - The Employment Network and Resume Database
- Entry Level Job Seeker Assistant - dedicated to helping people who have never held a full-time permanent job in their field or have less than a year of experience.
- Euroleaders.com - offers resumes of European graduate students.
- Future Access Employment Guide - add your resume or view resumes from all over the world free.
- GO Jobs - free job searching and resume posting service.
- GroupWeb Employment Services - accepts job openings. Create and post resume or resumes online; includes info on employment agencies, resume preparation and human resources links.
- HeadHunter.net - post your resume or view job listings for free.
- HVAC Jobs Online - job and resume bank serving the HVAC, refrigeration, and energy management controls industry.
- Independence Bank - resume bank exclusively for individuals with disabilities.
- InPursuit's Employment Network - Offering a wide range of products and services including: a resume center, professional resume writing, career counseling, job posting, and more.
- InstaMatch Resume Database - professional resumes. Resume search engine and reply service.
- Internet Job Locator - database search facilities combined with job, resume, and newsgroup posting. Job recruiters and employers may instantly post open positions.
- InterNetworking - a resume is the marketing of your career, so why limit yourself to a small audience.
- Isla Vista Network - searchable resume database for Isla Vista, CA residents.

- JobBank USA - provides employment networking and information services to job candidates, employers, and recruitment firms.
- JobExchange - resume/employment database for those seeking a job or career change, and for companies/recruiters to search for candidates to fill available positions.
- JobSearch UK - submit your CV or search for vacancies.
- JobSite - contains vacancies from many industries. Provides job listings by email and distributes CVs to recruitment agencies.
- Minnesota Jobs - lists of technical and non-technical jobs and resumes. Access is free, with no registration.
- Net-Temps - resume banks, contractor resources, and thousands of jobs from hundreds of employment agencies.
- Online Career Center - info on career assistance, career fairs and events, campus recruiting, and various forums.
- PeopleBank - international database of job-seekers, from a wide range of providers who can be matched instantly to employers requirements; requires registration.
- Price Jamieson - recruitment and job search firm with listing of jobs; submit your resume online.
- PursuitNet Jobs - provides standard resume and job requirement forms.
- Recruitment Database - offers worldwide coverage for job seekers and employers alike.
- Resumail Network - locally focused job search site, including a college recruiting center, resume database, and job fair listings. Download free resume software.
- Resume Advisors - volunteer resume advisory organization consisting of recent university graduates who have been successful in their job hunts.
- Resume Bulletin Board - post a summary of your resume or help wanted ad for free in our help wanted section and resume bulletin board.
- Resume Canada - post or view resumes free, post or view career opportunities free.
- Resume Malaysia - job and resume listing services for Malaysian employers and job-seekers.
- Resume Plus - professional resume service. Consulting, professional writing, and online posting.
- Resume Posting Board - provides job seekers with URLs and homepages for a fee.
- Resume'Net - a source for job-seekers wishing to make their resumes available on the Internet.
- Resume-Net - serving the Silicon Valley computer industry; free for employers; first month free for job seekers.
- ResumePATH - pick employers to send your resume to.
- Resumes On The Web - resumes and job postings, categorized by job category and searchable by job title, state, more! Submit at the site, view for free!
- Resunet - provides job seekers and HR managers access to resumes.
- Shawn's Internet Resume Center - post your resume on the Internet and make it available to millions. Other services: resume & career counseling and resume creation/job assistance.
- SiamJob - Thailand's first job fair on the Internet.
- Staffing Page, The - allows job seekers and company human resource managers to simultaneously e-mail multiple employment agencies with their resumes and job orders.
- TAPS - The Appointments Section - UK recruitment site where you can search and apply for a new position, create your own web resume, and be notified of new developments via email.
- Virtual Job Fair
- VirtualResume - free resume and portfolio database.
- Web Directory: Where to Send Your Resume
- Work Access - resume and job database for bilingual professionals.
- WorkSite - career and job resources for professionals, entrepreneurs, students and college graduates.
- World Wide Employment Network
- Usenet - misc.jobs.resumes - Postings of resumes and "situation wanted" articles.

Appendix 2
Value Chain for resume.com

Inbound Logistics:	Operations:	Outbound Logistics:	Sales and Marketing:	Service:
Computer mainframe capable of handling large amounts of data. Payments to internet server/provider. Lease of storage server to hold data. Software for inputing resume/ job requirement information. Resumes. Employer position openings.	Maintenance of web server, web site, and cutting edge technology. Filling advertising space on web site/banner ads.	Ownership of domain name. Software allowing employers to download resumes. Building and maintaining relationships with employers through sales staff.	Alliances with universities and career centers. Presence at promotional events at career fairs. Strong visibility in major metropolitan career sections of newspapers.	Customer contact via e-mail, small support staff to answer questions, resolve problems, and conduct satisfaction surveys.

Technology/Product R&D:	Detailed industry analysis of what services are offered and where differentiation lies. Cutting edge data entry methods and searching capabilities. The largest database with the best searching capabilities. Rapid downloading abilities. Capability to handle numerous users simultaneously.
HR Management:	Persuasive, friendly, and customer service oriented sales force. Talented MIS manager responsible for maintaining and keeping database trouble free.
General Administration:	Limited overhead costs. Salaries to personnel. Possible alliances with internet search engines and internet providers.

Appendix F-1: resumes.com
Consolidated P&L Statement

	2001 E	%	2002 E	%	2003 E	%	2004 E	%	2005 E	%
Income Statement										
Number of Clients / Users	1,000		1,050		1,208		1,389		1,527	
Client Growth		5%		15%		15%		10%		
Annual Revenue per Client	$ -		$ 1,200.00		$ 1,320.00		$ 1,452.00		$ 1,452.00	
Fee Growth				10%		10%		0%		
Total Annual Revenues	$ -	100%	$1,260,000	100%	$1,593,900	100%	$ 2,016,284	100%	$2,217,912	100%
Direct Labor	34,000		25,200	2%	31,878	2%	40,326	2%	44,358	2%
Direct Materials	6,000		1,260	5%	1,594	5%	2,016	5%	2,218	5%
Total Cost of Goods Sold	40,000		26,460	2%	33,472	2%	42,342	2%	46,576	2%
Gross Profit	$ (40,000)	98%	$1,233,540	98%	$1,560,428	98%	$ 1,973,942	98%	$ 2,171,336	98%
Expenses										
Officers (management) Salaries	255,840		206,640	16%	286,902	18%	383,094	19%	443,582	20%
Salaries (others)	200,000		113,400	9%	143,451	9%	181,466	9%	199,612	9%
Rental Expense	46,800		37,800	3%	47,817	3%	60,489	3%	66,537	3%
Research & Engineering	250,000		100,800	8%	127,512	8%	161,303	8%	177,433	8%
Product Development	100,000		37,800	3%	63,756	4%	80,651	4%	88,716	4%
Selling & Advertising Expenses	600,000		315,000	25%	398,475	25%	504,071	25%	554,478	25%
General & Administrative Expenses	55,000		12,600	1%	15,939	1%	20,163	1%	22,179	1%
Total Expenses	$1,507,640		$ 824,040	65%	$1,083,852	68%	$ 1,391,236	69%	$ 1,552,538	70%
EBITDA	$ (1,547,640)		$ 409,500	33%	$ 476,576	30%	$ 582,706	29%	$ 618,797	28%
Depreciation			12,600	1%	15,939	1%	20,163	1%	22,179	1%
EBIT	$(1,547,640)		$ 396,900	32%	$ 460,637	29%	$ 562,543	28%	$ 596,618	27%
Interest Expense	112,000		98,560		86,061		74,437		70,937	
Net Income from Operations	$(1,659,640)		$ 298,340	24%	$ 374,576	24%	$ 488,107	24%	$ 525,682	24%
Other Income(Expense)	$ 18,000		$ 27,000		$ 36,000		$ 42,000		$ 52,500	
EBT	$(1,641,640)		$ 325,340	26%	$ 410,576	26%	$ 530,107	26%	$ 578,182	26%
Less: Income Taxes	-	28%	91,095	28%	114,961	28%	148,430	28%	161,891	28%
Net Income	$(1,641,640)		$ 234,245	19%	$ 295,615	19%	$ 381,677	19%	$ 416,291	19%
Net Profit Margin				18.6%		18.5%		18.9%		18.8%

Appendix F-2: resumes.com
Consolidated P&L Statement

	2001 E	2002 E	2003 E	2004 E	2005 E
Cashflows					
Net Income	$ (1,641,640)	$ 234,245	$ 295,615	$ 381,677	$ 416,291
Depreciation	-	18,000	36,000	54,000	72,000
Gross Cash Flow For Debt Service	(1,641,640)	252,245	331,615	435,677	488,291
Current Maturities of L-T Debt	80,000	192,000	178,560	166,061	166,061
Net Cash Flow After Debt Service	(1,721,640)	60,245	153,055	269,616	322,230
Less: Dividends Paid	-	-	-	-	-
Net Cash Flow After Financing Activities	$ (1,721,640)	$ 60,245	$ 153,055	$ 269,616	$ 322,230
Cash Flow/Cmltd	(20.52)	1.31	1.86	2.62	2.94
Cash Available For Debt Service					
Net Income After Taxes	$ (1,641,640)	$ 234,245	$ 295,615	$ 381,677	$ 416,291
Depreciation	-	18,000	36,000	54,000	72,000
Interest Expense	112,000	98,560	86,061	74,437	70,937
Cash Available for Debt Service	$ (1,529,640)	$ 350,805	$ 417,676	$ 510,113	$ 559,227
Debt Service	192,000	290,560	264,621	240,497	236,997
Historical Coverage Ratio (Cash Avail For Ds/Cmltd + Interest)	(7.97)	1.21	1.58	2.12	2.36
Free Cash Flow	$ (1,641,640)	$ 252,245	$ 331,615	$ 435,677	$ 488,291

business**PLAN**

Whole Fish/Seafood Restaurant and Market

Ray Van Gilder

Harald Van Gilder

Background

This business plan was written for an individual who was interested in starting a new fresh seafood restaurant in Kansas City, Missouri. Much of the organization and development of the restaurant was patterned after a very successful, existing restaurant that is located in St. Louis, Missouri. The individual did not want to own or manage the restaurant, but was interested in serving as a general manager in the development of a chain of fresh seafood restaurants. If successful, the individual wanted to franchise the restaurant. The individual had commitment of financing to support the establishment of the first restaurant. Part of the pre-launch planning included identifying and arranging for a young man, who would become head chef in the restaurant, to attend culinary school in New York.

Purpose of the Business Plan

The purpose of the business plan was to describe the restaurant concept and demonstrate the feasibility of the organizational plan. Due to the focused nature of the business plan, no attempt was made to develop or forecast cashflow or other financial statements. Since capital had already been committed to the project, financial information was not deemed important. It was assumed that restaurants identical to the very successful restaurant in St. Louis would also be successful.

The organization and themes of the plan closely followed the preferences of the individual for whom the plan was written.

Concept

The individual for whom the business plan was written believed that one of the main competitive advantages of the restaurant was in his ability to develop and access a network of suppliers of fresh seafood from around the world. A supplier system providing fresh seafood to the Midwest has the potential of being very successful due to the long distance from the ocean. This individual personally knew the owner of an existing and very successful fresh seafood restaurant in St. Louis, Missouri, and would be able to obtain the list of suppliers of the fresh seafood from the owner of this existing restaurant. The supply of fresh seafood to the proposed restaurant would be a duplicate of the existing restaurant. A critical component of the concept was close proximity to an airport having good air transport services. Because of the ability to access a network of fresh seafood, the individual for whom the plan was written also wanted to open a market where he could serve as a wholesaler for other restaurants and general public in the local area.

An important aspect of the proposal was the organization and linking of corporate structure. The business plan described the creation of three legally sepa-

---

- Would you fund this start-up business with your hard-earned money?

- What makes sense to you and what doesn't?

- What part does location play in the siting of new business?

- Do you get a good mental picture of what the business will look like and how it will operate? Would you go to this restaurant?

- Did you understand the franchise offer? Would you buy this franchise?

- Do you understand the industry from this analysis?

- What do you know about the financial projections from this plan?

- Will this business be successful?

rate, by operationally integrated corporations: Management Corporation, Franchise Corporation, and Real Estate Corporation. Each corporation would be responsible for distinct aspects of the overall business system and managed by individuals who had much expertise in the operational area managed by their respective corporation.

Background and Role of the Prospective Owner

The prospective owner had been responsible for the construction of over 300 convenience stores in the Midwestern USA, and was previously the owner of several convenience store franchises. From this experience, he developed a considerable background as a general contractor. His role in the restaurant would be to provide general oversight of the construction and management of the initial launch of the restaurant. After the proposed restaurant was operating smoothly, the prospective owner would have little input into the day-to-day operations. Instead, his role would be to provide strategic vision and development of similar restaurants throughout the USA. Other future potential locations for the restaurant included the Pacific Northwest, Hawaii, and Florida.

Table of Contents

Business Description

The Whole Fish & Seafood Market and Restaurant is comprised of three distinct businesses located within the store's location. A restaurant and bar, a fresh carry-out seafood market, and the distribution of fresh seafood to other restaurants in the area.

Restaurant and Oyster Bar

The unique and distinguishing feature of the restaurant is the freshness of all the food served. Fresh seafood is flown in daily from a network of suppliers from all over the world, including, for example, New Zealand, Hawaii, the Gulf of Mexico, Singapore, and the North Atlantic. To insure the highest quality products, the restaurant buys directly from fishermen or their brokers, instead of processors or other wholesalers. This concept cannot be claimed by any other restaurant in the current location's market area. The restaurant will be open seven days a week. Its specialty is fresh seafood entrees which may be either steamed, grilled, sauteed, or blackened. The menu includes selections such as cold appetizers (oysters, smoked salmon, shrimp cocktail), hot appetizers (clams, mussels, shrimp mushrooms, crab cakes), soups (clam chowder, Creole seafood gumbo), salads (shrimp, seafood supreme, tuna, garden), fried specialties (fish and chips, shrimp clam, oysters) and sandwiches (tuna, salmon, halibut, shrimp). The entree selections include lobster, catfish, halibut, mahi mahi, orange roughy, oysters, rainbow trout, rock shrimp, salmon, scallops, shrimp, swordfish tuna, and walleye pike. Daily specials will be offered featuring selected seafood items that feature either special cooking styles or seafood that is in-season.

Other menu alternatives are also available. Grilled sandwiches served on a Kaiser Roll or wheat bread, the finest Iowa corn fed beef and poultry, and pasta. A few combination platters are available with mixed choices of seafood and a steak and lobster option. Cholesterol-free fried seafood specialties are included on the menu. A full selection and description of several white, blush, and red wines are served as well as house wines by Inglenook. Several varieties of domestic, import, and non-alcoholic bottled beers are available in addition to a few draft beers. A light lunch menu is also available. All meals are served with a dinner salad and hot, fresh sourdough bread. The meal will be attractively served to ensure the customers dining experience will be relaxing and enjoyable. A high quality and broad range of dessert selections will provide an excellent complement to the seafood specialties that complete the menu.

The interior of the restaurant will have an "ocean" type theme and atmosphere. Pictures, models, and stuffed fish adorn the walls. Replicas of items representative of the fishing industry will also be displayed. The presentation will be such that a business meeting or family dining may be both suitable and appropriate (highchairs are provided for small children.) Preparation of the meals may be observed in the "Galley" located to the rear of the restaurant. Tablecloths will not be used; rather, paper products will be used for place mats, napkins, and condiment containers. The oyster bar area is partitioned off from the restaurant with accessibility from two sides. The oyster bar area contains an "L" shaped bar with an island in the middle of the room with chairs surrounding it. Booths again line the insides of the walls. Sushi may be served one night a week in the bar. All in all, the restaurant and bar, with its enhanced interior decor that matches the seafood menu, creates an atmosphere that promotes a feeling of dining close to the sea.

The restaurant seating will include comfortable booths around the perimeter and tables in the center areas of each room. Most booths and tables will accommodate 4 customers. In addition, a few booths will seat 6 customers, and a few tables will seat 2 customers. This arrangement will provide flexibility and take advantage of all available seating areas in the restaurant. The oyster bar will have 3-4 booths where customers may enjoy a meal, appetizers, or alcoholic beverages in the oyster bar atmosphere. The restaurant will have approximately 35-40 tables and a seating capacity of about 150-160. The oyster bar will have a seating capacity of approximately 60-70 customers.

Carryout and Seafood Market

The seafood market, located in one section of the restaurant, contains three large refrigerated counters filled with fresh fish fillets, fish steaks, medium and jumbo shrimp, mussels, and scallops. Another smaller frozen counter contains lobster tail, king crab legs, and clam strips. A live well containing lobsters is provided so that patrons of either the restaurant or the market may choose their lobsters for restaurant dining or carry-out. Cooking accessories and utensils such as specialty seafood knives, cookbooks, spices, shrimp and crab boil, and many other items are sold. Waterfront recipe cards are available at the counters. A bulletin board that will be placed towards the front of the seafood market will provide newspaper and magazine articles describing the health rewards of fresh seafood.

Distribution to Other Restaurants

Whole Fish & Seafood Market and Restaurant also ships live and fresh seafood at regular market prices and guarantees freshness. With just a phone call, the market will ship the finest fresh seafood available in the Midwest. The products will be shipped in insulated corrugated boxes filled with leak-proof polyethylene liners. Products will be kept cool with frozen refrigerant packs. Whole Fish & Seafood Market and Restaurant will ship products by either next day overnightdelivery to homes or businesses, or by commercial bus the same day.

Supportive Sales

Whole Fish & Seafood Market and Restaurant will also sell seafood-related, nonfood merchandise that will complement and support the other restaurant activities. For example, seafood spices, cooking utensils, and cookbooks will be available for customers. Employees working at the restaurant will be knowledgeable in the use of these items to provide customers with advice and expertise.

Building

Each restaurant will be constructed with approximately 6,000 square feet. Free standing structures will be preferred. Construction of the buildings is expected to take 4-5 months. Approximately one-half acre will be required to accommodate each free standing restaurant and provide the required parking lot. However, depending on the availability of building sites and market structure, restaurant units may also be placed in existing facilities. The perimeter where customers sit will be composed primarily of glass. The use of glass will permit a high level of natural light to enter the eating areas in the restaurant. This natural light will accentuate the restaurants' image of providing fresh seafood. Exterior landscaping will include high quality planting of trees, shrubs, and bushes. Customers eating in areas located close to the perimeter glass walls will overlook this exterior landscaping. This arrangement will enhance the relaxing dining environment and improve customer enjoyment of the dining experience.

Restaurant Industry

National and Regional Trends

The restaurant industry has been described as entering the "mature" phase in its life cycle. However, solid growth should be experienced nationwide in 1995. According to the National Restaurant Association, restaurant sales in 1995 are expected to increase 4.7% over sales in 1994. Coupled with similar gains in 1994, the period 1993-95 is expected to be the industry's best two-year growth period since the late 1980s.

Similarly improved but modest growth for the restaurant industry is expected in the West North Central states region (Minnesota, Iowa, South

Dakota, North Dakota and Nebraska). Reflecting this growth, restaurant sales are expected to increase by 4.6% in 1995 as compared to 1994, while employment is expected to increase by 4.5% in 1995 over the 1994 levels.

Eating places currently account for two-thirds of the food service sales. In 1995, restaurant sales are projected to reach $201 billion nationally, which is a 4.9% increase over 1994. Since the 1970s, the fast food segment of the restaurant industry has been the fastest growing market segment. In 1995, about 49% of the industry sales should occur in the fast food restaurants, which continues to be the fastest growing market segment within the industry.

Full service restaurants are the second largest segment of the restaurant industry. This type of restaurant is expected to experience great competitive pressures as a result of customers who are increasing their expectations regarding almost every aspect of their dining experience and from new restaurants entering into an already crowded market. As a result of the increasing competition, successful restaurants should focus on offering customers high quality food and service at an attractive price. In addition, the architecture, decor, ambiance, landscaping, and site location are becoming much more important. The greatest burden of this pressure will be experienced by independent operators as the larger full-service restaurant chains continue their ambitious expansion.

However, the independent operators have several special competitive advantages in the market. For example, they are in a much better position to react and adjust to changing customer needs and expectations than are the larger chain restaurants. Many consumers are tired of a steady stream of negative news from the mainstream press. Socializing with family and friends in a pleasant environment offered in a full-service restaurant offers the opportunity to "reconnect", and an alternative to the cocooning home lifestyle that has become increasingly popular. Finally, the greater number of women entering the work force will translate into greater household disposable income and, resultingly, increased demand for full service restaurants offering a relaxed and enjoyable environment.

Trends in the Kansas City Metroplex

The Kansas City metro area is expected to experience strong economic growth during 1995, which should benefit and be reflected in performance of the restaurant industry. The industry trends have showed a growing and vibrant industry. For example, the number of restaurants in Kansas City increased from 717 in 1991 to 995 in 1992, and from 686 in 1991 to 903 in 1992 in surrounding suburbs. Gross restaurant sales in Kansas City increased from $394,659,000 in 1991 to $479,027,000 in 1992, and from $242,770,000 in 1991 to $264,901,000 in 1992 in surrounding suburbs (most recent data available). Employment in the restaurant industry increased from 91,577 in the 3rd quarter of 1993 to 94,043 in the 3rd quarter of 1994. Finally, projected increases in employment and disposable income should increase restaurant sales to a 5.5% increase in 1995 over 1994.

Full service restaurants should account for 30.3% of total food service sales in 1995. Industry sales are expected to increase by 2.9% in 1995 over 1994. As consumers increase their expectations for a "total dining experience," restaurants need to focus on architecture, decor, landscape, location, and accessibility in addition to the quality, service, and price in all restaurants.

Business Organization

Organizational Structure

The business units, which will be organized around functional responsibilities, will include the Franchise Corporation, Management Corporation, Real Estate Corporation, and individual Franchise Restaurants. This organization structure offers the following advantages:

- Separation of ownership responsibilities into autonomous units that correspond to specific responsibilities within the restaurant. Each corporation would be responsible for fulfilling interdependent roles.
- Separation of tax liabilities according to separate corporate liability.

This unique aspect of the organizational form allows investors in each corporation to accrue tax benefits independent of other corporate units.

- Accounting and financial reporting support for each restaurant. Each restaurant will have a normal operating account and a payroll account. All revenues will be allocated among all investors accounts and deposited in proportion to sales at each restaurant location. Likewise, all expenses will be handled in a similar manner. The Franchise Corporation will be responsible for this activity, which will simplify the operational responsibility of the other corporate entities.

Business Goals

Short Term Goals

The short term goals are to develop, open, and operate four successful restaurants in the Kansas City, Missouri area. To accomplish this, it will be necessary to set-up and integrate the different corporate entities, attract the necessary capital, hire and train all staff, and confirm that the existing supply networks used in the St. Louis market. In addition, the general concept of franchising the Whole Fish & Seafood Market and Restaurant must be proven.

Long Term Goals

The long term goals are to continue opening similar restaurants in different locations in the USA and, perhaps, the world. After the short term goals have been accomplished, the franchise concept will expand through the opening of new restaurants in other locations. Preliminary target locations have been identified and are currently being explored.

Franchise Restaurants

The franchise restaurants will be operated as subchapter S corporations issuing Internal Revenue Code 1244 stock. Under Internal Revenue Code 1244 (herein referred to as IRC 1244), a domestic small business corporation may issue stock, either preferred or common, voting or nonvoting, that will qualify as TRC 1244 stock if certain procedures are followed.

"Section 1244 stock" may be issued if the following conditions are met:

- at the time of issuance, the corporation was a small business corporation

     (For a corporation to be considered a small business corporation, the aggregate amount of money and property received by the corporation for stock shall not exceed $1,000,000.)
- the stock was issued for money or property
- the corporation must derive more than 50% of aggregate gross receipts from sources other than passive income for the previous five taxable years or the period of the corporations existence until the date of the loss (if not in existence for five years).

Implications of Tax Rules

Owners of stock qualifying as IRC 1244 stock are entitled to take an ordinary loss deduction for any loss sustained on the stock's sale, exchange, or worthlessness. The loss deduction is limited to $50,000 for single taxpayers or $100,000 in the case of a husband and wife filing a joint return.

The advantages of filing under IRC 1244 essentially allow a risk free investment. If a married couple were to invest $100,000 and the restaurant was not able to maintain the outstanding success of the current restaurant, an ordinary loss deduction is allowable up to the amount recognized on the loss with a maximum of $100,000.

Initial Financing Structure

The funds required to launch the restaurants will come from franchise investors. As described above, IRC 1244 allows an investment of $1,000,000. Franchise investor(s) will invest $1,000,000 in each restaurant. The allocation of these funds is as follows:

- $50, 000 will be paid to the franchise. The franchise will apply these funds to expand the restaurant concept into other locations.
- $450,000 will be available and used as a source of operating funds for each restau-

rant. This capital will be available for use by the Management Corporation and can be used for operating requirements.
- $500,000 will be used to pay for leasehold improvements at each restaurant.

     At the end of the first year, the franchise investors will receive a repatriation of any invested capital that has not been spent. It is anticipated that this will amount to $150,000 after the first year.

Franchise Corporation

Description

The Franchise Corporation will be the umbrella organization that coordinates much of the activities and provides the most important integration aspects of the business activities. The Franchise Corporation will assist in the financial and accounting management, insure standardization, facilitate various aspects of operations, and provide all maintenance of all franchise units.

Responsibilities

(1)The Franchise Corporation will be responsible for expanding the restaurant concept into other markets. Initially, the franchise corporation will manage the opening of four restaurants in the Kansas City metro area. This figure has been chosen based on the ability of the market to sustain this number of restaurants as analyzed by a site selection firm. The four restaurants will be located in Lenexa Lee's Summit, Ray Town and Kansas Park. Each franchisee will be granted ownership at a particular address rather than a market area. After these four restaurants have been successfully launched, the franchise corporation will begin working to open four new restaurants on the Hawaiian Islands. Subsequently, the franchise corporation will begin working on launching restaurants in Ft. Meyers, Florida. The franchise corporation will continue opening new restaurants in other markets, such as, perhaps, Vancouver, Canada.

For planned expansions of the franchise, the corporation will hire an Iowa State University finance graduate and a hotel, restaurant, institutional management graduate and send them to the Culinary Institute of America (Ithaca, New York). This nationally renowned culinary institute is an eighteen month program that will prepare the personnel for the management and operation of the franchise expansions.

(2) The Franchise Corporation will be responsible for managing the restaurants' commissary operations. The commissary will be responsible for the purchase, supply, and management of all food products for each restaurant. The commissary will be located at or near the airport in each market in order to ensure fresh and efficient handling and delivery of the seafood. The commissary will bake and prepare all food items that it can do cheaper and of the same quality as its suppliers.

The commissary will develop and maintain the network of seafood suppliers throughout the world. The commissary will be responsible for placing orders with the suppliers for the seafood requested by each restaurant. The commissary will pick-up the seafood from the airport immediately upon delivery. Subsequently, commissary personnel will process the fresh seafood according to the restaurants' orders. After processing, the seafood will be delivered to the restaurants. Each commissary will necessarily include kitchen facilities and kitchen staff that will process the seafood that arrives at the airport and prepares selected menu items as agreed upon by the restaurants.

A very close and supportive liaison relationship between the commissary and restaurants must be maintained in each market. This close relationship will enable the commissary to respond quickly to the needs of each restaurant and provide a flexible working relationship with each restaurant.

The commissary will also be responsible for preparation of soups and desserts that are served at each restaurant. Fresh soup and dessert selections will be cooked and delivered daily according to the orders placed by each restaurant.

(3) The Franchise Corporation will be responsible for maintenance at all restaurants including snow removal. To accomplish these tasks, the commissary will hire and train the required staff. Initially, the Franchise Corporation will contract-out all maintenance work. As the level of maintenance activity increases, the Franchise Corporation will hire full time maintenance employees.

(4) The Franchise Corporation will be responsible for all accounting and financial management of the franchisees. To accomplish this, the Franchise Corporation will hire a highly qualified accountant, such as a Certified Public Accountant. The financial records of each franchise unit will be kept separately. Account integrity will be maintained. At the end of each business day the registers at each restaurant will be cleared and deposited at a designated banking institution into the franchisees accounts. The accounts will then be swept every night and transferred into very liquid and secure short term securities (expected to yield 2-3% per year).

Each state will have a regional franchise office. The Franchise Corporation office will be located in a central location, possibly Lenexa, Kansas.

Fees

The initial franchise fee charged to each new franchisee will be $50,000. In addition, a yearly fee of 3% of gross income will be charged to maintain the franchise and provide all the required services previously described. Any investor wishing to withdraw their investment must find a replacement investor. The franchise corporation may assist in this search.

Management

This corporation will be owned and managed by

Management Corporation
Description

The Management Corporation will be an umbrella corporation under which all training activities occur. These training activities will include all restaurant personnel (cooks, table servers, hostess, etc.), franchise corporation (accountant, manager, etc.), and commissary (food preparation, delivery, purchasing, etc.).

Responsibilities

The management corporation will be responsible for staffing, training, and managing all restaurant personnel, as well as managing all activities and operations of the restaurant. To maintain continuity and minimize the inherent "learning curve" associated with launching new restaurants, some employees from the St. Louis restaurant will transfer to restaurants in Kansas City area. Employees who transfer to the Kansas City area will be assigned to management positions in charge of training and direct supervision of new restaurant employees. The mixture of experienced with new employees will limit the amount of employee training that will be required since the transferred employees will be familiar with the menu and operations of the restaurant. In addition, as new restaurants are opened in new markets, employees will be given career advancement opportunities by transferring to new locations.

Fees

The Management Corporation will receive $25,000 per restaurant per year. This fee will cover all training activities of new employees at existing locations, new employees at new locations, and continuing training of all employees. The training will include employees at the Franchise Units, Franchise Corporation, and Real Estate Corporation. To insure continuity over a long period of time and consistency in the training and operations of all franchise locations, a long term contract will be negotiated with the Management Corporation.

Management

The Management Corporation will be owned and managed by Ray Van Gilder, who is the current manager and owner of the existing Whole Fish & Seafood Market and Restaurant in St. Louis, Mo. Van Gilder will be responsible for developing personnel in the Management Corporation to insure training continuity for both the short and long term requirements. These requirements will include training of personnel at new franchise locations in the Kansas City area as well as new markets that are developed in the future.

Real Estate Corporation

Description

The Real Estate Corporation will acquire the land necessary for the franchise units. In addition it will construct, own, and maintain all franchise units. It will be located in one central location, possibly Lenexa, Kansas. The Real Estate Corporation will work directly with architects in developing building plans, meeting local municipal building code requirements, and adapting the facilities to local market requirements. In addition, the Real Estate Corporation will be responsible for site selection in new markets.

Responsibilities

The real estate corporation will be responsible for site selection, acquisition of property, construction of buildings, and furnishing of all interior facilities. Using the assistance of an electronic site selecting firm, four sites have been identified in the Kansas City area on which to establish the first four franchised restaurants (Lenexa, Kansas Park, Lee's Summit, and Raytown). The Real Estate Corporation will work with the architects in developing the architectural plans for the physical facilities. In addition, the Real Estate Corporation will hire and work directly with a general contractor during the construction phase of each restaurant. All initial financing for the land acquisition, construction, and leasehold improvement costs associated with each restaurant will be handled by the Real Estate Corporation.

After the initial building construction, the Real Estate Corporation's responsibility will be limited to maintenance activities. These activities will include such responsibilities as landscaping, mowing, snow removal, and cleaning the parking lot.

To achieve greater market recognition and consistency among the various locations, the Real Estate Corporation will attempt to develop similar freestanding restaurant buildings at all locations. The exterior design, landscaping, interior decoration and seating layout will be similar. All buildings will be constructed to permit the identical delivery of service between the time the customer enters and departs the restaurant. The design and construction of the buildings is important in insuring a consistent flow of food orders, preparation, and delivery. Identical building designs will also enable the Management Corporation to train the new employees at each new restaurant with greater efficiency.

Fees

The Real Estate Corporation will charge each franchise unit a fee of the higher of:

- the base mortgage payment plus insurance, taxes and maintenance costs (triple net lease) or,
- 6% of gross sales

In addition, each restaurant must pay the Real Estate Corporation a fee for all maintenance work. This fee will be limited to the actual costs of the maintenance activity as incurred by the Real Estate Corporation (commonly known as common area maintenance-CAM).

Management

The Real Estate Corporation will be owned and managed by Harald Van Gilder. Harald has an extensive background in the construction, operations and management of franchise businesses. He previously was a general contractor in Kansas City. In this capacity, he was responsible for building over 300 Seven-Eleven Stores in Texas, Oklahoma, and Kansas. In addition, he was a franchise owner of several of the SevenEleven Stores.

appendixA

Interview Participants

Baye, Timothy—associate professor, Business Outreach, University of Wisconsin-Extension. Previous entrepreneurial experience includes ownership of businesses in food manufacturing and distribution, consulting, software development, farming, agricultural product research and development, large-scale landscaping, and a lumberyard.

Brockhaus, Bob (Robert H.)—Coleman Foundation Chair in Entrepreneurship, Saint Louis University. Director of the Jefferson Smurfit Center for Entrepreneurship and its Family Firm Forum. Previously owner of several restaurants in Missouri.

Bryant, Hattie—creator of *Small Business 2000*, the public television series, and of *www.SmallBusinessSchool.com*. Hattie has owned her own business since 1979 and is the author of *Beating the Odds*. Prior to developing television and online training, Hattie taught sales, customer service, and management classes inside hundreds of small companies.

Dennis, William—senior researcher, National Federation of Independent Business (NFIB) Foundation.

Godfrey, Joline—CEO and founder of Independent Means, Inc. (IMI), the leading provider of content, programs, and products for the financial novice. In addition to establishing and running her own companies, Godfrey's standing as an expert on girls and money is buttressed by her research and writing on the subject. She is the author of *Our Wildest Dreams: Women Making Money, Having Fun, Doing Good* and of *No More Frogs to Kiss: 99 Ways to Give Economic Power to Girls*, both published by Harper Collins. Her third book, *Twenty $ecrets: The Dollar-Diva's Guide to Life*, is available from St. Martin's Press. Godfrey has also been a contributing writer for *Inc.* and *Hues* magazines and is a syndicated columnist for both womenconnect.com and lycos.com.

Heller, Rodney—founder and chairman, Foodusa.com, an Internet-based business-to-business meat exchange. Former food broker and lifelong entrepreneur. Leading authority on understanding the intricacies of launching a business to business exchange in the new Internet economy and on creating the investor excitement needed to get the venture funded.

Hofer, Dr. Charles W. (Chuck)—Regents' Professor of Strategy and Entrepreneurship, University of Georgia. Author, *Strategy Formulation and Analytical Concepts.*

Hoy, Frank—director of the Centers for Entrepreneurial Development, Advancement, Research, and Support and chair for the Study of Trade in the Americas at the University of Texas at El Paso (UTEP). Served as dean of the UTEP College of Business, 1991-2000. Also directs the Family and Closely-Held Business Forum. Participated in managing and launching multiple businesses, including some with family members. Currently an investor in his son's most recent venture in Mexico City.

Kiesner, Fred—Hilton Chair of Entrepreneurship, Loyola-Marymount University. Previously owner of a community newspaper, an import/export business, and an incubator and private enterprise training center in Russia. Industry experience included being a commercial manager for a Bell Systems firm, and product manager for girdles and garter Belts (stop laughing, somebody had to do it) for an intimate apparel firm. Began teaching entrepreneurship in 1969.

Kuratko, Donald F.—Stoops Distinguished Professor of Entrepreneurship and executive director of the Midwest Entrepreneurial Education Center, College of Business, Ball State University. Previously in family business, operating funeral home, limousine service, and consulting firm in Chicago area.

Lonier, Terri—CEO of Working Solo, Inc., a consulting company advising companies targeting the SOHO market. Author of the *Working Solo* series. Previously an entrepreneur/potter.

Meeks, Michael—doctoral student, University of Colorado-Boulder. Previous entrepreneurial activities ranged from engineering to martial arts instruction to construction to computer software.

Meyer, G. Dale—Anderson Chair in Entrepreneurial Development, Graduate School of Business Administration, University of Colorado-Boulder. His previous business and entrepreneurship experience was in consulting and as the founder of three successful startups. His biggest success was with the Western Management Corporation, which assessed entrepreneurial growth companies and from this portfolio matched them with capital sources for capital infusions and/or friendly acquisitions. The WMC took equity positions in many of these brokered deals.

Reiners, Jack—business counselor, Small Business Development Center, University of Wisconsin-Madison School of Business. Previous business experience includes commercial bank lending, software development, and consulting to small businesses.

Solomon, George—adjunct professor of management-entrepreneurship, at George Washington University. Currently responsible for the nationwide Business Information Center program for the Small Business Administration. Previously, entrepreneur while in undergraduate and graduate school, constructing modular furniture for libraries and schools.

Zach, David—futurist. Owner of Innovative Futures, a consulting firm working with a diverse client base of corporations, associations, and educational institutions, helping them with strategic understanding of key trends and issues. Previously, he worked in strategic planning for Northwestern Mutual and was a trend analyst for Johnson Controls.

Business plans were submitted by the following:

Timothy Baye, University of Wisconsin Extension
Lloyd Fernald, Jr., Ph.D., University of
    Central Florida
Joan Gillman, University of Wisconsin
Robert Shepard, Ph.D., Boise State University
Howard Van Auken, Ph.D., Iowa State University
Joan Winn, University of Denver

appendix**B**

Resources

General Business

- Small Business Development Centers (SBDCs) —Check with the U.S. Small Business Administration to locate the SBDC nearest you.
U.S. Small Business Administration Web site: *www.sbaonline.sba.gov*
- Technical colleges—often have marketing, personnel, and other resources for business.
- Service Corps of Retired Executives (SCORE) and Active Corp of Executives (ACE)—These are programs established by the U.S. Small Business Administration to help all types of small businesses gain access to business counseling from experienced business operators and executives.
- Private consultants

Marketing

- American Marketing Association— Contact the national office for a chapter in your community.
American Marketing Association
311 S. Wacker Drive
Suite 5800
Chicago, IL 60606
800-AMA-1150
312-542-9000
Fax: 312-542-9001
Web site: *www.ama.org*
- Simmons Market Research Bureau (a powerful mix of marketing and media data users of consumer products)
Simmons Market Research Bureau (SMRB)
309 West 49th Street
New York, NY 10019
212-373-8900
Fax 212-373-8918
Web site: *www.smrb.com*
- Local universities and colleges, for students looking for internships or practicums

Personnel

Finding the right people:
- State job centers or unemployment offices
- College placement offices
- Technical school training/apprenticeship programs

Financial

General financial information:
  Dun & Bradstreet
  One Diamond Hill Road
  Murray Hill, NJ 07974-1218
  908-665-5000
  Fax: 908-665-5803
  Web site: *www.dnb.com*
Financing sources:
  Small Business Administration, Department of Commerce
  U.S.D.A. Rural Development programs (for those outside the boundary of a city of 50,000 or more and immediately adjacent urbanized areas)
  Micro Loan Programs offered by the SBA
  Community Development Block Grants
  Veteran Loan Fund
  Check with your SBA office, SBDC, or financial institution for information on financing sources in your community.

Legal Advice

The bar association for your state may have a business assistance program, which you can take advantage of at no cost. Typical programs offer small and emerging businesses several hours of counseling services from a business lawyer free of charge. Your volunteer can help you identify problems affecting your business and develop a plan for solving the problems. This is offered as a public service by the bar association. Participation does not imply further obligation. Contact your state bar association to find out if it offers such a program.

Adams Media Corporation Resources
Streetwise Advisor Series
Streetwise Complete Business Plan, Bob Adams
Interactive software for preparing financial projections

Books
There are so many good books on business planning! A browse on the Internet or in a bookstore will bring many fine titles to your attention. These books were specifically recommended by our interview participants.

- *First, Break All the Rules: What the World's Greatest Managers Do Differently* by Marcus Buckingham, and Curt Coffman
- *The Millionaire Next Door: The Surprising Secrets of America's Wealthy* by Thomas J. Stanley and William D. Danko
- *The Future and Its Enemies: The Growing Conflict over Creativity, Enterprise and Progress* by Virginia I. Postrel
- *The Seven Habits of Highly Effective People: Powerful Lessons in Personal Change* by Stephen R. Covey
- *First Things First: To Live, to Love, to Learn, to Leave a Legacy* by Stephen R. Covey, et al.

Books of interest to women:
- *The Best Way in the World for a Woman to Make Money* by David King and Karen Levine
- *The Managerial Woman* by Margaret Hennig

Magazines
Wired
Fast Company
American Demographics
Entrepreneur

Television Shows
Small Business 2000 (Hattie Bryant)

Web Sites
Here are a few of my favorite Web sites:
www.fsi.org
The Family Firm Institute (FFI) is an international professional organization dedicated to assisting family firms. FFI acts as a clearing-house for the media, family business owners, other professional associations, and members of the public who are interested in learning more about the latest trends and developments in the field of family business.

priceline.com
expedia.com
I travel extensively. These travel-related sites help me reduce the cost of my trips.

These sites provide useful tax-related information:
www.irs.gov
Download IRS forms and publications, plus links to state forms.

www.ey.com/pfc
Ernst & Young offers substantive tax help here.

www.1040.com
This site keeps up-to-date information on IRS regulations.

www.quicken.com
This site offers tax chat rooms.

The following Web sites were recommended by Terri Lonier of Working Solo, Inc.
www.sba.gov
Small Business Administration, the "mother ship" of government information

www.score.org
SCORE, featuring free online business mentors/counseling

Valuable SOHO Web sites:
www.lowe.org
Edward Lowe Foundation, with strong content and resources

www.inc.com
Inc. magazine online, with its rich archives

www.sbinformation.miningco.com
The Mining Company, with online guides

www.workingsolo.com
News and insights on the small office/home office market

appendixC

Generic Business Plan Outline

This generic business plan outline provides you with a general framework for writing your business plan. Because a business plan is tailored to your business, you may need to adapt this outline by expanding some areas while eliminating or providing limited information in others. Although there are many business plan outlines available, all have similar sections:

- description of your business and its product/service offerings
- documentation of the need in the marketplace for your service or product (including competitor information)

- marketing strategies
- production/operations plan
- organizational structure/personnel
- financial projections and needs

Books and/or workbooks at libraries and bookstores can provide additional guidance.

Generic Business Plan Outline

I. Cover Sheet
   A. Title of the Document
   B. Presented to
   C. Applicant
   D. Date

II. **Table of Contents**

III. **Executive Summary (usually written last)**
   A. Brief Description of the Business
   B. The Opportunity
     - Market
     - Industry
     - Competition
     - Niche/strategy
   C. Financials
     - Sales projections
     - Profit potential
     - Growth potential
   D. The People
   E. The Offering

IV. **The Business**
   A. The Nature of the Business (type and legal structure)
     - Start-up or existing business
     - Type of business
        manufacturing
        wholesale
        retail
        service
     - Legal structure
        proprietorship/partnership
        corporation
     - General information
        location
        hours of operation
   B. Product/Service
     - What is the product/service?
     - What are you selling?
        price
        selection
        service
        quality
        convenience
     - How will the product/service be produced/marketed?
     - Who will buy it?
     - Proprietary information
   C. History of the Business
     - Date the business began operations
     - Chain of ownership
     - Significant changes in the business
        product/service line
        location/facilities

        marketing strategy

        capitalization

   • Summary of sales and profit history

D. The Business Opportunity

   • Sales by size/dollars/units

   • Profitability

   • Market share

   • Based on market analysis

V. The Industry

A. Present Status

B. Trends Impacting the Business/Industry

   • Technology

   • Economy

   • Political

   • Legal

   • Demographic

   • Social

C. Data sources

   • U.S. Census (WISPOP)

   • County Business Patterns

D. Trade Sources (i.e., Sales & Marketing Management)

   • Survey of current business

   • Census of Retail Trade

VI. The Market

A. Define the Market

   • Customer category

       consumer

       business

       industrial

       institutional

       government

   • Define <u>need</u> for product/service

   • Geographic coverage

       distance

       time

       traffic patterns

       topographic considerations

       social and cultural considerations

   • Demographic target

       age

       income

       sex

       employment

       education

       residence

       family status

       race

       religion

   • Psychographic characteristics

B. Quantify the Market
- Size
- Trends
- Local issues
- Based on demographic and geographic definition of the market

C. Profile the Competition
- Who are your competitors?
- Where are they located?
- How do they/you compare?
- Nature and status of each competitor

D. Marketing Strategy
- Competitive focus (price, quality, service, selection, convenience)
- Marketing methods
- Marketing channels
- Channels of distribution
- Advertising/promotion plan

VII. **Location**

A. Site
- Size
- Physical character
- Legal constraints on use

B. Facilities
- Buildings
- Storage

C. Linkages
- Traffic
- Accessibility
- Convenience
- Exposure
- Parking
- Suppliers
- Competitors
- Market

VIII. **Business Objectives**

A. Annual Profit Targets
B. Annual Sales Growth Rate
C. Rate of Return on Investment
D. Rate of Return on Equity

IX. **Technical Considerations**

A. Process/Technology
- Present
- State-of-the-art
- Special applications, considerations, constraints
- Trends

B. Raw Materials/Inventory
- Requirements
- Sources/availability
- Suppliers

C. Proprietary Information
- Patents/tradenames/trademarks/copyright
- Process
- Product

X. **Management/Personnel**
  A. Organization
     • Organizational chart
     • Major responsibilities of key managers
     • Ownership structure
     • Board of directors
  B. Management Team
     • Resumes of key management personnel
     • Strengths and weaknesses
     • Personnel
     • Compensation
         wages and salaries
         benefits
     • Level of investment by managers

XI. **Potential Risks and Problems**
     • Plan to meet risks

XII. **Financial**
  A. Projected Income Statement
     • Three years minimum
     • Assumptions
  B. Projected Balance Sheet
     • Three years minimum
     • Assumptions
  C. Cash Flow Statement
     • First year monthly, second and third years quarterly
     • Assumptions
  D. Business Valuation
     • Methodology
     • Assumptions
     • Estimated value
  E. Break-Even Analysis
  F. Sensitivity Analysis
     • Assumptions
     • "What if" analysis

XIII. **The Offering**
  A. Capitalization
  B. Terms
  C. Sources and Uses of Funds
  D. Ownership Structure
  E. Projected Return to Investors

XIV. **Supporting Documents**
     • Organization
     • Credit reports
     • Letters of intent or sales agreements
     • Lease and purchase agreements
     • Options
     • Copies of leases
     • Contracts
     • Permits and licenses
     • Insurance
     • Letters of reference
     • Business development schedule

ABC COMPANY
Projected Income Statement

	Year 1	Year 2	Year 3

Sales

    Cash
    Credit

    Total Sales

Cost of Goods Sold

    Beginning inventory
    Purchases
    Ending inventory

        Total Cost of Goods Sold

Gross Margin

Operating Expenses

    Wages and salaries
    Commissions
    Payroll taxes
    Benefits
    Rent
    Advertising
    Utilities
    Telephone
    Insurance
    Supplies
    Repairs and maintenance
    Travel
    Auto and truck
    Office expense
    Accounting and legal
    Taxes (other)
    Miscellaneous
    Other
        Total Operating Expenses

Profit/Loss

ABC COMPANY
Projected Cash Flow

(Year 1)

	Jan.	Feb.	Mar.	Dec.
Beginning Cash Balance				
Cash Inflows				
Cash sales				
Collections on acct.				
Loan proceeds				
Add'l. investments				
Other				
Total Cash Inflows				
Cash Outflows				
Payments on acct.				
Payments for expenses				
Income tax payments				
Owner's draw				
Loan retirement/interest				
Capital expenditures				
Other				
Total Cash Outflows				
Ending Cash Balance				

ABC COMPANY
Balance Sheet

(Opening Day) Current Assets
    Cash
    Accounts/Receivable
    Inventory
    Supplies
    Other current assets
        Total Current Assets

Long-Term Assets
    Land
    Equipment
    Machinery
    Other long-term assets
    Total Long-Term Assets

TOTAL ASSETS

Current Liabilities
    Accounts payable
    Salaries payable
    Taxes payable
    Interest payable
    Notes payable
    Other current liabilities
    Total Current Liabilities

Long-Term Liabilities
    Notes payable
    Mortgage notes payable
    Other long-term liabilities
    Total Long-Term Liabilities

TOTAL LIABILITIES

Owner's Equity
    Invested
    Retained earnings
    Draws
    Total Owner's Equity
    Total Liabilities and Owner's Equity

ABC COMPANY
Sources and Uses of Funds

<u>Sources of Funds</u>

Bank Loans		
1st National Bank	$80,000	
1st Federal Savings & Loan	70,000	
Equity		
Personal	40,000	
Other	<u>50,000</u>	
TOTAL		$ 240,000

<u>Uses of Funds</u>

Equipment	$50,000	
Truck	20,000	
Building	100,000	
Inventory	50,000	
Working capital	<u>20,000</u>	
TOTAL		$ 240,000

appendix D

Worksheets

Worksheet 4.1

Business Description

All businesses: answer these questions.

What business are you in? _____

_____

What is the status of the business (start-up, going concern, turnaround, division of a larger business)?

_____

What is the structure of the business (sole proprietorship, partnership, limited liability corporation, corporation)?_____

_____

Why is your business going to be profitable? _____

_____

How will your business achieve growth?_____

_____

What will be the status of your business in five years? In 10 years? _____

_____

When did (will) your business open? _____

What hours of the day and days of the week are you (will you be) in operation?_____

Is your business affected by seasonal factors? _____

New start-up businesses: answer these questions.

Why will you succeed in this business? _____

_____

What is your experience in this business? _____

_____

Have you spoken with other people in this kind of business? _____

What did you learn from them? _____

_____

_____

What will be special about your business? _____

_____

_____

What managerial or technical help will your trade suppliers provide? _____

_____

_____

What trade credit will you offer? _____

If you will be doing contract work, what are the terms? _____

_____

_____

How will you offset slow payment by your customers? _____

_____

Worksheet 4.1

Worksheet 4.2

Developing the Vision and Mission Statement: Who Are We?

Objectives:

Identify the values and beliefs upon which the organization is based.

Develop a collective vision of what the organization could be five to 10 years in the future.

Develop a draft vision and mission statement that states what the organization does and for whom, and what it aspires to be.

Thought Provokers for Vision and Mission Statement

1. Focus on who you serve.

Describe the target market for your product or service offering. It might help to focus on one or two of your best customers. What are their characteristics? _____

_____

Describe unique features of your offering. What is your business uniquely good at? This is your competitive advantage. _____

_____

Describe the benefits that your competitive advantage delivers to your customers. _____

_____

_____

2. Focus on the nature of the business.

What is your geographic domain? _____

(Warning: this is a trick question. Since the arrival of the Internet, your domain may be a community of interest spread throughout the world rather than a specific geographic locality. If so, describe that community of interest.)

What role does technology play in your business? _____

What are your plans for growth? _____

3. Focus on your philosophy.

Describe the self-concept of your business. What are your attitudes? How formal is the workplace? If your business were a car, what sort of car would it be? _____

_____

_____

What is your public image? How do you want to be thought of in the community? _____

_____

_____

Describe your concern for your employees. _____

_____

4. Focus on how you will put this mission into action.

What are the primary goals for the company? _____

_____

What concrete actions will you take to achieve these goals? _____

_____

5. Company Values and Beliefs
Describe the primary company philosophies, values, beliefs (written or unwritten).

1. _____
2. _____
3. _____
4. _____
5 _____
6. _____

6. Mission Statement Components
Describe in one or two sentences your "ground rules" with regard to each of the following. Come up with a few words or phrases that describe your business.

Customer/Market
"We seek to serve the . . . with solutions to . . ."

_____

_____

Product/Service
"We produce/provide . . . designed to . . ."

_____

_____

Geography
"We serve the . . . area of . . ."

_____

_____

Technology
"We apply technology in these areas . . . .We plan to stay current by . . ."

_____

_____

Growth
"We will conduct our operations to grow (rapidly) (moderately) (in pace with our industry's growth rate) . . ."

_____

Philosophy
"We are committed to . . ."

_____

_____

Self-Concept
"We are a . . . with strong . . . and respect for individual. . . . We have a desire to improve (quality of life) (opportunity for all) (conservation of natural resources) . . ."

_____

_____

Concern for Public Image
"We must be responsive to the concerns of the public, including . . . . We will be perceived as . . ."

_____

_____

7. Now you're ready to write the vision and mission statement.

The fundamental, unique purpose that sets your business apart from your competition and identifies the scope of your operations.

Answer these questions: What business are you in? What markets (customers) do you serve? What products/services do you provide? What customer needs do you fulfill? What do you want them to be?

Worksheet 5.1

Market/Industry Description

Describe current changes taking place in this industry. (For example, consolidation or a trend toward specialization . . .) _____

_____

_____

What were trends for this industry for the past five years? _____

_____

_____

According to industry journals and other sources, what are the projected trends? _____

_____

_____

Describe technological developments affecting this industry. When will new technologies be available? What impact will this have on your business? _____

_____

_____

_____

Describe economic developments affecting this industry. What are the prospects for economic health within this industry? _____

_____

_____

Describe the regulatory environment affecting this industry. What laws and regulations do you have to comply with? What legislative changes are likely to occur that might affect your business? _____

_____

_____

What risks are specific to this industry? _____

_____

_____

Is this industry dominated by large or small firms? _____

How does the failure rate for this industry compare with that of others? _____

_____

_____

Describe the target market(s) for your product or service offering. _____

_____

_____

_____

How big is the market? _____

Is the total market growing or shrinking? _____

How might economic changes—for example, incomes, prices, savings, and credit—affect your business?

_____

_____

_____

What are typical company sales? _____

What are profit percentages accepted throughout this industry? _____

Describe demographic shifts affecting this industry. What are current or emerging trends in lifestyle, fashion, and other components of culture? How will these trends affect the makeup of your target market? How will these affect the demand for your product? _____

_____

_____

_____

What share of the market do you think you can capture? _____

Research needs

Make a list of market research that you need to obtain to make this section stronger.

_____

_____

_____

_____

_____

_____

_____

_____

_____

_____

_____

_____

_____

_____

_____

_____

_____

Worksheet 5.2

Customer Analysis

Who are or will be key customer groups? _____

_____

_____

_____

_____

_____

What characteristics define each group? _____

_____

_____

_____

_____

_____

What products and services have they purchased? _____

_____

_____

_____

_____

_____

What customer needs do your products and services satisfy? _____

_____

_____

_____

_____

_____

How profitable is each customer segment for your business? _____

_____

_____

_____

_____

_____

Worksheet 5.3

Competitor Analysis

List your major and minor competitors. Rank this list of competitors, and/or categorize them into distinctive groups that compete with you in specific areas.

_____

_____

For each firm from whom you experience significant competition, answer the following questions.

What products and/or services do they provide?

_____

_____

What territory do they sell in?

_____

_____

Who are their prospective customers?

_____

_____

What is their market share?

_____

_____

What is their price/value position?

_____

_____

What are their plans for growth? Market expansion? New products?

_____

_____

Describe their strengths and weaknesses.

_____

_____

Describe their financial capacity.

_____

_____

Describe their managerial capacity.

_____

_____

What are their marketing strategies?

_____

_____

Evaluate their advertising. What benefits are emphasized? What media are they using to distribute their message?

_____

Worksheet 5.4

Features into Benefits Exercise

List as many product/service features with their corresponding benefits as you can. A single feature may offer different benefits to different audiences, so have a particular target market in mind when you do this exercise.

Features   Benefits

_____   _____
_____   _____
_____   _____
_____   _____
_____   _____
_____   _____
_____   _____
_____   _____
_____   _____
_____   _____
_____   _____
_____   _____
_____   _____
_____   _____
_____   _____
_____   _____
_____   _____
_____   _____
_____   _____
_____   _____
_____   _____
_____   _____
_____   _____
_____   _____
_____   _____
_____   _____

Worksheet 5.5

Product/Service Description

What are you selling?

_____

_____

_____

_____

What are the benefits (as opposed to the features) of what you are selling?

_____

_____

_____

_____

_____

Rank these in order of priority held by your most profitable target market.

_____

_____

_____

_____

_____

How do your products or services differ from competitive products or services?

_____

_____

_____

_____

If your product is new or state-of-the-art or otherwise unique, what makes it different? What makes it desirable?

_____

_____

_____

_____

If your product or service line is not special, why would people buy from you?

_____

_____

_____

_____

Worksheet 5.6

Place (Distribution) Description

Describe the selling process for one of your products or services.

Example: How does the product/service get from you to the ultimate end user? What steps are involved? What type of people and businesses are involved along the way? You could write this out or diagram it.

What distribution strategy will you employ?

How will you accomplish your distribution strategy?

Worksheet 5.7

Price Strategy Worksheet

Covering your costs sets the floor for your prices.

1) What will it cost to produce (or purchase from a supplier) your products and services? This equals your cost of goods sold. Include both materials and labor.

_____

_____

Competition and the customer's perception of the value set the ceiling for your prices.

2) What is your estimate of the ceiling price you could charge?

_____

_____

3) What are your pricing objectives? Market share, maximizing profits, building up a new product line, remaining competitive? Remember that pricing is only one way to reach your objectives, and low pricing is not the best way for small businesses.

_____

_____

4) What is your gross profit margin (%) for the product/service? _____

5) What are your monthly and annual fixed costs of operation? _____

6) How many units of your product/service do you estimate you can sell in a month and annually?

_____

7) How many units at a certain price do you need to sell to break even annually? _____

Checklist of Pricing Concerns

8) Do your customers expect a certain price range? _____

9) What is the balance between price and quality in your market? _____

10) Is demand for your offering elastic or inelastic? _____

11) Have you tested the impact of price strategies on your markets? _____

12) How does the nature of the other "four Ps" of the marketing mix affect your price? Does the nature of your products/services, or the method of distribution, or your promotional policies influence your price strategy?

_____

_____

_____

_____

Worksheet 5.8

Example

Competitive Category: WOMEN'S CLOTHES
Dimensions of competition: Price and quality

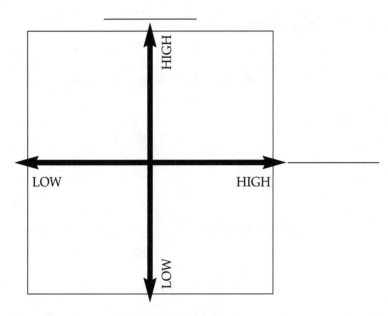

Consider the positions held by your competitors: on what dimension are they considered "best"? They might be known for product features, or selection, or convenience—you get the idea. Positioning is about finding or creating a dimension in which you can become known as "best".

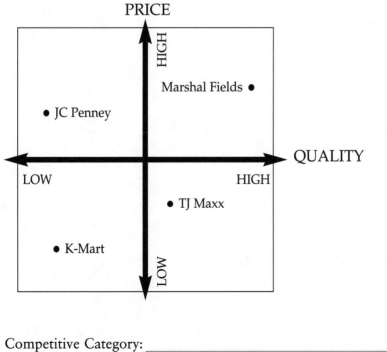

Competitive Category: _____

Dimensions of competition:_____
     and_____

Worksheet 5.9

Your Positioning Statement

Use this worksheet to develop a one-sentence positioning statement for your company, product, or service.

_____

(name of product, company, or service)

is the _____

(competitive category; type of business, company, or service)

that provides/makes/gives/offers/brings _____

(benefit)

_____

for _____.

(target market)

Worksheet 6.1

Management Depth: Internal Assessment

	Your Performance					Its Importance				
	Poor				Excellent	Not				Very
Pricing skills	1	2	3	4	5	1	2	3	4	5
Promotion skills	1	2	3	4	5	1	2	3	4	5
Selling skills	1	2	3	4	5	1	2	3	4	5
Distribution system	1	2	3	4	5	1	2	3	4	5
Knowledge of customers	1	2	3	4	5	1	2	3	4	5
Personnel policies	1	2	3	4	5	1	2	3	4	5
Compensation policies	1	2	3	4	5	1	2	3	4	5
Employee morale	1	2	3	4	5	1	2	3	4	5
Teamwork/cooperation	1	2	3	4	5	1	2	3	4	5
Organizational structure	1	2	3	4	5	1	2	3	4	5
Management skills	1	2	3	4	5	1	2	3	4	5
Supervisory skills	1	2	3	4	5	1	2	3	4	5
Operating procedures	1	2	3	4	5	1	2	3	4	5
Technical competence	1	2	3	4	5	1	2	3	4	5
Equipment	1	2	3	4	5	1	2	3	4	5
Quality control	1	2	3	4	5	1	2	3	4	5
Financial resources	1	2	3	4	5	1	2	3	4	5
Availability of capital	1	2	3	4	5	1	2	3	4	5
Cash flow	1	2	3	4	5	1	2	3	4	5
Supplier relationships	1	2	3	4	5	1	2	3	4	5
Information availability	1	2	3	4	5	1	2	3	4	5

Worksheet 6.2

Management Planning Tool

Duties and Responsibilities

1. Who does what?

_____

_____

2. Who reports to whom?

_____

_____

3. Who makes the final decisions?

_____

_____

Salaries

4. What are the comparable salaries for comparable management positions?
(Check out Help Wanted ads and trade associations for information.)

_____

_____

5. How much money do you (realistically) need to live on? _____

Resources Available to the Business

6. Who is:
   Your accountant? _____
   Your lawyer? _____
   Your banker? _____
   Your major trade supplier? _____

7. Who handles your insurance? _____

8. Who else might help your business become more profitable?

_____

_____

_____

_____

_____

Worksheet 6.3

Manager's Background Survey

1. What is your business background?

   _____

   _____

2. What management experience have you had?

   _____

   _____

3. What education (including both formal and informal education) has a bearing on your managerial abilities?

   _____

   _____

4. What is your age; what are your special abilities and interests, reasons for going into business; where do you live, etc.?

   _____

   _____

5. Are you physically up to the job? _____

6. Why are you going to be successful in this venture?

   _____

   _____

7. What is your personal financial status? _____

Related Work Experience

8. What is your direct operational experience in this kind of business?

   _____

   _____

9. What is your managerial experience in this kind of business?

   _____

   _____

10. What other managerial experience have you had—in different businesses, in a club or on a team, in civic or religious organizations, or in some other area? (need not be a paid position)

    _____

    _____

Worksheet 6.4

Survey of Personnel Needs

1. What are your personnel needs now?

_____

_____

2. What jobs will you have to fill during the next 12 months?

_____

_____

3. What jobs will you have to fill within the next five years?

_____

_____

4. What skills does your business require?

_____

_____

5. Are the people with those skills available for hire? Where?

_____

_____

6. Will you have full- or part-time employees (or a mix)?

_____

_____

7. Will your employees be salaried or hourly?

_____

_____

8. What fringe benefits will you offer?

_____

_____

9. Will you pay overtime?

_____

_____

10. Will you have to train people to meet the job requirements?

_____

_____

Worksheet 6.5

Family Business: Goals and Expectations

Lifestyle Goals

1. How many hours do you expect to work each week? _____

2. What is the maximum number of hours per week you could conceivably work in a busy period, and for how many weeks could you keep that up?_____

3. How many hours do you expect others in your family to be putting in? _____

Personal Goals

4. What do you expect the business to allow you to do, as an individual?

   _____

   _____

5. How are you going to develop your skills and your interests?

   _____

   _____

6. How do you anticipate the business will allow your loved ones to develop their skills and interests?

   _____

   _____

Financial Goals

7. How much debt are you willing to assume? _____

8. How much money are you willing to put into the business, as equity?_____

9. What kind of rate of return, and what kind of salary, do you expect? _____

Worksheet 7.1 **Income Statement**

Worksheet 7.1

PRO FORMA INCOME STATEMENT This document produced on:

	Sep-97	Oct-97	Nov-97	Dec-97	Jan-98	Feb-98	Mar-98	Apr-98	May-98	Jun-98	Jul-98	Aug-98	YEAR	% of Sales
Expected Monthly Sales														
Cost of Goods Sold	=====	=====	=====	=====	=====	=====	=====	=====	=====	=====	=====	=====	=====	
Gross Profit														
Overhead Expenses														
Utilities & Telephone														
Insurance														
Advertising & Promotion														
Travel & Entertainment														
Repairs & Maintenance														
Shipping & Postage														
Office Supplies														
Other (inc. rents & leases)														
Property & Other Taxes														
Total Overhead Expenses														
Depreciation														
Machinery & Equipment														
Buildings & Intangibles	=====	=====	=====	=====	=====	=====	=====	=====	=====	=====	=====	=====	=====	
Operating Income (EBIT)	=====	=====	=====	=====	=====	=====	=====	=====	=====	=====	=====	=====	=====	
Interest Expense	=====	=====	=====	=====	=====	=====	=====	=====	=====	=====	=====	=====	=====	
Taxable Income (EBT)														
Est. Income Tax Obligation**														
Tax Credits														
Estimated Income Taxes**	=====	=====	=====	=====	=====	=====	=====	=====	=====	=====	=====	=====	=====	
Net Profit														

NOTES:

Worksheet 7.2 **Balance Sheet**

PROJECTED BALANCE SHEET:

Period:

ASSETS	Beginning	Ending
Cash		
Receivables		
Inventory		
Total Current Assets:		
Equipment		
Facilities/Bldgs		
Deprec. Intangibles		
Land & non-deprec.		
TOTAL ASSETS:		

LIABILITIES		
Previous Debt		
New Debt:		
Short-term		
Medium-term		
Long-term		
TOTAL LIABILITIES:		

EQUITY
TOTAL LIAB. & EQUITY:

LEVERAGE RATIOS

Debt/Asset:
Debt/Equity:
Fixed Charge
Coverage:

LIQUIDITY RATIOS

Current Ratio:
Quick Ratio:

New Investment in Budget Period
Depreciable Equipment
Depreciable Building
Depreciable Intangibles
Land & Non-Depreciable Assets
Working Capital/Inventory

OTHER FINANCIAL INFORMATION

Total Sales:
Gross Profit:
Taxable Profit:
Net Profit:
Cash flow from
Operations:
Sales Breakeven
Point:

PROFITABILITY RATIOS	
Gross Margin:	%
Taxable Profit	
Margin:	%
Net Profit	
Margin:	%
Cash flow from	
Operations/Sales:	%

YEAR-END RETURN RATIOS

(based upon cash flow)	
Return on Total	
Assets:	%
Return on Dep.	
Assets:	%
Return on	
Begin. Equity:	%

Short-Term Debt	190,000
130,000	
302,000	
Total	

Notes: Accounts payable estimates are not developed by the model. New (acquired within the planning period) short-term debt is assumed to be the only current liability.

Worksheet 7.3 **Cash Flow Budget**

PRO FORMA CASH FLOW FROM OPERATIONS STATEMENT

	Aug-97	Sep-97	Oct-97	Nov-97	Dec-97	Jan-98	Feb-98	Mar-98	Apr-98	May-98	Jun-98	Jul-98	Aug-98	13 Month
Cash Sales														
Collected Receivables														
Other Income														
Total Operation Cash Inflow														
Operation/Overhead Costs														
Direct/Raw Material Costs														
Interest Expense														
Income Taxes Paid **														
Total Operation Cash Outflow														
Total Cash Flow From Operations														

NOTES:

Worksheet 7.4 **Sources and Uses of Funds**

PRO FORMA CONSOLIDATED STATEMENT OF CHANGES IN FINANCIAL POSITION: SOURCES AND USES OF FUNDS

	Aug-97	Sep-97	Oct-97	Nov-97	Dec-97	Jan-98	Feb-98	Mar-98	Apr-98	May-98	Jun-98	Jul-98	Aug-98	13 Month
Sources of Funds														
Cash Flow from Operations														
Increase in Short-Term Debt														
Increase in Medium-Term Debt														
Increase in Long-Term Debt														
Increase in Payables/Accruals														
Sale of Assets/Investments														
Cash (Equity) Contribution														
Total Sources:														
Uses of Funds														
Short-Term Debt Retirement														
Medium-Term Debt Retirement														
Long-Term Debt Retirement														
To Purchase Equipment														
To Purchase Bldg/Land/Intang.														
Other (includes Oper.Exps.)														
Total Uses:														
Changes in Financial Position:														
Estimated Ending Cash Balance:														
Changes in Inventory (2):														
Changes in Receivables (3):														
NOTES:														

Worksheet 7.5

Worksheet 7.5

Financial Assumptions: Examples of Information to Include

Balance Sheet Items
1. Facility costs
2. Equipment costs
3. Capital investments
4. Loans and terms

Income Statement Items
[Fixed Costs]
1. Inventory costs
2. Salary expenses
3. Benefits, including FICA, UC, WC
4. Insurance
5. Supplies
6. Services
7. Vehicle costs
8. Travel
9. Education
10. Telephone
11. Utilities
12. Rent

[Variable Costs]
13. Sales price per unit
14. Number of units sold
15. Variable costs associated with sales/promotion

Worksheet 9.1

Self-Evaluation for Prospective Entrepreneurs

In deciding to go into business for yourself, evaluate your attitudes and resources.

Question	Definitely	Probably	No/Not Sure
Marketing • Is there a real market for the product or service? • Can you access the market? • Is your product or service competitive with others? • Is there a realistic need for this business?			
Risk • Could you personally survive a failure?			
Finance • Is the cash flow projected from operations adequate? • Will your projected income be adequate for your needs? • Can you obtain the necessary financing/capital?			
Personal • Do you have your family's support? • Do you have the initiative, desire, tenacity, and leadership abilities? • Are you capable of being realistic and objective about your business concept?			
Production • Is there a reliable supply of the materials to make the product or ingredients for the service? • Can you obtain the required professional and technical assistance when necessary?			
Human Resources • Can you find enough good people to staff the organization?			
Feasibility • Do you have adequate knowledge to conduct the business and its management? • Is promotion ability and charisma required, and do you have it? • Can you work well with customers and others? • Can you work comfortably with regulations, government permits, and restrictions? • Has this business been tried before? If not, are you sure it can be done?			

Answer as honestly as you can. Have friends evaluate you/your business idea as well. If there are a number of areas where you rate yourself as "No/Not Sure," re-evaluate your plans.

Some entrepreneurs gain additional experience by working for others in the industry. Others bring a partner into the business whose strengths balance their weaknesses.

Develop ways to protect yourself and your business in those areas where you are weakest as you develop your business enterprise.

Worksheet 9.1

appendix**E**

Glossary

Accounting: the art of recording, classifying, and summarizing in a significant manner and in terms of money, transactions, and events that are, in part at least, of a financial character, and interpreting the results thereof.

Assets: anything of value owned by an individual or business, including, but not limited to, inventory, equipment, furniture, rights, and accounts receivable.

Balance sheet: shows financial position, weighing the balance of assets to liabilities. A balance sheet consists of sections describing assets, liabilities, and owner's equity.

Brand identity: consists of the associations and expectations that come to mind when exposed to a name or a logo or a package. Through repeated exposure, brand identity comes to represent the positioning you want your customers to think of when they see your brand.

Break-even point: the point at which a company's costs exactly match its sales revenues. At break-even, the company has neither incurred a loss nor made a profit.

Cash flow statement: shows the cash inflows and outflows over a period of time. A cash flow statement consists of four sections: beginning cash balance, cash inflows, cash outflows, and ending cash balance.

Concierge: an emerging professional category of people who help other people get things done.

Corporation: a legal form of business enterprise consisting of a voluntary association of persons and treated by law as an individual entity.

Data mining: the process of developing and using information from research data, particularly when data from multiple sources is overlaid to give a more complete picture or to isolate a group sharing specific traits.

Distance learning: the bringing of an educational environment to individuals regardless of their location, using a variety of approaches, including online resources.

Elastic demand: a situation in which demand for a product or service is strongly affected by price, as when plenty of alternatives and substitutes are available.

Entrepreneur: one who organizes, operates, and assumes the risk for a business venture.

Equity: the owner's investment in a business. Calculated by subtracting the liabilities of a business from its assets.

Executive summary: a statement that briefly describes the business concept, the current situation, and the success factors that give a particular business a competitive edge. The executive summary alerts the reader to the purpose for which the plan was prepared.

Four Ps: product, place, price, and promotion, the four elements of the marketing mix that a business controls in response to external factors.

Franchisor/franchisee: a company that creates and sells franchises is called a *franchisor*. An individual who has purchased a franchise is called a *franchisee*. Their franchise agreement usually gives the franchisee exclusive rights to a specific geographic area in return for a fee and, usually, a percentage of gross sales.

Income statement: summarizes the operations of a company over a specified time period. An income statement consists of four main sections: revenues, costs of goods sold, expenses, and net income. Also called a profit and loss statement.

Inelastic Demand: a situation in which demand for a product or service is unaffected by price, as when relatively few alternatives or substitutes are available.

Liabilities: the debts of a business; anything of value that is owed by a business to its creditors.

Limited liability corp. (LLC): a legal form of business enterprise that functions like a partnership with the exception that none of the members of an LLC are personally liable for the LLC's debts.

Logistics management: an emerging field that uses sophisticated information about production, transportation, and consumption of goods to reduce unnecessary warehousing and transportation costs.

Marketing: the process of creating a product then planning and carrying out the pricing, promotion, and distribution of that product by stimulating buying exchanges in which both buyer and seller profit in some way.

Marketing mix: consists of the "four Ps" of product, place, price, and promotion; the components of a marketing program that a business controls in response to external factors.

Mission statement: a brief description of the fundamental, unique purpose that sets a business apart from other firms of its type and identifies the scope of its operations.

Offering: a product, service, or combination of product and service attributes created to fill anticipated market demand.

Owner's equity: the owner's total investment in a business minus any profits or losses incurred. Calculated by subtracting the liabilities of a business from its assets.

Partnership: a legal form of business enterprise joining two or more persons who will share any profit and accept liability for any debt.

Positioning: the act of designing a company's offering and image so that they occupy a meaningful and distinct position in the customer's mind.

Profit and loss statement: summarizes the operations of a company over a specified time period. A profit and loss statement consists of four main sections: revenues, costs of goods sold, expenses, and net income. Also called an income statement.

Pro formas: projected financial statements prepared using the format of standard historical financial statements.

SOHO: acronym for "small office/home office." The transition to a knowledge-based economy has created business opportunities where physical inventory is not required. Technological advances have brought business equipment that is affordable, portable, and simple to use, plus the resources of the World Wide Web. The result of these trends is a rapidly growing market of SOHO operators.

Sole proprietorship: a legal form of business enterprise involving one person as owner. The personal assets of the sole proprietor have no protection from the liabilities of the company.

Venture capital: money provided by investors outside traditional sources.

Vision statement: a brief description of a positive possible future and the preferred long-range outcome of current strategies and operations.

index